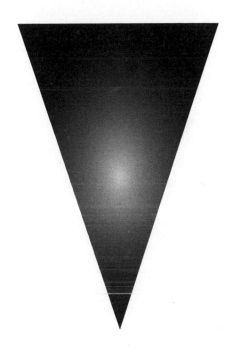

Television Production

6th EDITION

TELEVISION PRODUCTION
Disciplines and Techniques

THOMAS D. BURROWS

California State University, Northridge

LYNNE S. GROSS

California State University, Fullerton

DONALD N. WOOD

California State University, Northridge

WCB Brown &
Benchmark
PUBLISHERS

Madison, Wisconsin • Dubuque, Iowa

Book Team

Editor *Stan Stoga*
Developmental Editor *Kassi Radomski*
Production Editor *Debra DeBord*
Designer *Lu Ann Schrandt*
Art Editor *Brenda A. Ernzen*
Visuals/Design Freelance Specialist *Mary L. Christianson*
Marketing Manager *Pamela S. Cooper*
Production Manager *Beth Kundert*

WCB Brown & Benchmark

A Division of Wm. C. Brown Communications, Inc.

Executive Vice President/General Manager *Thomas E. Doran*
Vice President/Editor in Chief *Edgar J. Laube*
Vice President/Marketing and Sales Systems *Eric Ziegler*
Vice President/Production *Vickie Putman*
National Sales Manager *Bob McLaughlin*

Wm. C. Brown Communications, Inc.

President and Chief Executive Officer *G. Franklin Lewis*
Senior Vice President, Operations *James H. Higby*
Corporate Senior Vice President and President of Manufacturing *Roger Meyer*
Corporate Senior Vice President and Chief Financial Officer *Robert Chesterman*

Cover photographs: top © S. Gazin/The Image Works; center © John Maher/The Stock Market; bottom © Mug Shots/The Stock Market

Copyedited by Cynthia Cechota

Interior design by Karen Mason

A Times Mirror Company

Library of Congress Catalog Card Number: 94–71284

ISBN 0–697–20131–7

Printed in the United States of America by Wm. C. Brown Communications, Inc., 2460 Kerper Boulevard, Dubuque, IA 52001

10 9 8 7 6 5 4 3 2

To our many students
who have helped
make teaching
the most rewarding
of all professions.

About the Authors

Thomas D. Burrows (Tom Burrows) now holds the title of *Professor Emeritus* in the Radio, TV and Film Department at California State University, Northridge. Retirement from full-time teaching has provided him the opportunity to pursue a number of activities relating both to his academic background and to his work as a professional broadcaster. In addition to ongoing teaching and advisory activities, Professor Burrows is a member of the Educational Programs and Services Committee of the Academy of Television Arts and Sciences. This committee oversees national student awards and internship programs in addition to a yearly television production seminar for broadcast professors. During his earlier career as a producer and director in commercial and public broadcasting, he received the Christopher, Emmy, and Peabody awards. He holds an M.A. degree from the School of Journalism at the University of Southern California.

Lynne Schafer Gross has taught television production at a number of United States colleges, including California State University–Fullerton, Pepperdine University, UCLA, Loyola Marymount University, and Long Beach City College. She has also taught production internationally at Queensland University of Technology in Brisbane, Australia; Georgetown University in Guyana, South America; Swaziland Broadcasting Corporation in Africa; and IPTAR in Kuala Lumpur, Malaysia. Her professional experience includes serving as director of programming for Valley Cable TV and producing a number of local and regional television series. She is presently chairperson of the Broadcast Education Association and has served as a board member and committee chair for the Academy of Television Arts and Sciences. She has published ten other books and numerous journal articles.

Donald N. Wood, professor of radio-TV-film, has been teaching at California State University, Northridge, since 1970. He also has taught at San Diego State University, The University of Michigan, and Westminster College (Pennsylvania). His professional background has been largely in educational broadcasting. He was program coordinator for National Educational Television, area coordinator for the Midwest Program on Airborne Television Instruction, and director of ETV for the Hawaii State Department of Education, during which time he was executive producer for more than eight hundred television productions. Dr. Wood is the author of *Mass Media and the Individual* and the textbook *Designing the Effective Message* and is coauthor of *Educational Telecommunications*. His B.A. is from Earlham College in Indiana; his M.A. and Ph.D. degrees are from The University of Michigan.

Contents

The first edition of this text was written some twenty years ago. Since that time much has changed in the field of television. In chapter 1 we have presented a short chronology of recent technical developments as a way of introducing the component systems and related terminologies that are in use at the present time.

Any person who has had access to the best of professional equipment over the past several decades cannot help but be very impressed with all that can be achieved today through the use of the new switchers, editing equipment, and computer generated graphic units. What is also somewhat startling is that the *rate of change* from year to year is definitely accelerating.

But, while the *techniques* of television may be changing, the *disciplines* that serve as the underlying strength of any operation remain much the same. The basic concepts of advance preparation, the constant checking of detail, and the necessity for teamwork assume a position of even more importance as technology becomes more complex. We are speaking here of a number of attitudes and behaviors involving responsibility, self-control, initiative, and respect for the work of others. These disciplines are in many ways the most important part of any university level production course. It is the authors' firm belief that these disciplines can be learned only within the structure of production exercises that involve full class participation and the rotation of students within the various crew positions.

This edition of the book has undergone some major changes to reflect what is happening in the industry. As already mentioned, a new section has been added to the first chapter to give students a history of production. The chapter has also been largely rewritten to take into account all forms of electronic media and the job possibilities they present.

The technical parts of both the audio and camera chapters have been simplified somewhat because of developments that have made this equipment easier to operate and control. The chapter on pictorial elements has been largely rewritten and moved forward from where it was placed in the last edition because of the expanding role of computer graphics and their connection to the switcher. The videotape chapter has been significantly revised to take into account the new smaller formats. Likewise, the chapter on editing has been changed to include the concept of nonlinear editing, although the linear editing systems that most schools still use are the main focus of the chapter.

A chapter on producing has been added so that graduating students can be more versed in what has become a crucial item in television production—budgeting and cost control. The two directing chapters have been largely reorganized and now incorporate much of the material that was in chapters dealing with acting and the production crew in the previous edition. Some of the production crew information is also included in the first chapter so that students can start the course knowing what their duties will be. The final chapter, on field production, has been reorganized so it serves both as a review of the rest of the book and as an introduction to single camera production.

Some of the production projects given in the appendix have been changed, and the rate card material given in the appendix of previous editions now appears, in updated form, in the producing chapter. Both the glossary and bibliography have been largely rewritten.

As in previous editions we have presented equipment that in our view serves as an example of the technologies that students are working with in their institutions or will be working with as they first enter the job market. Some equipment used for illustration will be close to state of the art, but in other cases we have deliberately shown some older, proven units because they are typical of the technology in general use.

The *training exercises* that in previous editions were at the conclusion of each chapter will now be found only in the *Instructor's Manual,* along with suggested exam questions and other related information for each chapter.

It is our wish to again provide a text that serves as an efficient teaching and learning vehicle for introductory and secondary courses in television production. As always we welcome suggestions and corrections from our colleagues through our respective universities or the publisher.

We have had the advice and assistance of many colleagues and students in putting this text together. While we cannot single out everybody, we would specifically like to thank those who reviewed the previous edition. Their comments provided us with ideas for this sixth edition text. They are David Cardwell, Xavier University; Joseph Chuk, Kutztown University; and George Quenzel, Emerson College.

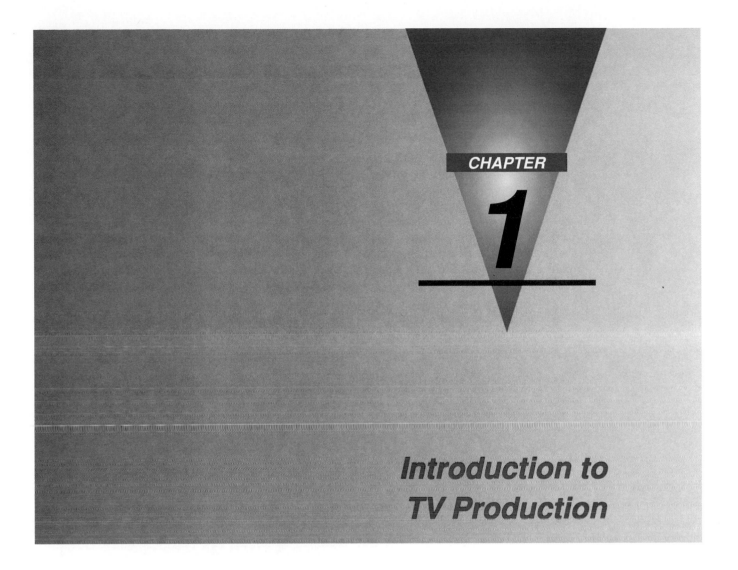

Introduction to TV Production

The electronic mass media are the primary forms of communication in America today. Those working in the field of TV production are part of an industry that has a great deal of authority and responsibility. There has been a mixed reaction to the fact that most people now receive the majority of their information, education, and entertainment from broadcast television, radio, cable, and motion pictures. A commonly accepted figure states that the average graduating high school student has spent 18,000 hours watching television and only 15,000 hours in the classroom.

With the advent of satellite transmission and the merging of a number of other communication organizations, the influence of these media upon our lives can only increase. Some educators have expressed a concern over statistics that show a steady decline in all cognitive skills and have blamed this on the influence of television. Others see the electronic media as an important adjunct to the field of education.

Whatever the case, most of those who work to organize and deliver the media message must themselves be very adept at traditional verbal and scientific abilities. A better than average reading and writing test score often serves as the gateway to success in media related areas such as *critical analysis, research,* and *business training.* Each of these can be an important prerequisite for long-range employment in the communication field.

To the outsider, and probably some of the newer entry level workers, television production seems to be an endlessly fascinating combination of glamour and excitement. While it is true that status and income levels are often impressive and the intensity found in many production situations can make the pulse race (see figure 1-1), the attractiveness of television as a career is rather more sophisticated.

Most video professionals feel a definite sense of pride in being able to function as a part of a team that creates a product, generally valued by our society. Whether one works on a news program or works to produce an industrial training tape, there are a number of things about being a part of this communications team that strongly appeal to intelligent, well-motivated people. Because the effort requires many different and exacting skills, the process of working together and accomplishing this worthwhile and very viable end product makes for a strong sense of continuing inner satisfaction as well as a good deal of mutual respect among colleagues. (See figure 1-2.)

FIGURE 1-1

Fast breaking stories can create a number of last minute, on-the-air changes in the five o'clock newscast. Those changes are possible because the director has calmly talked through the basic structure of the program with key operating personnel in a session that goes right up to airtime. Note clock.

Photo courtesy of KABC-TV

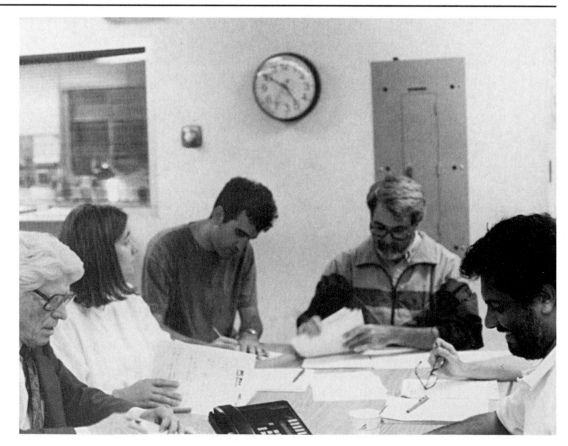

FIGURE 1-2

Prior planning pays off when the production team can coordinate an hour of studio anchored news with live location pick-ups and the split second insertion of videotaped inserts. This group took over from the crew of the previous hour which returned again to do the six o'clock program.

Photo courtesy of KABC-TV

1.1 DISCIPLINES AND TECHNIQUES

In the study of electronically based media production it is important that students develop an understanding of the ways in which the creative process is linked to the technology of the media. Such an understanding can really only be gained through "hands-on" experience in operating such components as switchers, cameras, audio consoles, and lighting control systems that are essential to the production sequence. As is evident by the title of this text, it is the opinion of the authors that there are two related but differing aspects to the operation of studio and field equipment.

First there are the basic *techniques* of knowing how and when to move levers, push buttons, and turn knobs so that a component can do what it is intended to do. The operator must follow the designated *logic* of the control system or the machine does not operate. The second aspect of equipment control is at a much more personal level of activity. This is the matter of *discipline*—the way in which skill and attitude are brought together in what is usually considered a creative effort. For the professional this more subtle level of operation may be the end product of a lifetime of work.

To further define these two terms, let's take the example of one camera operator who uses off-air time to double-check all aspects of focus for upcoming shots, allowing for possible unexpected variables in camera-to-subject distance. Another operator does only a cursory check at several positions of the zoom lens and figures to make last-second adjustments if changes occur. Both individuals may know the specific *techniques* needed to operate their cameras equally well. But only one will be prepared for the unforeseen but all too common surprises of an ongoing production.

For a professional director, the *discipline* exhibited by the well-prepared camera operator is an enormously important quality. It is what makes "live" and "live-to-tape" sports, news, and music television possible. It exists when one is motivated to combine operational skill with a sense of responsibility. This text takes a number of opportunities to extend the idea of self-discipline into the related concept of *teamwork* and the skills that are necessary for one to function as a part of a production team. (See figure 1-3.)

The authors have sought to stress the importance of both the *technical* and *organizational* aspects of television while preparing the material presented here. They are well aware that for many individuals college level production courses are their first opportunity to gain an understanding about the way the production process operates. The text has been designed so that the instructor can provide a somewhat realistic introduction to both studio and field operations by means of a number of scripted exercises and production examples.

FIGURE 1-3

The calm authority of news anchors Harold Green and Ann Martin is only possible with the support of many highly skilled people behind the camera. At KABC-TV nearly 200 people work to produce five and one half hours of news per day.

Photo courtesy of KABC-TV

The law of averages would indicate that while many students will follow a career in production-based positions, others will gravitate to office jobs such as operations, programming, sales, or management. Whatever the case, nothing has been wasted. Management decisions constantly revolve around what is done in the studio and how efficiently it is done. People in all facets of the industry, from unit managers and scriptwriters to advertising executives and general managers, will do a better job if they have a good understanding of the production techniques presented here.

Today the need for a good background in studio and field operations also directly relates to the important process of getting that first job. The competition for internships and entry level jobs at cable companies and independent production houses is such that it is almost mandatory to have some experience in directing, producing, and writing along with many of the operating skills of lighting, audio, editing, and graphics.[1]

As a television production student, you have entered into a long process of *individual development* that must continue throughout your career. You must be concerned with the *techniques* of knowing precisely how to use all of the equipment as well as developing your own sense of production *discipline* so that others will be able to depend on you with confidence. In fact, one of the most revealing tests of your production capabilities is to answer this simple question: Do other people really want you on their production team?

1.2 DEVELOPMENT OF A PROFESSIONAL ATTITUDE

When people work together in what sociologists call *task-oriented groups*, ongoing

1. Gross, Lynne S. *The Internship Experience*. 2nd ed. Prospect Heights, IL: Waveland Press, 1993.

5

FIGURE 1-4

These students are discussing professional methods and attitudes with Erica Hanson, a producer with Fox Entertainment News.

success is very much a matter of what other people—especially those in charge of getting things done—think of you. In these circumstances we are judged by a set of values that are usually summed up under the term *professional attitude*. (See figure 1-4.) How do others view your manner of approaching those tasks that fall within your area of responsibility?

Dependability is probably the most basic virtue in a time-oriented industry like telecommunications. Do you make a conscious effort to be on time, and to be in the sort of physical and mental condition that enables you to give your best effort? Do you handle your equipment with proper care to avoid costly maintenance work? Do you make an attempt to communicate your suggestions as well as your uncertainties to those in charge? Do you show respect for the work of others and for their operational needs during the production sequence? Finally, and of great importance, have you learned to discipline yourself to remain calm and focused upon your tasks, especially when difficulties begin to occur?

The answers to these and similar questions are what determine how we rank with our peers. It may be hard to believe in the early college years, but for many students their important career contacts will go back to the people in their classes—especially in their production courses. In terms of future employment it is not so much *who* you know, as it is the status of the people who *think well of you.* It therefore behooves all students, beginning on the first day of class, to quietly but confidently start doing those things that go into creating the impression of being one who is articulate, reliable, and skilled. Yes, there are those big talkers who for a while can make an impression without much to back it up, but the realities of production eventually are their undoing.

Attitudes and Self Image

In this process of interpersonal relationships it is important to keep in mind that the opinions that others have about us in many ways relate to what we think of ourselves. There has been much discussion recently about how young people need *self esteem.* The reality that is often ignored in this is that people do not simply *get* self esteem—they *earn* it. On a production crew you earn the good opinion of others by consistently doing the sort of job that brings approval and, along with it, that very important sense of self-satisfaction. People know, and the word gets out. Good work does not just happen. It comes from thinking through the things that one must be prepared for in order to function in any given position.

Do you really understand the signal flow through the audio board or are you planning on figuring it out during the setup period? Where are the tight places in the script when a lot of things happen at once? Do the others working with you understand their responsibilities or should you double-check them on equipment and procedures? Minutes spent in preparation can save a tenfold wasting of precious time during final production.

Competition and Team Functioning

An interesting process of interaction becomes evident as groups of four and five persons begin to work together on a project. Such teams quickly find it difficult to function properly if everyone tries to have an equal say on all matters. There must be one designated person who has responsibility for final decisions after making sure there has been a good exchange of ideas on the content and approach to the project. The successful leader maintains his or her position not only by presenting a good plan of action, but also by adopting other team members' ideas, especially in their areas of assigned responsibility. Teams usually function best when everyone has a chance to exhibit his or her skills and leadership abilities. This delicate combination of cooperation and competition usually produces very positive results. (See figure 1-5.)

The authors have seen this process of "equal opportunity in action" occur in countless classes. The course starts out with a new mix of students. Some are old friends and some are just getting to know each other. There are usually a few who would like to think of themselves as "the talented people." In early production work the truth or myth of their superiority is proven by results. During a normal process of organization and competition, some new people begin to emerge both as leaders and/or as persons with other special talents that are very important to a project. No one has really been "put down," but some have had a chance to learn some very important lessons about hard work and accomplishment. Those with sufficient *ego energy drive* make adjustments and in later classes work to regain the good opinion of their peers. The need for status and respect motivates us all.

FIGURE 1-5

For this student crew, field production day was the culmination of a month of planning that included subject research, scriptwriting, and location surveys.

1.3 THE EXPANDING SCOPE OF VIDEO PRODUCTION

In his 1991 book, *Three Blind Mice*,[2] author Ken Auletta tells the fascinating story of how some aggressive and imaginative people in the cable business captured a considerable amount of the traditional network audience. They did it by providing low cost programming that appealed to smaller, select audience groups. Called **niche programming,** it included a number of "talk" shows featuring some rather bizarre people, channels airing commercial-free movies for a fee, top musical hits accompanied by visual images, and news twenty-four hours a day. It wasn't all pretty, but the networks were caught napping and lost many of their viewers.

2. Auletta, Ken. *Three Blind Mice.* New York: Random House, 1991.

This sequence of events accelerated the already changing shape of video production in this country. In the "good old days" the networks produced many of their own programs or had them tailor-made by a very select group of production companies. With the new opportunities on cable, a whole new group of production companies began to turn out numerous attractive, low budget shows.

Employment Patterns

While many prime time network and cable shows are still produced in large, fully equipped video studios often located on movie lots, an increasing number of programs are done in much smaller **production houses,** with or without union sanction. They employ many recently graduated students working at entry level wages. The reality is that all too often one must trade experience for money during the early years of a media career.

Another negative trend is the employment of most workers on a **daily hire** basis. These workers are not on staff and, even though they may work regularly three or four days a week, they are not eligible for health or other benefits. The result of this **freelance** employment is that many people now make their living working simultaneously in cable, corporate, and broadcast production. The production techniques and equipment are very much at the same level. Except for the larger broadcasting stations and networks, crew members are often called upon to perform a wide range of engineering tasks such as audio, lighting, camera, and graphics. Those wishing to do directing and producing are selected from these crew positions.

For those about to graduate, all of this may seem to be a bit on the down side. The good news is that in many areas of employment, things are expanding at a

8

very healthy rate. Most of those who can survive the difficult early years will find themselves in responsible positions with a fairly secure future. One can take heart in the knowledge that those early career problems being faced by students today are not very different from what entry-level people have faced over the past four decades. The problem of an oversupply of young people wanting to get into TV production continues to exist.

One of the burgeoning areas is *corporate video*. Large and small companies produce a variety of material such as orientation tapes for new employees, training tapes to teach people specific jobs, promotion tapes for new products, and video "newsletters" to keep employees up-to-date. Sometimes these companies have people on staff using company equipment to produce the material; other times they hire freelancers or people who have formed small production houses. In both cases, jobs are created for people with television production skills.

Educational institutions also employ people in media related jobs. Today many universities use **Instructional Television**

Fixed Service (ITFS) to transmit courses over specially designated channels. At many universities this service is a part of a media center that also trains instructors in the use of video in their own classrooms.

Interactive video, made possible by the instant access possibilities of the **CD-ROM** and other digital technologies, is seen as having an important impact on television and is creating many new jobs for those seeking careers in telecommunications.

During the 1980s the FCC approved the use of commercial *low power television* (LPTV) by educational institutions and other organizations. With its transmission distance of only 15 to 20 miles and the difficulty of competing with an ever increasing number of cable channels, its ultimate success remains in question, but it provides excellent entry level jobs.

One of the largest fields is *government media*. Local, state, and federal agencies are involved in a myriad of telecommunications projects. The federal government is probably the world's largest television and film producer. Military applications, including the Armed Forces Radio and Television Services, account for worldwide operations—as does the United States Information Agency (USIA) and its worldwide satellite operation, Worldnet.

Possibly the most rapidly expanding area is in the field of *medical and health services*. More than 80 percent of the 7,000 hospitals in the country use television and related media for patient education, in-service training (staff development), and/or public and community relations. (See figure 1-6.)

Another active field is that of *religious production*. The production level seen on many of the broadcasts of some of the evangelical groups rivals many network programs. At least five such church bodies operate their own satellite networks.

One of the more intriguing applications of the video and computer technologies is **desktop video.** A number of manufacturers who are new to the field have been marketing relatively inexpensive but very efficient editing and graphics equipment that allow people to do some very effective video production work right in their own home. Most of the peripheral production areas like *event video* (weddings, graduations, and yearbooks) have gotten into this format with very good results.

An idea of the significance and magnitude of all of these various nonbroadcast production operations can be gleaned by simply looking at respective employment figures. According to United States Department of Labor statistics, in 1990 there were well over 200,000 people employed in broadcast operations, including both stations and networks. By contrast, it is estimated that close to 300,000 people were employed in the nonbroadcast areas just discussed (cable, corporate, educational, interactive, low power, government and military, medical and health, religious, and event video). It is probably safe to say that the later 1990s could add another 50 percent to both figures and not be too far off the mark.

1.4 PRODUCTION APPROACHES

During its first several decades much of what was seen on broadcast television was either a **multiple-camera** "live" production that was edited through the **switcher** as it was being broadcast, or a **single-camera** film production that was shot much like a movie and edited on a machine called a **movieola.** News programs were a successful combination of both techniques.

The development of truly portable cameras and the **helical scan** tape formats, which made editing possible, changed all this. News programs were first to use portable equipment because the footage shot could be shown instantly without having to wait for film processing. As a result, the equipment became known as **electronic news gathering** (ENG) equipment. But portable equipment also opened up a whole series of new production possibilities far beyond the area of news programs so has frequently been referred to as **electronic field production** (EFP) equipment. Recently both the cable and the broadcasting networks have been successfully using EFP equipment for a number of new documentary formats including "police in action" and other crime related productions.

At a somewhat higher level, many professional observers have been impressed with the way ABC's *Nightline* has combined studio, field, and documentary techniques while functioning under the strict deadlines of a five-night-a-week live program. It maintained its ratings against an impressive array of late-night talent.

Multiple-camera production was invented by television. It remains the only way of broadcasting news, sports, and other events whose value is related to the immediacy of presentation. The same is true of daytime talk shows like *Donahue* where the spontaneity of the discussion can only work properly with the "live" technique. With dramatic presentations, the decision to use multiple-cameras relates more to budgetary matters. An hour of network prime time drama costs more than a million dollars to produce if it is shot with a single-camera film technique. Most situation comedies use multiple film or electronic cameras to shoot complete three to five minute scenes for postproduction editing. (See figure 1-7.) The shows that use single-camera film transfer the film to videotape for all editing and effects work.

All daytime soap operas are shot using multiple electronic cameras. Scenes are shot straight through from beginning to end with an occasional pickup shot edited in later to correct minor problems. Most of the sets are permanently erected in large network studios. The production

10

FIGURE 1-7

Network level multiple-camera production continues as a cost efficient production method, especially for public broadcasting, commercial network situation comedies, and soap operas.

Photo courtesy of KCET-TV Los Angeles

methods are very efficient. Sometimes two directors will be working the same day on different program segments. A typical program budget costs approximately $500,000 for five hour-long shows. It is quite usual for all five programs to be completed within a four day work week.

1.5 A QUICK SURVEY OF WORKING AREAS, EQUIPMENT, AND CREW POSITIONS

From the beginning, a network television **studio** has been an impressive place in which to work or even just to visit. There is a special something about the way the crew and talent work together that is unforgettable. This is also very true of the spirit of cooperation that develops in most university level production courses. (See figure 1-8.)

Your own studio, be it large or small, will contain several elements common to all production studios since the beginning of television. Suspended just below the ceiling is a light **grid** consisting of a series of connected pipes on which a number of different sized lighting instruments are hung. The illuminating device within these lights will usually vary in strength from 500 to 5,000 watts of power. In most studios there are a sufficient number of instruments so that they are not moved from one location on the grid to another. Each light has a number that corresponds to the same number on a **patch panel** where each is further connected to a lighting **dimmer board.** The lighting director and his or her crew set the lights before the production begins. (See figure 1-9.)

Covering at least two of the walls will be a floor-to-ceiling stretched cloth called a **cyclorama.** It is anchored at the top by chains to a track that allows it to be moved

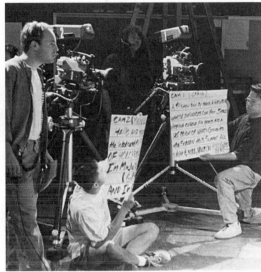

when not needed. In addition to the usual basic light grey color, some "cycs," as they are also known, may have black or dark blue sections to provide a variety of backgrounds. The lighter cloth textures reflects a variety of colors when a transparent colored **gel** covering is placed in front of a lighting instrument. The cyc is only one form of background used for television productions. Many other sets are needed, so most studios have a nearby area where set pieces and props can be stored and constructed. A **production designer** or **art director** is usually in charge of selecting and constructing proper sets and other artistic elements.

The studio also contains the **cameras** used to obtain the pictures that will be shown over the air and the microphones that will pick up sound. Camera operators frame the proper shots during production. Sometimes cameras have **teleprompters** on the front from which the talent reads the script. If this is the case someone is needed to run the script material through the teleprompter, keeping up with the reading rate of the performers.

12

Audio operators place microphones on the set or talent before taping begins. Sometimes an operator is needed to move a microphone, such as one mounted on a **boom,** during production.

Another person who operates from the studio during production is the **floor manager** (also known as the **floor director** or **stage manager**). This person is in charge of dealing with the talent and relaying the director's instructions to them.

The cameras in the studio are connected to a separate room called the video **control booth.** (See figure 1-10.) During production the producer, director, assistant director, technical director and often the lighting director will be working out of this area. Located directly in front of these crew members are a series of video **monitors** showing the picture coming from each camera and from all of the other picture sources being used in the production. The people working in these five positions use the visual information seen on the monitors along with what is heard on audio monitors to make ongoing decisions as to the moment by moment structure of the production. While the scope of each of these positions may vary according to the nature of the program, the basic areas of responsibility are those described below.

When programs are done in a continuous, start-to-finish style of assembly, the **director** is usually in a position of complete control. It is his or her voice that dominates what one hears on the **intercom** system. With this microphone/earphone **headset,** the director talks to most members of the crew, giving precise commands to do certain things and also making sure that they are aware of the upcoming sequence of events. Their brief replies are an informational feedback that is important to the director. (See figure 1-11.)

Some network level news and sports productions operate with the **producer** also on the headset. This is in line with the concept that on such shows the producer has the responsibility for making final

FIGURE 1-11

To control the ongoing production sequence, the director must use the intercommunication system in both a precise and considerate manner.

program decisions even during airtime. On most other types of programs, however, producers are more concerned with long-range planning, budgets, and personnel matters. Most of the creative thinking on exactly how those policy and artistic decisions will be executed is the province of the director. Because these two areas of responsibility all too often overlap, discretion is needed to avoid tension.

The **assistant director** works directly in support of the director. He or she may be delegated to provide timings, set up camera shots and alert crew members to the upcoming sequence of operation.

The **technical director** operates the switcher during production, selecting the director's choice of video inputs and video effects such as wipes and picture inserts. This position has the larger responsibility for coordinating all technical aspects of production from the initial planning stages through studio wrap-up.

The **lighting director** works at the lighting dimmer control board usually located in the video control room for convenience of communication with the director. During a production there may be a number of changes in lighting that must occur on cue from the director. The lighting director is responsible for drawing up a lighting plan and overseeing the work done to adjust each instrument for coverage and intensity.

Adjacent to the video control room and sometimes viewed through a large window is the **audio control booth.** Here the main audio operator and assistants work at an **audio board** to mix and balance the feeds from microphones, audio and video tape machines, audio disc players, and other sound sources. Prior to the production they design and check out the audio plan for the positioning of microphones in the studio. Often, a soundproof **announce booth** is adjacent to this room where the off-camera announcer can make appropriate input.

Much of the equipment needed for television production is located in a separate area or areas often still called **master control** (MC). (See figure 1-12.) Here one finds the **camera control unit** along with the **waveform monitors** and **vectorscopes** that are essential to establishing camera brightness and color quality. Video operators use this equipment to make sure the cameras are producing their best technical pictures. The MC area also usually houses the **sync generator** to keep all video equipment in synchronization along with a

number of **videotape recorders** and their accompanying audio and video monitors. Nearby will be other equipment used during production such as the **character generator** and **computer graphics** unit. These equipment operators must be wearing intercom headsets to receive cues to start tapes or change a graphics feed.

In some production facilities there may be no MC as such. All this equipment is located right in the video control room. With the separate room location, however, a master control supervisor is responsible for overseeing the whole operation. This master control equipment is usually linked together through a patch panel so that it can also be used for editing work.

Editing, itself, is usually undertaken in small or medium-sized rooms called **editing suites.** These are usually close to, but not part of master control. They contain videotape recorders, monitors, edit controllers, and sometimes peripheral equipment such as CD players or character generators. The editors who operate this equipment often

FIGURE 1-12

In many teaching institutions the master control area contains the picture synchronization equipment, camera control units, videotape machines used for program material, computer controlled graphics, and character generator equipment. Each requires its own picture monitor or other graphic readout.

work in tandem with the director. The director conveys what should be edited and the editor actually accomplishes it.

With your first studio tour you will undoubtedly find some variations from the structure described above. A number of basic designs are possible, depending upon the size and designed purposes of a particular studio. It is to be hoped that your equipment goes beyond the basic facilities described here, but do not despair if this is not the case. The nature and scope of one's training is ultimately what is important. It should be noted that the descriptions of crew positions are of an introductory nature and will be dealt with more completely in later chapters.

1.6 TECHNICAL ASPECTS OF TV PRODUCTION

At the beginning of this decade, most people had very little reason to believe that their personal computer (if they had one) had much in common with their television set. Then, with the development of digitally based audio and video systems, these two miracles of the electronic age were given the ability to "talk" to each other. The result has been a veritable *quantum leap* of communication options and efficiency. This new technology will increasingly affect the way in which we relate to each other as individuals and to the way in which we perceive world events and their meaning in our own lives. We can see this by examining how Cable News Network and similar operations have changed our perspective on the world in the past years.

At the other end of the scale, increasing numbers of people have discovered the corporate and personal uses for desktop video. It is now possible for a single individual to do camera-work, graphics, and editing right in their home and, in the process, create some very impressive work.

Between these two poles, the field of traditional media production has undergone an enormous growth, brought about by an almost exponential increase in the use of the electronic media in our society.

In this, as in previous editions of the text, we follow the lead of much of the industry and use the term "television production" in its broadest sense. It will simply apply to all of those video and sound operations that go into the assembly of productions distributed by cable and broadcasting, as well as those done for the educational and corporate areas.

1.7 BACKGROUND TO TODAY'S TECHNOLOGY

In earlier days, the term television production described a much smaller realm. When one of this text's authors was first working in television in the late 1950s, much of the daytime programming seen on a major city station was either a "live" studio production (with such stars as Johnny Carson and Liberace), a rerun of a prime time network program produced on film, or an old movie. Commercials for locally advertised products were usually done live in the studio. Commercials for nationally advertised products were produced mostly on film.

While film was an important part of local news programs, it was used carefully because of the cost factor. Footage was shot as a black-and-white negative. Editors and reporters had to do their work looking at this negative film which was then projected on the air as a positive picture through the action of **polarity reversal** in the broadcast projection camera. Sound was recorded on a magnetic strip on the film. Because of the location of the sound pickup head in the projector, editors had to leave an extra second of picture on the film before making an edit. This meant that the audience would often see a moment or so of a speaker's lips continuing to move at an edit outpoint.

The only way to record a "live" program was to utilize the **kinescope** film process. With a few refinements, this was basically a matter of placing a film camera in front of a TV set. In the late 1950s many people in the western states were still seeing prime time network programs by means of these filmed recordings as they waited for the coaxial cable to get to their town. Programs had to be aired one week late in these areas and, to make things even worse, the "kine" caused a noticeable loss of audio and picture quality.

Compared with today's technology, the mostly black and white programs of the late 1950s and early 1960s may sound somewhat primitive. However, truth of the impact of this new medium upon the American public is another story. The audiences loved television and so did those of us who worked to put it on the air.

Impact of Recorded and Edited Television

Technically, much began to change with the introduction of **videotape.** The first **VTRs** (video tape recorders) were large and viewed with reverence and wonder. CBS first began to use them in 1956 for delaying the feed of news programs to the western states, but it took much of the next decade before videotape was in general use. At first, editing was done with razor blades and plastic adhesive tape. With this method, about every third edit would cause breakup in the picture and it had to be re-done.

Then, electronic **transfer editing** using two machines was tried. In the beginning it was also a hit-and-miss affair. The proposed **edit in** and **edit out** points were synchronized by rolling the tape to the hoped for edit point, stopping the tape, and then making a mark on the tape with a grease pencil. One must keep in mind that the old **quadruplex** VTR machines could not produce a picture unless the tape was kept running at full speed. Both big reels (holding two inch wide tape) were then rolled backwards by hand to prepare for a roughly five second **pre-roll** period. Playback and record tapes were then rolled together. The director watched both monitors, and at the right moment said, "NOW!!!" as the editor pushed the record button. It was called "crash editing" and after a few hours you felt like somewhat of a wreck yourself.

By the early 1970s two important developments were providing editors with precise control over tape movement and, as a result, segment location. These factors resulted in the concept of **frame-accurate editing.** The first was the development of the **helical scan** recording format. Each slanted top-to-bottom scan of the tape produced a complete picture **field.** As a result, tape speed could be varied to allow both **still frame** and slow-motion pictures. An editor could now stop the tape or move it slowly back and forth while viewing picture fields. This gave the operator the necessary control for locating the precise inpoints and outpoints of an edit.

The development of **SMPTE** (Society of Motion Picture and Television Engineers) **time code** was of equal importance in the improvement of editing techniques. Called an **address system,** it assigned a specific hour, minute, second, and frame number to each of the thirty frames per second produced by the camera or other video source when recorded on tape. Picture location could be precisely linked to numbers. With the combination of these two elements, editing ceased to be a chore and was on its way to becoming an art.

Advances in Field Production, Film Transfer, and Graphics

Field production (then called a **"remote"**) was a matter of taking a converted bus, three very large cameras, that huge tape recorder and a noisy gasoline powered generator mounted on a trailer, to someplace where it all stuck out like a sore thumb. It was a big operation and fraught with possibilities for "Murphy's Law" to catch up with you.

Again the helical-scan format came to the rescue. When combined with the invention of the **cassette** tape, it allowed for the development of the first truly portable cameras and recorder units and eventually led to the camcorder. (See figure 1-13.) These advances totally changed the way electronic field production was shot. When combined with newly developed editing techniques the result was a whole new concept of postproduction. (*Wide World of Sports* is the primary example.)

Eventually much of this same technology was applied to studio-based shows giving them an entirely new look. The economics of all this meant these programs could compete in prime time with the more expensive filmed productions.

By the 1980s most programs being shot on film began to use a **flying spot scanner** such as the Rank-Cintel unit that transferred film to video for all editing, titles, and effects work. Using the CMX editor or similar equipment, programs were assembled and reassembled in a work print **off-line** test stage before finally being put together in the **on-line** assembly stage. Again economic factors resulting from new technology brought about a major change in production techniques.

Also in the 1980s the whole world of **computer generated graphics** seemed to just explode upon the scene. Hooked up to the incredible speed of micro-chip electronics, artwork produced directly onto a TV monitor was something never seen

FIGURE 1-13

This portable electronic news gathering equipment revolutionized news coverage and greatly improved sports programming as well.

Photo courtesy of ABC news

before. Units with names like *ADO, Chyron,* and *Paintbox* costing hundreds of thousands of dollars, were talked about with a certain awe. As more and more of this work began to be done with animated movement, the public was irrevocably drawn to its stunning effect.

The Beginnings of a New Video Standard

This graphics breakthrough, and much more that was to follow, became possible because American scientists discovered a new way to encode video and audio signals into **digital** form. A video signal is created by the action of the camera which turns light into amplified waves of electromagnetic energy. These are referred to as being an **analog** of the original light waves in that they retain a similarity of form. Through a process called **sampling,** various qualities (frequency, wavelength etc.) of these waves are converted into a digital equivalent of the same signal information. In their new "0" and "1" **bit** form, they are virtually impervious to outside interference and, of even more importance, are now in a form that is the basic language spoken by computers.

It became obvious that the digital signal carried the promise of greatly improved technology in all areas of video as well as audio production. The first digital video tape machine was the Sony DVR 1000, which appeared in the mid 1960s. It also utilized the new concept of separating the video signal into separate brightness and color **(luminance** and **chrominance)** feeds. This **component** video in a digital format soon became known as **D-1** to differentiate it from a later **D-2** tape format put out by the Ampex Company. This was also a digital format but it returned to a **composite** (combined brightness and color) signal that did not necessitate as much expense in studio

conversion costs. The numerical tradition continued when Panasonic later brought out its **D-3,** a half-inch digital composite format. To add to the confusion, while both the **S-VHS** and **Hi8** formats also split their signals into separate luminance and chrominance feeds, the manufacturers do not claim this format to be a true component video.

For a number of years some editors were not completely satisfied with the restrictions of **linear** videotape based editing. The problem is that one cannot insert additional material to expand a segment once the edit transfer is made. With **nonlinear** editing, the **laser disc** and/or **hard drive** technology, with its digitally produced pictures, has been combined with the computer's ability to control an almost instantaneous **random access** to pictures. In a manner that resembles the operation of a word processor, an editor can insert new video material within an existing segment. This is similar to the way in which film has always been edited in that no material has to be removed to make way for the new insert.

Engineers who had been working on the concept of **high definition television (HDTV)** soon realized that digital technology offered tremendous opportunities for improving all phases of video production, especially those relating to the new FCC approved over-the-air broadcast system. During the past decade the television picture seen by Americans has been in the process of evolving away from the original **NTSC** (National Television Standards Committee) form dating back to 1941. With its 525 scanning lines, analog signal, and composite video signals it has served us well, but is now seen to contain a number of flaws that will be improved upon with the implementation of the new FCC high definition broadcast standard. It will eventually have a component digital video with double the number of **scanning lines** of the older system. This new picture will be scanned *progressively* instead of the older **interlace** system that produces the sequence of odd and even line fields. To solve the problem of the large increase in **bandwidth** necessary for digital transmission, the new concept of **bit rate reduction** (**compression**) has been of great importance. This development eliminates the repetitive parts of the picture signal during all phases of production, editing, and transmission. The result is a savings in equipment size and a reduction in required channel capacity. Above all, the quality and reliability of this new system is seen by many as opening up new vistas for the use of the television product.

1.8 TECHNOLOGY AND TEAMWORK

In every edition of this text we have spent some time discussing the relationship of technology to the academic study of media production and specifically to the career goals of students. The above material on the status of current technology has been presented to emphasize the scope and rate of change during the relatively short period of television's development. To those of us who have been a part of this process, there would seem to be several conclusions that can be drawn from a careful look at this impressive history.

First it must be noted that those who ignore technological advances do so at their own peril. For too long the American video industry failed to do the research and development necessary to keep even a small share of VCR and set manufacturing in this country. Our computer hardware and software manufacturers seem to have learned an important lesson and continue to be very competitive in that area. In terms of actual program production, this country sets the pace. One must

be especially impressed with the areas of news and sports where innovations based on new techniques of editing, graphics, and camera-work have set standards that are copied around the world.

It must be noted, however, that advances in operational technology can too easily become an expensive exercise in futility and waste if there is not a well-functioning team to turn the best scriptwriting and planning into a program. One of the most important things that students learn in production courses is an ability to work as a part of a team. With these interpersonal work skills, experience is the best teacher. Those who have helped manage a fast food outlet or trained in competitive sports often have an advantage in understanding the concept of *teamwork* and how it applies to video production.

The team experience is essential to those who aspire to work eventually in positions of *leadership*. The directors, technical directors, producers, and program executives of the future are those in your classes (possibly yourself) whose ideas and efficiency of communication are such that they can motivate groups of people to work together toward a common purpose. Much of being a successful leader is a matter of getting people to move beyond just "doing a job" to the level of *creativity*. Being creative is itself often defined as the ability to project a previously learned skill into a new situation. By that definition a lighting director, carefully lighting the face of an actress to fit her role, shows the same sort of *creative initiative* that one looks for in directors or scriptwriters. The process of getting writers, planners, and equipment operators all moving toward a creative whole is indeed an exercise in leadership and cooperation. There may be problems and there is always tension, but the process is usually a very rewarding one at all levels of creativity and responsibility.

SUMMARY

Television production is a complex, difficult but usually rewarding enterprise. Each individual member of the operating team must master and demonstrate an exacting combination of *techniques* and *disciplines*—knowing the proper use of the equipment and being able to interact productively with every member of the team. This is true whether you are involved with *television production* at the network, station, or cable level, or *nonbroadcast telecommunications* (corporate, government, medical, and educational applications), or the personal format media (event recording and desktop media). Similar techniques and disciplines must be mastered whether you are involved with *multiple-camera* live production (in the studio and on location) or if you are working with *single-camera* techniques (for either dramatic or journalistic purposes).

In any kind of TV production situation, you must be concerned with a wide variety of working areas and tools of the medium—the *computer/word processor, studio facilities, sets, graphics, lighting instruments, cameras* and *microphones*, audio and video *mixing areas, editing equipment*, and various *engineering and control facilities*. Students in beginning TV production must also be familiar with the jobs of the *producer* and *director*. As producer, you must assume ultimate responsibility for the entire program—from its initial conception to final audience feedback. As director, you are responsible for the specific elements of production—preproduction planning, creative use of the medium, control room execution of the production, and, if necessary, editing. Each position entails its own set of techniques and disciplines.

It is also important for students involved in video production to know the fast-paced history of equipment and techniques from the early days of *live* or *kinescoped* productions through advances in *videotape recording, editing, field production*, and *graphics* up to the new evolving standards developing through the use of *digital technologies, compression*, and *high definition television*.

Most of what has been presented in this chapter is of a general overview nature. The rest of the book will handle in more specific detail the equipment and concepts touched on in this chapter. In chapter 2 we begin our look at the audio elements of television production.

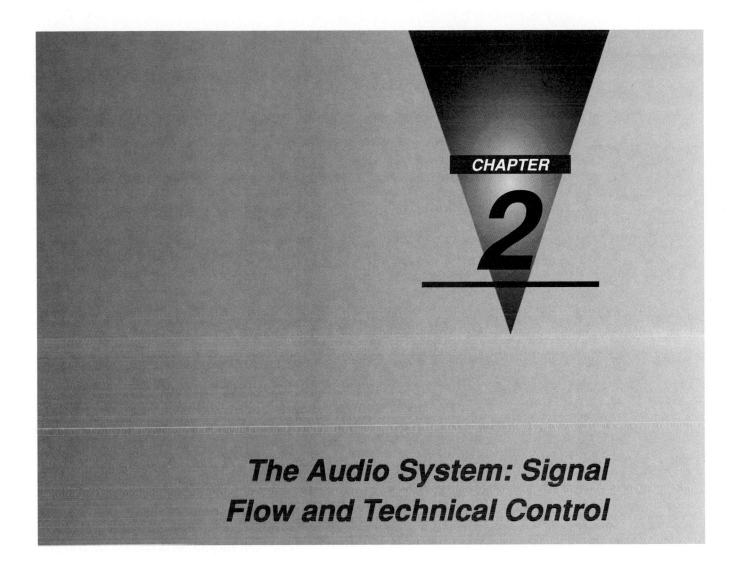

The Audio System: Signal Flow and Technical Control

The audio system is an excellent place to begin comprehending the basics of television. In most ways the function and operation of audio equipment is easier to understand than video, and the model provided by audio production methods gives students an advantage in understanding the more demanding complexities of the audio/video production.

For most students their first examination of an **audio console** is an impressive and somewhat intimidating experience. However, as each component part of the console is approached in terms of its *function*, all the faders, knobs, lights and other indicators make good sense. The equipment in the **audio control booth** is designed to do one or more of *seven basic control functions*, and to do them quickly and efficiently. Once these functions are understood, learning to work with the equipment is a matter of combining hands-on practice with a continuing study of the *disciplines* and *techniques* of audio production.

2.1 TECHNICAL AND CREATIVE FUNCTIONS OF AUDIO

As the nature of the production sequence becomes clearer, one begins to understand that operators utilize their equipment to perform both *technical functions* and *creative functions.* Electromagnetic energy is such that certain basic requirements must be met simply to get an adequate sound or picture (technical function). It is also possible to manipulate these and other control factors in such a way as to achieve certain aesthetic effects (creative function).

In the audio system, we will initially be concerned with the basic *technical requirements* needed to reproduce original sound with some degree of fidelity. We will start with the study of microphone construction and usage. With this knowledge we can then better understand how voice signals are moved through the various components of the audio console. Within this audio "board," as it is sometimes known, we will also see how the quality of voices can be adjusted and mixed with other sound sources. From the first practice exercises each assigned audio operator should be seeking clear, blended sound at adequately balanced levels of volume.

The *creative side* of audio production may have as its goal a specific *mood* or *emotional setting,* achieved through the specialized use of microphones and other sound sources. For example, the voices in a tender love scene must be heard at a very low level with a husky or whisperlike quality. To get this intimate effect, special mics are placed very close to the performer. Another simultaneous goal could be an *illusion of reality* achieved by purely technical devices, such as a special filter that can create the distinctive voice quality heard in a telephone conversation. A further artistic effect would be produced by the use of music and sound effects.

Several of these elements are discussed in this and the next chapter: mixing and shaping the audio signal (see section 2.2); microphone selection and use, including such considerations as acoustical differences, mic distance, sound balance, and audio perspective (see sections 3.3 and 3.4); and adding other audio sources (see section 3.5).

2.2 THE SEVEN BASIC CONTROL FUNCTIONS

Each piece of equipment in the studio or control booth can perform one or more of seven basic control functions. If you look carefully at your own audio booth and adjoining studio, you will find that audio facilities are generally designed to move, modify, or otherwise control a signal in these seven ways: (1) **Transduce:** converting sound waves into electrical energy and back again; (2) **Channel:** routing the signals, sending them wherever necessary; (3) **Mix:** combining two or more sound sources; (4) **Amplify:** increasing the signal strength; (5) **Shape:** creatively changing or improving the quality of a sound; (6) **Record** and **playback:** retaining a sound in permanent electronic form for later use; (7) **Monitor:** hearing the quality and volume of individual or combined sound sources at various stages of control.

While examining this list, many examples of these functions will probably come to mind from your experience in operating a home entertainment center with recording and playback capabilities. As you apply the previously mentioned characteristics to your unit, you will begin to see that some components perform more than one function. For example, the speaker that *transduces* a signal into listenable sound is also obviously a *monitor.* The bass and treble controls that *shape* the final output of the unit do so by allowing for separate levels of *amplification.*

Keep in mind that the terminology used to define the various components and their functions may vary slightly with time and location. There is, however, a basic structure of functional design common to all audio control rooms. Understanding the essential elements of this structure in your own facility is the necessary prerequisite for successful operation of the equipment in any production situation.

Transduce

The process though which sound (voices, music, etc.) is converted into an audio signal (electrical information) is referred to as *transducing*. Figure 2-1 shows in simplified form how the transducing elements—the microphone components that actually change sound waves into electrical energy—perform this function in one type of microphone.

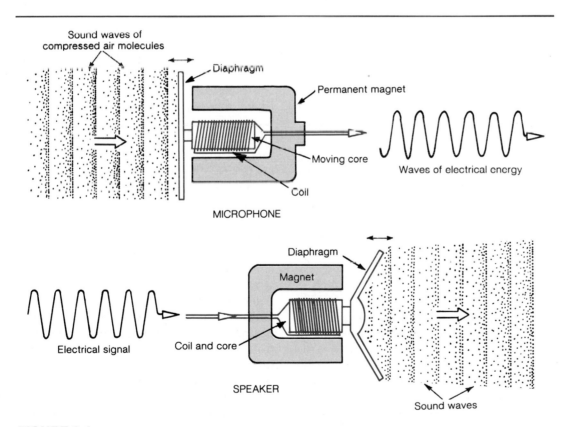

FIGURE 2-1

Transducing element of a dynamic microphone and corresponding speaker elements.

When sound waves from a voice or musical instrument strike the diaphragm of the microphone, the waves of compressed air molecules cause the attached coil to vibrate. As the coil moves back and forth within the magnetic field of the permanent magnet, a small fluctuating electric current is produced. This minute current, which will be amplified many times, carries the same information as the original sound waves. At the receiving end, when this minute electrical signal reaches the speaker coil, it produces fluctuations in the magnetic field that then cause the diaphragm of the speaker to vibrate, creating sound waves that reproduce the original sound picked up by the microphone.

The tone production of a human voice or musical instrument creates pressure waves in the molecules of the air. If these waves are produced at a constant rate of 440 **cycles per second,** the result is the musical tone of A above middle C.[1]

These audible sound pressure waves move through the air and come in contact with the **diaphragm** of the microphone. Their force causes the attached **coil** to vibrate within a part of the permanent **magnet.** When this coil moves within the resulting magnetic field, a small electric current is produced. This signal is now in its new electronic form but retains the original **frequency** pattern of 440 oscillations per second.[2] (More information on wave theory is contained in Appendix A.)

The electronic waveform at this stage is said to be an **analog** of the original sound pressure wave since the electronic wave retains those essential elements of wave frequency, length, and amplitude that characterized the original sound pressure waves. With the newer **digital** playback and/or recording systems the audio signal goes through an additional encoding/decoding stage. Using computer technology, these characteristics of the signal wave (frequency, amplitude etc.) are measured to be further converted into groups of off-on digital pulses. (See section 2.3.) In this digital form, the signal is almost invulnerable to nonsignal **noise** and can therefore reproduce a much higher quality sound.

The transduced microphone signal is amplified at several stages in its journey through the audio control room and is then sent to a recording machine or transmitter. Several more changes take place if the signal is **modulated** for broadcast. In this case the signal is superimposed onto a **carrier frequency** specifically assigned to the radio station and amplified more than a million times for transmission. As an electronic signal, the broadcast carrier wave makes no change in the molecules of the air or any other material through which it passes. In fact, it is this same type of signal that can travel millions of miles to and from spacecraft in the vacuum of space.

Figure 2-2 illustrates that this modulation phase is just part of the total broadcasting sequence.[3] At the receiver a series of events take place that are almost the exact reverse of what took place in the broadcast studio. When picked up by the antenna, this relatively weak broadcast signal is first removed from the carrier wave in a process called **demodulation.** It is then amplified, sent through tone and volume controls and then to the speaker of the TV set or radio receiver. The speaker is also a *transducer,* something like a microphone with the elements—a coil and a magnet—now operating in reverse order. The electrical energy of the signal puts the diaphragm into pulsating motion, pushing against the air molecules. When it moves at

---

1. The term *cycles per second* (cps) is used as the basic unit of measure for sound pressure waves and, in the past, for electromagnetic waves. In recent years, engineering terminology has, for the most part, replaced the term *cycles per second* with the term *hertz* (abbreviated *Hz*), in honor of Heinrich Hertz who first demonstrated the existence of electromagnetic waves.

2. Actually, the A 440 cps frequency in our example is only the fundamental tone. It is by far the most prominent of many tones that are simultaneously produced when a voice or an instrument is sounded. The other tones, which are much softer in volume and occur at higher frequencies, are called "overtones" or "harmonics." Their presence and relative volume are what produce the distinctive quality of any individual voice or instrument. To reproduce any single complete tone accurately, all these resultant frequencies must be picked up and simultaneously transduced into the electrical signal. A more complete explanation of the overtone series is presented in Appendix B.

3. For a simplified explanation of how a carrier wave is theoretically modulated, both by amplitude modulation (AM) and frequency modulation (FM), see Appendix A.

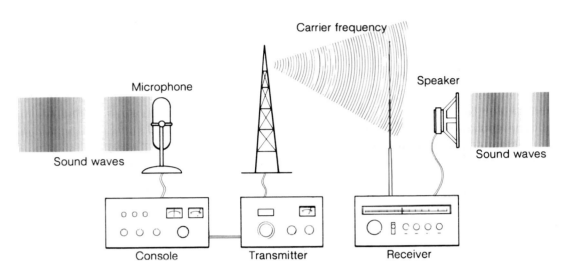

FIGURE 2-2

Modulation and demodulation in the broadcasting sequence.

The original sound waves are transduced into an electrical current that, at the transmitter, is modulated or superimposed over the assigned carrier frequency of the broadcasting station. (During this process, the original signal has been amplified many times its original strength.) This carrier wave is the specific broadcasting frequency assigned by the Federal Communications Commission—either part of the television channel, or, in the case of radio, a separate part of the electromagnetic spectrum (see Appendix A), for example, 690 kiloHertz ("six-ninety on your radio dial"). The TV or radio set then receives this carrier frequency and demodulates (or strips off) the superimposed electrical signal, which is the program information, and the speaker transduces the electrical energy back into sound waves that the ear can perceive.

a rate of 440 cycles per second it creates sound pressure waves reproducing the original tone of A above middle C.

Channel

The term *channel* is used as a verb when it refers to the procedure of moving signals from one place to another and as a noun when it describes the actual pathway the signal follows through cables and other equipment from its source to its final destination. Figure 2-3 shows how the audio operator would plan the *sequence of signal flow* of the feed from a studio mic, going through a **patch bay** connection, into and through the audio console, and then back to the patch bay where it is available to be sent to a video recorder or any number of other destinations.

The process starts when a microphone is connected to a cable which is in turn plugged into a studio microphone input. These numbered wall receptacles are located at different points around the studio. This connection might also be made into a component called a **snake** which has receptacles for twenty or thirty mic inputs all located together in a box-like component connected to the audio booth by a large cable. These permanent lines terminate at the patch bay where there is a similarly numbered receptacle called a *mic output*. (See figures 2-4 and 2-5.)

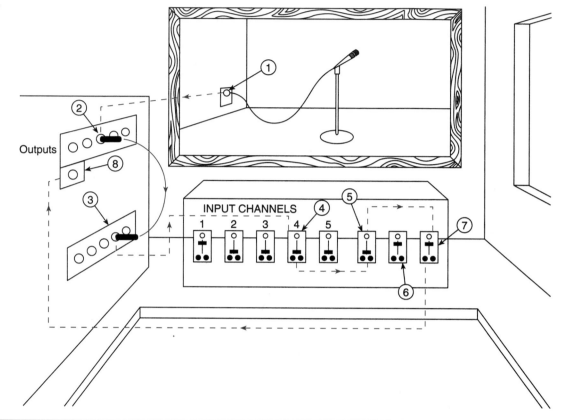

FIGURE 2-3

Audio signal flow model.

(1) Studio microphone wall receptacle input. (2) Patch bay output from studio. (3) Patch bay input to console. (4) Input channel #4. (5 and 6) Group master faders. (7) Master fader for program output. (8) Program-out patch bay receptacle.

FIGURE 2-4

Diagram of a simplified patch bay.

This diagram shows the configuration of a simplified patch bay. The top row of receptacles are source outputs. The lower row are input receptacles leading to numbered input channels at the audio console. Hard-wired (normalled) connections are indicated by a dotted line. A sample signal pathway is shown in red.

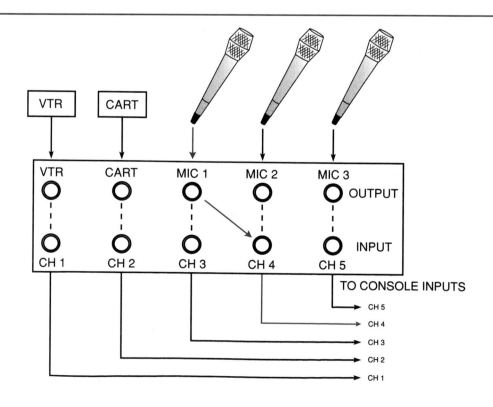

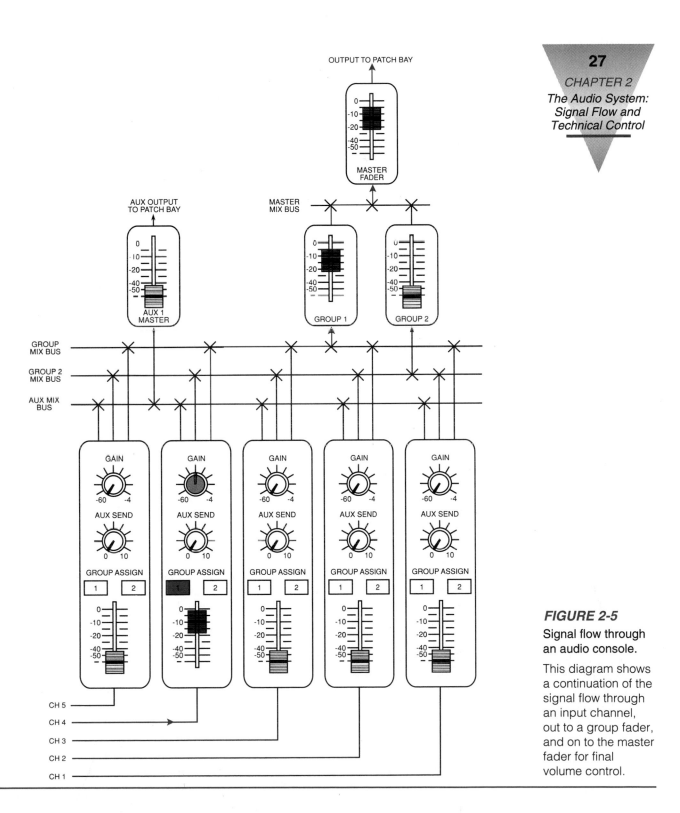

FIGURE 2-5

Signal flow through
an audio console.

This diagram shows
a continuation of the
signal flow through
an input channel,
out to a group fader,
and on to the master
fader for final
volume control.

In addition to a number of other mic outputs, the patch bay will contain outputs from components such as cart (cartridge) machines, CD players, and audiotape and videotape machines.

Usually located just below these output receptacles, another row of input receptacles will lead to the numbered *input channels* within the audio console. In figure 2-4 we show "mic 1 output" being connected down and over to "input channel 4" by means of a **patch cord.**

Normalled Connections

We could have patched mic 1 into input channel 5 or into any of the other available input channels depending upon our *audio setup plan.* However, had we wanted to use input channel 3 (just below the output), we would not have needed to use a patch cord to make the connection into that input channel. Notice the dotted line running from mic 1 to input channel 3 (and the similar dotted lines for the other corresponding vertical pairs). It denotes that in our model patch bay, as on most equipment, a permanent hard-wired connection already exists between these two points. This is called a **normalled** connection because it is *normally* in place. It saves time as the operator does not have to make a patch for the input of equipment constantly in use, such as audiotape and videotape recorders and certain basic studio microphones.

All normalled connections are designed so that the existing connection is broken (separated) any time a patch cord is placed in either the input or output receptacle. Some people prefer to patch all mic connections to set up a left-to-right sequence of faders on the console that matches the left-to-right position of mics in the studio as a way of enhancing operator control.

The Audio Board

With our patch between "mic 1 out" and "input channel 4," we have moved our signal into the audio board itself. (See figure 2-5.) Since at this point we are mostly concerned with the concept of *signal flow,* the input channels depicted have been simplified to show only **gain** and **fader** controls for the main feed, along with one gain control used for an **auxiliary send** feed. This *send* feature is a special audio feed that allows a performer in the studio to hear the mixed program output or even a selected videotape feed through an earphone during the ongoing production.

We have also included another very important routing device known as a **group assign switch** for each channel. This channeling control allows any input channel to be fed through any of the **group master faders** (also known as **submasters**). These faders in turn feed into a final **master fader** for control of the volume of **program line out.** If the board was designed for stereo, the input channels, group faders, and master faders would work in pairs—along with some special controls (**pan**) to handle the left and right channels of stereo sound.

The capacity of an audio console can be greatly increased by the use of a **routing switcher** that can allow for two or more inputs to be fed into any one input channel. While not included in our simplified depiction, it is usually located just "**downstream**" of the patch bay, which is immediately after the signal comes out of the patch bay. Its value is based on the concept that while some productions will feature a heavy use of pre-recorded feeds such as videotapes, carts, or CD material, others will have a heavier emphasis on the use of studio microphones. With the routing switcher the operator has a choice of *either* a mic *or* a recorded signal being fed into a channel, in addition to an ability to switch quickly between the two sources without repatching.

The importance of the *input/output* concept cannot be stressed too often. As a signal moves through any system, it is repeatedly going into, through, and out of a series of controls and other components. The *output* of one component becomes the *input* of the next. A thorough knowledge of the *sequence of signal flow* within any system is the key to being able to set up and test audio in any production situation. When trouble occurs, a point-by-point sequential check is the most efficient way to find the button that was not pressed, the fader that was not opened, or the component that is not functioning properly. In later chapters it will become evident that this same *discipline* has applications to lighting, video, and the setting up of any video editing/graphics operation. Many students find that the equipment is never intimidating as long as they can keep a clear picture in their own minds of how the signal moves through the components.

Mix

It seems obvious now that the ability to blend and control a number of sound sources and to control separately the volume levels of each would be seen as a primary requisite for any type of audio production. History tells us, however, that early radio studios had only one microphone and that volume control was accomplished by placing people and musicians closer or farther away from that one mic. Fortunately, radio broadcasters in the late 1920s came up with the idea of a common line **mix bus** being fed by several individually controlled microphones. The idea is not only still with us, but has been greatly advanced over the years.

The basic concept involved in **mixing** several sound sources is not complicated. Take the example of an audio operator who, for a segment of a program, wishes to make one channel's sound louder than sound from two other channels (for example,

voice over background music and sound effects). Because of normal fluctuations of volume in the speaker's voice, the music, and the sound effects, the audio operator will make a continuing series of volume control adjustments with the *fader* for each individual channel. (See figure 2-6.) This is the only way the operator is able to maintain a proper **balance** among the three separate sound sources while making sure the voice predominates.

Looking again at figure 2-5 we see that any of our input channels can be fed to either of the group master faders. The purpose of this arrangement is to allow the operator to "group" together any number of the individual input channels for special purposes.

As an example, consider that in our simplified model of an audio console studio mics 2 and 3 have been designated to cover the small orchestra, and studio mic 1 is for the announcer. Using the **group assign switch** on each of the input channels, the operator can separately control the musical and speaking elements of the program by sending mic 1 to the group 1 master fader and mics 2 and 3 to the group 2 master fader. Now multiply this simple example and envision twenty-four or even forty-eight input channels controlled by eight to sixteen group masters. Such combinations of multiple microphones call for the use of separate group masters for more precise control over percussion, brass, woodwind, and string sections. The process is known as **submastering** and it is quite important when handling any large audio operation.

If it is becoming evident that an understanding of signal flow is essential to the mixing function, then it will come as no surprise that the functions of *amplifying* and *shaping* are equally related. These functions, along with a necessary ability to *monitor* results, are all interactive aspects of signal control.

FIGURE 2-6

Potentiometers/faders.

Left: Older audio consoles use rotary potentiometers (or "pots") to control the signal level or volume.

Right: Newer boards use slide-faders. This board has channel-select "assign" switches (enabling the operator to select different output channels for each fader or input channel) and a rotary "pan" knob (allowing the operator to balance two stereo channels).

Amplify

Radio broadcasting was only possible after the invention of the vacuum tube with its ability to increase the power of a signal while maintaining its original waveform. Its function has long since been taken over by the transistor and all the other marvels of semiconductor technology that create and control signals of increasing diversity. An audio console must be able to handle them all. For example, signals that come out of an already amplified audio source such as a videotape machine are at what is termed **line level.** The feed from amplified instruments, such as a guitar or an electronic keyboard, is less than line level but still much stronger than the relatively weak signal generated by a microphone.

Mic level feeds are further divided into two subtypes, **low-impedance (Lo-Z)** level and **high-impedance (Hi-Z)** level with most studio mics and lines being in the first category. The term **impedance** refers to a measured amount of opposition to signal flow through a line. It is a part of the way in which all signal strength is measured. For further information on impedance and the additional considerations regarding the differences between **balanced** and **unbalanced** lines, see section 3.2.

Contemporary audio consoles can cope with varying input levels by having a number of small amplifiers (**preamps**) at key points in the console, as well as a number of strategically placed devices called **pads,** whose function is to absorb or reduce signal strength.

FIGURE 2-7

Modern audio boards feature numerous input channels, each with its own VU meter, and a variety of sound quality controls as well as signal flow options as in this Yamaha MR 1642 Audio Mixing Console.

Photo courtesy of Yamaha

To explain how this works, a careful look at an input channel in a professional level audio console is necessary. Figure 2-7 shows a Yamaha MR 1642 mixing console. This type of unit would be ideal in an industrial video studio or an educational institution doing broadcast quality production and class instruction. It is a stereo board with sixteen input channels making it ideal for medium sized "live-to-tape" productions. It also has a number of features that would make it useful for the teaching of multi-track music recording techniques.

At the top of the **input channel** shown in figure 2-8, we have examples of the controls that deal with varying levels of input. *Control #1* is a **tape switch** that works in conjunction with *control #2,* a **pad switch.** These switches are needed because on the back of the audio console each input channel has four different input receptacles. Each is of a different type allowing the channel to be matched with signals from microphones of differing impedance or other signals of varying strengths.

In effect, these multiple inputs increase the capability of the board by expanding the capacity of each channel. For example, an input channel can be used for a microphone during the first part of a program and then switched to a videotape feed later when needed. By pressing *control #1* (the tape switch), the videotape signal is brought into the input channel at line level. This is roughly forty decibels stronger than microphone level. If amplified guitars and electronic keyboard instruments are part of the production, then *control #2* (the pad switch) is used to vary the strength of those signals by up to twenty decibels. These inputs are then further adjusted by the use of *control #3* (the gain control), that can adjust levels within a range of forty decibels (shown as –20 decibels to –60 decibels).[4]

If a microphone (with the usual low impedance level feed) is being fed into the

4. A decibel is actually one-tenth of a larger unit, the *Bel,* named for Alexander Graham Bell of telephone fame.

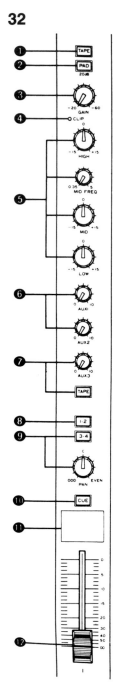

FIGURE 2-8

Schematic drawing of an input channel for the Yamaha 1642.

input channel, then neither the tape nor pad switches need to be used. Once the proper settings are established, *control #12* (the **channel fader** at the bottom of the input channel) is used to maintain consistent sound levels. *Control #4* (the **clip LED indicator**) is a light-emitting diode monitor that will be discussed along with the monitoring section.

Shape

The function of *shaping*—of altering the tonal characteristics of the sound—is to a great extent a creative function. A number of subtle but important things can be done to affect the quality of a sound signal. In both a technical and a creative sense, much of the technique and discipline of a trained audio engineer results in the ability to reproduce the same quality and dimension as existed in an original sound pressure wave—replicating the natural sound as we would hear it without electronic intervention. A related goal is that of creating an enhanced version of that original sound so that it sounds like the tone the listener *expects* to hear in a given program situation. The problem of turning natural sound into electronically reproduced sound is that much of what shapes the quality of the sound is strongly affected by the physical conditions of the recording location as well as by the microphones and other audio equipment utilized.

The musical notation chart in Appendix B shows the way in which the quality of sound from a musical instrument (or voice) is shaped by the presence of a number of higher frequency **overtones** produced by the instrument in addition to the fundamental note. These tones vibrate at different degrees of loudness according to the resonating qualities of each instrument. Brass reflects differently than wood. A trumpet has a different sound from a clarinet because its overtone pattern (as can be seen on an oscilloscope) is very different

from that of the clarinet. In addition to this, the sound of a trumpet, as produced in a studio, is further affected by a number of other things such as soundproofing on the walls and cloth material in a cyclorama. These surfaces cause the overtones to be absorbed or reflected in varying degrees. Tone quality can be considerably altered.

The electronic components of the audio system further shape the tone of the original sound—for example, the ability of the microphone to capture and reproduce most of the frequencies being fed into it. Mics vary greatly in their designed capacity to capture overtones at varying distances and levels of loudness. They should only be used for the purpose for which they were intended. The all-purpose mic designed for an outdoor public-address system is not able to reproduce the subtleties of musical tones required in a recording studio. (See sections 3.1 and 3.3.)

Equalizing

For a variety of reasons, including microphone type and the resonance qualities of a studio, a human voice or other instrumental sound may not always produce the tonal quality that is desired. For example, professional singers will complain of day-to-day changes in their voice quality. The Yamaha MR 1642 in the example has audio components designed to help solve such problems by altering the frequency balance of a voice *after* it has been picked up by the mic. In figure 2-8, the four knobs of *control #5* (the **three-band equalizer**) are used primarily to *strengthen* any of those overtone frequencies that make a trumpet sound like a trumpet. Going one step further, these same controls can *reinforce* additional frequencies to create an even more mellow trumpet sound than the original.

The controls function in three separate frequency ranges—*high, medium,* and *low.* If, for some reason previously mentioned, the trumpet sound is deficient in the higher level overtone frequencies, we can use these controls to **equalize** the incoming frequencies to produce a tone color that is very close to the quality of the original sound. Since the mid-band of frequencies is the one most important for both voice and instrumental sound reproduction, there is a fourth control knob that allows the operator to "*sweep*" across this range to continually enhance the tone with selected frequencies.

Additional Components

Although not a standard part of this Yamaha mixing console, some additional components are sometimes added to existing equipment for special purposes. A **limiter** might be used to cut off levels when they reach a volume that is too strong for equipment to handle without creating distortion. An audio **compressor** can be used to compress the distance between the lowest and highest volume levels; in effect, raising the lowest levels to bring them up close to the loudest levels the system can handle. **Echo** and other **reverberation** devices, often used for musical programs or certain dramatic effects, also fall into this shaping classification.

Monitor

While it is true that certain types of video production do make use of the stop-and-go methods of film, much of the work being done live and on videotape utilizes the ongoing, multiple-camera style that is the essence of television. For the audio operator who is in a continuous process of amplifying, mixing, and shaping a number of sound sources, this requires constant awareness as to the status of the signals going through the audio console. Fortunately, a basic understanding of the components that provide this important feedback of information is not difficult to achieve. But as with the other elements of a large audio console, the skillful use of this equipment should be looked upon as a never ending study.

The most important of these components is the primary audio monitor or **program speaker** in the audio booth. Its obvious function is to provide the operator with a high quality reproduction of the sound being fed out over the **program line** as the final mix of all combined sound sources. In a live broadcast situation, there might also be a separate **air monitor** to pick up and check the quality of the actual transmitted signal.

In larger productions one may need the ability to monitor separately any of the single sound sources from among the ten, twenty, or even more channels that are being mixed for transmission or recording. This is done by means of a preview or **cue channel.** Each input channel and each group master channel will have a **cue button** (see figure 2-8, *control #10*), which when pressed will send that channel's output into a common line. At this point the signal becomes a part of a totally separate sound system with its own amplification, gain control, and speaker. The operator can select either one single mic or a group master for audition purposes while the full orchestra is playing. Of necessity these selected cue channel feeds would be heard on their own speaker in the booth.

The VU Meter

The **volume unit (VU) meter** provides visual description of volume levels and the degrees of difference among the ongoing level changes. Some VU meters, such as the one in figure 2-9 have needles to indicate volume; others have a series of LEDs—green ones at the bottom and red ones at the top that glow when the volume is too loud to be reproduced effectively by the equipment. Individual meters for each channel are now common on many consoles.

In spite of the marvelous structure of the human ear, even highly trained personnel are not always able to discern differences in volume accurately enough to exert

FIGURE 2-9
Volume Unit (VU) meter.

On all newer VU meters the "0" point indicates
a recommended "peak" level of volume. Higher
decibel readings hold the possibility of signal
distortion as indicated by a red line. The
parallel percentage of modulation scale (shown
here) is often seen on older equipment.

the precise control necessary for controlling amplified electronic signals. This is often critical because there is a point of amplitude at which the shaping and amplifying components lose their ability to process the signal properly. As the amplification of the signal is increased beyond this point, not all frequencies are equally amplified, and the sound becomes distorted. When levels drop below an acceptable minimum they are not processed by the system and are lost.

On audio consoles comparable to the Yamaha MR 1642, there is a VU meter for each group master channel as well as one for the final program feed. For stereo applications, both left and right group and master faders would have VU meters. Most of the newer audio consoles have a VU meter for each input channel.

The VU meter readout uses a **decibel** (**dB**) scale. Slightly to the right of the top of the arc is *zero point*. The zero does not signify a lack of volume; rather, it indicates the point where the signal is at its *optimum* level. All differences in signal strength are measured from this point either in **plus decibels** (to the right) or **minus decibels** (to the left). As you can see in figure 2-9, the range of measurement goes down as far as minus twenty decibels and only up to two or three decibels on the plus side. Keep in mind that the decibel is not an absolute unit such as an ounce or a foot. Decibel readings indicate a *ratio* of the strength of one signal as compared to another or to the amount of variation occurring in a signal at continuing points in time. There are logarithmic charts that show how differing decibel measurements relate to the varying strengths of electrical energy applied to the signal (amplitude). The resistance (impedance) to the flow of current in a wire is also a part of this equation.

As an operational introduction to these concepts, two basic rules and some simple example numbers may provide a basis of understanding. *1. For every three decibel increase, the power of a signal has been doubled. 2. Whenever a power is ten times another, it is 10 dB greater.* If 1 watt of power is used to produce a "0" level (see above) calibration point of volume, then 2 watts of power will produce a 3 dB level and 4 watts will produce a 6 dB level. It takes 6.3 watts to make an 8 dB difference from our original "0" level. Conversely, a *decrease* of 10 dB would result in the power of a signal being one-tenth of its previous strength.[5] It should be noted that in addition to measuring electromagnetic wave energy, the decibel also measures

5. Davis, Gary, and Ralph Jones. *The Sound Reinforcement Handbook*, Milwaukee: Leonare/Yamaha, 1987.

the relative intensity of audible sound waves such as factory noise or jet planes taking off.

In most operational applications, the audio operator adjusts the fader knobs to have the needle oscillate between a point in the area of minus two or three decibels swinging up to the optimum "0" point. Ideally the needle is always made to **peak** (reach the highpoint of its swing) at the "0" position. This process of using the fader or other gain control to maintain a consistent level of volume is called **riding gain.**

During the pre-production setup period for any program, audio inputs from all sources must be checked and noted so that uniform levels of volume can be maintained during production. The audio operator *sets mic levels* by having each performer speak into his or her microphone in a normal voice. The operator then sets the channel fader at the zero (optimum) position and adjusts the gain knob to get the VU meter to peak at "0." Similarly, all pre-recorded audio sources such as CDs, carts, and videotapes are checked for their signal levels. All these procedures will be covered in considerable detail in chapter 3. As we shall see, the concept of the "0" dB optimum level is very important in calibrating the levels of all feeds to and from the audio console.

Other Monitoring Capabilities

One small but important type of monitor is to be found in figure 2-8 at *control #4.* In this case it is the **clip LED** (light-emitting diode) **indicator** that shows that the *#3 gain control* has been properly set. It is designed to show an optimum audio level by continuously flashing. If it is constantly on or off, levels most likely need to be adjusted.

Previously mentioned was the *auxiliary send* feature, located at the midpoint of the input channel shown in figure 2-8. One of its main purposes is to provide on-the-air talent with a small monitor (earphone) in

their ear, with an audio monitor for selected feeds. This earphone monitor setup is referred to as an **interrupted feedback (IFB)** system. The volume knob, *control #6* in figure 2-8, could be used to provide studio talent with either instructions from the director on the intercom or program sound from a field reporter. *Control #7* would be used to send the news anchor sound from a videotape insert.

Two final controls complete the structure of our example input channel. *Controls #8 and #9,* as shown in figure 2-8, are the *group assign switches,* which send the output of the input channel to the group master faders. On this model, they are in a stereo configuration and would work in conjunction with the pan control, used for balancing L and R channels, located just below them.

Playback and Record

Much of the equipment in television production is designed to be used in both the *playback* and *record* modes. While the setup procedures may be much the same for both operations, the operational *disciplines* and *techniques* can be somewhat different. Some examples of these differences can be seen in the process of getting program sound recorded on videotape and being prepared to feed sound from videotape inserts into a program. One of the audio operator's most important tasks is to make sure the output of his or her audio console is properly connected to the videotape recorder (usually by patching from the audio board to the master control room). The audio operator must constantly be aware of the total signal flow pattern. Another top priority for the audio operator during any recording session is simply "getting the sound right." Is the mic quality appropriate? Is there proper balance between voice and music? Is the stereo balance right? (See section 3.3.)

On the other hand, the essential factor involved in playing back an audio segment recorded on cartridge involves an alert preparedness that enables one to react quickly to operational cues from the director. Section 2.3 discusses some specific audio playback sources (videotape, audiotape, cart machines, and CD players), and section 3.4 details some particular techniques and cuing procedures. The work of the audio operator in controlling both the production use and the quality of signals coming into and going out of the console during the ongoing program operation is always a stimulating challenge.

2.3 SOURCES OF TV AUDIO

In preparing for even the simplest program, the person in charge of audio should always develop a definite plan of operations. In thinking through how resources will be used, it is often convenient to organize such things as patching and the setup of the audio console in terms of the various sources of the audio. The majority of production inputs are going to be microphones, pre-recorded tapes, and digitally based materials, and even possibly some electronic instruments.

Microphones

The microphone comes in a wide variety of types and sizes, designed for a multitude of specialized purposes. They vary in **frequency response:** some will pick up low frequencies well, while others respond best to higher frequencies. They also differ in **pickup pattern:** some (**omnidirectional**) will pick up sound equally from all directions. For others (**cardioid**), the performer should stand directly in front of the microphone in order to be heard well. They will vary in the technical construction of their *transducing elements*—the way they actually transform sound waves into electrical energy. As a result, some are more rugged than others. Microphones vary in *physical design,* to be used in different ways. Some are to be placed in mic stands or hand held while others are worn around the neck or attached to special boom stands.

These different distinctions and differences are discussed in chapter 3. By becoming familiar with the different microphone classifications and characteristics, the audio operator will be able to select the most appropriate microphone for each application. Which microphones should be used for talk shows? Drama? Musical productions? What kinds of mics are best suited for outdoor (location) productions? Which microphones are used for picking up sound from a great distance? What if you want a microphone that can be concealed or hidden? These are just a few of the considerations that an audio operator must consider.

Pre-recorded Sound Sources

For the most part, the audio operator will think of pre-recorded sound used in a production situation as coming from one of several basic sources: the *videotape* soundtrack, *audiotape* units for both cassettes and cartridges, compact disc players, or even possibly one of the newer *digital audio delivery systems.* Reel-to-reel tape, twelve-inch vinyl recordings and film sound may occasionally be used when dealing with older library sources. Most professionals prefer to **dub** these older formats over to cartridges or digital systems for production use.

Videotape Audio Tracks
Many types of productions will have videotape inserts, in which a short, previously recorded videotape segment is incorporated into the body of another television

production. The insert videotape machines are usually located in a separate area along with computer graphics, camera control equipment, and similar facilities. This is the **master control** area mentioned in chapter 1. The videotape machine operator is responsible for making all patched connections and testing them, and operating the unit during production.

Audio Tapes

Out of necessity, all audio-only playback and record equipment is located in the sound booth. Until the advent of the compact disc, the audio **cartridge** unit, or **cart machine,** had been the workhorse of most audio control rooms. Figure 2-10 shows a typical three-channel cart machine. Since there are no variations in tape speed, track configuration, or reel size, they were a big improvement over vinyl discs. At the conclusion of a segment, the cartridge automatically rolls on to any subsequent **cue** point and comes to a stop. This means that each tape may be programmed to contain one or several cue points which saves the operator from having to change cartridges during a very busy production. Perhaps its biggest virtue is that the technology used to record on cartridge is inexpensive and available at most learning institutions. For these reasons, cart machines are still an integral part of many audio operations.

Audio **cassette** tape recorders (often the same ones used by consumers) are also used for video production. They are harder to cue than cart tapes because they do not stop at cue points, but they are frequently used for background music or other material that does not need to be tightly cued.

Compact Discs

The **CD player** has found a secure spot in most modern audio booths. Digital signal and control technology has produced equipment with the highest sound fidelity coupled with a number of benefits. The laser acquisition system permits cue points to be held indefinitely in the *pause* position with no wear to the disc. A precise minutes and seconds read-out allows the disc to be easily programmed for sequential cue points with almost instantaneous access to each when needed. When several units are "ganged" together (see figure 2-11), there is an almost unlimited source of quickly presented program sound feeds. Complete libraries of sound effects and stock musical selections have been released on CDs. The compact size of the disc makes for large improvements in storage and handling.

FIGURE 2-10
Audio cartridge player designed to access nine different carts on three different channels.

FIGURE 2-11

The CD (compact disc) player has become a standard audio playback unit in most radio and TV stations because of its crisp digital sound and its ease of cuing. Station KLOS uses a bank of three units and controllers to enable the operator to play back one CD, have a second unit cued up in the standby mode, while previewing a third CD.

Photo courtesy of KLOS-FM

Digital Audio Delivery Systems

The new multi-purpose digital audio delivery systems will probably not replace the CD players, but they are increasingly being found in radio stations and TV production facilities. While the initial cost is at present relatively high, their flexibility of use and ease of operation can make them easily worth the cost in many production situations.

An example of this state of the art technology can be seen in the DAD 484X manufactured by Enco Systems. Each unit is actually a computer with a large **hard drive** capacity that is used to store, edit, and play back large numbers of instantly retrievable sound inserts. Instead of operational control being done by means of a keyboard, there are five or more different **matrix touchscreen displays** which, depending upon the mode of operation, are put up on the monitor. (See figure 2-12.) These displays, designed to look very much like sections of a standard audio cart control panel, perform all operations of the unit at the touch of a finger. Each unit can store 144 announcements, music cuts, or effects for instant access. Segments can be edited by means of the visual graphic waveform display. Figure 2-13 shows the wave structure of sound on left and right stereo channels. Each separate word or short sound is seen as a frequency burst separated by little or no modulation. Editing is done by moving one's finger along a timeline displayed between the two channels to the point of edit and then pressing other controls to execute the cut. During this process one hears all the sound relating to the edit preparation and final execution. More than ten other control panels display a

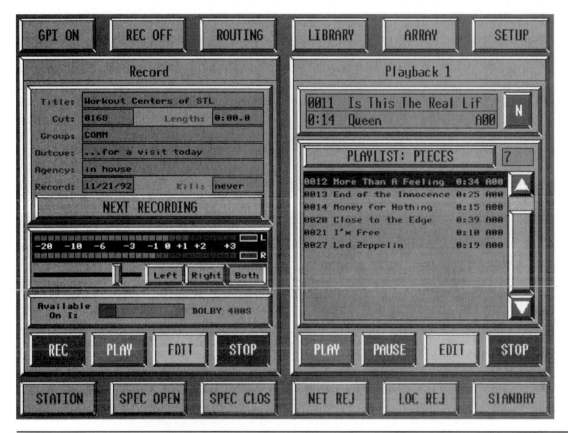

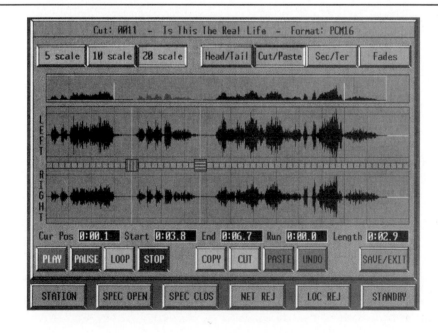

FIGURE 2-12

This matrix touchscreen display from the DAD 484X Audio Delivery System is the actual operating control board. The controller operates the unit by touching points on the display. Music or sound cues already loaded into the machine are available on a split second basis.

Illustration courtesy of Enco Systems

FIGURE 2-13

Another display example from the DAD 484X is a control board for audio editing. One simply moves a finger along either or both of the stereo waveforms to make edits. One hears the sound in relation to the speed of the moving finger.

Illustration courtesy of Enco Systems

number of additional control and delivery features, including lists of all available insert pieces by name and number.

SUMMARY

As an introduction to the audio system, we have been concerned more with *technical* functions than with *creative* functions. The seven *basic control functions* are *transducing, channeling, mixing, amplifying, shaping, monitoring,* and *recording for playback.*

These control functions were traced through the *audio signal flow* pattern—typically from studio *microphone input,* through the *patch bay,* into the *audio console,* through an *input channel,* through the volume control or *potentiometer/fader,* into a *submaster* channel, through the *master* potentiometer, out the board through the

line out, and back to the program-out position on the patch bay.

The *microphone* remains the basic ingredient in audio production along with some of the established *audio tape* technology such as the *cartridge* and *cassette.* Playbacks from *videotape* are often integrated into productions, and the *CD* has become widely used. The newer *digitally based audio equipment* is impressive and will make it possible for an operator to handle increasingly complex assignments with enhanced precision.

It must be kept in mind, however, that technology itself can never replace training in terms of *technique* or preparation as it relates to *discipline.* In chapter 3 we will go into more detail as to how microphones and playback equipment are used during the production sequence.

CHAPTER

3

Fundamentals of Audio Production

I n chapter 2 the reader was introduced to the microphone that turns sound
pressure waves into electromagnetic signals, as well as to a number of other
components that direct and adjust those signals for broadcast and/or recording. From a technical standpoint alone this process is an impressive accomplishment. There is also an additional dimension of knowledge that relates the designed capabilities of a component to its optimum production use. In this area
we are dealing with the reasons *why* one type of microphone, for example, will
have definite advantages when used in one set of operational circumstances but
have some limitations in another.

We will look more closely into the operational *techniques* for audio equipment and various *disciplines* necessary for individual as well as group effort. This
chapter is an introduction to the mechanics of production—the skills that enable
one to follow instructions on a split second basis, or to act on one's own initiative
so that all elements of planning occur at the required time. The material is designed

to prepare students to work together on an audio production exercise and provide the opportunity to put material presented thus far into practical use.

3.1 THE ROLE OF FREQUENCIES

As explained in chapter 2 and Appendix B, the differing combinations of **overtone** frequencies that resonate along with any single **fundamental** tone are what give various musical instruments their individual tonal qualities. While these overtones (also known as "**harmonics**") are produced at much *lower amplitudes* (loudness) than the fundamental tone, they are very definitely picked up by the human ear. What we hear ranges from a low rumble at 20 **cycles per second (hertz)** up to a possible high of 20,000 cycles per second. The ultimate quality of any microphone is judged by the accuracy with which it is able to transduce these sound pressure waves, especially those in the higher frequency ranges.

The importance of overtones is best exemplified by comparing the sound on AM radio with FM radio and compact discs. AM radio has a top limit of only 7,500 hertz **(Hz)** and for a variety of reasons many stations do not even take full advantage of this potential. As a result, music has always been much more impressive on FM with its ability to reproduce frequencies up to 15,000 Hertz. This additional bandwidth encompasses the critical range where all of the overtones contribute so much to sound fidelity. Under ideal circumstances the compact disc technology, with its digital signal and a number of other component improvements, is able to encompass almost the entire range of our hearing. The result is consistently impressive sound reproduction.

Television sound is an FM signal with the potential of transmitting up to 15,000 Hz. While many stations are equipped to transmit these upper frequencies and do so in stereo, some individual productions do not opt to spend the money on hi-fidelity stereo production.

3.2 THE MICROPHONE: FUNCTION AND CONSTRUCTION

Keeping in mind that an electronic signal is a complex combination of a great number of fundamental and overtone frequencies, imagine a 100-piece symphony orchestra, each instrument of which is producing not only a fundamental tone but also ten or more related overtone frequencies. It is truly impressive that a relatively small number of specially designed and properly placed microphones can transduce the majority of those frequencies necessary to produce a professional recording of the orchestra.

Microphones are manufactured in a large variety of types to suit a wide range of needs. Some have very specialized uses while others are intended to satisfy a number of differing applications. Every good mic is designed to balance the need for durability and sound fidelity within the market realities of cost.

Pickup Patterns

In most professional circumstances a priority is usually given to the fidelity factor. Each mic has its own set of **specifications** ("specs") in printed form available at the time of purchase. In addition to matters of structure and levels of power output, there is always the important information relating to what a microphone's **frequency response** will be in a given set of circumstances.

Simple graphic charts are possibly the most useful part of this information. One is the **polar pickup pattern** that depicts

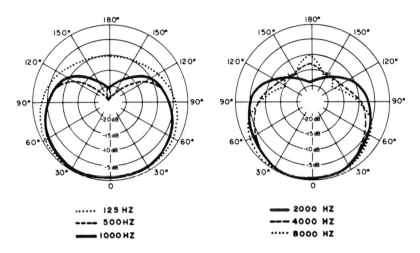

FIGURE 3-1

The different lines in these two polar pattern projections show the directional sensitivity of the Shure SM 58 mic at eight different frequencies. The heart shape traced by the lines indicates a **cardioid** pickup pattern with least receptivity at the rear of the mic.

Pattern courtesy of Shure Bros. Inc.

the *directional* sensitivity of the mic at several different frequency levels. Figure 3-1 is the actual pattern for the SM 58 professional mic manufactured by Shure Bros. Inc. pictured in figure 3-2. The directional sensitivity is shown as dotted or continuous lines. The heart shape traced by the lines on the diagram classifies it as having a **cardioid** pickup pattern with a decreasing response to sounds coming from the rear of the mic. All such patterns are only two dimensional depictions of an actual sphere as shown more clearly in figure 3-3.

While the 0 degree point may be placed at either the top or bottom of the circle's outer ring, the front of the mic is always oriented directly toward that 0 degree point. Do not be confused by the minus dB numbers (a measure of less volume) that get larger closer to the mic in the center of the circles. The -dB numbers denote the declining decibel level for each smaller circle. Note how the heart shaped

FIGURE 3-2

The SM 58 mic is well-known in professional circles as an all-purpose hand/stand mic with a dynamic transducing element.

Photo courtesy of Shure Bros. Inc.

44

FIGURE 3-3

All pickup patterns
are actually a three-
dimensional sphere
as depicted in this
cardioid type.

Illustration courtesy of
Shure Bros. Inc.

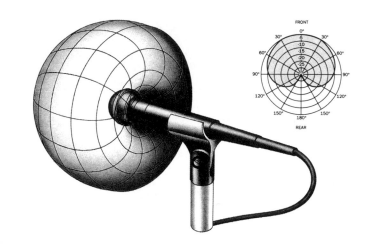

FIGURE 3-4

Omnidirectional
microphone pickup
pattern.

The omnidirectional
mic picks up sound
equally well from all
directions.

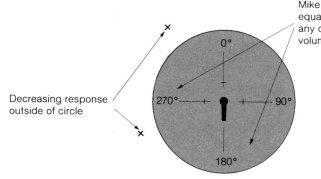

Mike responds to sound
equally well from
any direction if
volume is constant

Decreasing response
outside of circle

response pattern develops when the response lines come in to the larger -dB numbers at the rear of the microphone's position. As stated above, it is this position directly behind the mic that pickup is least effective.

With high quality microphones, the information presented in a pickup pattern is often also expressed in terms of the distance between the sound source and the microphone. Section 3.4 discusses the way in which some sounds coming from outside the pickup pattern will be transduced and amplified, but not with the correct balance of frequencies. The result is an **off-mic** distortion of the original sound caused by a substantial loss of higher frequencies.

The whole idea of **directionality** is largely a matter of mics being designed to acknowledge the effects of differences in source-to-mic distances. The **omnidirectional** pattern seen in figure 3-4 produces an equal response to sound from all directions. Obvious advantages in this pattern include its ability to pick up a large number of people, often including an audience.

The opposite effect is achieved through the use of a highly directional pickup pattern found in the specialized long-distance **shotgun** mics. (See figure 3-5.) This mic often presents a trade-off involving some loss of quality for the ability to get a fairly good pickup at a distance of 20 feet. To further increase their sensitivity, these mics

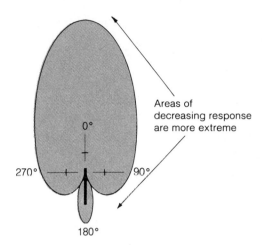

FIGURE 3-5

Highly directional microphone pickup pattern.

The highly directional microphone is designed to pick up sound in a narrow response pattern from relatively long distances.

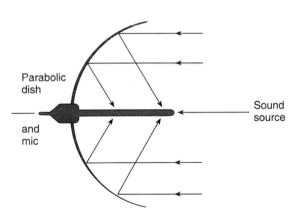

FIGURE 3-6

The parabolic dish increases the range of a shotgun directional microphone by focusing sound sources into the transducing element.

are often used in conjunction with a **parabolic dish,** which can collect and concentrate an even more distant audio source and reflect this focused audio beam directly into the microphone. (See figure 3-6.) This equipment is often used at sporting events and similar outdoor occasions.

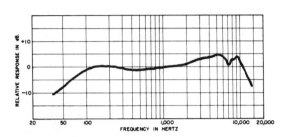

FIGURE 3-7

The frequency response chart gives the audio operator an accurate and quick indication of how a mic will perform at all frequency levels.

Equally important pickup information is expressed by the **frequency response chart.** This linear graph shows how consistent the mic is in transducing frequencies at all the various points of the hearing spectrum. Many professional mics have what is called a "flat" response with more or less a straight line representing frequencies in the 50 to 15,000 Hz range. Figure 3-7 shows a mic frequency response chart with what is called a "shaped" response. It has increasing strength in the middle and higher frequencies and then a rather rapid decline after 10,000 Hz. This chart would represent a typical professional mic used more for voice applications than for the recording of classical music. Such a mic would help compensate for the fact that lower and louder male voices have the effect of sounding closer to a mic than a female voice.

Transducing Elements

Since the invention of the first microphones, a number of transducing elements have been used to accomplish the delicate matter of turning sound pressure waves into an electronic waveform. Carbon granules and foil ribbons as well as ceramic and crystal elements have been used. Most microphones in use today are of two basic types.

The classic mic described in chapter 2 is called a **dynamic microphone.** It utilizes the basic **coil** and **magnet** combination found in all electric engines. This structure makes it able to tolerate rough handling as well as temperature and humidity extremes. The majority of microphones in use are of this type.

Like the dynamic mic, the **condenser microphone** has a movable diaphragm to receive sound waves. Its difference lies in its use of an electrically charged **backplate** just behind the diaphragm. The two elements form what is called a **capacitor,** enabling the unit to generate voltage in response to sound wave pressure. This structure not only produces very high quality sound but also allows the unit to be as small as a clip-on lapel mic. While a dynamic mic can generate its own charge, this condenser unit must have a source of electricity to function. Batteries are located in the handle, or, with a **wireless mic,** they may be part of the portable unit that transmits the signal. Another solution to the need for power is accomplished by the use of what is called "**phantom power.**" A "phantom power" is another possible power source. A small current is sent to the mic from a controlling component in the audio console and through a specially designed cable. **Electret** condenser microphones that have a permanently charged backplate are another option.

Impedance Levels

In our discussion of the audio console amplifying function (see section 2.2), reference was made to differing **impedance** levels. Impedance refers to opposition to the flow of an audio signal through a component or cable. Professional studio microphones and cables are always of the **low impedance (Lo-Z)** type. Because there is less resistance to signal flow in the mic cable, the signal can be carried a great distance to the audio console where it is amplified. Low impedance cables are less susceptible to hum, static, or other forms of outside electrical interference. Most *professional* field video recorders are also designed to work with low impedance mics and lines.

Most amateur and some industrial level video recorders, however, call for **high impedance (Hi-Z)** mics and cables. These mics produce a stronger electrical signal than Lo-Z units, but the signal deteriorates rapidly because of the higher resistance; therefore, relatively short cable lengths must be used with Hi-Z mics. Care should be taken not to mismatch microphones, cables, or inputs intended for differing impedance levels. Unless a transformer is used, sound distortion will result.

Mic cables also vary in that most professional uses call for mic cables with two lines to carry the audio signal as well as an additional grounding wire. This is called a **balanced** line and utilizes what is known as an **XLR (Cannon) connector.** Most other protruding plug connectors (see figure 8-15) are of the **unbalanced** type with only one line for audio and one grounding wire. They are usually used for high impedance applications.

3.3 MICROPHONE USAGE CATEGORIES

No single all-purpose microphone has ever been designed. The most expensive microphone would have limitations in some situations. Instead, manufacturers provide a wide variety, each of which may combine a number of qualities suited to differing needs. Rather than discussing an impressive but unwieldy list of microphones by category, we shall instead offer a rather simple method of classifying the types of instruments generally found in teaching institutions. It is felt that this introduction to the process of classification will enable students to feel comfortable with microphones starting with the first hands-on exercises in the studio. We therefore suggest the following three broad practical categories: (1) hand and/or stand mics, (2) limited-movement mics, and (3) attached personal mics.

These categories are obviously very general designations devised for learning purposes only. (For instance, you will never find a section of a microphone cabinet labeled "limited-movement mics.") These classifications, however, should help you think about the different ways in which microphones can be positioned and used—keeping in mind the positive qualities and limiting factors of each grouping. Also, note that these are not mutually exclusive categories—there is obvious overlap. Many mics could fit into two of the groups.

Hand and/or Stand Mics

The most versatile group of mics are most likely the medium-sized, elongated instruments designed to work best at a range of six inches to three feet from a speaker or musical performer. Although a few require a fixed mount, most are structured to fit into a holder on a desk (for a news program or panel show) or in a floor mic stand (for a performer). The same microphone is used as a hand-held mic for an on-location news event or for spontaneous interviews with members of an audience. This category can overlap both the stationary and mobile distinctions. For example, a performer begins a number by using a mic stand (stationary) and then removes the mic from the holder and concludes the number using it as a hand mic (mobile). (See figure 3-2.)

Resistance to the rugged handling of a rock or rap performer is an important quality for such a mic. Most microphones in this category are the *dynamic* types utilizing the coil and magnet transducer. Many such instruments have a **pop filter** (a metal or foam ball placed over the top of the mic)

that minimizes the plosive effect of sounds such as *T*s, *K*s, and *P*s. Such a mic is all the more useful if it is designed to function in the outdoor conditions of news and sports remotes. These instruments require a fairly wide angle of sound acceptance and are usually either *omnidirectional* or *cardioid* in their pickup pattern.

Limited-Movement Mics

This category encompasses several different microphone applications from stationary, fixed-position uses to a considerable amount of movement on large **perambulator booms.** Generally microphones in this category are larger than those intended to be hand-held. Almost always, mics in this grouping are not intended for use on camera—they are seldom seen by the audience. As off-camera mics, they are required to have good pickup qualities at relatively moderate to long distances.

The label "**boom mic**" can cover a wide variety of applications. The big boom, or *perambulator* (see figure 3-8) is a large three-wheeled movable platform that holds the boom operator and has a long counterweighted boom arm that can be extended and tilted while the microphone itself can be rotated in almost a full circle. It is a large cumbersome piece of equipment requiring two operators—one dolly pusher and one mic manipulator—and is effective only in spacious studios. Perambulators are often used in pairs, for example to cover guests on a talk show such as *The Tonight Show.*

The smaller boom, similar to that in figure 3-9 is the **giraffe**—a counterweighted boom arm supported by a tripod on casters that can be operated by one person. Although not as flexible as the big boom, the giraffe can be moved more easily and takes up much less floor space. Even though it is thought of as a movable boom, the giraffe is usually stationed in a fixed position for an entire production.

Figure 3-8

Two large studio perambulator booms used to cover a drama.

Photo courtesy of KCET-TV, Los Angeles

FIGURE 3-9

A giraffe, or tripod, microphone boom.

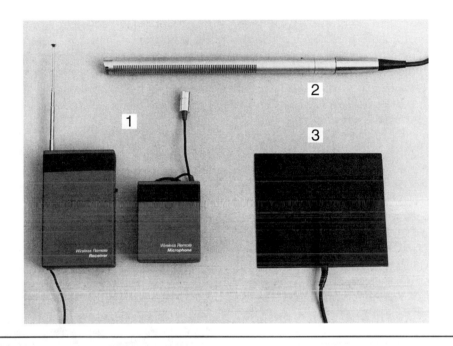

FIGURE 3-10
Three very different methods of picking up sound.

(1) A lapel mic used in conjunction with wireless transmission and receiver units; (2) A highly directional long distance "shotgun" mic; and (3) A pressure response, surface mount mic.

Finally, consider the use of the **fishpole**—literally a small, lightweight pole to which the mic is attached. The operator hand-holds the pole to continually get the best audio position in any changing scene or situation. These are quite often used in the video coverage for an impromptu appearance of a celebrity or politician.

Most production situations calling for boom, dolly, and even fishpole mics utilize some variation of a highly directional type of mic. As mentioned in section 3.2, the long distance *shotgun* mics have found an important place in the world of outdoor video production. News and sports programs as well as all *reality based* productions in the early 1990s were greatly enhanced by the very effective use of these mics in conjunction with the parabolic dish. While earlier models had a limited range of frequency response, some of the newer, more expensive, top-of-the-line models have produced impressive sound quality and are used in outdoor stage and concert work. (See figure 3-10.)

The limited-movement category has recently been expanded to include some very different adaptations of mic structure. One of the most successful is the **surface-mount mic** (also known as a **PZM**™ **mic**). They have a flat base with angled sides and are designed to be placed on a large table, floor, or even ceiling. The operating concept is based on the principle of physics claiming that sound pressure waves are intensified as they gather and move along a flat surface. These mics are best used on a desk or table top. When used on a floor they can pick up a lot of unwanted vibration. (See figure 3-10.)

Attached Personal Mics

Television created the necessity for an unobtrusive instrument that could move with the performer. The **lavaliere** (suspended by a cord around the neck) and the **lapel mic** (clipped inside the clothing or to a tie or lapel) are the result. Most early lavaliere models were effective omnidirectional mics although they were limited to the frequency range of the human voice. Later models filter out unwanted noise caused by clothing rubbing against the mic. The more recent lapel models have a frequency response more than adequate for instrumental pickup. (See figure 3-10.)

The problems caused by mic cords have resulted in the development of the **RF** (radio frequency) or *wireless microphone*. A miniature transmitter—either a part of the mic itself or in a concealed pack—sends an FM signal to a portable receiver that can be placed as far as several hundred feet from the performer. Although these systems have obvious advantages for television production, a propensity for dead spots in the transmission pattern and some limitations in frequency range have been the major limitations to their use. Recent progress with sophisticated receivers, however, has eliminated many of the problems. Most stage productions and musical videos have made the wireless mic almost indispensable in contemporary programming. Their advancing reliability and miniaturization make them increasingly popular for talk shows, remote productions, musical numbers, audience participation segments, etc.

3.4 USING THE MICROPHONE

The proper procedures for microphone utilization are largely a matter of common sense application of a few simple principles. With this section, we specifically probe the area of creative functions of audio production. Most successful audio/microphone usage is just an extension of three basic considerations: (1) selection of the correct microphone; (2) proper placement of the microphone; and (3) application of the principles of balance and perspective.

Microphone Selection

In previous years at many small stations and teaching facilities, the question of microphone selection was sometimes an exercise in futility. Those who controlled the finances too often felt that one microphone was very much like another. Fortunately things have changed, and now a choice of mics for different uses is seen as being as quite important.

When selecting the proper microphone, first define the audio job to be done. Let's take, for example, the task of picking up a well-tuned concert grand piano. Mics should be selected on the basis of their known positive and negative qualities. Voice-frequency-range lavalieres and older long-distance shotgun mics are not going to pick up all the true tonal quality of the piano. However, any of several condenser mics placed either inside or underneath the instrument can do this satisfactorily. As with the pickup of most musical instruments, the source-to-mic factor is crucial.

If one is concerned with recording a pop vocal personality, it is best to take into consideration whether or not the singer wants to use a microphone as part of the performance—as a hand prop. If the singer does, you would want to use a fairly rugged dynamic mic. If, however, the production calls for an off-camera boom mic, then a full frequency condenser microphone might be used, especially if fidelity to the musical quality is uppermost.

When producing a news program or panel discussion, the full frequency range of a condenser is probably not necessary.

Depending upon the "look" of the production, you may decide on either a dynamic desk mic (desk mics are often subject to considerable table pounding and verbal abuse) or lavalieres.

Suppose you are to handle a remote assignment covering a parade or sporting event. You would probably want a rugged, relatively sensitive cardioid dynamic mic for the narrator/announcer (to allow him or her to work closely to the mic, cutting out as much background noise as possible) coupled with a highly directional shotgun mic to pick up selected crowd or parade sounds as desired.

The first task, however, is always the same: define the job to be done in terms of frequency response needed, appropriate pickup pattern, and the amount of physical abuse to which the microphone will likely be subjected.

In selecting microphones correctly for a particular audio pickup, one must be aware of two critical considerations. One is *aesthetic* and the other is *acoustical*. In a dramatic production, the mic must not be seen as part of the picture. Usually, directional long-distance pickup mics mounted on movable booms are used. In some cases, wireless equipment may be used. On the other hand, if you are working in a news, public affairs, or sports situation, the use of a hand mic is accepted by the audience—as is an occasional camera shot that reveals an operator holding a shotgun mic mounted in a parabolic dish. Sometimes one must compromise between aesthetic and acoustical needs. In the telecast of a symphony performance, for instance, the quality of sound is very important. A number of mics must be placed relatively close to the musicians to assure proper balance and timbre. This is especially true of string and woodwind instruments. An unobtrusive, sensitive microphone located on a small stand is now generally accepted by the audience.

Microphone Placement

Several important basic rules apply to the placement of microphones in all situations. These rules seem so obvious to those who work with sound reinforcement and recording that they are sometimes overlooked in a general discussion of operating procedures. Since this textbook is concerned with basics, this is the perfect place for them to be set forth.

1. Place microphones as close to a desired sound source as practically possible. The very nature of the transducing element in a mic is such that proximity must be given priority. If a mic is too close and distortion results, the mic can always be moved farther away. Quality loss from too distant a position, however, may never be noticed unless the closer position is tried first.

2. If studio audio monitors are needed as a part of a production, be sure that microphones are not aimed in their direction. The audio **"feedback"** effect of a high pitched squealing sound is caused when a microphone is aimed at a speaker and picks up output that is then fed through the amplifying system. This creates a circular monitor-mic-amplifier-monitor situation with the amplification being escalated and distorted with each cycle. When recorded sound is to be used behind a person talking or singing on a live studio mic, careful testing of safe levels is required prior to production. With any public address system the speakers should always be placed *in front* of the microphones.

3. Observe instructions relating to directionality and source-to-mic distance patterns to avoid picking up

unwanted ambient sound that is present in almost all situations. Outside traffic, building machinery, and even air conditioning may not be noticeable during setup in a busy studio, but often greatly detract from an otherwise efficient production.

4. Avoid a placement situation where two nearby microphones pick up the same sound source. When signals from each mic get to the audio console the similar waveforms tend to cancel each other out. This is called a **phasing** problem. The "**three to one rule**" states that if two singers (or other performers) are standing side-by-side, each working at a distance of *one foot* from their respective mics, then the two mics must be at least *three feet* apart. If source-to-mic distance is increased, mic separation must similarly be increased. A further application is that if a person wearing a lavaliere mic walks over to a standing mic, one of the mics must be turned down. These considerations are part of a much larger area of study of how the length and construction of cable (**timing**) and the overlapping of pickup by two mics can have serious effects on the signals being mixed in the console.

These general rules, along with the other *disciplines and techniques* discussed below should serve to remind students that the operations needed to utilize all the seven basic control functions require careful planning along with a sense of respect for the equipment and the manner of its use. The right mic, used with the best of intentions, cannot do the job if the realities of the specific pickup pattern of the mic have been disregarded. A microphone that works well at one location may be inadequate in a slightly different position. Sound, especially the higher frequencies, diminishes in loudness (amplitude) very rapidly as it passes through the air. This loss directly relates to the amount of energy it takes to propel the pressure waves through the molecules of the air.

The rate of drop-off is scientifically described by the **inverse square law**. Although this text is not the proper place to attempt to describe all the principles of physics involved, the operating concept is easily understood: *as microphone-to-source distance is doubled, the loudness is reduced to one-fourth.*

Therefore, if you have an audio source (voice) giving you a constant level of sound at a distance of one foot from a microphone, and then you move the mic back to a distance of two feet, the strength of the sound pressure (loudness) hitting the microphone will be only one-quarter of what it was when the mic was one foot from the source. If you again double the distance and place the microphone four feet from the source, it will again reduce the loudness level to one-quarter of what it was at two feet. The level is now one-sixteenth of what it had been at a distance of one foot. When working with relatively short source-to-mic positions any distance change can be critical.

Putting this principle into simple operational terms, suppose you have checked the sound level of a performer speaking one foot away from a desk mic. (See section 3.8.) Once the program starts that person then decides to lean back just one foot to be more comfortable. You have lost close to 75 percent of that person's volume! On the other hand, if you have a performer working ten feet from a long-distance directional microphone, and that person moves one foot backward, there will not be much of a noticeable difference because the performer has only increased his or her distance by a factor of one-tenth.

In addition to the above *source-to-mic distance* effect, it is equally important to

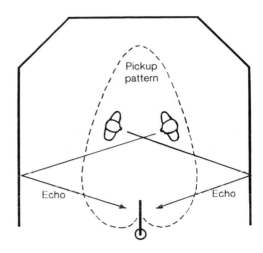

FIGURE 3-11

Incorrect placement of directional mic between two performers.

Although the two actors are standing "in the pattern" of the directional mic, their voices will be picked up with a hollow "off-mic" quality because they are not facing toward the mic; they are directing their voices away from the microphone.

consider the *source-to-mic direction* factor. This refers to the degree to which the main source of projected sound of a voice or musical instrument is in a straight-line path to the primary receiving area of the mic. Sound waves do not curve around corners. When sound is reflected by several angled surfaces there is a noticeable loss in both volume and quality.

Let us take as an example two actors playing a dramatic scene. As in any conversation, they would normally face more toward each other than toward the "audience" area. The audio operator must work closely with the director to determine the various speaking positions of the actors as they move about the set. Untrained people often make an error in this situation. They decide to place a one-directional mic in the "audience" area in an attempt to pick up both voices. (See figure 3-11.) The

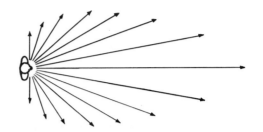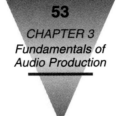

FIGURE 3-12

The sound pressure waves of the human voice begin to decline in intensity beyond a 45 degree angle from those projected directly to the front of the speaker.

actors would seem to be within the pickup pattern of the directional mic. One must keep in mind, however, that each sound source has a *projection* pattern that is somewhat similar to the pickup pattern of a microphone. With the human voice, the shape of the mouth and lips tend to focus the strongest pressure waves in a relatively narrow channel as represented in figure 3-12.

This illustration shows why mics placed at a side angle (sixty or more degrees from the straight-ahead direction of the sound pressure waves) result in a considerable drop-off in audio level. If you attempt to turn up the amplification to compensate for this loss, you will also begin to hear the reflected (echo) sound waves coming back from the set and walls of the studio. The result is an *"off-mic"* distortion of the original sound. While these reflected echoes are always a part of any sound pickup and contribute to the effect of natural room "presence," they should be heard only in their original proportion to the primary sound waves and not become the primary source itself.

The proper placement of microphones for a two person conversation is shown in figure 3-13. Using two mics, the audio operator positions one mic directly in the

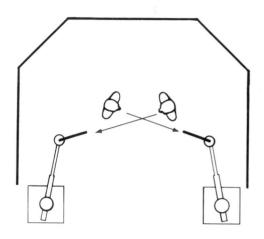

FIGURE 3-13

Correct placement of directional mics.

To achieve optimum audio pickup from two actors facing each other, it is necessary to use two directional microphones—a separate mic placed directly in the vocal path of each actor.

path of each voice to pick up the best and most direct voice quality. If the two persons move about the set during the conversation, the perambulator dolly is necessary—the boom arm is extendable and the angle of the mic can be changed to keep the proper distance and mic direction in relation to the actors.

Determining the correct distance from a source to a microphone starts with a check of the polar pickup pattern provided by the manufacturer. Ultimately it is also a matter of simply listening carefully to what the voice sounds like. A professional may work for years to gain a knowledge of just how the voice should sound given the "specs" of the mic and the natural voice quality of the source. Depending upon the type of microphone and the audio quality desired, the optimum speaking distance may be anywhere from a few inches to several feet. A typical shotgun directional mic might give fairly good audio pickup as far away as fifteen or more feet while the average hand mic works best at about 12 inches. With so many

variables the factor of experience becomes more and more important. From a student's first opportunities to work with the sound system, it is important to begin to keep mental, or even better, written notes on how different mics respond in differing production situations. One needn't be a musician to develop a trained ear and other disciplines necessary to successful audio work.

Balance and Perspective

In establishing the overall quality of sound in a production, the audio director must always consider how each individual sound is being heard in relation to all the other sounds that make up the ongoing audio **mix**. No frequency response chart, polar pattern or VU meter can replace the human ear in determining the proper combination of sounds for a program.

Keeping in mind that each individual sound relates to all the other sounds in the mix, one seeks the right proportions (**balance**) of volume from the different sources. Are the musical instruments balanced? Is there too much piano for the vocal group? Are all the panelists being heard at the same level? Can a proper balance be achieved simply by adjusting volume levels with the faders, or is the quality of sound such that microphone placement should be altered?

This last question leads into the area of audio **perspective**—an especially important concept in dramatic audio. Actors must all appear to have an audio **presence** that matches the subconscious perception of "distance" between the viewer and sound source on the screen. While this sometimes can be a matter of relative volume of a source, it more often has to do with vocal *quality*. In an intimate love scene, each subjective close-up shot puts the viewer in a visual perspective of one of the lovers. From this perspective the sound that would be heard would usually be characterized by a soft and low voice quality. Were one lover to get up and walk to a distant door, the voice quality would become entirely different, possibly diminishing slightly in volume as the person approaching the door is seen from over the shoulder of the other lover.

While the skills necessary to create these types of artistic effects are obviously developed over long periods of time, they are not beyond the abilities of beginning students, at least in an experimental, training sense. Students should be encouraged to work toward these more subtle uses of the audio vocabulary. Most will find they are usually rewarded by the results of trying the very things that they have seen on television and in the movies over thousands of hours of viewing time.

Stereo Considerations

The current competitive nature of the broadcast and cable markets has had the fortunate effect of an increasing use of **stereophonic sound** in much of the available programming. For many productions the increased costs are easily affordable when put in the perspective of million dollar plus budgets for one hour of prime time television. One less car crash per program probably more than pays for the time of several talented audio engineers. While true professional stereo involves some complicated elements, very effective results can be obtained through some rather practical methods. In its simplest configuration, stereo audio pickup requires two microphones or a single unit containing elements for both a left channel and a right channel.

The simplest setup would be the **spaced (split-pair) mic** setup shown at the top of figure 3-14. In this configuration, two mics are placed parallel to each other facing into the set—roughly analogous to the placement of your stereo speakers at home. Cardioid or omnidirectional mics can be used. Since most of the rules about mic

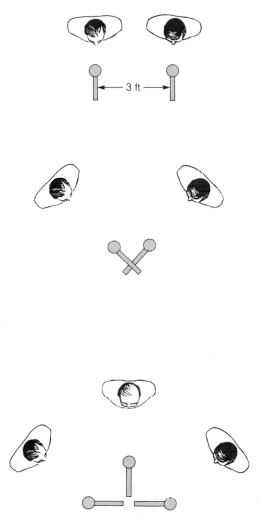

FIGURE 3-14

Three basic stereo microphone patterns.

Top, the split-pair setup works only if the microphones are at least three feet apart and are receiving somewhat different sound inputs.

Middle, the X-Y (crossed pairs) is a simple but effective approach in that it allows the mic angle to be easily changed to suit the situation.

Bottom, the M-S (mid-side) setup is a more complex approach in that it requires balancing the center mic with the two side mics.

placement similarly apply to stereo, the mics should be anywhere from three to ten feet apart depending upon source distance.

A second and usually more effective technique is the **X-Y (crossed-pairs) mic** placement. This is known as a *coincident* microphone technique. It involves placing two cardioid microphones like crossed swords, forming (as seen from above) a perfect X and Y axis (figure 3-14, center). The angle actually can be anywhere from 60 to 120 degrees, depending on the specific production requirements—the wider the angle, the greater the apparent stereo separation.

A third configuration, also a *coincident* pattern, is the **M-S (mid-side) mic** technique. This involves three microphones arranged somewhat like an inverted "T" forming two 90-degree angles (figure 3-14, bottom). This is a more technically sophisticated setup in that it requires a transformer matrix or mixer. The matrix decoder can then combine the middle mic (M) with the two side mics (S) separately to form the two complementary stereo channels. Although it involves more electronic juggling, the result can be very effective because the audio technician can often manipulate spatial perspectives and stereo effects without having to move either microphones or audio sources. Another variation of this technique involves only two mics, one of which is a bi-directional mic (picks up from two sides) and the other a cardioid pattern. Here again there is some complicated mixing and separating of channels requiring some equipment that is not always available.

As with the creative uses of sound presence and perspective mentioned earlier, students should be encouraged to experiment with stereo sound so they can make some early decisions as to how difficult or feasible its use really is. It is the experience of the authors that most classes are usually pleasantly surprised by the results of their efforts.

3.5 ADDING OTHER SOURCES

Up to this point we have been concerned entirely with the microphone as the source of television audio. We now turn our attention to other sources of recorded sound (as outlined in section 2.3). Most pre-recorded audio sources generally come from one or two locations—either the audio control room or a master control room.

Those record and playback units located in the audio booth—CD players, cartridge machines, cassette machines, and the occasional reel-to-reel deck—either will be **normalled** (permanently wired) into specific channels in the audio console or must be *patched in* by means of the **patch bay** in the booth. In most audio control rooms there is a patch bay so an operator can patch into any of these units for recording purposes. (See figure 3-15.)

FIGURE 3-15

This KABC-TV News audio booth gives the operator separate video monitors for cameras, remotes, video cassettes, and other possible picture/sound sources. Note patch bay at right.

Photo courtesy of KABC-TV

The same is true of those audio sources coming from master control. The videotape machines, possibly a **CD ROM** or other digital unit, would be normalled *into* the audio console. There would, however, have to be a patch bay so that studio output could be fed into any of the several video record machines. This patch bay is also designed to connect all the playback and record machines to any of the various editing units that are generally located somewhere in the same vicinity. In professional postproduction houses there are giant patch bays and even switchers that allow all available facilities (entire editing suites, as well as banks of separate record and playback units) to be interconnected as the need arises.

3.6 PRODUCTION COMMUNICATION

In all types of studio productions, the crew must operate, at least part of the time, within the demands of a *time continuum.* Each pause costs considerable money in terms of time lost. To keep the production going there is a carefully organized audio system that allows a director to give specific instructions to a crew of as many as twenty or more people. All crew members and performers must be prepared to follow those instructions on a split second basis because the director is actually editing the program (or segment) as it progresses.

The system by which all production elements are brought together at the precise moment that they are needed in a program is the **intercom** network. It is sometimes still referred to as the **PL** or **private line**. It is, in essence, a closed-circuit audio network that connects all primary production and engineering personnel by standard **headsets** that have an earpiece and a small microphone or mouthpiece. Thus, during a production, the director can talk to the **stage manager**[1] without the conversation being picked up by any of the program microphones. Technically any crew member with a headset can talk to anyone else. In practice the technical director makes heavy use of the system during setup time and the director is heard most of the time during a production. (See figure 3-16.)

A **double headset system** is often used by the audio personnel. This enables the audio operator in the booth and boom operator(s) to hear the PL with one earpiece and to monitor the program audio with the other earpiece. This is invaluable for a boom operator who is following a fast moving piece of dialogue among three people. For instance, he or she can directly monitor the *balance* and *perspective* being picked up while manipulating and adjusting the boom position.

In some large network productions, separate intercom networks may be set up for engineering and production personnel. Thus, the audio operator and technical director can work on a problem during a production without interfering with the director and floor crew.

In many live news and sports productions there is an adjunct system called the **interrupted feedback** or **IFB** line. On-camera talent wears an unseen **earphone** that carries the output of the program line. When the director needs to give the talent instructions, a button is pressed and his or her voice interrupts line audio.

The **studio address (SA),** or **studio talkback** system, occupies yet a different position in the production communication system. The SA talkback microphone in the control room (there is usually also one for the audio operator)

---

1. The terms "stage manager," "floor manager," and "floor director" are used interchangeably in this text. Used in different parts of the country, by different kinds of production centers, they all refer to the chief crew member on the floor—the director's surrogate in the studio production area.

FIGURE 3-16

The successful use of the intercommunication system both before and during production is not only essential for the director but also for lighting, audio, and assistant director duties.

Photo courtesy of KABC-TV

enables the director to activate a special studio speaker so that he or she can talk to everyone in the studio, regardless of whether or not they have on PL headsets. Most studios also have the talkback feature with a mic hanging in the studio so that anyone in the studio, including lighting crews up on a ladder, can be heard in the control rooms. Obviously this system can only be used prior to production, during breaks, or while a videotape is being fed into the production. (The SA speaker automatically cuts out the regular program microphone input to guard against any unintentional feedback which could overload the audio system.)

An important discipline of any television director is knowing when to use the SA (to communicate efficiently and quickly with the whole crew and all talent simultaneously) and when to rely on the stage manager to properly serve this function as the director's representative in the studio.

The total intercommunication system is further extended—to the performing talent during the production—by the hand and arm signals of the stage manager. This is the pantomime system by which different directions can be given to persons while they are on camera without having to vocalize any commands and thereby possibly unintentionally getting these directions picked up as part of the program audio. (See Appendix C for illustration of basic hand and arm signals.)

COPY: INTEGRATED SOUND CORP. COMML.

TIME	DIRECTOR COMMANDS		
-:10	Stand by music & announcer		
:00	Music up full	MUSIC:	UP FULL 10 SEC. AND UNDER
:05	Stand by music under & annc.		
:10	Music under, cue announcer	ANNC:	THE INTEGRATED SOUND CORPORATION IS PLEASED TO PRESENT ITS NEWEST HOME STUDIO COMPLETE SOUND SYSTEM FEATURING A CD PLAYER, DIGITAL TUNER, TURNTABLE AND CASSETTE DECK ALL HEARD ON SKEAKERS WITH 120 WATTS OF POWER FOR EACH STEREO CHANNEL. THESE COMPONENTS FEATURE A REMOTE CONTOLL FOR CONVENIENCE.
:25	Stand by music up full		
:30	Music up full and stand by announcer	MUSIC:	UP FULL 5 SEC. AND UNDER.
:30	Music under, cue announcer	ANNC:	DO YOUR OWN HIGH QUALITY DUBBING FROM RADIO, CD OR TURNTABLE USING METAL OR NORMAL AUDIO TAPE. THE FIVE-BAND GRAPHIC EQUALIZER LETS YOU SHAPE THE SOUND TO YOUR TASTE. SPEAKERS EACH HAVE A TWELVE INCH WOOFER, A FIVE INCH MIDRANGE AND A THREE INCH TWEETER.
:45	Stand by music up full		

FIGURE 3-17

This example shows how each of the director's commands is given at a precise point in time during the ongoing production sequence. Each command requiring some action by a crew member would be given slightly ahead of its actual execution to allow for the normal reaction time of an equipment operator.

3.7 VOCAL COMMAND PROCEDURE

The voice commands that are the organizational backbone of all ongoing video production had much of their origin in military operational techniques for tank and aircraft crews. Early live television saw the utility of a system that separates commands into two phases—preparation and execution. The *commands of execution* are those cues that directly affect what goes out over the line monitor. "Fade in music" or "Cue the announcer" call for an immediate action at a precise point in time.

For a crew member or performer to be able to respond with this immediate action, however, he or she must be given adequate preparation time to be mentally ready and/or physically prepared to perform some action or operate equipment. For this reason, all commands of execution must be preceded at some point by a related *command of preparation*. Figure 3-17 shows how the commands fit into the time frame of the production sequence for a simple audio exercise. (The commands and their timing are shown for the first paragraph of a longer radio commercial written to be performed as a "round-robin" production exercise by all members of the class. The complete script is found in Appendix D-1.)

The term *"standby"* (announcer, music, record, and so forth) is probably the most functional preparatory command for our present needs. It should alert the audio operator—and all other personnel—to listen carefully for the subsequent command of execution. The verb *"cue"* is quite often used as the first word of a command followed by the specified object of the phrase like *"music"* or *"announcer."* Complete voice command procedure for a total television production is, of necessity, somewhat more complicated than what we have presented here. More complete commands involving video will be discussed in conjunction with the explanation of video switching procedures. (See section 8.5.)

Most successful television directors work to develop a calm, articulate manner when using the intercom. Whenever possible they speak in a very casual style and even use a bit of humor. Those not used to being on the intercom net should not be misled by this apparent easygoing banter. It is designed to mask the intensity and ongoing pressure under which the director and all key members of the crew are working. Good directors know that to betray anxiety is to risk losing the confidence of the crew. Inexperienced directors who speak in loud and commanding voices are very hard to put up with on a long-term basis. Crew members listen much more carefully when the director's voice is calm and assuring. All directorial commands, whether they are for preparation or execution, must be delivered with practical consideration of the realities of the production. To request that the audio operator do too many things in too short a time is to invite a series of problems. Once an operator falls behind in a sequence, there can be a

"domino effect" which can put a whole series of production elements at risk. The wise director knows what is possible and what is not.

Since most of the operational commands, as well as a considerable amount of general information, is coming *from* the director, the crew must always maintain the *discipline* that the director has first priority at all times. Professional crew members are quick to learn the intercom style of a director. With this style in mind, and an understanding of the basic sequence of the production, they know when it is safe to talk and when it is not. Often the director specifically asks crew members for information that is needed for a quick decision. Crew members must remain alert and respond rapidly.

3.8 AUDIO SETUP PROCEDURES

Prior to the initial class audio production exercise, we should outline some basic steps needed in preparing the studio and the audio control booth for operation. During this *"setup"* period the audio assistants will follow the primary audio operator's instructions as to which studio mic inputs to use and where to set up the mics after the stage manager has seen that tables, chairs and other facilities are in place. All this is an important introduction to the concept of how *cooperation* and *responsibility* function within the chain of command.

For example, while the director can have microphones placed anywhere he or she wants them, the decision is usually the result of a consultation process. The director outlines *what* is required and leaves it up to the audio operator to decide exactly *how* that result is to be achieved.

The person in charge of audio should have the entire sequence of the flow of signals from each mic—through the console and to the recorder—clearly in mind before the mics are connected. That way if a mic does not work there can be a step-by-step signal flow check-out to find the problem. With two separate communication channels available for the setup period, it is important that their use be carefully designated and kept segregated. Generally the audio operator in charge should speak to his or her assistants in the studio through the stage manager by means of the *intercom system.* This leaves the *studio address system* free for the director or the lighting director to give instructions to other personnel without an overlap in either system. The use of these two channels could be reversed if it seemed more practical in a special circumstance.

Once each microphone has been connected, it should be checked off as being in operating condition. Later, when the performers are all in place there must be an additional test of audio **voice levels** for each performer. The audio engineer must have the help of the stage manager in ascertaining that performers are in the same position that they will occupy during the program and that they are speaking at the voice level that will be used during the performance. All too often in beginning exercises one hears the audio operator say "have him speak louder," or "have her move closer to the mic." There are two reasons why this is a very wrong approach. First, the person who moves in to the mic or speaks louder during the test will probably go back to the more natural position and voice quality that they were using previously. In this situation the operator is using the VU meter incorrectly and wasting the testing procedure. (See section 2.2.7 on the function of the VU meter.) It is also wrong because the position and the voice quality of a performer are strictly the domain of the director.

The radio commercial production exercise (full script in Appendix D-1) may at first appear to be a rather simple exercise. However, as each member of the ten-person team takes his or her turn in the different talent and operational positions, he or she soon discovers how important it is to be able to think ahead and focus one's attention upon the performance of a single task at a precise point in time. There is no better way to gain an understanding of the disciplines of production than this sort of "hands-on" exercise.

SUMMARY

As part of the *technical* requirements for audio production, it is important to know the basics of microphone design in terms of *pickup patterns, transducing elements, frequency response,* and differences of *impedance* in both cables and microphones. It is also important to know whether the mic will be *hand-held* or on a *stand,* require *limited movement,* or be *attached* to a person. These factors in turn affect a number of creative considerations. The audio director must be concerned with the way microphones are used—*selection* and *placement* of the mics, and audio *balance* and *perspective.* Moving into *stereo* production adds additional complication to the usual problems.

In adding other pre-recorded sound sources, the audio operator must also be familiar with *signal flow* to and from various facility areas, in additional to operational techniques such as *mixing* procedures.

In preparation for the first audio production exercise, it is equally important that all students understand the basic television production procedures, the *intercom network,* the *studio address,* the *IFB,* the *vocal commands,* and the audio setup operations.

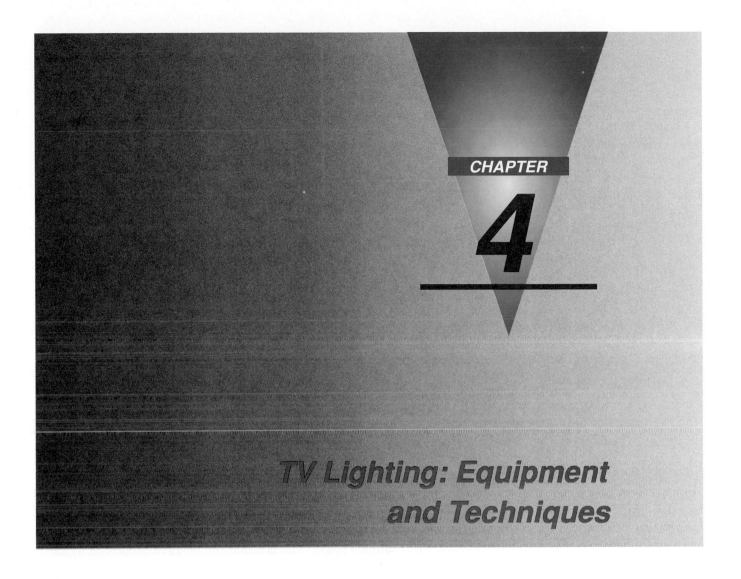

CHAPTER

4

TV Lighting: Equipment
and Techniques

Television production consists basically of two elements—audio and video. Chapters 2 and 3 dealt with audio while chapters 5 and 6 deal with obtaining video through a camera. Before we can look at how cameras and lenses work, however, it is necessary to spend time looking at that physical phenomenon that makes all vision possible—light! Without light there would be no video. With good lighting, all video is greatly enhanced.

4.1 TYPES OF LIGHT: INCIDENT AND REFLECTED

Light comes to us in two different forms. Light that comes directly from a source such as the sun, a light bulb, or a candle is called **incident light.** As important as this light is, it conveys little besides the fact that we are looking at a light source.

Our ability to see is the result of a second kind of light that has been reflected from and, as a result, altered by the surface of a material substance. This **reflected light** transmits information to us regarding our environment; the brain has been conditioned to respond to this information as perceived by the eye.

As children, we constantly reinforced our developing visual sense by touching the objects in our immediate environment. We were, in effect, programming our computer-like brain so that we could "believe our eyes." Looking out on the world, we see a series of flat planes and curved surfaces occurring at various angles. The reflected light from these diverse surfaces comes to our eyes in differing intensities—depending upon the position of the incident light sources. Our brain learns to translate these variations of light and shadow into the concept of shape and texture.

Take as an example the instructor's desk in a classroom. The dimensions of the desk's top are defined for us by the uniform intensity of the light reflected from all points of its hard, smooth surface. The light reflected from the side of the desk is of a different intensity, possibly somewhat of a shadow; this tells us that these side surfaces are at a different angle from the top and indeed are the sides of the desk. Other features, such as the drawer handles and the legs, are defined by the shadows that the light source "molds" around them.

Reflected light also tells us much about the *texture* of a surface. The even, shiny quality of light reflected from the desk top denotes a hard, uniform surface. Cloth is much more light absorbent. We can perceive the texture of a heavy cloth material by the many tiny shadows created by the design of the weave. Illumination for video production, as we shall see, is an art that involves the proper use of lighting equipment to control the light that is reflected *from* the subject *to* the camera. It is the way we shape and control this reflected light that determines what the TV camera perceives as a picture.

4.2 LIGHTING OBJECTIVES: BASIC ILLUMINATION

When the lighting director (LD) designs the lighting plan (see section 4.6) for any type of video production, he or she must think in terms of two interacting concerns. On one hand, important considerations grow out of the *artistic* or *creative needs* of the program. These will be examined in section 4.3. On the other hand, the LD knows that the creative aspects of lighting must exist within the larger context of *general illumination,* which is necessary to meet the technical needs of the camera system. These two categories—basic illumination and artistic concerns—correspond to the basic technical and creative functions as introduced in section 2.1.

The term sometimes used to refer to the general illumination of an area is **base light.** It is not to be thought of as a separate planning entity. Rather, it is the sum total of specialized and general lighting used throughout the set. Whether one is shooting a news story on location or a mob scene in a large studio, there must be a minimum amount of light present in all areas that may be photographed. A specialized artistic effect light falling on a performer may also illuminate parts of the set and thereby contribute to the total base light effect. To accomplish an even base light, the LD must take into consideration two technical aspects of the lighting conditions (whether artificial or natural sunlight)—*intensity* (contrast ratio) and *color quality* (color temperature).

Contrast Ratio

Contrast ratio deals with the complexities of the video camera pickup **CCD** chip or **tube** (see section 5.2) and the way it reacts to differing degrees of brightness within a single picture. For example, in an evenly lit living room scene on a wide shot, the colors are correctly balanced and the detail of the picture is clear. Now, as we introduce into this shot a person wearing a white raincoat who fills the left-hand quarter of the frame, several rather drastic things happen. The camera's **automatic gain control** (**AGC**) reacts to the introduction of the very bright area by decreasing the intensity of the rest of the picture. Without any changes in either the lighting or the camera controls, the right-hand three-quarters of the picture will suddenly become much darker. The colors will have a muddy tone, with the details of the set obscured. The raincoat will be an out-of-focus blur and the person's face, a dark spot. Stated in simple terms, the acceptable range of contrast between the brightest and darkest elements of the picture has been greatly exceeded. The light level that was previously sufficient for a picture has been "compressed" by the introduction of an overpowering amount of light.

The human eye can accept a **contrast ratio** of up to 100 to one. In other words, the brightest thing you are looking at can be 100 times brighter than the darkest thing you are looking at and the eye allows you to see both. A conservative but safe figure for the television camera would approach thirty to one. This means that the brightest area of a picture should not be more than thirty times as bright as the darkest elements.

A common error often occurs as students are learning the techniques of balanced lighting. For example, consider a picture in which the faces appear to be darker than the background. To solve the problem the novice LD adds more light to the set. If this light, aimed toward the dark faces, also falls on a too brightly lit background, the problem has actually been made worse. As this additional light illuminates the background, the camera's automatic gain control compensates for the generally brighter video, and that adjustment darkens the entire picture. The face remains dark in its relationship to the brighter background. A similar problem occurs if too much light reflects from hair, shoulders, or a desk top. (See section 4.5.)

Light Meters

It may be surprising to some that the human eye is much *less* sensitive than the video camera in detecting *differences* of light intensity. The relatively narrow range of what is acceptable to the camera as an adequate light level is difficult to judge with the unaided eye. For this reason, all lighting for television should be done with the aid of a **light meter.** Using the **footcandle** (**fc**) as a unit of measurement, the meter visually indicates the intensity of light coming from the direction in which the meter is pointed.[1] Some light meters have a scale of footcandles and a needle that indicates the number of footcandles being registered. Other light meters give a digital readout of the number of footcandles. (See figure 4-1.)

The intensity of television lighting is measured two different ways. We can find out how much *incident* (source) light is falling upon a subject by holding the

---

1. One footcandle (fc) is the amount of light that would fall upon a surface placed at a distance of one foot from an established theoretical source approximating the brightness of one candle.

FIGURE 4-1

Photo of a digital light meter and drawing of an analog light meter.

Although construction may vary from one light meter to another, most register light falling on the meter in terms of footcandles (fc).

Photo courtesy of Minolta

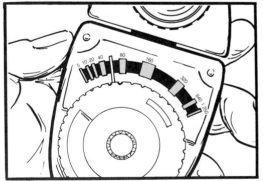

The second and possibly more important method of measuring intensity is achieved by the *reflected* light reading. It indicates how much light is reflected *from* the surface areas of subjects *into* the camera lens. For this reflected light reading, point the meter directly at the subject from the perspective of the camera. The meter should be held close to the subject, but care must be taken to avoid blocking the light source.

These two methods of measuring light produce very different readings of intensity because the texture of every surface absorbs a considerable amount of the light that falls upon it. The two different meter readings are, therefore, used for two rather different purposes. In the primary stages of setting up a lighting pattern one is looking for more general matters of intensity and coverage as it comes from the source. The LD first adjusts the strength of individual lighting instruments and then again uses the meter from different points in the set to find *hot spots* where overlapping projection patterns have caused the intensity to exceed the average level. These readings, however, do not tell the whole story.

In the more subtle aspects of lighting, we are working with the reflective qualities of the texture and color of a surface. While only a small percentage of the original source light is reflected back to the cameras, this is the light that really matters. A light green knitted dress might reflect 30 to 40 percent of the illumination falling upon it, whereas a black knitted dress might reflect less than 10 percent. A white vinyl jacket, on the other hand, might reflect well over 90 percent.

Different elements of the set may also have large variations in reflected light bounced back to the camera. These reflected hot spots coming from the set or the performers must be measured by reflected light readings with the meter pointed toward the subjects at close range. (See color plate D.)

meter very near to the camera subject and pointing it directly toward the light source. This incident light measure tells us how much light arrives at a given point, but it by no means tells the LD all that must be known to light for the camera. (See figure 4-2.)

Incident
light reading

Reflected
light reading

FIGURE 4-2
Incident and
reflected light
readings.

An incident light
meter indicates in
footcandles the
actual amount of
light coming from
the light source. A
reflected light
reading indicates
the amount of light
reflected back from
the surface of the
subject being lit.

It is these reflected light readings that can tell the LD when the contrast ratio for a given camera has been exceeded. For example, if the brightest spot the camera is aiming at is 600 footcandles and the darkest spot in the picture is twenty footcandles, this is a ratio of thirty to one; the camera probably will not handle that too well. If, on the other hand, the brightest spot is 450 footcandles and the darkest is thirty footcandles, you have a contrast ratio of fifteen to one. In the right circumstances this could be acceptable. If the contrast ratio is too great, either the bright hot spots must be toned down or the darker areas must have more light.

While the preliminary work of establishing overall light levels is best determined by a direct incident light meter reading, contrast ratios are best determined by a comparison of reflected light from the brightest and darkest elements in the picture. Divide the brightest reflected light reading by the darkest reading to determine your contrast ratio.

Color Temperature

One other factor must be taken into consideration when working with all light for television. You have probably noticed that light, itself, will exhibit differences of color in varying situations. Many fluorescent bulbs give off more of a bluish light compared to the reddish light given off by the tungsten bulb used in the home. This is the phenomenon of **color temperature,** and it is measured on a scale of **Kelvin (K)** degrees. What is being measured is neither brightness nor heat but, the **frequency** of the lightwave. One rule of thumb to remember is that, the redder the light source, the lower the Kelvin temperature; the bluer a source, the higher the Kelvin temperature.

Most studio lights are about 3,200 degrees Kelvin and have a slight red tint. Outdoor light for most of the day is about 5,000 degrees Kelvin and is quite blue. Not surprisingly, red sunrises and sunsets go down to about 2,000 degrees.

If a light is connected to a device that allows for gradual changes in applied voltage, the light wave frequency and color temperature will decrease as the light is supplied with less and less voltage. (See section 4.6.) Thus a lighting element that produces a white light when operated at full intensity of 3,200 K will gradually begin to produce an increasingly reddish tint as less and less voltage is put through it. The opposite effect results in a bluish white tint. This distortion is not readily perceived by the naked eye, but the camera is very sensitive to any drop in color temperature over a couple hundred degrees Kelvin.

The **dimmer board** designed to increase and diminish the intensity of lights is a holdover from the theatrical tradition. It does have uses in television production but should not be used as a way of adjusting the brightness of lights during setup. Section 4.4 explains how the **controlled-beam spotlight** is used to accomplish this purpose by spreading its beam over a wider surface and thereby lessening its intensity.

Shooting in an outdoor setting where sunlight becomes a major source of illumination necessitates an added awareness of Kelvin temperature. Depending upon haze and cloud conditions, outdoor color temperature readings can range anywhere from *2,000 degrees Kelvin to over 10,000 degrees Kelvin.* In these situations, video cameras must be adjusted for the abundance of bluish light by changing the built-in color temperature filter (see section 5.4) and/or by resetting the white balance (see section 5.5). One of the main problems with outdoor shooting occurs as the sun moves across the sky or as weather conditions change. Scenes shot during sunset will have a much lower color temperature than scenes shot at noon, and therefore may not edit well together.

4.3 LIGHTING OBJECTIVES: CREATIVE PURPOSES

As a creative or artistic factor in video production, lighting can be said to have four main purposes: (1) to define the shape and texture of physical form and, by extension, to create a sense of depth and perspective within the elements of the set or location; (2) to imitate the quality of light characteristic of a situation or setting in reality; (3) to establish and enhance the psychological mood of a performance or setting; and (4) to focus attention upon a single performer or aspect of the production and thereby separate that subject from any feeling of relationship with setting or location.

While this last concept usually has a specialized application, the other three purposes should be thought of as principles that can be simultaneously applied within a given production situation. The same light that gives shape to a person's features can also provide mood, and at the same time, relate to the setting itself (for example, a beam of sunlight coming through a window and falling on the heroine's face). At first glance, it might seem that some of these purposes apply only to dramatic productions. This is not necessarily true. These principles apply to all types of programs, from game shows to live news remote transmissions.

Perspective, Shape, and Texture

When a light source is placed right next to a camera, the light waves reflected back into the lens will be of a generally uniform quality. This effect is *flat lighting* because the illumination has "filled" the hollows and curves that are the distinguishing features of the subject. When the light source is moved so that the beam comes from an angle, the resulting shadows "etch" the features so that the eye can perceive depth and texture. The camera system functions best when there is an exaggeration of contrasting light values within the video picture. The art of creating the illusion of depth on a flat video tube is largely a matter of accentuating the illumination patterns that we utilize in the normal process of vision.

The experienced lighting director knows it is the manipulation of shadows, rather than bright spots, that can most effectively add form and texture to any object. Light coming from the side or rear of an object will throw shadows in certain shape-defining ways. Extreme side lighting (at right angles to the camera position) will emphasize textural quality by exaggerating shadows, making any object look much rougher than it would otherwise appear.

The heightened sense of perspective necessary to the video picture is simply an application of this basic concept in the context of the entire set. Performers and foreground objects can be separated from the background when the angle and intensity of the light beam are adjusted to create a slight "highlight" effect (see section 4.5).

Reality

Light operates on our conditioned responses in other equally important ways. We all have tuned in to the middle of a television play and watched a series of close-up shots. Either consciously or unconsciously, we are soon aware of being indoors or outdoors and of the time of day by the quality of light on the actor's face. It is probably outdoors and near noontime if the light is relatively bright and there are definite shadows under the eyebrows,

nose, and chin of the actor. If the scene has been shot inside a studio, the *imitation of reality* is a product of the lighting.

Other specific shadow and lighting effects suggest certain kinds of realistic situations. Shadows of venetian blinds or prison bars cast on the rear wall of a set help to suggest a particular locale. Other *off-camera* lighting effects help to pinpoint a setting: a low-angle flickering light indicates a campfire or fireplace; a continually flashing red light indicates the presence of an emergency vehicle. Other effects help to carry forth the dramatic narrative: a shaft of light coming from under a door of a room previously unoccupied indicates the presence of an intruder; a flashlight probing around a darkened room helps reveal evidence of a burglary.

Mood

Similarly, the psychological *mood* of a performance or production can be reinforced by the quality of light and its abundance or absence. Comedy is bright; therefore, **high-key lighting** is used to give an intense overall illumination with a fully lit background. Situation comedies, game shows, and big musical numbers in a variety show rely on this kind of lighting to establish a light-hearted mood.

Conversely, tragedy or fear are communicated when the area surrounding an actor is dark or dimly lit. **Low-key lighting** refers to selective illumination that highlights only the necessary elements of a picture—usually the background is dark, extreme lighting angles may be used, and only part of the picture is disclosed. Again, specific dramatic moods may be reinforced by special effects—a flashing neon sign outside a sparsely furnished hotel room suggests a seedy part of town; lightning flashes create an eerie mood; lighting from a low angle gives a character a sinister, unnatural appearance (see figure 4-3).

FIGURE 4-3

Sinister lighting effect.

Lighting from unusual angles or sources can give unnatural or symbolic effects; for example, lighting from a low angle usually results in a foreboding, sinister appearance.

Focus of Attention

When a high contrast exists between the light on a subject and the light falling on the background area, the eye is drawn to the subject. The most obvious example is the use of a **follow spot** on a performer in a musical or variety show. Another variation of this technique is **limbo lighting,** where the subject is placed "in limbo" against a softly lit cyclorama or some other nondescriptive, neutral background. (See section 10.2.)

Another way of achieving focus of attention is with **cameo lighting**—the performer is lit, but the background is completely dark. (See figure 4-4.) A **silhouette** effect—with the performers kept in darkness but outlined against a brightly lit background—may be desired for a dance routine or other special situation. (See figure 4-5.) A

FIGURE 4-4

Typical cameo lighting: figure against a dark background.

FIGURE 4-5
Representative
silhouette lighting:
dark figures against
a light background.

single shaft of light may be used to accent a contestant in a suspenseful climax of a game show. The host of a documentary may be accented with a strong back or side light. Subtle lighting highlights may be used in many other dramatic and nondramatic settings to control focus of attention.

So, above and beyond the necessity of using enough base light for basic illumination, the lighting director must also plan creative lighting to add shape, texture and perspective, heighten the illusion of reality, create and enhance a specific mood, and focus attention.

4.4 TYPES OF LIGHTING INSTRUMENTS

A visit to a commercial supplier of theatrical and television lighting equipment can be a dazzling experience in every sense of the word. Hundreds of highly specialized pieces of equipment are on display or in the catalogs. One sees a range of instruments designed for the largest studio set as well as the newest lightweight portable gear for EFP and ENG uses. In section 4.5 we will examine the basic studio lighting techniques as a way of establishing a

foundation for all video illumination. These principles will be adapted to small format and EFP production in chapter 14.

Our understanding of lighting technique is made easier by the fact that most lighting instruments fall into one of two basic categories—the controlled-beam **spotlight** and the diffused-beam **floodlight.** (Many lighting professionals use the term *hardlight* to refer to spotlights, distinguishing it from the "soft" light of a floodlight.)

Controlled-Beam Spotlights

The classic controlled-beam spotlight illustrated in figure 4-6 is the workhorse of studio lighting. The spotlight is used wherever a highly directional beam of light that can be shaped and focused is desired. Its chief characteristic is the ability to throw a spot of light on any particular area or performer. It is commonly referred to as a **Fresnel** (pronounced without the *s*), although each manufacturer will have a different name for it.[2]

2. The lens generally used in the instrument has a series of raised concentric rings on the outer face that help to dissipate the tremendous heat buildup in the enclosed structure. Augustin-Jean Fresnel was a nineteenth century scientist who did important research into the nature of light.

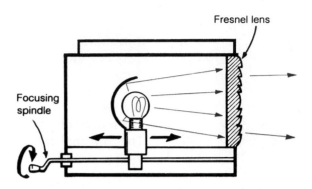

Fresnel lens

Focusing
spindle

FIGURE 4-6

Focusing mechanism of the Fresnel spotlight.

By turning the focusing handle or spindle, the bulb-reflector unit can be moved toward the lens or back to the rear of the housing. When in the forward position, the spotlight beam is "spread" to cover a relatively wide area. When moved to the rear of the housing, the beam is more narrowly focused, or "pinned," on a smaller area.

In addition to its characteristic lens structure, the spotlight's other distinguishing feature is the movable assembly that allows the illuminating unit (bulb and reflector) to be moved back-and-forth between the rear and front of the instrument.[3] With the bulb in the rear **"pinned"** position, the light rays are focused in a narrow beam of high intensity, perhaps spreading no more than ten degrees. As the bulb is moved forward in the housing, the beam becomes **"spread"** and its intensity is diminished. In its full-forward spread position, the beam forms approximately a 60-degree angle.

The models of spotlights most generally in use range from 500 watts to 10,000 watts. In a 2,000-watt instrument (commonly called a "junior"), a spotted (pinned) light will produce an intensity of 600 footcandles

3. The focusing mechanism described here (and pictured in figure 4-6) is moved forward or backward by turning a crank or focusing spindle. Other spotlights accomplish this by means of a focusing ring or (on smaller quartz instruments) a horizontal focusing lever.

when measured at a distance of twenty-five feet. In the fully flooded (spread) position, the intensity of the same instrument drops to roughly sixty footcandles, but the light now covers an area six times larger in diameter. Fresnel spots are also classified by the diameter of the lenses. The most common studio sizes are the 6-inch, 8-inch, 10-inch, and 12-inch models.

Some newer lights are designed to be fully adjustable from the floor with a *light pole* such as that seen in figure 4-7. The Fresnel lamp in figure 4-8 has knobs located on either side of the yoke and on the lower assembly that can be engaged by a connector on the end of a matching pole. The light can be spotted and flooded, adjusted up and down, and moved sideways back and forth without having the crew member climb a ladder.

The **ellipsoidal,** or **leko,** spotlight diagramed in figure 4-9 gains its name from its fixed reflecting mirror at the back of the unit. By means of its tube shape and focusing lens, it projects an intense directional beam that is well-defined at its edge point.

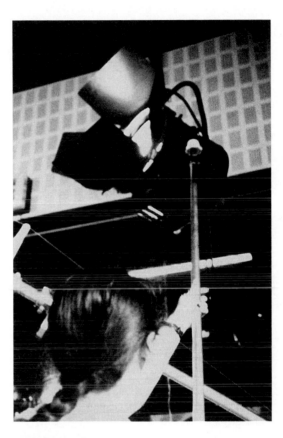

FIGURE 4-7

This special pole, which fits into knobs on the lamp, can be used to tilt and focus the lighting.

The beam can be further shaped by movable metal shutters (also known as *cutters*) located inside the lamp housing, behind the lens. At this point—where all the reflected rays of light are in sharp focus—there is also a place to insert a patterned metal design cutout. The shadow of this **cucalorus** or **cookie** or **kook** is then projected to add visual interest to large, plain background surfaces. Some common kook patterns include prison bars, arabesques and Moorish motifs (see figure 4-10), venetian blinds, crosses, squares and other geometric designs, and cloud patterns.

Because it throws a very harsh beam, the ellipsoidal spot is rarely used as the basic instrument in lighting a person or an object for television. It is more likely to be used as a special effects light.

Several other varieties of fixed-beam spotlights exist. One popular type is much like an auto headlight with the lens, bulb, and reflector built together as a single unit. This **internal reflector spotlight** is common as a portable source of light, or as a light clipped to a portable stand. Often it is used to fill in and highlight areas with inadequate lighting.

Another type of portable spotlight is the **external reflector** model—a highly efficient quartz lamp in a small housing with no lens. Although not as controllable and precise as a Fresnel spot, this model is lightweight, easily moved (often with a clip-on attachment or a lightweight tripod), and more than adequate for most remote lighting assignments.

Floodlights

When we examine the specific techniques of lighting (see section 4.5), we see that the effects of the focused-beam spotlight are balanced by the use of softer light from a different angle. The purpose of this light source is to soften and thereby control the shadows that are created by the angle of the focused spotlight. When a number of floodlights are used in a set, the effect is a soft, diffused light that eases the harshness of the shadows.

To help achieve the shadowless effect of a large source area, the floodlight does not use a lens; it will probably have a diffusing reflector, which has the effect of spreading out the source; it may use a softlight bulb with no exposed filament at all, and; it may use a **scrim**—a soft, spun-glass filter or other translucent piece of material in a rigid frame attached to the front of the instrument (see section 4.6).

The classic model for a floodlight is the one-half hollow globe structure known as a **scoop** (see figure 4-11). Its large reflecting

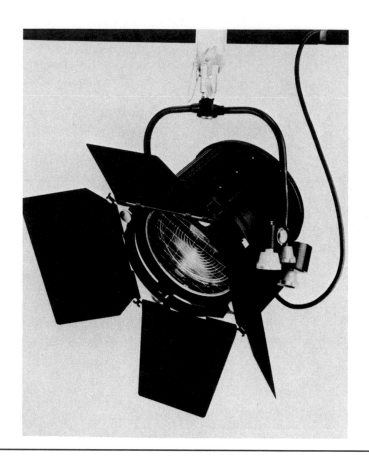

FIGURE 4-8

A 2,000-watt Fresnel
spotlight equipped
with knobs for a
lighting pole.

Photo courtesy of
Strand Lighting

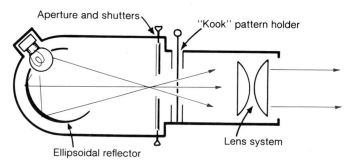

FIGURE 4-9

Lens system of the ellipsoidal spotlight.

Light rays are reflected from the fixed reflector and focused through the aperture. At this point the shutters can be adjusted to precisely shape the beam of light or cucalorus patterns which may be inserted to project hard-edged shadow designs through the lens system.

FIGURE 4-10

Left: ellipsoidal spotlight.

Right: example of a shadow pattern cast by a "cookie" inserted in a leko (ellipsoidal) spotlight.

(Left) Photo courtesy of Strand Lighting

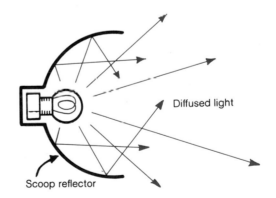

Diffused light

Scoop reflector

FIGURE 4-11

The basic scoop is the main source of fill light. Using either quartz or incandescent elements, the popular sizes for most television studio applications are the 14-inch and 16-inch diameters.

Drawing indicates the diffused pattern of reflected light rays.

Photo courtesy of Strand Lighting

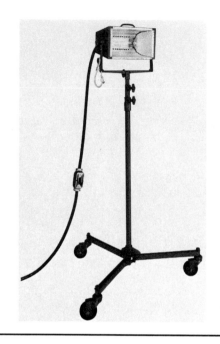

FIGURE 4-12

The *pan* shape of the reflector or the *broad* beam provided is the source of the name that describes this lighting instrument.

Left, pan mounted on a floor stand; *right,* ColorTran 1-K broad with barn doors.

(Left) Photo courtesy of Mole Richardson

FIGURE 4-13
Strip lights.

area is made of a light-diffusing material that spreads the illumination in a nonfocused scattered pattern. Floodlights built in a rectangular shape are known as **pans** or **broads** (see figure 4-12). Some have controls that allow for an adjustment of the degree of spread. Their square shape makes possible the additional use of blocking devices known as **barn doors.** (See section 4.6.) Another type of floodlight is the **softlight.** It is constructed with the bulb positioned so that the light is reflected off the back of the lamp housing before leaving the housing; the reflection material diffuses the intensity of the light coming from the bulb. A 2,000-watt floodlight will have a pattern of illumination that is more than twice the area of a 2,000-watt Fresnel spotlight in the maximum spread position.

When a series of pans are constructed in a continuous side-by-side row, they are called **strip lights.** They are used frequently with colored **gels** in lighting the background **cyclorama** (**cyc,** pronounced "sike") or other large set surfaces (see figure 4-13). Each individual lamp will typically be from 500 to 1,000 watts.

For larger studio productions, huge multi-bulb instruments such as that pictured in figure 4-14 may be used. Such an 8,000-watt "super-softlight" may either be mounted on a floor stand or hung from a lighting grid (see section 4.6). The eight 1,000-watt bulbs can be separately controlled to produce a variety of intensity levels. The bulbs are positioned so that only diffused light is sent out from the large reflector.

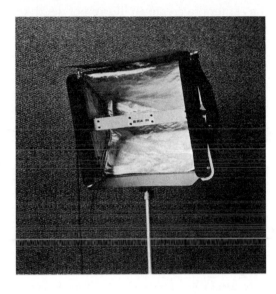

FIGURE 4-14

Super-softlights.

Left. In this 8-K *super-softlight,* there is no direct light from the eight 1,000-watt quartz bulbs; all light is reflected by the large, curved surface.

Right: The Lowel Softlight 1500 has two bulbs that bounce light off the canvas reflector impregnated with foil for a diffused light.

(Left) Photo courtesy of Mole Richardson

Today, most spotlights and floodlights are designed to use the **quartz** bulb. The term "quartz" is applied to a variety of quartz-iodine, tungsten-halogen, and similar illumination sources that have largely replaced the incandescent bulb. Its advantages are that it is smaller, longer lasting, more efficient (producing more illumination per watt), and does not darken with carbon deposits as it gets older. It does, however, tend to lose some of its Kelvin temperature as it ages—producing a slightly yellowish light.

This brief review of lighting instruments barely suggests the scope and variety of available equipment. In the past

decade, leading manufacturers have developed a whole new generation of highly efficient, lightweight, and portable lighting systems. This section has been presented to provide a practical background for an understanding of the principles on which all stage, film, and television lighting is based.

4.5 FUNDAMENTAL LIGHTING CONCEPTS

As noted in section 4.3, creative lighting is largely a matter of careful control over the

effects of light and shadow. The manipulation of these two factors is what permits the camera to create an illusion of depth on the viewing screen.

Three-Point Lighting

The specific techniques through which these effects are accomplished can be easily understood by examining the classic lighting setup borrowed from motion pictures. It is known as **three-point lighting** because it involves the use of three different light sources—the **key light,** the **fill light,** and the **back light.** Each has a separate effect upon the subject being lit because the three lights differ in relative angle or direction (or apparent source), level of intensity, and degree to which they are either focused or diffused. Taken together, the cumulative effect is that of a balanced and an aesthetic unity—what

Rembrandt called a "golden triangle" of light. Figure 4-15 illustrates how the three sources are used in a typical situation. This three-point lighting arrangement not only provides the *base light* but also meets the *creative purposes* of form and texture, reality, mood, and focus of attention.

It is important to keep in mind that our three-point lighting model is an ideal, based upon a concept that was developed for film production where a *single* camera shoots the subject or subjects from one angle only. Each shot could be separately set up and lit. The ways in which this underlying concept is modified to apply to multiple-camera, continuous-action video production are discussed throughout the rest of this section. (Single-camera EFP video production, of course, can come closer to the filmic model of separate setups with balanced three-point lighting carefully plotted for each shot; see section 15.8.)

FIGURE 4-15

Three-point lighting.

The key light and fill light should normally be placed approximately 30 to 45 degrees from a line drawn straight in front of the talent (with the fill being more directly in front of the talent). The back light is always behind the talent at a steeper angle than the key or fill lights.

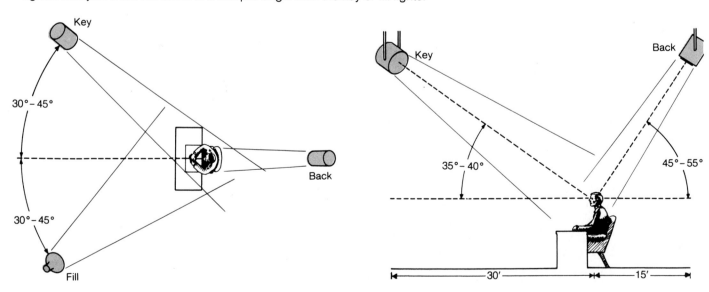

Key Light

The most important illumination in any lighting plan is the *key* light. It is the apparent source of the light hitting the talent and provides the majority of the light that is reflected into the camera lens. (See figure 4-16.) Almost invariably, a spotlight is used for the key light; its strength and directional beam emphasize the contrast of light and shadow, defining the shape and texture of the subject. It is the use of the key light that brings out the features of the face and illuminates the eye itself.

While more extreme angles can be used to produce special dramatic effects, the optimum result is achieved by placing the key off to one side of the face of the subject, coming in at an angle between thirty and thirty-five degrees. (If the key light is placed directly in front of the talent, the result is a flat, washed-out appearance with no shadows, no sculpting or molding of the face.) The height of the key will depend to some extent upon the facial contours of the talent. It should be placed high enough to produce a slight shadow under the chin and nose, yet low enough to get the light directly into the eye socket itself. (If the talent has deep-set eyes and the key light is at too steep an angle, the result is simply two dark shadows under the eyebrows.) A good rule of thumb is that the key should normally be placed at a 35- to 40-degree angle above the vision line of the subject.

In setting all lights—but especially the key—you must consider carefully the angle of the light hitting the subject as it relates to the intensity of the light being reflected back into the camera lens. In terms of the basic laws of optics, *the angle of incidence equals the angle of reflection;* or, reflected light bounces off a flat surface at the same angle as the incoming light hits the surface.

If you have a light source projecting a beam perfectly perpendicular to a flat surface, that beam would reflect directly back upon itself. However, if you raise the light source as to create a 30-degree angle above the perpendicular, as in figure 4-17, the reflected beam will bounce back downward at a corresponding angle of thirty degrees. If the subject being lit has a

FIGURE 4-16
Subject with key light only.

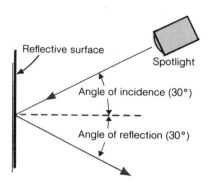

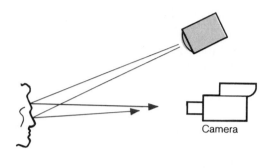

FIGURE 4-17
Angles of incidence and reflection.

Basic laws of optics tell us that the angle at which the rays of light hit a flat reflective surface (angle of incidence) will equal the angle at which the reflected rays (angle of reflection) bounce away from the surface. Depending on the angle, a reflective surface such as metal or the talent's shiny forehead may send an unwanted glare or highlight back into the camera.

rough texture or an uneven surface, the reflected light will be diffused and this angle is not important. However, if you are lighting a smooth and relatively polished surface (such as vinyl or even oily skin), this angle can become very critical.

Applying this principle to the way light is reflected from the face of a subject, you can see how the relatively smooth (and sometimes oily) surfaces of the forehead and nose can create shiny, highly reflective "hot" spots as light is bounced back directly into the camera lens. This same effect may occur many times over within a large set with its various angles and planes. Similarly, productions using studio graphics or photographs mounted on cards may have trouble with reflected glare—unless a dull matte surface is used or the cards are properly angled to reflect the light away from the camera lens.

Fill Light
In order to "fill in" on the dark side of the face or object being lit, some sort of *fill*

light is needed. It should come in at an angle on the side opposite from the key. Ordinarily a floodlight (such as a scoop or broad) would be used, although a spotlight in its *flooded* position can often be effective. In any case, a soft diffused light is desired. (See figures 4-18 and 4-19.) It is used simply to soften the shadows and give some illumination to the otherwise dark side of the talent. Fill light should not be as strong or directional as key light; it should not compete in creating shadows or countering the shaping qualities of the key.

Often a great amount of fill light is used to achieve a consistently even *wash* of illumination over the entire set. In this application, the fill light comes close to serving the same purpose as base light. (See section 4.2.)

Back Light
As the name implies, *back* light comes from behind and above the subject. A spotlight is virtually always used so that the light can be directed and focused like the key. The back

FIGURE 4-18
Subject with fill
light only.

FIGURE 4-19
Subject with
balanced key and
fill lighting.

light falls upon the subject, and as a result, accentuates such features as hair, shoulders, and top surfaces of set elements. (See figures 4-20 and 4-21.) This highlighting effect separates the talent from the background, adding to the illusion of depth within the total picture. Without adequate back light, the subject appears flat and tends to blend in with the background, as in figure 4-16.

Back light requirements will vary with the color of the subject, the background, and the desired effect. Hair color and texture are especially crucial. For example, blondes require relatively little back light. Their natural hair color separates them from the background. Also, tightly curled hair generally needs extra back light because it does not reflect light well.

FIGURE 4-20
Subject with back light only.

FIGURE 4-21
Subject with balanced three-point lighting (key, fill, and back light).

Auxiliary Light Sources

Several other terms refer to more specialized types of lighting. One of these, the **kicker,** is a *back* light that also functions partially as a *key* light. It is hung so that it comes in over the right shoulders (camera left) of a line of guests as shown in figure 4-22. It brightens up the camera left side of the face without disturbing the intended three-point light effect.

One of the most important additional sources of illumination is the **set light** or **background light** (not to be confused with the *back* light). This is the major source of lighting for the cyclorama or background set behind the performers. In addition to helping fill in the overall picture (basic illumination), background lighting can give form and texture to the setting, provide a sense of reality, or suggest

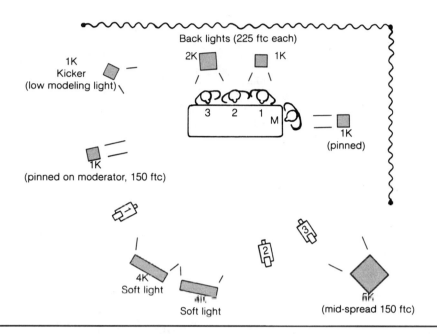

Back lights (225 ftc each)

1K
Kicker
(low modeling light)

2K   1K

3 2 1 M

1K
(pinned)

1K
(pinned on moderator, 150 ftc)

4K
Soft light

Soft light

(mid-spread 150 ftc)

FIGURE 4-22
"Plan A" lighting plot.

Modified three-point
lighting plan
designed for
participants
primarily addressing
the audience.

mood (creative functions). Colored gels on a plain cyclorama can help establish mood on a production.

In one function or another, most types of lighting instruments can be appropriately used for background lighting. Floodlights (scoops or strip lights) are often used for general illumination of a cyclorama or flat space. Spotlights can be used to highlight certain areas or present dramatic lighting effects (for example, strong diagonal slashes of light or selected low-key elements). And, of course, the ellipsoidal spot can be used with a variety of cucalorus patterns for various shadow effects. (See figures 4-10 and 10-22.)

Other special lighting effects depend upon careful background lighting. A good *silhouette* demands an evenly lit background, balanced from top to bottom as well as from side to side. A good *cameo* effect, on the other hand, requires a complete lack of any light hitting the background; front lighting must be carefully controlled to make certain that no spill is reflected onto the set behind the talent.

Actually, in any moderately complicated lighting setup, the illumination is coming from many directions and angles. In addition, the subjects—the persons being lit—will be moving within the set. The concept of key, back, and fill lights should be used as a guide, not as a rigid set of rules. Auxiliary lighting and special effects will be added as needed for certain creative purposes. The important consideration is that the lighting director be in total control of the *direction, intensity, quality* (harsh shadows or diffused), and *color* (if applicable) of light falling upon performers and set.

Multiple-Camera Lighting

As previously mentioned, the concept of three-point lighting was developed for the motion picture single-camera technique— always concerned with lighting from the viewpoint of the camera. With this approach, every shot has its own lighting setup. When the subject and camera are moved, the lighting is changed. Detailed care can be taken to sculpt the face and other features of the subject with the key light, blended with back and fill lights.

With television's multiple-camera formats and continuous action productions, lighting directors have found it difficult to adhere to the concept of classic three-point lighting. In the talk show format, for example, the host or hostess moves to people in the audience and the cameras must shoot from many angles. The solution to this situation is to create an overall *wash* of illumination throughout the entire set. Many soft fill lights (fewer keys) are used from all possible camera angles. The result is what is called *"flat"* lighting because the faces take on more of a flat look as differentiated from the *"shaped"* effect of shadows created by a strong key. It is a workable solution to a common lighting problem.

Some situation comedies shot with electronic multiple-camera techniques have had substantial success in overlaying the concept of three-point lighting within a flat-lit set. Working together, the TV director and lighting director can select points within the scene where the actors will remain in place for a period of time; in these spots careful three-point lighting can be used for close-ups. When portions of the scene contain physical movement, the action is picked up by the cameras on wider shots (see section 6.2) so the flat lighting will not matter as much. Close-ups are kept to a minimum in the areas lit by flat lighting. It is a compromise, but it works fairly well.

Daytime serials ("the soaps") that crank out an hour a day of multiple-camera production are hard pressed to work much with delicate lighting, but using the previous technique they manage to achieve an overall satisfactory lighting effect. Since productions of all types operate within tight budget constraints, lighting directors never have all the time and crew they need to do a perfect job. They simply do the best

they can with what resources they have. But in all video production, three-point lighting—with its potential for texture, depth, modeling, perspective, and focus—remains the standard against which all lighting work is measured.

Two Different Lighting Techniques

To examine some multiple-camera lighting problems—as well as their solutions—let us look at the example of a four person discussion program such as the one suggested by the "Frame of Reference" script in Appendix D-2. The participants are seated in an "L" shape with the host on the camera right side. This arrangement allows the host to keep eye contact with the three guests while leading the discussion.

If the three guests speak to the host or straight out to an audience area behind the camera 2 location, and the host addresses the viewers by means of camera 1, then we can use the "Plan A" lighting plot as shown in figure 4-22. In this illustration the key light is provided by the 5-kilowatt Fresnel spotlight, which is spread to cover all four participants. Its angle will create slight shadows on the faces of the three guests. It should be tilted so that its light also falls on the cyclorama in the background. Fill light is provided by the two 4-kilowatt *softlights* (see figure 4-14) from the camera left side. This is basically an application of the *three-point lighting* technique.

One possible problem may occur when guests one and two occasionally turn to their right to speak to guest three (on the camera left side)—they would have only fill light on their faces from the angle of camera 1. This problem can be solved by placing a spotlight *kicker* from over their right shoulders to provide a "modeling" effect from the camera 1 angle. To do its job properly, this controlled beam light should be hung somewhat lower than the two backlights. The host is covered by a

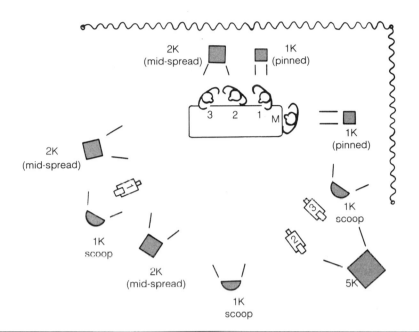

FIGURE 4-23

"Plan B" lighting plot.

Cross-key lighting may be appropriate when participants are involved in considerable give-and-take head-turning discussion.

pinned spot from a slightly different angle from the camera 1 shooting perspective. This gives the host's face some shape and definition. The host's fill light comes from the two *softlights*.

The back lights are located as indicated on the lighting plot. (See figure 4-22.) Whenever possible, their intensity should be adjusted to take into account the differing amounts of back light needed by blondes as opposed to brunettes. Differences in light or dark clothing around the shoulder area may also need adjustment. Light falling on the cyclorama must be checked to be sure that its brightness and color are the same behind all camera shots. Problems can be solved by placing additional scoops or broads to fill any dark spots on the cyc.

However, if the guests, for the most part, will be constantly turning to speak to each other and to the host during the course of the discussion, then the "Plan B" lighting arrangement (see figure 4-23)

would be more appropriate. It utilizes a **cross-key** lighting technique so named because the multiple key lights are aimed onto the set from different directions. Their beams *cross* each other as they light their respective subject areas.

The lighting must be done in this way because both guests 1 and 2 will at times be facing to their extreme right or left as they talk to their fellow panelists and the host. Note that cameras 2 and 3 have been moved farther to the right and camera 1 more to the left so as to be shooting faces at less than a 30-degree angle from a straight-on position. A well-lit camera shot showing the eyes and other facial movements tells us much about what an individual wishes to communicate to the audience and sometimes it betrays an important truth that was not necessarily intended. This effect is lost with a profile shot and should be avoided in most circumstances unless there is a specific artistic reason for its use.

Light	Footcandles	Relative Strength
Key	150 fc.	Reference point of 1
Fill	75 fc.	1/2 of key
Back	225–300 fc.	1 1/2 to 2 times key
Background	75–115 fc.	1/2 to 3/4 of key

FIGURE 4-24

Ratio of key, back, fill, and set lights.

It should be noted that figures 4-22 and 4-23 are not exactly drawn to scale. As mentioned earlier, all lights, and especially the *key lights,* should be sufficiently distant from the subjects to eliminate any possibility of dark areas around the eyes and unflattering shadows under the nose and chin.

Balanced Lighting Ratios

The first step a lighting director must take in creating a three-point lighting pattern is to decide on the relative strengths of each light source. There are some basic guidelines they use in making their preliminary plans. Figure 4-24 shows an average ratio of key, back, and fill lights that can be applied in most basic lighting situations. The footcandle figures represent incident meter readings that would be made at the point where light strikes the subject.

During the lighting setup period, there is a definite sequence of activity that should be followed by the lighting director and his or her crew. First, a generally optimum light level for the studio cameras should be ascertained from the person in charge of technical facilities. In average circumstances this could be around 200 footcandles of incident light. With this in mind, the ratios presented in figure 4-24 would be applied. As each light is turned on, its

strength must be measured using the light meter and adjusted to contribute its part to the final ratio. A big mistake made by novice crews is to first turn on all lighting instruments and then try to balance them. This does not work. Good lighting must be a well-planned, organized process.

The key light, being the primary light source, is given the reference point of *one.* Other light sources are then adjusted in relation to the strength of the key. The back light is typically up to *one and one-half* the strength of the key; the fill is roughly *one-half* the strength of the key.

Such ratios are only guidelines, of course. Once the lights are turned on, the lighting director can check the shot through the camera monitor and get a better picture of the reflective qualities of the subject and the rest of the set. The final lighting decisions have to be based upon many factors, such as the color and shading of the object being lit, the texture and shade of the background, the illusion of reality, and the desired mood. Particular care must be taken with skin tone and hair. Too much light on the hair and shoulders can cause the face to look relatively darker than it naturally is. If any picture elements appear out of balance, they should be checked by reflected light meter readings.

Of the three fundamental light sources, the back light is the most difficult to measure and work with. Achieving the desired effect of highlighting the hair, shoulders, and so forth, calls for considerable intensity. Because of the steep angle of the typical back light, much of this intensity does not reflect into the camera. The direct incident meter reading, therefore, will seem quite high in relation to the effect on the picture. Because it is usually much closer to the subject than the key light, the wattage needed in the back light lamps will often be less than that used for the key lights.

The light falling on the background, which usually has its own independent sources, also consists of some contribution (*spill*) by both the key and fill lights. For this reason, it is sometimes difficult to predict background light level accurately in the initial plan. The reflective quality of background materials varies considerably. The same amount of incident footcandles falling upon a light-colored cyclorama and dark wood paneling will produce considerably different amounts of light reflected into the camera.

When the performers are in place, there must be a final adjustment process that should utilize a more accurate set of reflected light readings. The footcandle readings will, of course, be on a much lower scale, but the same basic ratio will apply. Again, the final suitability of a picture should never rest with an arbitrary ratio and a light meter. Ultimately it comes down to how the picture looks on the monitor to the director and the lighting director.

Economy of Lighting

Frugality in the use of lighting instruments is an important consideration. Good lighting technique is often as much a matter of knowing when to take out or soften lights as it is of knowing how to add lights to a set. The modeling and texturing effects of a few well-placed key lights are easily wiped out by adding too many lights from too many directions. Newer cameras that require less light are making it increasingly possible to capture the subtle effect of natural light we are all used to seeing.

4.6 STUDIO LIGHTING PROCEDURES

Having looked at some of the basic television lighting requirements and concepts,

we are ready to consider the actual techniques and procedures involved in lighting a television setting. Several of these aspects also involve practice and discipline in the execution of specific lighting functions— for example, in the precise preparation and use of lighting plans and plots and in careful observance of all safety precautions.

Mounting Lighting Instruments

Our first concern should be with the way the lights are actually mounted or supported. How are they to be positioned and held in place? Basically, there are two ways—by *hanging* them from above or by mounting them on a *floor stand*.

Hanging Mounts

Every television studio is equipped with a **lighting grid** for mounting lights above the staging area. It is comprised of pipes and supporting mechanisms that place the lighting instruments in a position to produce a proper angle of illumination while leaving the studio floor uncluttered for camera and talent movement, microphone placement, and various set elements. Most studios have a pipe grid or **batten** system upon which the lights are actually suspended. The pipe grid is a rigid permanent arrangement of pipes several feet beneath the studio ceiling. A movable batten system allows the pipes to be raised or lowered by a counterweight system so that lights can easily be worked on from the studio floor.

After lights are hung in the right position, final adjustments (**trimming**) have to be made at the operating height, even on a counter-weighted batten. Some of these might be accomplished with a *light pole*, which can be inserted into the ring-focus mechanism on some spotlights to adjust the spot-flood position of the bulb-reflector unit. Some larger studios will have a **catwalk**, allowing lighting operators

FIGURE 4-25

High-tech it may not
be, but this type of
wooden ladder with
one alert person to
stabilize it provides
a quick and efficient
way to trim lights.

to move around on permanent scaffolding to reach the lights from above. In most studios, however, a special movable *lighting ladder* is used that allows lighting personnel to climb up to any instrument for final adjustments and focusing. (See figure 4-25.)

Lighting instruments may actually be connected to the grid or batten with a variety of fastening devices. Many are placed into position with a **C-clamp,** which connects the light firmly to the grid but allows for no vertical adjustment of the instrument. (See figure 4-26.) The clamp is always used in conjunction with an additional steel **safety chain** that prevents the light from falling should there be any accidental disconnection of the clamp.

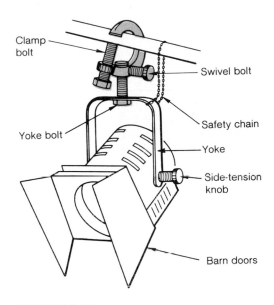

Clamp bolt

Swivel bolt

Yoke bolt

Safety chain

Yoke

Side-tension knob

Barn doors

FIGURE 4-26
C-clamp.

The C-clamp holding this Fresnel spotlight to a pipe grid has four adjusting screws or bolts.

Different types of adjustable rods are available that permit lights to be positioned several feet lower than the height of the main grid; a light is attached near the bottom of a rod, and the rod is attached to the grid. A **pantograph** can also be used to lower lights. It is a scissors-like, spring-counterbalanced hanger that allows lights to be pulled down or pushed up quickly and easily to any level. This is the most convenient arrangement for rapid adjustments and easy positioning of lighting instruments.

Floor Stands

In many kinds of studio arrangements, the suspended lights often have to be supplemented by lights mounted on floor stands. Although too many floor stands tend to clutter the studio floor and get in the way of other production elements, they do represent a certain degree of flexibility and simplicity of setup. Sometimes there are positions where it is simply impossible to position a light except on a floor stand.

Floor stands for studio use are usually mounted on a heavy metal base for stability. They come in a variety of weights and sizes capable of handling many different types of lighting instruments. Of course, for location productions (wherever supplemental lighting is needed), the portable floor stand is indispensable.

Lighting Control

The video camera system is extremely sensitive. Optimum performance is possible only when illumination is kept within certain carefully prescribed limits. To achieve the artistic and technical purposes of lighting, the lighting director must work within four separate yet interrelated parameters:

1. The level of intensity
2. The degree of focus or diffusion
3. The shape of the projected beam
4. The color quality

After the initial setup is completed, the lighting director, working with the director and camera operators, makes a continuing series of adjustments throughout the rehearsal period and prior to the final take. A number of mechanical and electronic controls are utilized during this process.

Intensity

We have already described the way in which the beam from a Fresnel lamp can be spread to lessen its intensity and at the same time cover a much wider area. It must be remembered that the *fully spread* beam has only a small fraction of the intensity of the strength of a *pinned beam.*

But whether a beam is focused or diffused, another factor has important implications in terms of intensity. Although

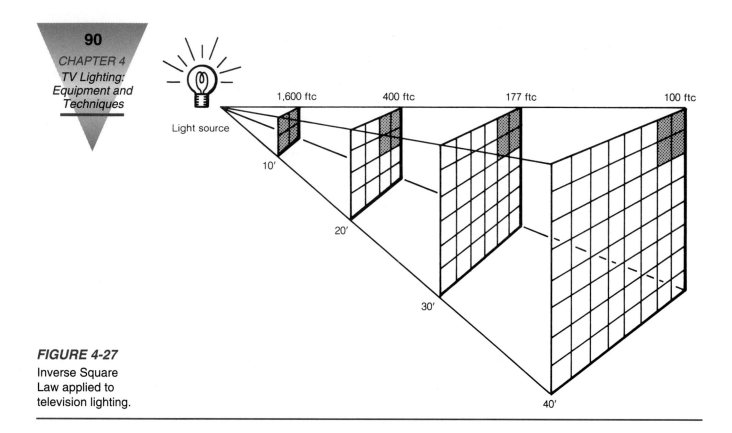

1,600 ftc   400 ftc   177 ftc   100 ftc

Light source

10'

20'

30'

40'

FIGURE 4-27

Inverse Square
Law applied to
television lighting.

it is not easily apparent to the naked eye, variations in the distance between a source light and the subject create large differences in intensity.

The same **inverse square law,** which in section 3.3 warned us how critical microphone-to-source distances can be, also applies to illumination. As with sound, the strength of a light source is reduced to one-quarter of its original strength as the source-to-subject distance is doubled. (And the strength is multiplied by four as the distance is cut in half.) As shown in figure 4-27, a light that produces 1,600 footcandles at a distance of ten feet is reduced to only 400 footcandles at twenty feet.

In terms of a practical field production example, let us assume a *clip-on* spotlight attached to a camera working twenty feet

from a subject produces a reading of forty footcandles. (Note that this is one-tenth of the reading illustrated in figure 4-27.) Should the subject move to within ten feet of the camera, cutting the distance in half, the reading would now be 160 footcandles. The illumination has been increased four times! This substantial increase would call for a large change of the **f-stop** setting—as well as an adjustment in the **white balance** setting of the camera. (See sections 5.5 and 15.9.)

On the other hand, in a studio situation where we are working with much stronger illumination and with the talent at greater distances from the lights, a change of ten feet in the source-to-subject distance should be noted but is not critical. Again using the ratios presented in figure 4-27, we can use the example of an actor performing at distances of thirty to forty feet from a light source. In this case, the range between 177 and 100 footcandles would probably call only for a minor change in the f-stop setting—if one were needed at all.

Therefore, as a general rule, the closer the lights are to the talent, the more critical the lighting and camera adjustments are going to be with every little movement the talent makes.

Located some distance from the actual lighting instruments—either in a corner of the studio or control room—is the patching and control equipment, which in any kind of sizable studio operation is centered around the *dimmer board*. (See figure 4-28.) Although dimmers vary tremendously in construction and operation, they all function on the same general principle: by controlling the amount of power that flows to the lighting instrument, the lamp gives off more or less light.

Patching and dimming equipment is, in many ways, analogous to the patch panel and console in the audio control booth. Apart from the creative considerations, we are concerned with power flow instead of signal flow. There is a basic routing system for getting power to a light.

This equipment varies greatly from one studio to another in both sophistication and capacity. Therefore, it would serve little purpose to attempt to describe all the possible techniques of a patching operation that would follow the many individual designs. This is best learned from the specific construction of the equipment in your own studio. As a frame of reference, it may help to consider some fundamental functions common to all lighting control equipment.

When a light on a grid has been connected to the nearby numbered line or grid outlet, the electrical power to turn on that light is available from two different sources in most studio setups—either a nondimmer circuit or a dimmer circuit. If no intensity control over the lamp is needed, a patch is made from the grid outlet or *load circuit* to a numbered nondimmer circuit and turned on at the switch or circuit breaker. This connection is normally referred to as a **hot patch.** If intensity control is called for, the patch is made from the load circuit into the dimmer board for a controlled power source. Here the circuitry may vary according to the design of the board.

In most boards, multiple units of lights can be connected into a single dimmer circuit. There is, of course, a definite limit to the amount of power that can be fed to any one circuit. This limit must be ascertained and always observed.

As mentioned in section 4.2, when there is a *reduction* in the amount of current being supplied to a bulb filament, there is a corresponding *lowering* of the Kelvin color temperature of the light. Care must be exercised so that key and fill lights are not dimmed into the yellow or red ranges. Because back lights do their job of separation without reflecting as much light directly into the lens, they can sometimes be dimmed into the yellow range without as much effect.

The final note on intensity is one that should seem obvious; however, it is one that is all too often forgotten in the pressure of production activity. The lighting director must choose the *correct* instruments and the correct *number* of instruments to do the job at hand. Frequently, lighting crew personnel will spend time trying to adjust a 2 KW (2,000-watt) spotlight when a 1 KW or even a 500-watt unit might be more suitable. Similarly, the use of too many instruments can enormously complicate the process of achieving proper lighting levels. Or, conversely, you might be trying to spread one spotlight too thin when you really need separate instruments to cover the areas to be lighted.

FIGURE 4-28

A patch bay (above)
and a dimmer board
(below).

Top photo courtesy of
KCET, Los Angeles

Focus and Diffusion

Diffused light is created and controlled in several ways to keep it in its proper perspective in relation to the focused key light. The primary control factor is that of adjusting intensity through some of the methods described previously. Placement is also very important. The best diffused light is achieved by using several instruments placed at differing angles.

Several devices are also important to the lighting director's toolbox. The most commonly used pieces of equipment for these purposes are either attached to the front of the instrument or mounted in front of it. A *scrim* is a wire mesh shaped to fit the front of the lighting instrument. (See figure 4-29.) It works by scattering the beam and cutting back on intensity. Scrims are used to soften a spread Fresnel light. To further soften scoops, pans, and broads, a cloth-like opaque filter made out of spun and pressed fiberglass is used. Available in three thicknesses, it greatly cuts down on the intensity and projects a soft, almost shadowless light. When shooting outdoors, using the sun as a key light, a foil **reflector** is often used to provide a relatively diffused fill light. (See figures 4-30 and 14-8.) It can also be used as a key light with the sun serving as the back light.

Shape

If lighting directors had to work with only the large raw beam projected by most instruments, their work would be difficult indeed. Fortunately, there are a number of shaping devices that are used to modify and block parts of the beam.

One of the main difficulties is that of controlling the overlap of multiple light sources. These can produce high-intensity hot spots. The most common solution to this problem is achieved through the use of *barn door* shutters, which are attached to the front of a spotlight. (See figures 4-8 and

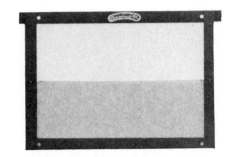

FIGURE 4-29
Lighting scrims: *top,*
half scrim; *bottom,*
full scrim.

Photos courtesy of
Mole Richardson

FIGURE 4-30
Foil reflector.

The two-sided reflector is an invaluable part of outdoor location shooting. The partitioned foil-leaf side (shown) produces a soft diffused light. A smooth silver paper surface on the other side produces a brighter, more intense light.

Photo courtesy of
Mole Richardson

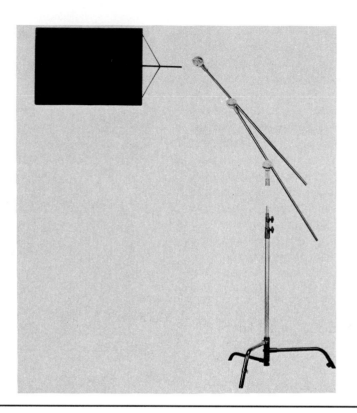

FIGURE 4-31

Flag.

Flags are used to block the light on specific areas of the performer or set. With their stands and extension arms, they provide an important final control over illumination.

Photo courtesy of Mole Richardson

4-26.) Used in pairs or sets of four, these hinged plates can provide an adjustable edge to the beam. By moving the shutters, both the height and width of the projected light can be limited. Most assemblies can be rotated to provide maximum adjustment. In a leko or ellipsoidal lamp, the movable shutters are inside the instrument (adjusted with outside handles) to provide an even greater definition to the projected pattern. (See figure 4-9.)

Sometimes the lighting director needs to create a small area of reduced intensity *within* a projected beam. For this a **flag** is used. Flags are rectangles of varying size made either of metal or of frames covered with black cloth. They can be hung from the lighting grid or mounted on a floor stand in a position to block out the light to a specific area. (See figure 4-31.) One use, for example, is to cast a slight shadow on

the forehead and top of the head of a person with thinning hair who otherwise might appear almost bald under bright lights on a close-up shot.

Occasionally, an added amount of light must be pinpointed at a particular area of the set. If barn doors cannot project quite as precise a pattern as needed, a **top hat** can be used to do the job. Inserted in the same frame designed to hold the barn doors, the top hat, a circle that ranges in diameter from four inches to a foot, can reduce the spotlight's beam to a smaller, clearly defined circle without increasing the intensity of the spot. Even portable lighting kits for EFP remote shoots will have holders for barn doors and other shaping devices. (See figure 4-32.)

The *cucalorus* (*cookie* or *kook*) is a cutout design that when placed in front of a spot projects a pattern upon a cyclorama or large set surface. Ellipsoidal spotlights are

FIGURE 4-32

ARRILITE 650/4 portable lighting kit.

This package, in addition to four 650-watt
instruments and stands, contains barn doors.
The lamps can be easily pinned or spread in
order to serve as either key or fill illumination.

Photo courtesy of Arriflex Corporation

FIGURE 4-33

Gel holder on a scoop.

Frames that hold a gel filter in place are
designed for all types of floods and spotlights.

Photo courtesy of Mole Richardson

designed so that smaller metal kooks can
be inserted into the instrument housing by
means of a "dipstick." (See figure 4-9.)

Color

There are occasions when a set or other
production location is simply too dull and
drab for attractive pictures with sufficient
color contrast. It may be that more
"warmth" from red-brown earth tones is
needed. Or possibly the "cool" effect of
green and blue is desired. To solve this
problem, variously colored *gels* are used to
add color to the setting and occasionally to
the performers' clothes and flesh tones.
The gel is a thin transparent celluloid material, available in a wide variety of colors.
The gels can be cut to fit a specially designed holder that slides into the same
frame that is intended to hold the barn
doors on a spotlight. (See figure 4-33.)

In using gels, the lighting director must
work carefully with both the video control
operator and the makeup artist. The effect
of projecting three or four different colors
onto a set can be subtle but must be carefully controlled. Since the camera system
tends to pick up and accentuate red, one
should be especially cautious with its use.

Because most normal makeup is in the reddish range, too much light through a red gel
will greatly exaggerate flesh tones. (See section 13.1.) A green gel, on the other hand,
has an unflattering effect on most people—
especially on those with darker complexions.

One of the most effective applications
for gels is that of using them with strip
lights to color a cyclorama. A wide variety
of color combinations and effects are possible. A continually changing dawn effect,
for example, can be created with the background shifting from a deep violet through
various reds and pinks to a light blue during the shooting of a scene.

Safety Precautions and Disciplines

Safety is the responsibility of everybody
connected with a television production. Any
unsafe situation can be avoided by using
common sense and observing basic precautions. Part of the *discipline* of television

production is the habit and attitude of *thinking safety.* Every crew member, whether or not part of the lighting team, should be disciplined to think always in terms of avoiding or correcting hazardous conditions.

When working in a studio, you should always "think overhead." Are all lights, mounts, and other equipment securely fastened? When heavy equipment is moved or repositioned overhead, is everybody warned and the area below cleared out? In addition, crew members should "think electrical." Is all equipment turned off before moving or inspecting it? Is the circuit turned off before it is plugged into an instrument?

Everyone should also "think hardware." Has the item of equipment been thoroughly checked out and is it ready for use? Has everything been connected? Tightened? Tested?

Whenever a lighting assistant is moving or trimming lights, there should be at least one person steadying the ladder from below. The person on the ladder should always carry a wrench (secured by a band or tie around the wrist to prevent dropping it on persons or equipment below) to tighten any lamps that may have become loose from excessive turning. When making any adjustment on any lighting instrument, the safety chain must always remain fastened, securing the light to the pipe or grid.

When changing the direction of a light, always loosen the thumb screw (swivel bolt) *first.* Do not mistake it for the bolt holding the lamp hanger to the clamp—loosening that bolt will detach the lamp from the lighting grid.[4]

4. The most common type of lamp hanger is the C-clamp. (See figure 4-26.) It is held in place on the pipe by tightening the *clamp bolt* against the pipe. At the bottom of the clamp there is the important *yolk bolt* that connects the yoke to the light itself. This bolt (Y-bolt or yolk bolt) should *never* be loosened. Instead the *swivel bolt* should be loosened to allow for left and right lateral movement of the lamp. The *side-tension* knob is used to allow for the vertical movement of the light.

When moving a light (clamp, hanger, and housing), always make certain that there are no people or equipment below the area in which you are working. Be certain the power to the lamp is off. Just because no light is being emitted does not mean there is no power coming through the cord. Damaged lights, burned-out bulbs, and short circuits are all potential dangers—that can kill. Again, be sure the power is off at the lamp's new location before plugging it into the grid outlet or load circuit. When moving an instrument from one location to another, the safety chain is always the last item to be unfastened, and it is the first thing to be hooked up when the instrument is repositioned.

In professional studios lighting instruments are rarely moved. A basic pattern of lights is established and the LD has a plot knowing where each light is located. There is a deliberate oversupply of instruments on the grid, much more than is needed for any single production. If one goes out during a production, the LD can replace its function very quickly and the audience is usually unaware that any difficulty occurred. Moving a light is also unwise from a financial standpoint. Rough handling, whether it takes place during movement or even during adjustment, greatly cuts down on the usable life of the bulb and/or lighting element.

When focusing lights, never look directly into a light. A light that measures 200 footcandles at thirty feet may approach 100,000 footcandles at the source. Studio lights are bright enough to permanently damage or even blind the naked eye.

A 2,000-watt lamp creates a dangerous amount of heat. After being on for only a few minutes, most studio lamps are hot enough to cause serious burns. Most studio lamps have handles—use them! Lighting technicians should also be furnished with heavy-duty, heat-retardant gloves. Use them! Special caution must be used when

FIGURE 4-34

In implementing the
original lighting plot,
the lighting director
works closely with
the director to
assure that camera
angles on faces and
elements of the set
can take full
advantage of light
placement.

Photo courtesy of
Dina Fisher

adjusting barn doors, as they are directly in
the path of the light source at only a few
inches and absorb a large amount of heat.

Make sure you never touch the surface of a quartz bulb with your bare fingers (even when the bulb is cold). Always
use gloves or some other cloth between
your hand and the globe. Quartz lamps
generate tremendous amounts of heat,
and even a small amount of finger oil or
acid on the face of the globe will interact
chemically to weaken the glass envelope
and hasten discoloration.

Preproduction Planning

One final note about production *discipline*
from the standpoint of lighting procedures:
in lighting—as in every aspect of television
production—it is imperative that as many
details as possible be taken care of before

walking into the studio for the production
setup and rehearsal. Every minute counts
in the studio. You cannot afford to start
your planning once you reach the studio.

The lighting director must use a lighting plan or **light plot.** (See figure 4-34.)
This plan will be worked out well in advance of the actual studio setup time. It
will include a schematic layout of primary
staging areas and lighting requirements for
each one. It should indicate each lighting
instrument to be used and the intensity ratios among the various instruments. Often
there is space for additional notes. Here the
LD will indicate which lights are to be
placed together on dimmer circuits or what
kinds of lighting effects will actually be
used on the air. Figure 4-35 represents a
sample lighting plan for a simple talk
show. Study also the examples used in figures 4-22 and 4-23.

98

Producer/Director: _____

Production Title: _____

Lighting Setup: (Date) _____ (Time) _____

Air/Recording: _____ _____

FIGURE 4-35

Studio lighting plot.

The lighting director would fill out a light plot on a form similar to this one after consultation with the director. The symbols are roughly to scale. The visualization quickly and efficiently indicates where the talent will be, how the numbered cameras will be positioned, and the type of instruments that are to be used. Note that lights are listed by their specific number in the grid so that the LD can easily coordinate the connection and trimming process with the floor crew and the dimmer board operator.

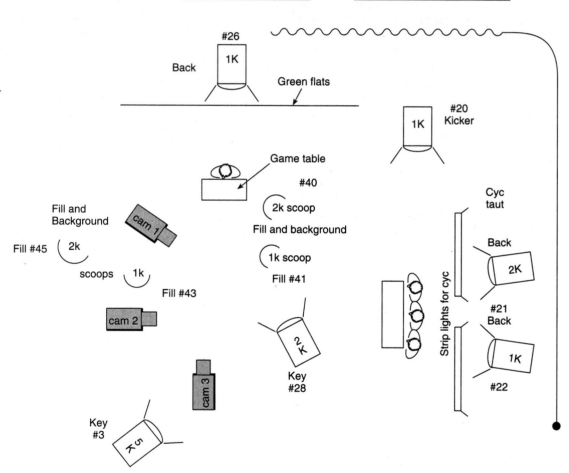

In many production situations, the lighting director will also prepare a more detailed set of working instructions—a work sheet that lists for each instrument to be used, the description of the light (spot, scoop); its size (500 watts, 2 KW); the staging area it is to cover; its function (key, kicker); the grid outlet or loadcircuit it is to be plugged into; the dimmer or nondimmer circuit it will be patched to, and so on. Again, the detailed preparation at this point will later save valuable minutes of studio setup and rehearsal time. The disciplined production person knows the importance of thorough *preproduction planning*.

SUMMARY

As with audio considerations, lighting directors must be concerned with both technical needs and creative purposes. In addition to establishing the correct amount of *base light* (usually determined by an *incident light* meter reading), the LD must also work within an acceptable *contrast ratio* (established by *reflected light* meter readings) and maintain the correct *color temperature* (3,000 to 3,100 degrees *Kelvin*).

The creative lighting objectives include *perspective*, molding *shape* and *texture*, establishing a feeling of *reality* (or nonreality), creating a *mood* or emotional setting, and *focusing attention*. All these functions are accomplished with *spotlights* that have a highly directional focused beam and/or with *floodlights* that give off a nondirectional diffused light.

Lighting a typical subject involves standard *three-point* lighting (*key* light, *fill* light, and *back* light). *Auxiliary sources* such as a *kicker* or *background light* may also be incorporated. When working with *multiple-camera lighting*, certain modifications and compromises in the ideal three-point lighting concept must be accepted—such as *cross-key* lighting.

As a starting point, lighting directors use a *basic ratio*, with the back light strongest, then the key light, with the fill being the weakest source. Complete studio lighting procedures also include knowledge of various *mounting devices* and, most importantly, various approaches to *lighting control* (intensity, focus and diffusion, shaping the beam, and color control). Finally, we must be concerned with essential *safety precautions* and the discipline of thorough *preproduction planning*.

All the lighting considerations, of course, are but a means of creating the picture that will be picked up by the camera and its lens system. Camera/lens structure and camera operations are discussed in the next two chapters.

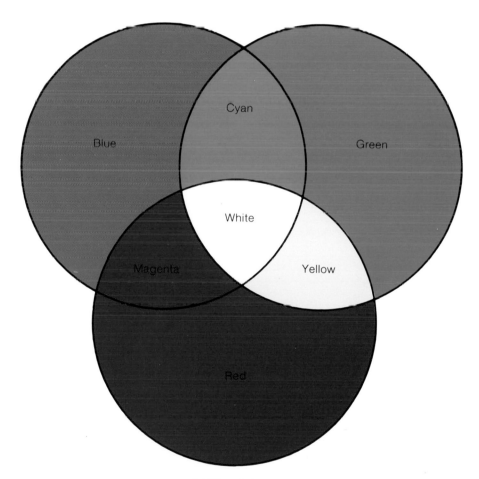

Additive Color

Additive color

Where any two of the three primary colors (red, green, blue) overlap, they form a secondary color—cyan (green-blue), magenta (blue-red), or yellow (red-green). Combinations of varying intensities of the three primary colors can produce all possible hues. When all three primary colors are combined in the specific proportions of 59 percent green, 30 percent red and 11 percent blue, the result is a pure white.

PLATE B

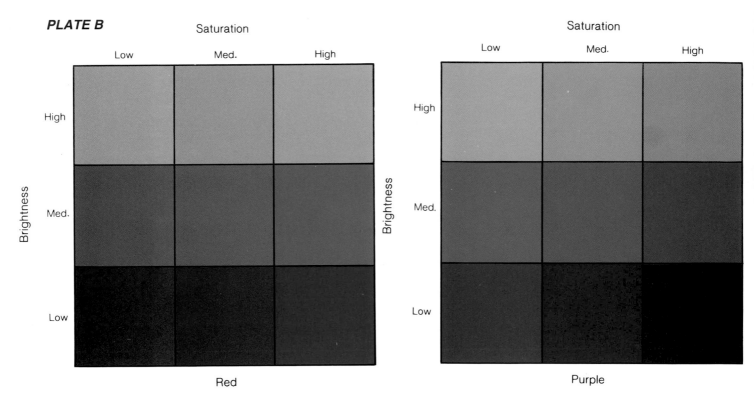

Saturation
Low   Med.   High

Brightness: High, Med., Low

Red

Saturation
Low   Med.   High

Brightness: High, Med., Low

Purple

The properties of color: hue, brightness and saturation

Each of these three boxes illustrate nine variations of one color that can result when the factors of brightness and saturation are varied in different combinations. With computer controlled graphics units, two or more colors can be mixed together with these innumerable gradations of saturation and brightness to produce (theoretically) close to one million individual color combinations.

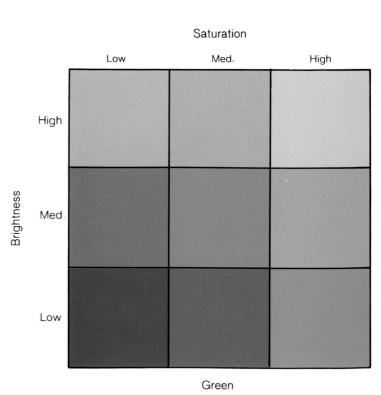

Saturation
Low   Med.   High

Brightness: High, Med., Low

Green

PLATE C

Which monitor is adjusted correctly?

The monitor looks as if it is adjusted correctly, but the vectorscope to the right shows that this color signal is out of adjustment. (The points on the green display are outside of the boxes etched on the overlay.) The phase of the color signal should first be adjusted (by a competent technician or engineer) and then the monitor should be adjusted so that it will reproduce the color signal *faithfully*.

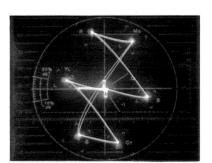

In this case the vectorscope shows that the signal is accurate, therefore the monitor is out of adjustment. This usually happens when the monitor is adjusted by someone trying to make a bad signal look better. The picture on the monitor should be corrected by a competent technician or engineer.

PLATE D

Typical video problems

The pictures on the right illustrate a number of video problems that should be watched for in every production. The top picture is getting too much light, as indicated by the "blooming" of the white shirt. This can be corrected by adjusting the lighting or adjusting the iris on the camera. While the white shirt makes the problem worse, it is also visible in the white patches on both faces. The middle picture shows the opposite problem—the scene is too dark. This may be due to improper lighting or incorrect iris setting on the camera, but it could also be caused by a low "pedestal" (black level) setting on the camera. (When the pedestal is too low, darker areas lose all detail and look completely black.) The bottom picture has color problems that could be due to (1) a camera that was not correctly "white-balanced," (2) a playback of a tape that is "out of phase" with the switcher, or (3) an improper monitor adjustment. To correct the picture, first check the white balance (for a camera) or the phase—using color bars and a vectorscope (for a tape machine). As a last resort, have a technician use a properly calibrated reference signal to adjust the monitor. Remember—do not adjust a monitor just because it does not look right!

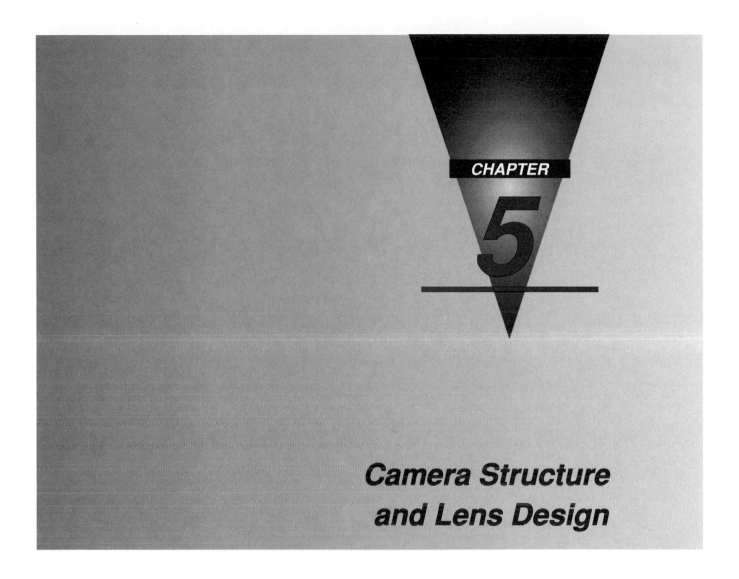

Camera Structure
and Lens Design

With this chapter, we begin an examination of the video system. It is usually referred to as the **camera chain** because there are a large number of components that shape and in other ways influence the video signal as it makes its way through this complex system. It should come as no surprise that over the past several decades, the video part of television has changed more than the audio portion. From both a technical and creative standpoint the pictures we now see as a part of cable and broadcast television are very impressive. What we will see within the next decade may be truly amazing.

5.1 VIDEO SIGNAL FLOW AND CONTROL FUNCTIONS

Just as we discussed the audio system in terms of audio signal flow, so also would it be helpful to think in terms of the *video signal flow* for the visual part of television production. The same *seven basic control functions* introduced in section 2.2 can be equally applied to the video system. In a simplified form figure 5-1 illustrates the basic units in the video signal flow.

The Seven Basic Control Functions

The first step, *transducing,* is accomplished by the camera itself. The camera receives physical energy (light waves) and transforms it into electrical energy (video signals) that is suitable for electronic distribution. Although considerably more complex than the microphone, the camera performs this same basic function.

Live camera and recorded feeds are *channeled* through the video **switcher** which is much more than just a routing device. It can *mix* picture inputs and also *shape* them in terms of both color and design. Camera signals first shaped by the **camera control unit** (CCU) are then further enhanced by switcher controlled digital effects or graphics units that make pictures whirl, twist, and explode in combination with two or more other video sources.

The *amplification* of the video signal may occur at several different points in the flow of the signal by **distribution amplifiers (DAs).** Amplification is necessitated by such things as cable distance and other factors that require the balancing of signal strengths. Our simplified diagram (see figure 5-1) does not attempt to show all the points where distribution amplifiers are placed throughout the system.

As with amplification, *monitoring* takes place at several different points within the system. In any regular studio production, the camera operators, like VCR and audio operators, must have monitors to provide an informational feedback needed for the control of their equipment. In the video control room the numerous monitors are crucial to the producer, director, LD, and AD in the performance of their duties. In this same area or in master control there may be several technically oriented monitors and scopes used for camera control. Learning how to get maximum use from these visual displays is an important attribute for all members of the television production team. (See the following section.)

In addition to the traditional videotape units, digital **hard drive** equipment is now being used for *recording* and *playback* of the television signal. (See chapter 9.) All these recorders now have provisions for a number of separate channels for various aspects of the video signal as well as several channels for stereo and other audio applications.

Control Components

The video signal is much more complex than the audio signal. It takes roughly 600 times as much "information" to produce a video signal as to produce sound within the same time frame. As a result the picture is vulnerable to a number of disruptive influences within the system itself. There must be several specialized components that monitor, adjust, refine, and stabilize the picture throughout the video signal flow. As has been previously noted, there are a great many impressive things that are now being done to enhance the visual impact of the television picture. What is discussed in the following paragraphs is on a very basic level. Some more sophisticated video effects equipment will be introduced in chapter 7.

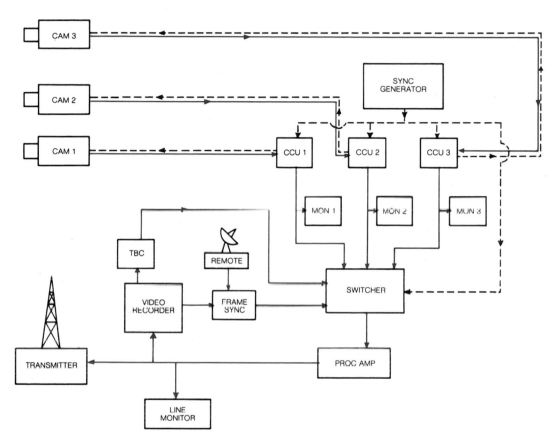

FIGURE 5-1

Simplified diagram of the video signal flow.

A portion of the synchronizing ("sync") pulse (dotted line) is sent out from the sync generator to each camera control unit (CCU) and on to each camera—keeping all cameras in perfect synchronization. The complete sync pulse is also sent to the switcher. Simultaneously, the picture information (solid line) flows from each camera to the CCU, where the video signal can be shaped and altered. The signal is then channeled into the switcher, with the picture information also being displayed on the video monitor for each camera. (In the diagram, from the CCU on through the rest of the system the solid line represents the complete video signal—color and brightness plus sync pulse; the dotted line is omitted for simplicity's sake.)

From the switcher, the composite signal can be sent through a process amplifier, to the line monitor, to a video recorder, and/or to the transmitter after audio is added. A video recorder also can be used, of course, as a picture source—sending its recorded program material through the time-base corrector (TBC) and on to the switcher or to the transmitter. Remote sources (satellite feeds, microwave links) can also serve as inputs to the switcher, flowing through the frame synchronizer that conforms the sync pulse with the other composite signals.

Synchronizing Generator

To coordinate the functioning of all components in the video system, the **"sync" generator** creates a series of timing pulses that lock together all elements of the video signal at every stage of production, switching, recording, editing, transmission, and reception. This sync pulse has often been called a system of *electronic sprocket holes* that keeps everything coordinated in a lock-step pattern. This timing pulse is based upon the basic 60-cycle alternating current used in the United States and in many other countries using the NTSC television systems.[1]

Process Amplifier

The *"**proc amp**"* takes the video signal from the switcher—color, brightness, and synchronizing information—and then stabilizes the levels, amplifies the signal, and removes unwanted elements or **noise.**

Time Base Corrector

Video signals from videotape recorders often have synchronizing pulses that have deteriorated or been slightly altered during the recording and playback process. The **"TBC"** takes these signals, encodes them into a digital form, and then reconstructs an enhanced synchronizing signal for playback and editing purposes.

Frame Synchronizer

An increasingly necessary piece of equipment, the **frame synchronizer,** takes video sources from outside of the studio control or video recorders, compares their sync pulses with studio sync, and adjusts the

differences between the two. The signals are put through a digitalized phase prior to output. Satellite and other out-of-studio feeds can thereby be coordinated through the studio switcher.

Color Bar Generator

This component sends a standardized pattern of vertical colored bars through the switcher. This monitor display (see color plate C) is used to calibrate the color values and adjustments on all cameras, video recorders, and monitors. The **color bars** are also recorded at the beginning of a video recording so that the playback machine can be matched to the color levels set at the time of the recording.

Waveform Monitor

The display on the **waveform monitor** (see figure 5-2) indicates the strength of a video signal, allowing a technician to compare and adjust the brightest and darkest elements in a picture.

Vectorscope

The display produced on the **vectorscope** (see figure 5-3) provides a visual readout on the accuracy and intensity of the color portion of the video signal. It shows the individual levels for the three **primary colors**—red, green, and blue—as well as the three **complementary colors**—yellow, cyan, and magenta. (See section 5.2.) These adjustments are crucial to every video production. Color plates C and D show problems that can occur when signals and monitors are out of adjustment.

Those well-meaning novices who "fix" bad pictures by adjusting the program line monitor are the source of many problems at educational institutions. Trained personnel continually maintain these monitors at the proper color levels through the relatively simple use of the color bar generator. Considerably more time is spent in adjusting the cameras by means of the waveform

---

1. In 1941 the FCC adopted the NTSC television system with the 525 line, 30-frame format described in this chapter. It presently remains in use in much of North and South America. Two other systems, PAL and SECAM, are used in other parts of the world. A number of countries, including the United States, have plans underway to convert to a new HDTV (high definition TV) standard.

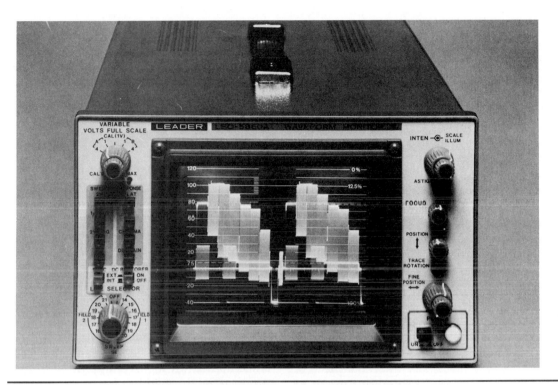

FIGURE 5-2

The waveform
monitor is used for
analyzing and
adjusting the
luminance portion of
the picture.

FIGURE 5-3

The display on the
vectorscope
provides information
on the status of both
hue and saturation
levels of the color
signal.

monitor and vectorscope. With VCR output, a time-base corrector is also involved. Once this work has been done, monitors must be left alone. But then along comes a *"video dodo"* who, unbeknownst to anyone, starts to mess with the monitor. The person in charge of video who does not know that this has been done, may be asked for last minute changes in camera or VCR settings based upon how the program monitor looks. All too often the result is a poorly balanced picture replacing the good one that could have been recorded.

5.2 THE COLOR VIDEO SYSTEM

While one must acknowledge the impressive graphics now being produced by digital computer technology, for most applications the camera is still the centerpiece of video production. Throughout much of television history, the heart of the camera was the **pickup tube**—that miraculous variation of the cathode-ray tube that transforms (transduces) frequencies of visual light into electrical signals. In recent years, however, an offshoot of the computer chip, the **charged-coupled device (CCD)**, has almost completely replaced the tube in both professional and consumer level cameras.

At the receiving end of the television system—the home TV set—the **cathode-ray tube** is still the primary element in the *display* of all video pictures. However, many portable TV sets utilize a newer **liquid crystal display (LCD)** screen technology.

Three Attributes of Video Color

Most professional cameras have three CCD image sensors (replacing the three pickup tubes). (Single chip cameras will be covered in the following discussion.) Because all video utilizes an **additive** color process, all shades and tones are the result of combining the three *primary video colors—red, green, and blue.* To do its job, the camera must first separate incoming light into these three primary colors by means of a **beam splitter,** made up of a glass prism and reflective mirrors. The three CCD chips are identical in structure. They are labeled red, green, or blue only because the beam splitter separates the three colors and directs just one designated color to each chip. To function properly the camera must be sensitive to the three factors that affect color as humans see it. There is the color tint itself (**hue**), the vividness of that color (**saturation**), and its relative brightness (**luminance**).

Hue

Color plate A indicates the three *primary colors* and shows how any two of them can be combined (in the overlapping areas) to produce the three additional *complementary colors—cyan* (a turquoise formed from blue and green), *magenta* (blending red and blue), and *yellow* (the combination of red and green). These primary and complementary colors are the basic pure hues seen when a prism breaks up white light into its constituent **wavelengths** (every hue has its distinctive **frequency** and wavelength) or when we marvel at a rainbow (which essentially is millions of droplets of water acting as tiny prisms to create the vivid primary and complementary colors—ranging from violet to red.[2]

We have known for centuries that a prism separates white light into its spectrum of constituent colors. Conversely when light waves of all three primary colors are added together in a proportion

---

2. As indicated in Appendix A, red, the lowest visible color in the electromagnetic spectrum, has a wavelength of 6,500 angstroms (each angstrom is one ten-millionth of a millimeter). Violet is the shortest wavelength we can see, with a wavelength as short as 4,000 angstroms.

that relates to the color sensitivity of the human eye (59 percent green, 30 percent red, and 11 percent blue), the resulting effect is *white*. Sometimes thought of as the absence of color, white is actually the *presence of all colors*. If you have trouble accepting this on faith, prove it to yourself by looking carefully at the individual grains of sand that make up a white sandy beach. The variety of colors that we are used to seeing in our daily lives result from the reflected combination of these primary colors.

As the proportions among the hues being combined are varied, an enormous range of colors becomes possible. For example, when red and green are added together, a range of pure hues from red to orange to yellow to green can be created. As the third primary color, blue, is added, you can achieve a wide variety of browns, tans, mahoganies, beiges, ochers, maroons, sepias, and so forth. Computer graphics programs have an almost infinite ability to mix ultra-fine gradations of color and, as a result, can create literally millions of different hues.

The concept may be hard to accept at first, but when we see a television picture containing what appear to be numerous colors, we are actually seeing the result of a continuous mixing process. (See figure 5-4.) Over 250,000 dots of red, green, and blue, glowing at varying degrees of brightness, are being rapidly combined in continually changing proportions to produce this effect of a myriad of colors in the eye of the viewer.

The calibration of these color values is accomplished by means of the *vectorscope*. Its clock-like readout has a point of light for each of the six primary and complementary colors. Each of these points of light must be in a precise location within a circular pattern for that color to be at its proper value. (See figure 5-3.) Red is displayed just to the left of the 12:00 position,

blue is at 4:00, and green is located at 7:00. The three complementary colors are displayed in between these locations.

Saturation

The intensity or vividness of a color is described in terms of its *saturation*. If we are dealing with strictly a red hue, then the intensity of that red can range from a highly saturated *vivid* red as shown in the lower right square of Color Plate B, to the less saturated *pastel* red shown at the top right square. The pastel red is achieved by diluting the color with white. Another effect is achieved by diluting the vivid red with grey producing more of a brown tone as seen in the far left corner.

As other hues are blended together, other color combinations result. Red and green hues combined in varying proportions with different amounts of white produce yellows. If increasing amounts of grey are used to dilute the saturation of the red and green factors in this yellow, a series of golden brown tones will result. Just as the saturation effect can be controlled on a scale leading to white, grey is on a scale of increasing darkness leading to black. Together, the *hue* and *saturation* portions of a video picture are termed the **chrominance** signal.

On the vectorscope the gradations of saturation are indicated by the position of the points of light, but in a different plane. The greatest saturation of a color is indicated when the point of light is closest to the outer edge of the circle. As saturation is decreased and diluted by white, the light spot moves closer to the center of the circle.

Luminance

It is really not possible to describe how hue and saturation interact to produce color without including the influence that the *luminance* factor (brightness) has upon the color picture. The illumination of a subject by a light source and the resultant

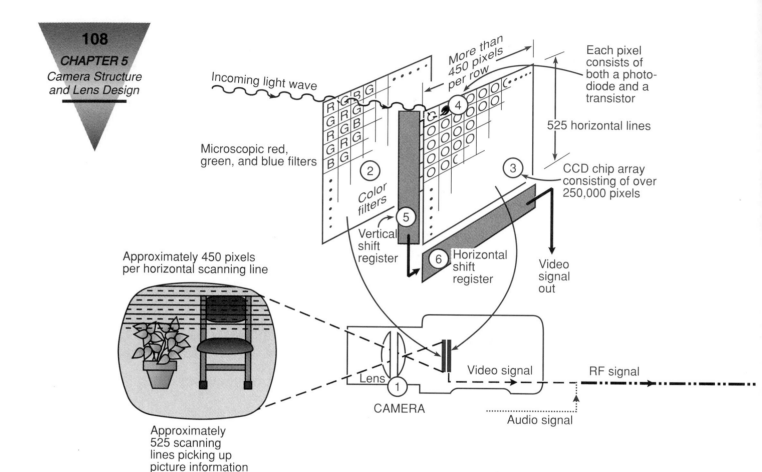

FIGURE 5-4

Cameras with only a single CCD chip can produce a normal color image through the use of filters placed between the lens and the chip. After the incoming image travels through the lens (1), it passes through a color filter consisting of a checkerboard pattern of red, green, and blue filter elements (2). The filtered color images are then focused on the two-dimensional image-sensing CCD chip located immediately behind the filter (3); therefore, there is a tiny red, green, or blue filter in front of each pixel on the chip. The precise alignment of these microscopic filters and corresponding pixels is crucial for a clear picture. Each pixel (4) consists of a photodiode (which generates an infinitesimal electric current in proportion to the amount of light hitting it) and a transistor (which stores the current for a tiny fraction of a second). When a trigger impulse is generated by the vertical shift register (5) (sixty times every second), the stored charge in each photodiode is transmitted along each row in sequence to the horizontal shift register (6). The information in the horizontal shift register is then shifted out and becomes one scan line of the video signal. This video information, along with the horizontal and vertical sync pulses, is now the video line output. For broadcast it is combined with the audio signal.

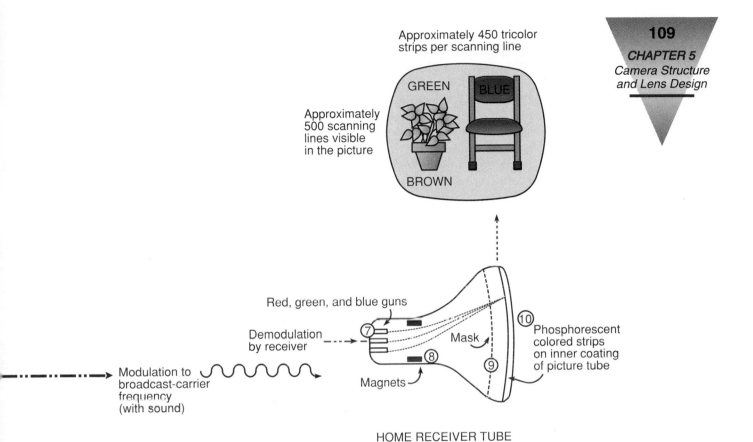

Approximately 450 tricolor
strips per scanning line

Approximately
500 scanning
lines visible
in the picture

GREEN   BLUE

BROWN

Red, green, and blue guns

Demodulation
by receiver

Mask

Phosphorescent
colored strips
on inner coating
of picture tube

Modulation to
broadcast-carrier
frequency
(with sound)

Magnets

HOME RECEIVER TUBE

At the receiving end, the picture and audio information are stripped from the carrier wave (demodulated), and the blue, red, and green information is sent to three electron guns (7) in the rear of the kinescope or picture tube. Each color gun shoots out an electron beam, which varies in intensity corresponding to the strength of the electric signal initially created by the CCD photodiode. This electron beam is directed back-and-forth (and up-and-down) by a ring of deflection coil magnets (8) controlled by the same sync pulse that triggered the vertical and horizontal shift registers in the camera. Thus, the scanning beam recreates the picture information for each color in the same pattern and at the same intensity as the signal from the camera. Each electron beam is precisely aimed through a mask (9) that directs the stream of electrons at the face of the tube with pinpoint accuracy. The electrons bombard the tiny phosphorescent strips or pixels on the inside of the tube—usually arranged in vertical bars or strips of the three primary colors (10)—making each one glow with an intensity that corresponds to the original picture signal. As the various red, green, and blue pixels are combined in varying intensities, the original image is recreated at the rate of sixty fields every second.

reflection of light from that subject into the camera starts a complex process. The picture focused through the lens is comprised of a number of colors in varying degrees of brightness as reflected from all surfaces of the subject. Important information about the shape and texture of the subject are made evident through the contrast of light and shadow in the luminance aspect of the image. It is what gives the picture a structure and creates whatever illusion of depth exists on the flat screen.

It must be kept in mind that luminance is generated by a response in voltage to the various brightness levels that make up the incoming picture. It relates to, but must not be confused with, the increase and decrease of video **gain** which is a matter of adding (or reducing) brightness of an entire picture through an amplification of the video signal. This adjustment is a part of the process through which color and brightness levels are controlled. The proper adjustment of video gain is important in ensuring that all cameras match each other within the variations of camera angle, set, and lighting conditions. In section 5.3, the way in which the lens also influences this complex combination of factors will be examined.

The differing bright and dark portions of the video picture are seen on the waveform monitor display as bar-like columns that change their structure as the picture changes shape. (See figure 5-2.) The highest point on the screen indicates the brightest part of the picture. If this registers above the "100" mark, the signal may be too strong and become distorted. It is also important to carefully observe the lowest part of the display representing the brightness level of the darkest part of the picture. It is called the **pedestal** and its adjustment is important in making sure that the darker portions of the picture do not lose their detail and become black blobs.

The Formation of the Video Signal

Originally all video signals combined the color (chrominance) and brightness (luminance) signals into one feed that was channeled into a single cable. It became known as **composite** video. In the late 1980s videotape formats such as **Betacam** were introduced that separated these two video signals and became known as **component** video. **S-VHS** and **Hi8** formats utilized the separate chrominance and luminance channel concept but did it in a slightly different manner. Later formats such as **M-II** actually utilized *two* chroma channels in addition to the luminance signal. In all these formats the separation of the two very different aspects of the video signal resulted in significantly better picture quality.

Other changes in the nature of the video signal have taken place in the past decade, most notably the additional encoding of the traditional **analog** signal into a more reliable **digital** form that is compatible with all the newer computer-driven editing and graphics equipment. In many of the newer cameras, the signal output is a component analog signal and the *interface* to a digital signal takes place later at the editing stage with the videotape machine. With the advent of **nonlinear** video editing equipment, however, camcorders are being introduced that not only produce a digital signal, but have the capacity to store it *in the camcorder* on a **hard drive** instead of on videotape. In the newest of the editing machines a **compression** of the signal takes place that eliminates redundant picture information and thereby simplifies the storage and transfer of electrical signals.

The Video Scanning Process

We have previously described how, in a *three-chip CCD camera*, a *beam splitter* separates the focused beam of the lens into three images consisting of the red, green, and blue parts of the picture. A yellow object such as a ball would have that image projected onto both the red and green chips. In the illustration of signal flow in a *one-chip camera* shown in figure 5-4, the entire picture is focused on that one chip, which is comprised of over several hundred thousand red, green, and blue **pixels** in the NTSC system.

Through the filtration process, lightwaves of each of the three colors are able to act upon a corresponding color pixel. The shape of a blue chair could be thought of as being outlined on a mosaic of blue receiving pixels. In the case of the yellow ball mentioned above, both the green and red pixels would be activated to produce the yellow color combination. The brightness and color information from each individual pixel are transformed into a minute electrical charge, depending upon the amount of light falling on the pixel. This infinitesimal electrical charge is passed on in an incredibly precise and rapid sequential pattern—one that resembles the way the electron beam scans the image target in the traditional camera pickup tube.[3]

The CCD Camera

This sequence of picture information is gathered by *vertical and horizontal shift registers* at the left side and bottom of the CCD chip. After the picture/electrical information from the first line is scanned from left to right, the current is momentarily turned off by a **blanking pulse** and

3. In the tube-type camera, the light image falling on the face of the pickup tube charges individual pixels on a "target" located at the front of the tube. The electrical charge on these pixels is then "read" by a beam of electrons that are being shot from an electron gun at the rear of the tube. This beam is pulled back-and-forth and up-and-down the face of the tube by magnets. As the beam *scans* back-and-forth across the pickup tube, it creates the electrical current that becomes the video signal.

pulled back to the left side of the chip by the **horizontal synchronization pulse.** Then the information on the *third* horizontal line of pixels is scanned. Sequentially, the process is repeated as all of the *odd-numbered* lines on the CCD chip are scanned. It takes one-sixtieth of a second to scan all of the odd-numbered lines (1-3-5-7 . . . down to . . . 521-523-525). This top-to-bottom half picture is termed a **field.** Because only half of the lines have been scanned (picking up information from only half of the pixels on the chip), this field represents only half of the total video picture. It is hard to believe that the CCD chip is roughly the size of a postage stamp. (See figure 5-5.)

Now a **vertical synchronization pulse** repositions the vertical and horizontal shift registers to start the scanning process all over again. This time, the *even-numbered* lines on the CCD chip are scanned to produce another "half-picture" field. These two fields, first the odd then the even-numbered lines, added together comprise a total picture that is referred to as a **frame.** Thus, thirty of these full frames are produced every second. The basic pattern of this scanning process is similar to that of your eyes reading across a line of type on a page and then jumping back to the left side of the page and starting on the next lower line—525 lines per page, thirty pages per second!

It is the transistor part of the pixel, with its ability to store and then quickly move small electronic signals, that allows the vertical and horizontal shift registers to gather the total signal of the multitude of pixels—thirty times per second. From this are generated the chrominance and luminance signals as well as the vertical and horizontal sync pulses so important to picture stability. All this electrical information is amplified and in other ways modulated within the camera to produce either the composite or component video signal. The

FIGURE 5-5

The model in the picture is showing the relative size of one of the three charge-coupled device chips used in this early CCD camera as compared to the tubes that would be used in a camera of the same size.

Photo courtesy RCA

resulting electrical message is the electronic signal that has just begun its long and complicated path.

The Receiver Picture Tube

Just as the radio speaker resembles the microphone, the TV set's picture tube mirrors the older technology of the camera pickup tube. By extension of the same analogy, it can be said that the display tubes of the future will probably relate more and more to the CCD and LED (light-emitting diode) technologies.

As the camera is picking up the picture—and during the subsequent channeling, mixing, shaping, amplifying, and monitoring—the signal remains in a "pure" line *video* format. Switchers, studio monitors, recorders, and editors all process this line level signal. However, for the picture to be transmitted, the audio signal must be added, and then the video and audio information must be converted to a **radio frequency (RF)** signal. It is this RF signal that can then be modulated onto a **carrier wave** that can be broadcast on a radio frequency in the **electromagnetic spectrum.**

The first task of the home TV set is to strip off the audio signal. Next, it **demodulates** the picture information. Then the red, green, and blue guns in the receiver tube each shoot out a stream of electrons. This electron beam, like the scanning beam in the older camera pickup tubes, is controlled by a ring of magnets that deflects and controls the beam to reproduce the left-to-right and top-to-bottom scanning pattern in the camera.

In most TV sets, the electron beams pass through a **masking plate** that focuses the electrons as they strike the designated

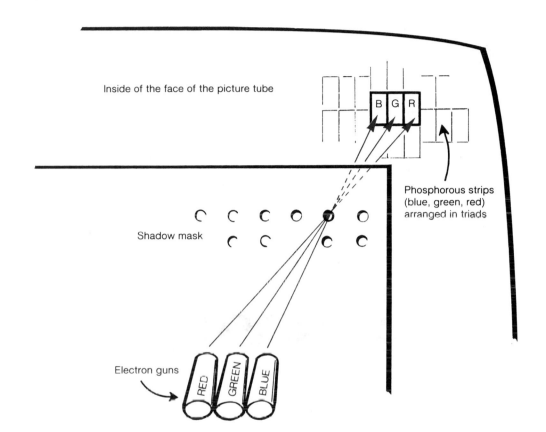

Inside of the face of the picture tube

Phosphorous strips
(blue, green, red)
arranged in triads

Shadow mask

Electron guns

RED GREEN BLUE

FIGURE 5-6

Shadow mask for
color receiver.

Most color receivers
utilize a shadow
mask, a thin metal
sheet perforated by
tiny holes. These
carefully aligned
dots or slots ensure
that as each of the
three electron
beams is pulled
across the face of
the tube in its
scanning pattern, it
will hit only those
phosphor strips
colored to
correspond with its
designated electron
gun in the rear of
the tube.

phosphor pixels on the inside glass of the picture tube. (See figure 5-6.) This inner coating can be either in the form of triad groups of red, green, and blue dots or in the form of tiny vertical phosphorescent strips of the same colors.

It is the control information on the synchronizing pulse (including the horizontal and vertical blanking intervals) that guarantees a synchronized scanning rate of sixty fields (thirty frames) per second. The TV receiver tube electron beams reproduce the video picture essentially as it was originally picked up by the camera tube.

Like the image picked up by the camera, the picture displayed on the receiver screen never actually exists as a single completed frame. The TV frame does not have a discrete existence the way a frame of motion picture film does. What we have is the linear tracing of a point of light moving at an incredible rate of speed. At any given microsecond, one "half-picture" field is always at some stage of the continual scanning process.

Because of the phenomenon of **persistence of vision** ("visual lag"), the brain perceives this incredibly rapid series of light flashes as a moving picture. The human eye retains images for a split second after the image has been removed. If about fifteen or more separate images per second are flashed before the eye, human perception will cause them to blend together, thus creating the illusion of motion. This persistence of vision is what makes simulated moving pictures possible—on celluloid film as well as on the face of a television tube.

5.3 LENS CHARACTERISTICS

Working in conjunction with the CCD image sensor, possibly the most crucial element in the whole pictorial process is the lens. Very little can be done if an improperly focused picture is presented to the beam splitter (or directly onto the CCD chip in single chip cameras). A good lens can help the cheapest camera but an inferior lens can turn the best professional camera into blurred trash.

Within five years of its introduction in the late 1950s, the **zoom lens** became standard equipment on virtually all studio television cameras. For most video production, this will likely remain true in the future. Indeed, most television production students will probably never see a **fixed-focal-length lens** on a television camera. The zoom lens by virtue of its numerous lens elements can quickly become any one of a wide range of lens types. However, this very technology prohibits it from being quite as optically perfect as a fixed-focal-length lens designed for one specified magnification. As a result, some feel that high definition television,[4] with its potential for much clearer pictures, may set the stage for a return to their use on at least a limited scale.

Most factors that characterize the zoom lens are based upon the optical principles underlying the traditional fixed-focal-length

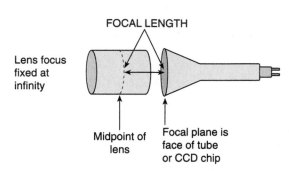

FIGURE 5-7

Measurement of lens focal length on a video tube.

The focal length is measured from the center of the lens to the point where the subject image is in focus on the surface of a CCD chip, a frame of film, or a video tube, shown here for purposes of illustration.

lens. Such characteristics as **focal length, focus, f-stop,** and **depth of field** are simpler to understand if the example of a nonzoom, fixed-focal-length lens is used. It is much easier to comprehend the concept of **long lens** compression of a picture or how a **wide-angle lens** gives a greater depth of field, if one visualizes the actual length and angle of the lens. We will therefore use these lenses as a reference point and return to the zoom for further consideration in section 5.4.

Focal Length

The *focal length* of a lens is measured from the optical center point of the lens (when it is focused at infinity) to a point where the image is in focus. This **focal plane** can be the film in a movie or still camera, a single CCD camera chip, or the face of the pickup tube in an electronic camera as shown in figure 5-7. Focal length is measured in either millimeters or inches (25.4 millimeters is equal to one inch).

4. Over the past decade numerous conferences were held in an attempt to agree on an international standard for the new high definition picture. At this writing a consortium of American and European manufacturers were completing work on a digitally based wide screen (probably 9 x 16) scanning system of roughly 1,000 lines.

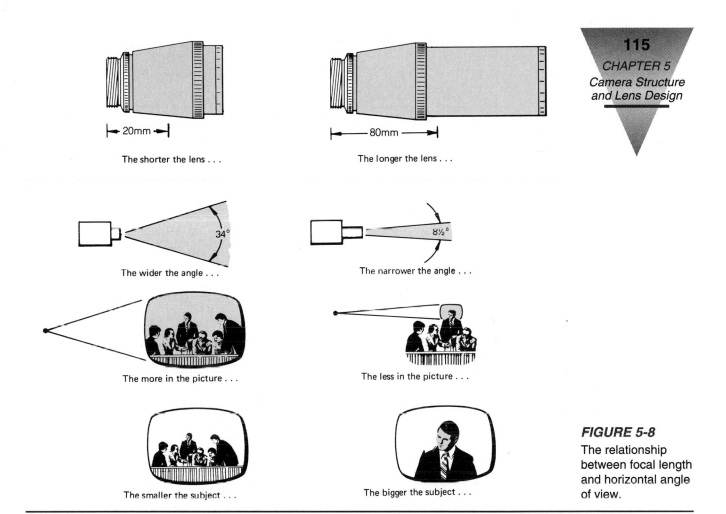

The shorter the lens . . .

The longer the lens . . .

20mm

80mm

The wider the angle . . .

34°

The narrower the angle . . .

8½°

The more in the picture . . .

The less in the picture . . .

The smaller the subject . . .

The bigger the subject . . .

FIGURE 5-8
The relationship
between focal length
and horizontal angle
of view.

Lenses of differing lengths are used primarily so that differing amounts of a scene can be included in the picture when shot from the same position. *The longer a lens is, the narrower its viewing angle will be, the less you will be able to get in the picture,* and therefore, *the larger individual subjects will be.* Conversely, a short focal-length lens will give you a wider viewing angle, thereby allowing you to get more in the picture, but individual subjects will appear smaller than normal. This *law of lenses* is illustrated in figure 5-8. Long lenses, therefore, can be used to obtain closer views of

objects. A long **telephoto lens** can get a relatively close-up view of an object from a great distance. On the other hand, a **short** (or wide-angle) **lens** will tend to increase distance and make things look farther away than they are. This fact can lead to distortion of distance.

A long lens (or a long-lens setting on a zoom lens) will *compress* distance. Two objects that are far apart from each other and at a great distance from the camera will be brought closer to the camera with a long lens and, consequently, will seemingly be brought closer to each other. A common

FIGURE 5-9

In the left picture the zoomed-in lens approximates a 54mm fixed-focal-length lens. Note the optical compression even though the children are nine feet apart. In the right picture the effect is quite different when viewed through a zoomed-out, 9mm lens. For this shot the camera was moved in to a much closer position.

example is the baseball shot of the pitcher and batter as seen with an exceptionally long telephoto lens from center field. Although the pitcher and batter are about sixty feet apart, the camera is perhaps 400 feet away. Thus, the two players are brought much closer to the camera, and consequently, the distance between them is apparently compressed—on the home screen they may look as if they are only ten or fifteen feet apart.

On the other hand, as we see in figure 5-9, a wide-angle lens (or a short-lens setting on a zoom lens) will *exaggerate* distance for exactly the opposite reason. The shorter the lens, the farther apart objects appear to be spread. In both shots the young man was standing nine feet behind his sister. The picture on the right was shot at the zoomed-out position (low magnification) on a video camera having a 6-to-1 zoom ratio. The camera "specs" list this as being the equivalent of a 9mm lens. The camera was four feet from the young lady in the foreground. Note the apparent separation. In the picture on the

left the camera was moved back to a distance of twelve feet from her, but the lens was completely zoomed-in to become the equivalent of a 54mm lens. This is the effect of *optical compression* mentioned above.

Figure 5-10 lists the horizontal viewing angles of lenses that were used on the last studio fixed-length cameras several decades ago. This chart, along with a review of figure 5-8 should provide some idea as to how different degrees of magnification affect the picture. We will now look into two additional variables that interact to have an even more significant influence upon picture quality.

Focusing Characteristics

Most fixed-focal-length lenses will have two adjustable rings. One will be the f-stop, or aperture opening, and the other will be the focusing ring. This focusing ring, which is common to all who have worked in still photography, can be adjusted anywhere from a few inches to infinity.

Lens Length	Viewpoint
10mm	Extreme wide angle
25mm	Wide angle
40mm	Normal
100mm	Narrow angle
200mm	Extreme narrow angle (telephoto)

FIGURE 5-10

Sample measurements of fixed-focal-length lenses.

Standard vidicon studio lenses. For reference, remember that 25.4 millimeters is equal to one inch.

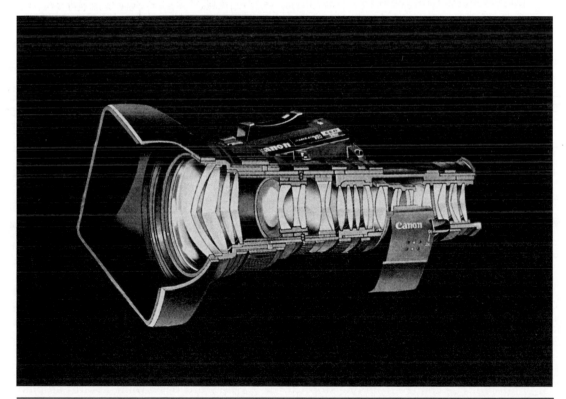

FIGURE 5-11

Cutaway illustration of movable lenses in a fourteen to one ratio zoom lens.

Photo courtesy of Canon

With zoom lenses, as we shall discuss in section 5.4, the focusing mechanism is slightly more complicated because of the number of lens elements that have to be rearranged within the housing of the zoom lens. (See figure 5-11.) Most contemporary TV cameras, including consumer camcorders, have zoom lenses where the focus automatically adjusts with the action of the zoom lens. This adjustment is usually accomplished on professional studio cameras by remote control from the rear of the camera—often on the **pan handle.**

The F-Stop Aperture

As we mentioned when discussing lighting and contrast range (see section 4.2), the television camera has a relatively narrow range of light tolerance as compared with the human eye. All camera lenses, therefore, have at the front of the lens an adjustable **iris** that can open or close the **aperture** by moving a **diaphragm** in and out. This opening is necessary so that the amount of light coming into the camera can be kept within acceptable limits. It does not affect the size of the picture the lens will pick up.

Most cameras with zoom lenses usually have the option of manual or automatic control of the iris. It is important, however, that students understand the following principles in order to comprehend how manual operation of the f-stop can affect the picture quality. As will be explained, many production situations exist where the camera operator will want to override the **automatic iris control** and adjust the iris manually for a variety of creative reasons.

The various sizes of aperture openings are identified by different f-stop numbers. The first rule to remember in working with f-stops is very simple, once you get it straight. *The lower the f-stop number, the larger the lens opening, and the higher the f-stop number, the smaller the lens opening.* (See figure 5-12.) For instance, f-22 is typically the smallest aperture found on most television lenses. The widest opening could be f-2.8 depending upon the structure of the lens. In between, the numbers would range through 4, 5.6, 8, 11 and 16. The change from one stop to another represents a doubling or the cutting in half of the amount of light being allowed to come into the camera. It is a precise measurement, hence the need for some decimal figures.

The most obvious application of the f-stop is to enable camera operators to adjust to varying light sources. If one is

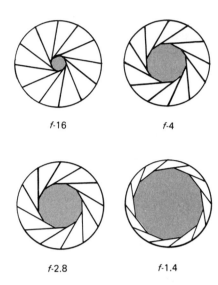

f-16   f-4

f-2.8   f-1.4

FIGURE 5-12

Diagrams of various f-stop openings.

The basic rule to remember with iris changes is the higher the f-stop number, the smaller the opening. Each marked position on the lens represents one full f-stop and each time the stop is changed one position, the light going into the camera is doubled or cut in half.

working under very poor lighting conditions, it might be advisable to open up to f-4. On the other hand, if you are working under extremely bright conditions (perhaps outdoors on a sunny day), you might want to "stop down" to f-11 or f-16. The *stop down* term that actually means a *closing up* of the iris at a *higher* number may take a little "getting used to," but it's the accepted phrase.

One word of warning about f-stop adjustments should be stated at this point. Generally speaking, the camera operator should not routinely think of the f-stop as a means of compensating for bad lighting. The f-stops, together with the various electronic camera controls, are often established for a given lighting situation by a trained studio technician and should only be changed after consultation. Bad lighting or uneven lighting should be handled by correcting the lighting, not by tampering with the camera adjustments. Increasingly, however, cameras in educational institutions are being set up with all cameras in the automatic iris setting. Again this setting should only be changed with the knowledge of some responsible engineer because all other camera controls have been coordinated with this setting. Overriding the automatic iris control may be a desirable creative effect, but the changeover should be tested and planned in advance.

Depth of Field

Our final factor in the consideration of camera focus has to do with the ways that one can determine the location of an area of consistently good focus within any picture. This so-called *depth of field* refers to *the distance between the nearest point at which objects are in focus, and the farthest point at which objects are in focus.* In a typical shot, objects close to the camera will be out of focus and objects too far away may be out of focus. Making sure that we can predict the location of this middle ground where objects are in focus is important in the production planning process.

Three different factors interrelate to determine the depth of field: *the f-stop* (the smaller the lens opening—only possible with adequate light—the greater the depth of field); *the distance from the subject to the camera* (the greater the camera-to-subject distance the greater the depth of field); and *the focal length of the lens* (the shorter the lens the greater the depth of field). Figure 5-13 illustrates these three variables.

Here a note of caution must be expressed. These optical rules apply well for fixed-focal-length lenses but applying them to the use of a zoom lens causes problems. The only factor that really gives you much flexibility with a zoom lens is

changing the f-stop. For example, you may have a medium shot but want to increase your depth of field. One way is to change the zoom lens to its widest angle, thereby decreasing the focal length of the lens. This would necessitate moving the camera forward to get somewhat the same framing. It might be satisfactory. The other option is to increase subject-to-camera distance. But this means moving the camera back and putting the lens in the zoomed-in position which, in effect, reduces depth of field. The best option is to stop down to a smaller lens opening, and as a result, you will need to add more light to the scene. Obviously, shots calling for a large depth of field must be planned in advance.

Occasionally, production students begin with the conception that the ideal lighting situation is one in which the lens can be stopped down to the smallest possible opening—thereby attaining the greatest depth of field (area of focus) possible. This, however, may not always be a desirable aim. For aesthetic reasons, the director may not want the background in focus as it may detract from the foreground action of the performers. Or the opposite may be true: the director may want the foreground to be out-of-focus (for example, he or she may be shooting through some unfocused leaves of a tree) in order to concentrate on the background action. This is referred to as **selective focus**—when either the foreground or background is deliberately kept out of sharp focus.

To achieve these effects, it is necessary to have a shallow depth of field—a wide-open aperture. This, of course, necessitates low-level lighting. Depending upon the exact lighting conditions, the camera operator may have to defeat the "auto setting" of the automatic iris.

Occasionally, for dramatic effect, the director may want the camera operator to **pull focus** to shift a shallow depth of field from a foreground object to the background, or vice versa. This also can be accomplished with a

The depth of field of a lens can be increased by altering any one of three different variables:

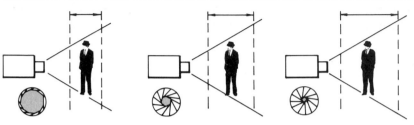

(a) by decreasing the lens aperture;

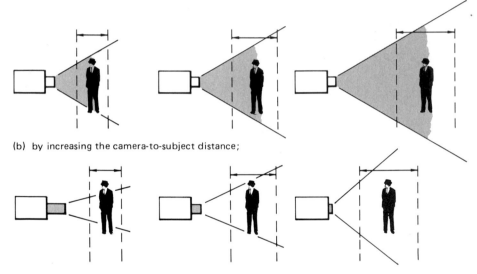

(b) by increasing the camera-to-subject distance;

(c) by decreasing the lens focal length.

FIGURE 5-13

Depth of field.

The depth of field of a lens can be increased by altering any one of three different variables: (a) by decreasing the lens aperture, (b) by increasing the camera-to-subject distance, (c) by decreasing the lens focal length.

wide-open aperture. For example, the director may want to open on a tight close-up shot of a half-empty glass close to the camera with the background out-of-focus; the camera operator could then change the focus (without otherwise altering the shot at all) to focus on the figure lying on the sofa while the foreground glass goes blurry.

Other factors may also necessitate a deliberate shallow depth of field. Perhaps the dramatic setting calls for **low-key** lighting, which means you have to operate with the lens aperture opened up. Another consideration is simply that of creature comfort; **high-key** lighting—solely for the sake of working with a greater depth of field—may not be worth the toll it takes on the performers working under more intense lighting for a prolonged period.

5.4 THE ZOOM LENS

The development of the *zoom* lens allowed camera operators and directors to achieve rapid and continuous adjustment of the focal length of the lens—and consequently

FIGURE 5-14

Canon J55X 9B IE "SUPER" field zoom lens.

This 55-to-1 zoom lens is one of the largest field production zoom lenses in professional use today. When it is zoomed in, its picture is fifty-five times larger than when it is zoomed out. It has a zoom range extending the unit from a 9mm lens to an effective 500mm lens. With its 2X extender, it doubles that figure to 18mm and 1,000mm. Weighing over thirty-seven pounds, it is almost twenty-two inches long, roughly ten inches high, and ten inches wide. It is used extensively for sporting events and similar productions.

Photo courtesy of Canon

to control precisely the size and framing of shots. It greatly changed the way directors approached visual continuity. In addition to giving the director and camera operator a wider range of lens lengths that are immediately available, the zoom lens also facilitates very smooth on-the-air movement. Its imaginative use was the foundation on which the incredibly successful era of network sports coverage in the 1970s and '80s was built. Figure 5-14 illustrates a large modern zoom lens used for these out-of-studio productions.

An optical as well as mechanical marvel, the variable-focal-length zoom lens is essentially an arrangement of gears and optical elements that allows the operator to shift these lens elements—moving them back-and-forth in relation to each other. This achieves varying focal lengths by changing the theoretical center point of the lens. While zoom lenses will vary greatly with price and manufacturer, those lenses designed for professional and industrial levels all share some of the same basic characteristics.

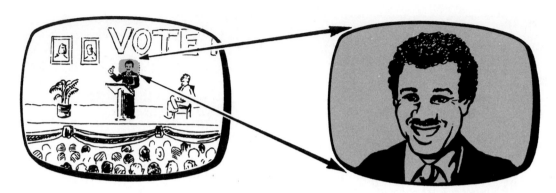

FIGURE 5-15
Range of a zoom lens.

These two views represent the extreme focal lengths of a 10-to-1 zoom lens: *left,* zoomed "out" to the shortest focal length (widest angle); *right,* zoomed "in" to the longest focal length (narrowest angle).

Lens Ratio

For most production situations, a 10-to-1 magnification ratio is common. On a typical lens this would result in focal lengths ranging from, maybe, 10.5mm at the wide-angle position to 105mm at the *zoomed-in* high-magnification or "long-lens" position. Figure 5-15 provides some indication of the range of shots available with a 10-to-1 **zoom ratio** lens. Consumer camcorders are often equipped with a 6-to-1 zoom lens with a still very adequate 9mm to 54mm range. For sporting events and other outdoor public events programming, zoom ratios of 30-to-1 and greater are not uncommon. The 55-to-1 ratio of the Canon J55X (see figure 5-14) can be doubled by the use of an **extender.** Its magnification strength is exceeded by only a few other lenses.

Movement Control

Virtually all zoom lenses will have a motor-driven zoom mechanism. Less expensive models may have only one or two rates of speed. This does not give you much artistic control over the effect you may want to achieve. Therefore, professional lenses will usually have *variable-speed* controls. Generally, professional zoom lenses will also provide an optional manual zoom control lever for those times when only the human touch will suffice. It should be noted, however, that serious damage will result if the manual lever is engaged while the power zoom control is in operation.

It is this ability to obtain smooth on-the-air zoom movement that gives the director production flexibility when using zoom lenses. It is possible to gradually (or quickly) *tighten up* a shot, going smoothly from a **long shot** to a **medium shot** to a **close-up.** The best zoom work usually goes unnoticed because it does not call attention to itself. The movement of a zoom produces a somewhat similar visual to the movement in and out of a camera. As mentioned previously, however, the lens characteristics produce very different relationships of subjects in the picture. This area is discussed in section 6.1.

Focusing

On all zoom lenses, the focus control is the slip ring located farthest toward the front of the lens. This ring is usually adjusted by remote control when cameras are set up for studio use. Staying in focus can be a problem with zoom lenses. As cameras are moved to different positions on the studio floor, there is a constantly changing distance relationship between the camera and the various subjects. Each change necessitates checking to be sure that the lens is set for a "zoomed-in" close-up shot—before it is needed. If it is not set, the operator coming from an in-focus wide shot may zoom into an out-of-focus close-up.

To preset a focus, zoom in all the way to the tightest shot you can get and adjust the lens focus. Now, zoom back slowly and check to make sure the subject is in reasonable focus throughout the entire length of the zoom. If not, the only slight adjustment you can make is with the zoom lens focus.

As long as you have a few seconds and you are sure that the talent is not going to move or the director is not suddenly going to ask you to get a shot of something at some other distance from the camera, you should be able to get the zoom focus preset. But problems do occur—especially when you quickly have to get an unexpected shot.

Macro Lens

This special adjustment has become a standard focusing feature of most newer zoom lens units. (See figure 5-16.) In the **macro** position, one can take extreme close-ups of printed material or small objects at distances of two inches or less from the lens. The procedure will vary with individual equipment, but the rather sensitive process of such delicate focusing is usually handled by adjusting the manual zoom lever and not the focus ring.

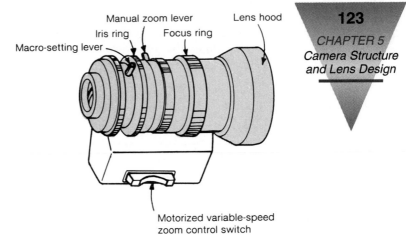

Diagram of a typical zoom lens.

In addition to the motorized variable-speed zoom control switch, adjustments on the lens include the macro lens setting, the iris (f-stop) setting, the manual zoom lever, and the focus ring.

Iris

As outlined in section 5.3, the iris (f-stop) position has an important relationship to picture focus. If incorrectly set, it can also greatly affect the quality of color in the picture. In a studio situation where light values are fairly constant, settings will stay within a narrow range. Operating instructions for each camera will usually provide optimum **lux** or **footcandle** levels as related to an f-stop setting.[5] For example, on many lenses an f-4 setting would be proper for a 200-footcandle reading.

As mentioned previously, many lenses have an automatic iris control that reacts to incoming light and continually adjusts the

5. The "lux" measurement is based upon an amount of candlelight falling upon an object from the distance of one meter. While not completely accurate, footcandle readings are often multiplied by ten to get a rough *lux* measurement (e.g., 40 fc = 400 lux).

f-stop as light values change. Some manufacturers provide a *temporary automatic* feature that allows the lens to hold any f-stop position set by the automatic sensor.

5.5 CONTROLS FOR CAMERA ADJUSTMENTS

Teaching institutions that have professional or industrial-level cameras possess sophisticated items of equipment having a number of controls that make possible high quality pictures. On the other hand, misuse of those controls will greatly diminish picture quality and even cause permanent damage. Each class should establish a definite policy as to which controls on the camera (or CCU) are for student adjustment and which are to be handled only by the instructor or trained staff personnel.

Those controls relating to zoom operation described earlier would normally fall within the realm of student control. Such controls should be checked for correct settings as part of camera setup. On the camera itself, however, there are several controls that, although they may not be designated for student operation, should nevertheless be understood so that settings can be checked for proper positions and levels prior to camera operation.

Color Temperature Conversion Filters

Professional cameras designed for both studio and field production usually have a built-in **filter** system to compensate for **Kelvin** temperature differences between indoor and outdoor lighting. Usually located in front of the beam splitter (see section 5.2), this filter component is an integral part of the camera system. Many industrial and educational cameras have a rotating disc of four filters for different lighting conditions: (1) iodine lamp and sunrise and sunset; (2) bright outdoor;

(3) cloudy or rainy; and (4) white fluorescent. It is interesting that sunrise and sunset have a color temperature that is very similar to artificial quartz-iodine light. This has to do with the angle of the light rays and the filtering effect of the atmosphere at those times of day.

One should also carefully follow the instruction book that comes with each camera, as some filters will screen out more total light than others. For instance, in the DXC 1820, outdoor positions 2 and 3 allow one-half as much light to get through as setting 1. This means that f-stop settings for indoor or outdoor shooting must be carefully adjusted with the filter position in mind.

White Balance

This is a control that establishes the correct color balance to produce a pure white. In a studio situation where all illumination is produced by lights having a consistent 3,200 degrees Kelvin temperature, it is possible to do most production work with the **white balance** switch at the factory established *preset* position. If, however, a camera is to be used for field production where Kelvin temperatures are constantly changing, the white balance procedure must be understood and utilized.

The alternate white balance switch position on most cameras is labeled *auto*, which simply means that the camera will automatically accomplish the necessary adjustment process. In this mode, with a white card filling the lens image, the camera color system senses any excess of either red or blue light and within a few seconds adjusts accordingly. The white card serves as a neutral reference point so that the camera can judge the balance between red and blue in the light source(s). On some cameras, additional fine-control adjustments permit the operator to subtly tint with additional amounts of red or blue without having to go through the entire balancing procedure.

To get the proper adjustment for flesh tones, the white card must be placed exactly where the subject's face will be for the shot. In field work where a change in the camera-to-subject angle may introduce a new light source, a new balance adjustment may be necessary. Also when shooting on location, lighting conditions will change throughout the day (the sun changes color when it descends; cloud covers vary) and occasional adjustments to the white balance will be necessary.

Video Output Level Selector

Many cameras have an **automatic gain control (AGC)** that automatically adjusts video levels to compensate for differing light conditions. However, other cameras have a **video output control** that allows the operator to adjust to some degree for low light levels. The "0 db" position is established by the manufacturer as the standard level of video output for the camera under prescribed lighting conditions. The video output control increases the decibels so that the camera can function at lower light levels than at the 0 db position. The term **decibel (db)** has been borrowed and slightly altered from its audio derivation; however as with audio, each 6-db increase means that the amplified signal is doubled. This control should never be thought of as a way to make a poorly lit picture better. All it can do is make the poor picture look a little brighter.

Viewfinder Visual Indicators and Controls

On some cameras the **tally light,** which tells both the operator and the talent/subject that the camera is feeding the switcher, will also light up to indicate that the white balance adjustment in the camera has been completed. On those cameras designed for field use, several **warning lights** may indicate *low battery power, insufficient lighting,* or an *abnormally high setting of the gain control knob,* which is causing excessive drain on the battery.

It should also be noted that the *brightness* and *contrast* controls are only for the viewfinder adjustment; *they do not have any effect on the video output of the camera.* Operators who are unaware of this basic fact can be a menace to any proper camera setup procedure. Such uninformed operators may take one look at their incorrectly adjusted viewfinder picture and—assuming the camera settings are wrong—mess up a perfectly good camera output by changing the f-stop, filter setting, and gain controls. The viewfinder controls—like the camera controls themselves—should be adjusted only while the operator is in headset contact with the person (usually the instructor or technical director) who is in charge of camera setup in the video control center.

Other Controls

Some cameras have several additional control units that, while not necessarily complicated, are best suited to an individualized-study approach. Such items as the **fade time control,** the **negative/positive selector,** and the **phase control selector** all have clearly marked "0" or neutral positions. The beginning student should be made aware of these *off* positions to be able to confirm their negative status during the process of learning camera operations.

Modern video cameras have incorporated numerous other internal monitoring systems, feedback circuits, and computer-based controls. Figure 5-17 shows the electronic complexity of the inner workings of the contemporary camera. An awareness of the fragile nature of these circuit boards should help the novice camera operator appreciate the need to treat these instruments with care.

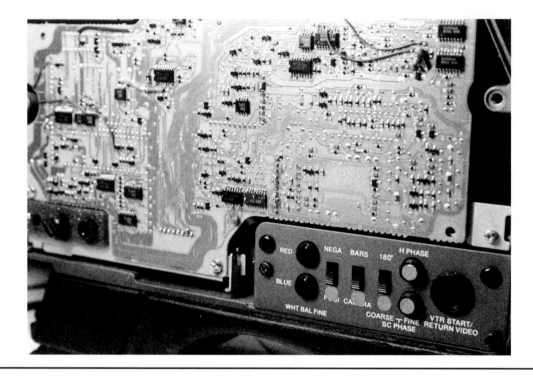

FIGURE 5-17

The circuit board of
a modern camera
gives some insight
as to its electronic
complexity.

SUMMARY

As with audio techniques and lighting considerations, a discussion of camera characteristics and operations could also be broken down into technical aspects and creative concerns. The sections dealing with the camera image-sensing devices (*CCD chip* or *pickup tube*), the *receiver picture tube*, the lens characteristics, and the *zoom lens* have been concerned largely with technical matters.

The *video signal flow* can be seen as parallel to the audio signal flow. The same functions apply to both audio and video control: *transducing, channeling, mixing, amplifying, shaping, recording* (and playback), and *monitoring*. Additional sophisticated *control components* are added to the video system—*sync generator, proc amp, time-base corrector, frame synchronizer, color bar generator, waveform monitor,* and *vectorscope.*

The color video system is concerned with accurately rendering three color components—*hue, saturation,* and *brightness.* The transducing function is identified largely with the *CCD* chip. Concepts important to the formation of the video signal are *composite* video, *component* video, *analog* processing, *digital* processing and *scanning.*

The three-chip color camera splits the incoming light into the three *primary colors* of red, green, and blue—each one being channeled to its own image sensor creating both a *luminance* and *chrominance* signal. The receiver picture tube, which can be thought of as a mirrored version of the old camera pickup tube, also has clear similarities to the newer CCD technology in that it is driven by the same *synchronization pulse* that keeps all elements of the production-distribution-reception system locked together.

Mechanical and optical considerations of the *fixed-focal-length lens* include *focal length, focusing characteristics, f-stop lens aperture,* and *depth of field.* While the *zoom lens* has several advantages pertaining to flexibility in selecting focal length and facilitating smooth movement, it also has a few drawbacks relating to focusing characteristics. Operating considerations of the zoom lens include *lens ratio, movement control, focusing, macro-lens setting,* and *iris control.*

Several other camera controls that students should be familiar with, although they would not necessarily be authorized to make such adjustments without explicit approval and supervision, are: *color temperature filters, white balance, video output level,* and *viewfinder picture adjustments,* among others.

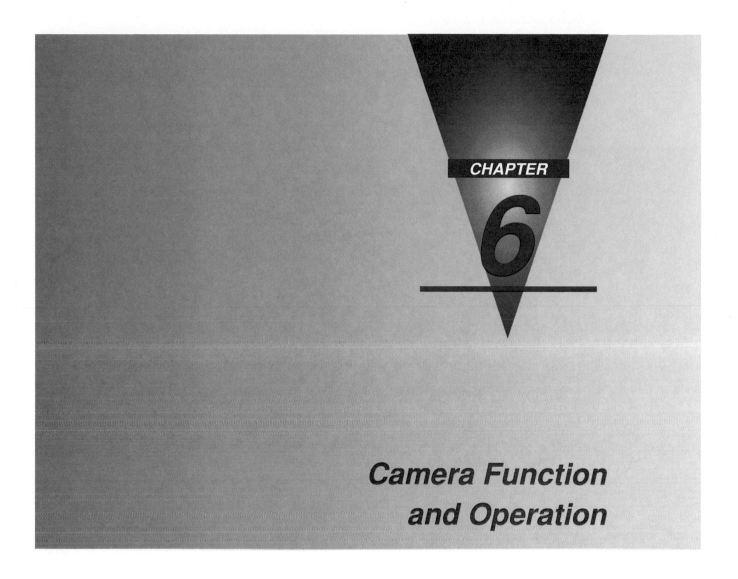

CHAPTER

6

Camera Function and Operation

I n the previous chapter we examined many of the technical aspects that go into the creation of the video picture by the camera. In this chapter we will study the various ways through which the electronic potential of the camera can be shaped and controlled by the operator to achieve the creative purposes of the director.

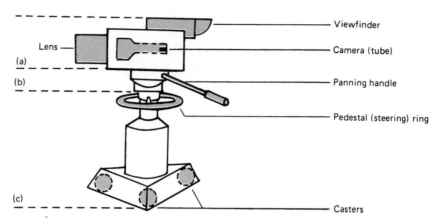

Lens

(a)

(b)

(c)

Viewfinder

Camera (tube)

Panning handle

Pedestal (steering) ring

Casters

FIGURE 6-1

Three basic parts of the camera.

(a) The video components of the **camera** itself including the lens, viewfinder, and tube or CCD; (b) the **mounting head** with the panning handle that controls camera movement; and (c) the **camera mount** that is the transport and support mechanism for the entire unit.

6.1 CAMERA OPERATION AND CONTROL

The efficient use of the video camera depends upon several primary factors that interact with one another during any studio production sequence. The first of these is simply the *position* of the camera in its relationship to a subject (or multiple subjects in wide-angle shots). The camera reveals the front, side or top of the elements in the picture according to where it is placed. A second factor involves changing the *direction* in which the camera is aimed to reveal different subjects.

There can also be a continuing change in the *point of view* of the camera as it is moved to reveal different aspects of a subject or sequence of subjects. This movement can also involve changes in the *elevation* of the camera, especially when an artistic effect is called for. The effectiveness of these operations is very dependent upon the hardware that provides movement and support for the camera.

Camera Head Movement

Figure 6-1 shows the basic parts of a studio camera unit, including: (a) the video components of the **camera** itself; (b) the mounting **head** containing the equipment used for movement of the camera; and (c) the **camera mount** which controls floor movement of the entire unit.

Shot changes involving vertical and horizontal movement of the camera are fundamental to video production. When these kinds of movements are continuous "on the air" moves, they require a skilled operator and a suitable mounting head with which to execute them. A horizontal movement to the left or to the right is known as a **pan.** (See figure 6-2.) When told to "pan right," the operator moves the camera lens in the direction of his or her right hand. This is the reverse of stage movements that are given from the standpoint of the performer looking out toward an audience.

Up-and-down movements of the camera are called **tilts.** The lens end of the

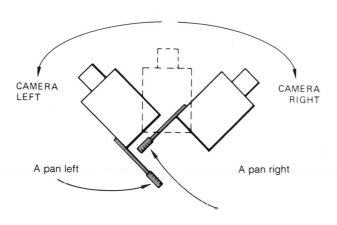

FIGURE 6-2

Camera panning.

To pan the camera in a given direction, the panning handle must be moved in the opposite direction. Thus, in order to execute a "pan left," the camera operator has to move the panning handle to the right.

camera is moved up or down to view elements at different elevations of the set. (See figure 6-3.) Both movements are accomplished by exerting pressure on the **pan handle** that projects from the right rear of the camera. Zoom and focus controls are usually located on this pan handle. In the mounting head area there is a coupling device such as a **cam** or **cradle** assembly that is important to a smoothness of motion, especially in a tilting action. (See figures 6-4 and 6-5.)

Camera Mounts

Any change of camera position, whether done as a continuing movement or simply for the purposes of changing the framing of a shot, is accomplished through some movement of the camera mount. Of the four types of camera and lens movements mentioned in this chapter's introductory paragraph, the last two—camera elevation and camera position—are both dependent upon the camera mount. The simplest and least expensive camera mount is the **tripod.** This three-legged stand is usually

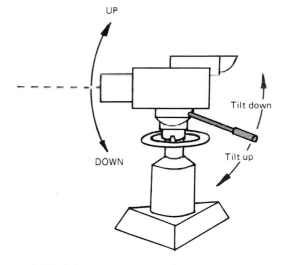

FIGURE 6-3

Camera tilting.

In tilting the camera up or down, the camera head is pivoted through the use of the pan handle. Several different cam and cradle mechanisms can be used for this assembly.

FIGURE 6-4

Camera mounted on
a cam head
assembly with an
adjustable tripod.

FIGURE 6-5

Camera with a
cradle head placed
on a compressed air
pedestal mount.

The ring is used to
turn the wheels for
movement.

fastened to a dolly base consisting of three casters. The casters can either rotate freely which facilitates quick and easy movement of the camera in all directions, or can be locked into a nonmovable position, resulting in a steady camera unit for straight-line movement.

The tripod illustrated in figure 6-4 has a crank-operated elevation adjustment that can be used to raise and lower the camera—although not smoothly enough to be used on the air. Many tripods have no way to adjust height other than the laborious process of mechanically adjusting the spread of the tripod legs. Thus, there is no way to achieve any elevation change during an actual production. The tripod, however, is lightweight, and most models are readily collapsible. This makes the tripod a desirable camera mount for most remote productions.

The **pedestal** mount (see figure 6-5) is a much heavier unit and is somewhat of a holdover from the days of much larger cameras that did not have **zoom lenses.** To get the variety of shots necessary for a production, those cameras were in constant movement around the studio floor. With its three covered casters, it maneuvers like any wheeled tripod, but its additional weight provides a more stabile movement. Its distinctive feature is the central pedestal that can be raised or lowered by an assist of counterweights or air pressure. It also has a steering ring that controls all three casters in a synchronized manner so that smooth, on-the-air camera movements across the studio floor can be achieved. This ease and steadiness in camera movement have made the studio pedestal a popular workhorse in many studio situations.

When more pronounced changes of position and elevation are called for, they are accomplished through the use of mounts such as the motorized **crane** and

FIGURE 6-6

Two powered mobile cameras used for Olympic coverage.

Left, a crab dolly adapted for field use, designed to move along tracks for trucking movements; *right,* special truck-mounted crane for following Olympic bicycling events.

Courtesy of ABC Sports

crab dolly shown in figure 6-6. With the crane, considerable differences in camera position are possible because there is a separate driver for the motorized base.

Inherited from the film industry, the *crane* is the largest and most flexible type of camera mount and comes in a variety of sizes. The camera itself is mounted on a boom arm that can be moved vertically or laterally without moving the crane base. Depending upon the model, the length of the arm extension is ten to fifteen feet for studio models and much more for a few very special field units. For everything from rock concerts to Olympic coverage, the moving crane shot has become an indispensable part of the visual language of television.

Figure 6-6 also illustrates a *crab dolly* adapted for outdoor use and mounted on tracks for smooth travel movement. This

is another legacy from the glory days of the film studios. The camera can be moved from floor level to over six feet in height. Newer models usually have power units for both movement and elevation. Other specialized mounts include everything from blimps to camera platforms built on vehicles for various racing events.

Camera Mount Movements

The entire camera and its mounting can be moved about the studio floor in several ways. One of the most obvious is moving closer to or farther away from the subject; this is referred to as **dollying** the camera. (See figure 6-7.) While the zoom lens has reduced the use of *dolly in* and *dolly out* movements when the camera is on, this move still has its uses. As pointed out in

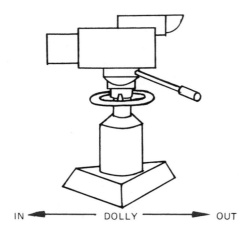

IN ◄──── DOLLY ────► OUT

FIGURE 6-7
Camera dollying.

In a dolly movement, the camera is simply moved closer to or farther from the subject.

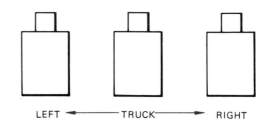

LEFT ◄────── TRUCK ──────► RIGHT

FIGURE 6-8
Camera trucking.

In a trucking movement, the camera and mount are moved laterally without any adjustment of the camera mounting head.

figure 5-9 there is a considerable difference in the way the zoom lens in a wide-angle mode sees two subjects separated by ten feet or so, and the way those two subjects are seen with the lens in the high magnification mode. Directors should experiment with the variables of lens **focal length** and **camera-to-source distance.** One interesting move is to dolly in on a wide shot and then continue the move toward the subject with the zoom.

Lateral movement of the camera and its mount is known as **trucking.** A change of picture is accomplished as the camera *trucks right* or *trucks left* because the camera moves sideways without panning to the right or left. (See figure 6-8.) In the field, dollying and trucking movements normally cannot be attempted unless special tracks have been laid down to facilitate smooth level movement. Usually, such movements are set up only for ambitious productions—expensive dramatic programs, major sporting events, and so forth.

A **follow shot** can utilize both the trucking and dollying techniques. In it a camera moves with the subject and maintains a constant distance from it while the background is seen to move past in a constantly changing panoramic sequence. An **arc** shot, is another variation of a trucking movement. The camera circles around the stationary subject to reveal different aspects of the subject. It is especially effective on facial features that have been well-sculpted by a **key** light. (See figure 6-9.) The crab dolly is recommended for this and other moves listed above.

In larger studios where the crane mounts or crab dollies are used, other effective movements are also possible. **Craning,** or **booming** (up or down), involves raising or lowering the crane or boom arm. The effect is similar to a pedestal movement, except that much greater vertical distances can be covered. A **crab** shot (left or right) is similar to a trucking shot but because of the presence of a separate driver and four coordinated wheels that turn together, the angle of movement can be easily changed in mid-course into a number of different directions.

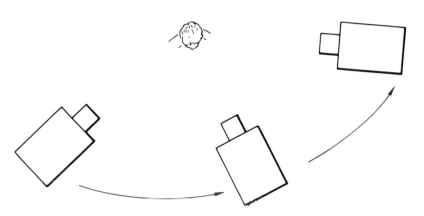

FIGURE 6-9

Camera arcing.

This move is accomplished mainly by a maneuver of the camera mount as the camera arcs around, keeping the lens pointed at the subject. The move is much easier to make with a crab dolly than with a tripod or pedestal mount.

One different kind of motion is the **arm move.** With a large crane, the boom arm or crane can be moved left or right in a lateral motion (while the base remains stationary). With both the crane and the crab mounts the camera operator retains control over the angle and tilt of the camera throughout all these moves.

An older move that is still used involves studio camera pedestals that were designed to facilitate a slight change in camera height. In this case, the word "pedestal" is used as a command verb as the camera operator is asked to *pedestal up* or *pedestal down.* (See figure 6-10.) Because these pedestal moves are limited to less than three feet at best, this effect is usually reserved for the crab dolly that extends from floor level to a height of more than six feet on most models.

It should be noted all these movements are difficult to accomplish when a zoom lens is at a position of high magnification (narrow angle). The slightest

unsteadiness during the camera movement is exaggerated because the **long lens,** while magnifying the subject, is also magnifying the shaky camera movement. To a lesser extent, the same problem is apparent with panning and tilting movements. Generally, *the longer the lens, the more difficult camera head or camera mount movement is going to be.*

Hand-Held Cameras

For out-of-studio production work, increasing use is being made of hand-held cameras. The shoulder-supported professional units, as well as the consumer oriented palm-sized camcorders, have popularized an informal and candid approach to production.

With amateurs, such hand-held camera work often results in poorly framed pictures, unsteady shots, and jerky camera movements (wobbly pans and shaky tilts) that may only be appropriate

FIGURE 6-10

Camera pedestaling.

In a pedestal
movement, the
entire camera and
mounting head are
moved straight up or
down by a system of
counterweights or
compressed air.

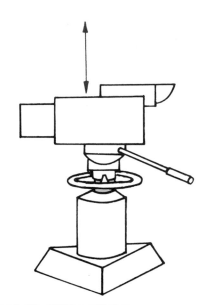

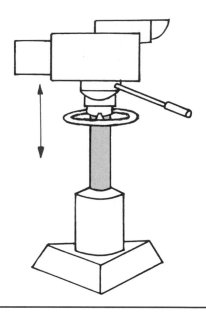

for small market news coverage and sub-
mission to *America's Funniest Home
Videos.* When used by professionals the
hand-held camera is considered indispensable for "reality based" television
and is used for both symphony and rock
concerts. It has long been recognized for
its contribution to news, sports, and public affairs productions.

Sophisticated gyroscopically balanced
systems are often used to steady hand-
held cameras for ambitious professional
EFP programs or film shoots. They are just
becoming available for smaller-scale and
amateur productions.

Robotic Camera Control

As a result of the rising costs of video production, the use of remotely controlled
cameras in news, public affairs, and sports
programs is on the rise. The cameras
shown in figure 6-11 are part of a group of
three that are operated from the studio

floor by one individual who is on a headset with the director. Most of the moves
and zoom changes have been programmed into a computer. Final control is
with the operator. For example, a camera
can be programmed to execute a shot involving a specific person, the location of
the pedestal on the floor, and the framing
of the zoom lens. "Joe, box shot left" describes the news anchor (to set pedestal
position) and the framing of a shot that
permits insertion of a video effect to left of
the performer. A final one touch control
makes this all happen.

6.2 CAMERA PERSPECTIVES

Before getting into specific camera operations, the beginning camera operator
should be aware of the different ways
that cameras can be employed in a television production.

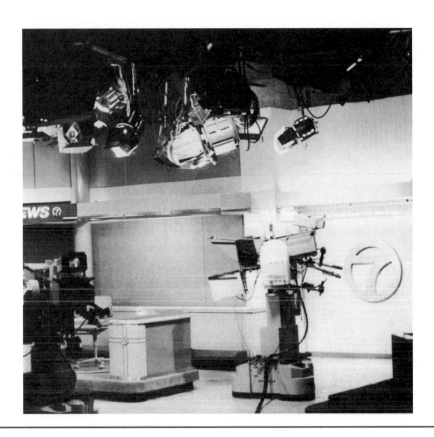

FIGURE 6-11

These Sony BVP 357 cameras are mounted on a robotics pedestal. They are part of a three unmanned camera system used in the production of the KABC-TV newscast. Three cameras are under the computerized remote control of an operator located in the studio.

Photo courtesy of KABC-TV

The Viewpoint of the Camera

Generally speaking, the television camera can be used to represent one of three different perspectives: **reportorial** (or **presentational**), **objective,** or **subjective.**

Reportorial (Presentational) Perspective

This viewpoint is used when a presenter or reporter is speaking directly to the audience through the camera. The speaker establishes eye contact with the camera and talks directly to the lens. This approach is most often seen in newscasts, corporate training programs, instructional TV lessons, some variety acts (for example, stand-up comedians), some political talks, demonstration programs, and so forth.

Camera work in this situation usually calls for a relatively close shot of the speaker—unless he or she has something to display or demonstrate for the camera. Basically, the camera-work is simply to give the viewer a reasonably comfortable look at the person speaking.

Objective Perspective

The easiest way to visualize this use of television is to imagine the camera as an eavesdropper. The camera is standing back, taking an objective look at what is going on. No one is addressing the camera directly; the camera is only observing the action. This type of camera work constitutes the bulk of what we see on television:

it includes virtually all drama, most variety and musical performances, talk shows and game shows (except when the host or announcer is directly addressing the audience through the camera), sporting events, and similar productions.

Camera techniques vary tremendously for objective production. A wide variety of panoramic shots, quick reaction shots, leisure camera movements, and rapid camera transitions are required for various formats. Virtually all techniques discussed in the remaining chapters are applicable to objective camera work.

Subjective Perspective

This particular camera use takes on special meaning when applied to dramatic productions. It refers to those occasional moments when the playwright director wants to place the viewer in the position of an actor. The camera actually becomes (usually for only a scene) a participant in the drama. It interacts with other players, and it views the world from the individual perspective of the character it is representing.

The camera, as the actor's eyes, is in the front seat of the car for the chase sequence; it is in the boxing ring, squaring off against the champion; it is trapped in the burning building, flames licking at the lens; it is drowning, with the waves lapping over the top of the camera-actor. The subjective camera is a specialized technique. Used with care and discretion it can have substantial impact.

These three perspectives are intermingled in many television productions. The newscast mixes reportorial and objective perspectives as the newscaster turns from the camera to interview an in-studio guest. The drama mixes objective with subjective techniques, and a touch of the reportorial-presentational is used as an actor turns to make a comment directly to

the audience.[1] The talk show jumps back-and-forth as the host and guests turn from their conversation with each other to talk directly to the viewer. As the camera operator is aware of these varying perspectives—and the production effects appropriate for each one—it is easier to achieve good camera work.

Field of View

The camera operator should be familiar with the various terms designating the size of the shot desired, or the **field of view.** Generally, most television shots can be related to three basic categories and one subtype. They are shown in figure 6-12.

The Wide Shot

The wide-angle shot is sometimes called a **long shot (LS)** in that its perspective is far enough away from a person that the entire body and quite a bit of the surroundings are included. Often, the features in the face of a performer are not exactly distinguishable at this distance. By its production use, is also known as an **establishing shot** when used in the beginning of a production (or segment) because it relates those people involved in a program not only to each other, but also to the setting and circumstances of that program. In drama and in other applications these wider shots are also necessary whenever people move from one part of the set to another. It can be used as a closing shot to signal to the audience that we are pulling back from the action—out of the drama—as it comes to a close. The wide shot could thus be said to generally communicate an *objective* view of the scene or situation.

---

1. The impact of mixing various camera perspectives can be quite striking and original, as in "It's Garry Shandling's Show" where the host/actor frequently breaks the proscenium arch to talk directly to the audience.

EXTREME CLOSE-UP
(XCU)

CLOSE-UP
(CU)

MEDIUM SHOT
(MS)

LONG SHOT
(LS)

FIGURE 6-12

Basic television shots.

In addition to these basic shots, many other designations and modifications are possible, such as the "extreme long shot," the "medium long shot," and the "medium close-up."

The Medium Shot (MS)

These shot designations are to some degree relative to their use and the artistic concepts of the director. What is a long shot for one dramatic segment could be considered a medium shot in another situation. Generally, however, a medium shot of a person includes most of the body or perhaps even two people. The medium shot is probably the basic shot in standard television production. It is used to convey much of the dialogue in drama and most of the action in talk shows, game shows, variety programs, and many other studio productions. Medium shots are designed to include gestures but not position moves. Depending upon their use they could be either *objective* or *subjective* in what they communicate.

The Close-Up (CU)

The close-up shot—with its sense of physical intimacy—can probe the individual and personal aspects of what a program is communicating. It is designed to be *subjective*. The eyes and facial expressions provide important insight into the full meaning of a person's words. In many dramatic situations—as well as in many reportorial-presentational

circumstances—the close-up is the only way we can get insight into the emotional state of a person or performer.

The close-up is usually defined as a shot consisting of the subject's head and top of shoulders. The **extreme close-up** (**ECU** or **XCU**) showing less than a person's full face (see figure 6-12) is most often used to intensify the emotion of a dramatic situation or musical performance. When these shots are used carefully, they can add the right artistic effect at the right moment. A close-up shot may, of course, be used to view objects other than a person. It may be a close-up of some item that has importance to the narrative of a drama. In a commercial it may be the product that is examined in more detail.

Many programs obviously call for a wider range of shots, or fields of view, than these three categories. Many times a director will want to establish a panoramic scene or cover the sweep of action with a very wide shot. If characters are so far away that they are hardly identifiable as specific individuals, the shot can be labeled an **extreme long shot** (**ELS** or **XLS**).

The process of alternating between the long shot and close-up segments of a program is possibly the most important element in the communicative language of both film and television. This basic principle was discovered by pioneers such as Edwin Porter and D. W. Griffith during the early days of the motion picture. They realized that by moving the camera into a closer position they could accomplish what is automatically done by the eye and the mind. While the scope of human vision is almost 180 degrees, we immediately isolate and particularize the focus of our attention to a single person or object when the brain is motivated by a stimulus such as motion or sound. Cutting from a wide-angle to a close-up camera shot is much the same process, except that the distance factor is greatly reduced by lens magnification.

6.3 PICTURE COMPOSITION

Much has been written on the subject of picture composition and the related concepts that deal with the cumulative effect of a series of picture images. As in motion picture, the main concern of television is usually the human element. Sets, props, and graphic arts have an important auxiliary function, but it is people we watch—the movements of their bodies and the expressions on their faces. When one considers the viewer sitting at some distance from a nineteen-inch or twenty-five-inch screen, the positioning of those faces and bodies assumes a critical importance.

As we discuss the following elements of framing, headroom, lead room, depth composition, angle of elevation, balance, and movement, keep in mind that these various "rules" that have evolved as part of the grammar of the medium should be considered *guidelines.* As with any artistic effort, there is always room for a new approach if it truly communicates to an audience. For the person who is just beginning to learn the disciplines of creative activity, the lessons passed on by more experienced people have much value. Once the rules have been mastered, they can be modified or even ignored as long as the creative person does so with a full understanding of the basic purposes of those guidelines.

Framing

Television directors (borrowing from the older traditions of their film cousins) have developed a simple terminology to describe the basic dimension of a shot to the camera operator. The scope of a shot is described in terms of that portion of the body that is to be cut off by the bottom edge of the picture. Thus a *full shot, thigh shot* or *chest shot* quickly communicates the desired framing of a person or persons in the picture.

Equally useful are the terms *single, two-shot,* or *three-shot,* which describe the number of people to be included in the shot. Other descriptive labels have evolved to specify certain kinds of desired shots. For example, an **over-the-shoulder shot (O/S),** as illustrated in figure 6-17 on page 143, might be called for in a situation when two people are facing each other in a conversation (such as a dramatic scene or an interview program). This is a shot favoring one person (who generally is facing the camera) framed by the back of the head and shoulder of the person with his or her back to the camera.

Headroom

An important discipline for all camera operators is that of consistently maintaining an adequate amount of **headroom.** This term refers to the space between the top of a subject's head and the top of the frame. When this distance is not observed, the results can be somewhat distracting. (See figure 6-13.)

WRONG   WRONG

CORRECT

FIGURE 6-13

Correct headroom framing.

Although it is largely a matter of subjective judgment and artistic "feel," it is important that the camera operator *always be aware* of the headroom on every shot. Too much headroom is as bad as too little.

FIGURE 6-14

Correct headroom on different-sized shots.

As a general rule—with many exceptions—the longer a shot is, the more headroom it should have.

It is especially important that headroom distance be uniform among all cameras on any production. A helpful guide for shot consistency is to place the eyes of subjects at the point of an imaginary line approximately one-third of the way down from the top of the picture. In close-up shots, the framing is best with the eyes slightly below the line; in wider shots, they should be slightly above the line. (See figure 6-14.)

There is a very good technical reason why headroom distance is carefully watched by camera operators and directors. Due to several factors, most home television sets lose up to 10 or 15 percent of the picture area at the outer edge. As a result, framing that would appear to be adequate on the studio monitor will actually result in a **cropping** of heads on the home receiver.

Lead Room

When speakers or performers directly address the camera (reportorial perspective),

BAD   BETTER   BEST

FIGURE 6-15

Proper lead room or "talk space."

The camera operator should always intuitively give talent additional space in the direction in which he or she is looking.

BAD   CORRECT

FIGURE 6-16

Proper lead room for a moving subject.

Whenever a person is moving across the screen, the camera operator should visually anticipate the flow of movement allowing the viewer to see where the subject is going.

they generally are centered in the frame, unless a foreground object or over-the-shoulder visual effect is to be included in the frame. When subjects are speaking to one another, however, as in a dramatic presentation or a public affairs panel discussion (objective perspective), the framing is much more attractive if there is an added amount of **lead room** (talk space) in the side of the frame to which they are speaking. By the same token, a distracting, crowded effect is created if the framing is such that the face of the subject is placed too close to the frame edge. (See figure 6-15.)

The concept of lead room applies even more strongly to moving subjects. If a person is moving laterally across the screen, it is important to allow lead space in front of the person. Lead the talent; do not follow. (See figure 6-16.)

Depth Composition

The television message is transmitted by means of a two-dimensional medium. To simulate some feeling of depth, the director has a number of options that involve lighting, camera work, the set, and the placement

FIGURE 6-17
Depth staging.

The over-the-shoulder shot (*left*) generally presents a more dynamic, interesting, and aesthetically pleasing picture than the flat double-profile two-shot (*right*). By shooting the person behind the desk from an angle (*left*), a more inviting and vigorous effect can be achieved than with a formal head-on flat shot (*right*).

of performers. One method is to make sure that the performers are separated from the set in the background both by their physical positions and by the constructive use of lighting. In this situation it is important to portray something familiar like the interior of a room or office so as to provide a feeling of scale or perspective. If a plain or abstract background is used, the viewer has no yardstick against which to gauge the distance from the subject to background.

Foreground objects can add significantly to the feeling of depth. By framing some nearby objects off to one side of the picture or along the bottom of the picture, the subject in the background is placed in greater relief. Care must be taken, however, not to force an unnatural effect for its own sake as this will undoubtedly appear contrived to the viewer.

Whenever possible, depth composition can be achieved with the arrangement (**blocking**) of talent. If several people appear in a scene, try to arrange them so that some are closer to the camera than others. Nothing is deadlier than three or four people stretched out in a straight line, all equidistant from the camera. In a two-shot, an over-the-shoulder shot as a rule is preferred to a flat two-shot of a double profile. (See figure 6-17.)

A feeling of depth can also be achieved by careful use of angles. If a shot calls for someone to be sitting behind a desk, the camera can get a much more interesting shot by trucking right or left and shooting the desk and subject from an angle. (Of course, the dramatic context might call for a formal head-on shot of a judge or stern employer.)

Angle of Elevation

For most conventional composition, you want the camera to be shooting at a relatively level angle to the subject. Generally speaking, try to place the camera lens at eye level with the talent. This is fairly normal when the talent is standing. With seated talent, however, this means that you must pedestal down so the camera is as low as the talent. To achieve this level angle, most "talk sets" (news programs, interviews, discussion shows, talk shows) will be staged on a raised platform or **riser** (see figure 6-18).

If you cannot avoid shooting down into an interview or discussion set, the steep angle can be minimized somewhat by using a longer lens setting and dollying back away from the set. The farther back you can get, the less steep the angle will be. Of course, you pay for this by demanding

FIGURE 6-18

This modern news set is staged on a platform to bring the newscasters up to camera eye level.

Photo courtesy of KNBC, Los Angeles

more studio space and by settling for potentially shakier camera work—the longer the lens, the more camera unsteadiness is magnified (see section 6.1).

There are times, however, when—for dramatic effect—you will not want to be shooting the talent at a level angle. To portray an actor as being overwhelmed, submissive, or downtrodden, you will shoot the actor from a higher elevation. Shooting from a high angle implies control and dominance over the individual. On the other hand, if you want to give a character power and authority, you should shoot that actor from a low angle. By placing the viewer in the lowered position, you endow the character with force and strength.

Balance

Many beginning camera operators try to achieve a pleasing composition by striving for **symmetrical balance.** They try to place the most important element directly in the center of the picture and/or try to balance picture components with equal elements equidistant from the center. This kind of mechanical or symmetrical balancing can lead to very stiff, dull, formal pictures.

A more dynamic kind of composition is **asymmetrical balance,** wherein a lightweight object some distance from the center of the picture can balance a heavier object closer to the center (similar to a seesaw with a light person at the end of the board balancing a heavier person seated close to the center).

Another way to avoid centralization of picture elements is to think in terms of the **rule of thirds.** Imagine the television screen divided horizontally and vertically into thirds. If major pictorial elements are placed at the points where the lines intersect, the result is a more pleasing balance than if perfect symmetry is achieved. (See figure 6-19.)

Movement

A final consideration of picture composition is the temporal and fluid quality of the medium. Since an important element of television is *movement* of one kind or another, pictures rarely remain static for any period of time. Even in a discussion program, the

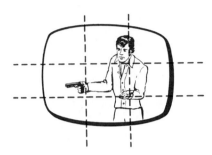

FIGURE 6-19

Asymmetrical balance and the rule of thirds.

Note how the two main focal points—the face and the hand holding the gun—are located at the intersections of the thirds.

guests will turn their heads as the conversation shifts to another person. In large musical or dramatic productions, the set and other background elements must be taken into consideration. For these reasons, proper composition involves a constant process of adjustment and an exercise of discretion in matters of balance and proportion.

6.4 OPERATING TECHNIQUES

At this point, the beginning camera operator should feel ready to start working with the cameras. A few words about some operating procedures—especially some safety precautions—should, however, be mentioned first.

Standard Procedures

The following are several basic standard procedures that every camera operator should always observe:

1. Put on your headset; make sure you are in contact with the control room before doing anything else.
2. Most cameras have some sort of lens capping device that shuts down the lens between operations. They

should always be used so that unattended cameras, especially those with tubes, are not damaged by bright lights.

Virtually every studio camera has provisions on the camera mounting head to lock the pan and tilt mechanisms. The pan and tilt locks should always be securely engaged whenever the camera is not in use. Release the locks, making certain you have a firm grip on the panning handle. Although all mounting heads should be balanced so that the camera head will not lurch forward or fall backward when unlocked, it is conceivable that something could go wrong and the camera could be damaged. Once you have the pan and tilt heads unlocked, *never let go of the panning handle* without first locking the mounting head.

4. In all camera operations, always be alert to the possibility of an accident, which could result in the camera falling over or off its mount. Check all tripod leg adjustments; make sure the camera mounting head is securely fastened. With lightweight tripods, be especially careful of the possibility of tipping over the whole camera mount (for example, by stumbling over a camera cable).
5. Never stand on the camera cable. The **coaxial cable** consists of numerous individual strands of wire. Any unnecessary pressure on the cable can break some of these fragile wires.
6. After the production, reverse the procedures you followed in setting up the camera. Lock the pan and tilt heads before doing anything else. Cap the lens and remove your headset.
7. Return the camera to its storage area and coil its cable in a figure eight pattern.

FIGURE 6-20

The efficient use of the setup and rehearsal time is the mark of a motivated cameraperson. Thinking through the sequence of shots and checking out framing always provide that extra edge during the production itself.

The process of developing all the above actions into the regular disciplines of your production activity is an important step toward professionalism.

Operating Hints

Aside from these rules, several other operational disciplines and techniques will help you in most studio situations. Check to see exactly what procedures are followed in your studio.

Camera Setup

Even before you are ready to set up your camera, see if you can help with other studio preparations. Can you be of assistance during the early stages of lighting and staging setup? In union studios, of course, this is not allowed; but in many university, corporate, and educational closed-circuit operations, all crew members are expected to assist in all positions. Always be ready to help out wherever needed. This is part of the discipline of a successful team member.

Check out all connections, locks, adjustments, and controls on your camera. Make sure everything is in working order. Do not try to adjust the specific camera controls (except for focus and viewfinder adjustments) without explicit guidance or permission from the person who has adjusted the brightness and color balance. (See section 5.5.) Check your f-stop to be sure that it conforms with what has been established by the technicians.

Many camera mounting heads have adjustments that will apply a variable amount of drag or resistance to the pan and tilt controls. Depending upon the explicit production requirements, you may want your pan and tilt controls rather loose and free or you may want them tightened up. Adjust them accordingly. (See figure 6-20.)

FIGURE 6-21

This Panasonic WV-F500 S-VHS camera is designed with multiple features but is priced to be within the range of educational and industrial production budgets. The video system utilizes three one-half inch 380,000 pixel CCDs. The camera setup for lighting conditions in five different scenes can be programmed into a memory unit for quick retrieval. There are four audio channels. Similar models have a direct "docking" feature that allows removal and separate use of the recorder section.

Photo courtesy of Panasonic Broadcast and Television Systems Co.

Rehearsals

In general, do not abuse the **PL intercom** (section 3.5). Quite a few production positions will be using the same line. Use it for speaking only when absolutely necessary and develop the ability to *listen* carefully. Directors and others who give instructions should develop the habit of clearly stating key information *one time* when they have everyone's attention. It saves endless repetition of the same information, especially while the setup period is in progress.

During the early technical or blocking rehearsal, familiarize yourself as thoroughly as possible with the production and your role in it. Make certain you have floor assistance wherever and whenever you need it—someone to handle any

graphics, someone to pull your cable in a difficult move. If you are working with a boom or crane camera, make sure you coordinate all moves with your camera assistants. Rehearse all dolly and trucking moves as well as pedestal changes. Make sure that helpers can provide plenty of cable for all moves. Practice all zoom transitions and related focus considerations. If you have been provided with a **shot sheet** (a list of your camera shots—see section 12.5), use it to think through the sequence of production.

The efficiency of the final production time is very dependent upon the care exercised by the camera operator during setup and rehearsal periods. (See figure 6-21.) Even the latest "state of the art" camera is of little value in the hands of an untrained and/or unmotivated person. However, when controlled by a caring, responsible operator, today's cameras become instruments of true artistic creativity.

On-the-Air Production

In general, be extra alert. Be prepared for anything. Anticipate problems. (Your camera cable may tangle; your zoom lens may go out of focus; your camera may get caught in a microphone cable.) Assume nothing. Television professionals (and others) have a phrase to describe this potential for things going awry at exactly the worst moment. Called Murphy's Law, it states, "Anything that can go wrong, probably will go wrong." It is really their way of reminding themselves to be constantly alert for the unexpected and prepared to quickly solve problems.

Prepare and anticipate all of your moves. Check your focus and if necessary preset your lens every time you get on a new long shot. If camera-to-subject distance changes significantly between shots, focus throughout the zoom move may not be maintained. Make certain that you are zoomed out to a sufficiently wide-angle position before attempting any camera moves (such as dolly, truck, arc). Even slight movements of the camera head are very noticeable when the zoom is in a highly magnified position. If you are using a free-wheeling tripod, be certain your casters are set, all pointing in the correct position, before trying any camera mount moves.

Always be ready for your next shot. Use your shot sheet if the director is working from one; otherwise, anticipate your next shot based upon the rehearsal. Every camera should be equipped with **tally lights** on the front of the camera (for the talent) and in the viewfinder (for the camera operator). These indicator lights signal that the camera is on the air or a part of a two-camera visual combination.

Watch your tally light; break to your next shot as soon as you are off the air—but not before.

If you are shooting a spontaneous, unrehearsed or a semi-scripted program, do all you can to help the director. Try to anticipate shots the director may need. Quite often directors will ask the camera operators to "hunt" for a shot of opportunity in an ad-lib situation. Do not, however, *ever* presume to tell a director what shot to take. In some panel or interview programs, the director will have good reasons for you not to move from your basic shot. That shot may be the constant cover shot around which other camera shots are able to be quickly changed. Stay with an assigned shot until other instructions are given.

Watch the talent for signs that will telegraph any moves on his or her part. When the talent leans forward, shifts feet, looks toward the next set element, it may mean a shift to or from your camera. If you are to do a follow shot, be ready to move with the first step or the rising from a chair. Again, anticipate; be alert and enjoy.

SUMMARY

Camera movements include those facilitated by the camera head and those facilitated by the camera mount. A *cradle* or *cam* head is used for *panning* and *tilting*. Various camera mounts—*tripods, pedestals, cranes,* and *crab-dollies*—are used for movements such as *dollies, trucks, arcs, cranes, booms, crabs, arm moves,* and *pedestals*. Sometimes cameras are *hand-held* or moved by *robotic* camera controls.

Three different camera perspectives can be employed: *reportorial (presentational)* (the camera is addressed directly); *objective* (the camera is an eavesdropper); and *subjective* (the camera is an actor).

The field of view of a camera can be thought of as consisting of *wide shots, medium shots,* and *close-ups*—with quite a few variations and combinations. In determining picture composition, shots are labeled descriptively—such as *full shot, thigh shot, chest shot, single, two-shot, three-shot,* and *over-the-shoulder shot.*

Headroom and *lead room* (talk space) are two important *framing* considerations. The illusion of *depth* in a television picture can be enhanced with proper background considerations, foreground objects, *blocking* of talent, and use of staging angles. Generally, the camera lens should be at *eye level* with the talent. *Asymmetrical balance,* which is generally more interesting than *symmetrical balance,* can be partially achieved by using the *rule of thirds.* Picture composition also has to be achieved in *movement*—as television is a temporal medium, constantly changing.

Before operating a camera, the camera operator should follow several *standard procedures.* There also are a number of *operating hints* the camera operator should be aware of during the setup period, during the rehearsals, and during the actual production.

Camera shots are combined with other pictorial elements. The sets and props used in the camera shots must be taken into consideration. Often the live camera shots are combined with graphics. These pictorial elements, sets and graphics, are the subject of the next chapter.

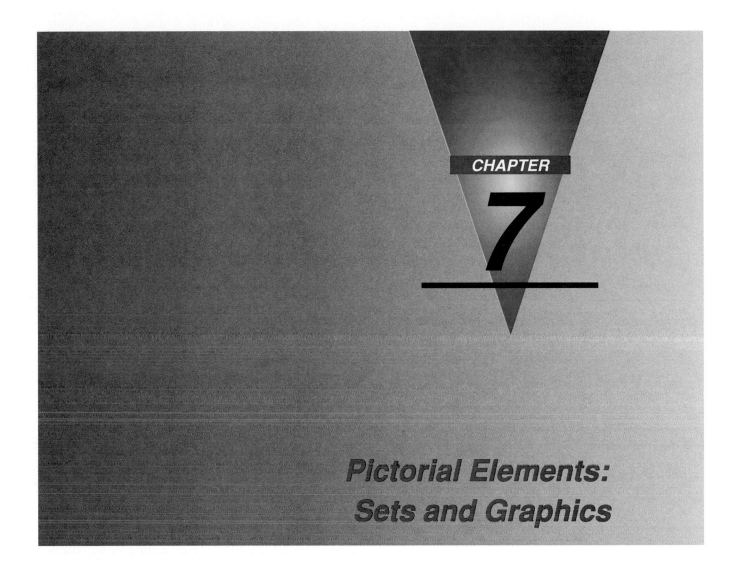

CHAPTER

7

**Pictorial Elements:
Sets and Graphics**

I n this chapter, we will examine the two major pictorial elements that make up the visual aspects of television production—graphics and sets. Although these two topics will be discussed separately throughout most of the chapter, they both encompass several concepts that will be considered first, namely pictorial design functions and pictorial design factors.

7.1 PICTORIAL DESIGN FUNCTIONS

Pictorial elements (like many other facets of television) are multifunctional. They can be used to convey information, and they serve to enhance or create emotional reactions within the audience members.

Informational Aspects

First, the *informational aspects of pictorial design* must be considered. They are concerned with conveying appropriate information cues to the audience as accurately and efficiently as possible. In the case of a dramatic setting, you ordinarily want to tell the audience as much as possible about the time and locale of the action. Where is the scene taking place? What is the historical period? What time of day is it? You may also want to give other pictorial cues. What is the status of the main character? Where does he or she live? (Of course, there are many dramatic programs where this type of information is deliberately concealed from the audience to create suspense or dramatic surprise.)

Nondramatic programs also need to convey this kind of information data. Are we in a newsroom? A classroom? A corporate office? Are we on a stage in front of a live audience? Are we in a pulpit? How much do we need to tell the viewers about where they are and what they should know about their surroundings? All television staging considerations should start out with these types of questions.

With graphics, the informational considerations are even more important. The overwhelming use of graphics—especially for simpler productions and basic formats—is to convey information. What is the name of the program? What is the name of the person talking? How much of our tax dollar goes to education? What does the race course look like? How does the piston work? How bad was the accident? In designing graphics, the need for clarity is paramount. The director and graphics person must always be asking, "How can I get this information across as clearly and efficiently as possible?"

Emotional Aspects

Second, the *emotional* or *psychological functions of pictorial design* must be considered. Many subtle messages can be conveyed by the total production design. All the scenic elements—sets, props, furniture—combine to give a "feel" or "image" to the program. In a news program, do you want the image of an advanced technological communications center, of an abstract setting (figure 7-1), or of a working newsroom (figure 7-2)? In an instructional TV program, do you want the image of a typical academic setting or of a research lab? In a religious program, do you want the image of a traditional church service or of an avant-garde contemporary movement? In a variety program, do you want the image of a conventional stage presentation or the electronic collage of a music video? Again, it is important that the director and designer begin with these types of questions before any decisions are made regarding the design or assemblage of set pieces or graphics.

In dramatic programs, of course, the overall *atmosphere* or *mood* is very important. Staging elements—combined with lighting—will tell us much about the mystery of an event, the state of mind of the hero, the lurking tragedy, the atmosphere of a family gathering, the majesty of an accomplishment, the power behind a particular move, the potential danger behind a closed door, the emptiness of a certain thought. The designer should always be concerned with maintaining or building the mood or feeling of every particular scene.

The emotional function of design also includes creating a given *style* or *continuity*

FIGURE 7-1

An abstract news set previously used for local news program.

Photo courtesy of KABC-TV, Los Angeles

FIGURE 7-2

A view of a working newsroom used as actual on-the-air background for a news set.

Photo courtesy of KCBS-TV, Los Angeles

to a program—helping to maintain a unity throughout the entire production. In the use of graphics, for instance, it would be jarring to establish a pattern of cartoons to illustrate a certain process and then suddenly switch to a series of detailed photographs. Several years ago, a church group produced a syndicated variety program dealing with the broad theme of the family. It was a composite of serious vignettes, vocal numbers, comedy sketches, talks, and dances and featured many different performers and guest stars. The production very easily could have fallen apart into many miniprograms; however, the entire program was held together by its scenic design. Every segment of the program was staged on and around one scenic unit—a large, white, abstract open set combining several different levels, platforms, and stairs. Because it had a scenic unity, the production had a continuity that it otherwise could have lost.

Thus, every pictorial design should serve both an *informational* function and an *emotional* function. The set should not only tell us what time of day it is, but also give us a hint as to what is going to happen this day. The graphic should not only give us information, but also emphasize how important the information is.

7.2 PICTORIAL DESIGN FACTORS

Artists and critics discourse long and eloquently about the many different factors that constitute aesthetic criteria—unity, harmony, texture, color, rhythm, proportion, and so forth. It is beyond the scope of this book to get into any detailed treatise on aesthetics of the still and moving picture. The beginning production student should be aware, however, of at least three pictorial design factors: (1) balance and mass; (2) lines and angles; and (3) tone and color.

Balance and Mass

The concept of balance was introduced in section 6.3 in connection with camera work. Asymmetrical balance is generally preferred over formal symmetrical balance. The larger a mass, the nearer it must be to the center of the scene in order to preserve a sense of balance with a smaller mass (figure 7-3). In addition, the placement of mass within a

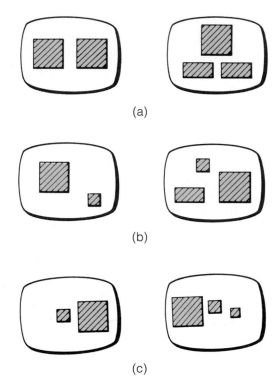

FIGURE 7-3
Symmetrical and asymmetrical balance.

(a) Symmetrical balance usually results in a rigidity and precision that is usually not desired—except for certain formal settings. (b) Asymmetrical balance usually is more interesting and dynamic, resulting in a more fluid and creative mood—and just as well balanced aesthetically. (c) An unbalanced picture can result, however, if care is not taken to position the asymmetrical elements with respect to their weight and mass. Temporarily, this may be desired.

scenic element will tend to affect the stability of the picture. A heavy mass in the bottom part of the picture implies firmness, solidarity, support, importance. A heavier mass in the top part of the picture projects more instability, suspense, impermanence (figure 7-4). These considerations of balance and placement have strong implications for the design of sets and graphics as well as for

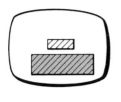   

(a)   (b)

FIGURE 7-4

Location of mass in the picture.

(a) Heavy weight in the bottom of the frame tends to give an impression of stability and security.
(b) If the top of the picture contains more mass than the bottom, the result is a feeling of
uneasiness and suspense.

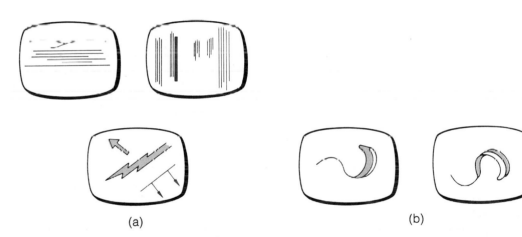

(a)   (b)

FIGURE 7-5

The effect of straight and curved lines.

(a) Horizontal lines are restful, inactive, stable. Vertical lines suggest solemnity, dignity, dominance.
Diagonal lines represent action, movement, impermanence. (b) Curved lines generally imply
change, beauty, grace, flowing movement. With an upward open curve there is a feeling of freedom
and openness. A downward open curve has more of a feeling of pressure and restriction.

camera composition. A graphic title with lettering in the bottom of the frame projects a solid, strong opening. A scenic unit with heavy ornamentation near the top implies a feeling of uneasiness and suspense.

Lines and Angles

The use of dominant lines is one of the strongest elements available to the scenic designer. Straight lines suggest firmness, rigidity, directness, strength. Curved or rounded lines imply softness, elegance, movement. The direction of the dominant lines in a picture will carry strong connotations. Horizontal lines represent serenity, inactivity, openness; vertical lines are dignified, important, strong; diagonals imply action, imbalance, instability, insecurity. (See figure 7-5.)

Lines and angles can also be used to reinforce or exaggerate perspective, giving

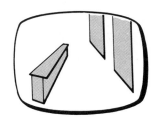
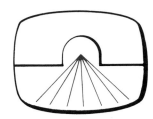

FIGURE 7-6

Lines and perspective.

A false perspective can be created by careful use of scenic elements and even by painting perspective lines on the studio floor.

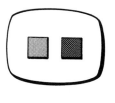
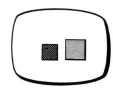

(a) (b)

FIGURE 7-7

Tone and balance.

(a) A darker tone tends to imply more mass; thus the darker tone will overbalance the lighter mass (*left*). A smaller dark mass can be used to balance a lighter mass that is larger (*right*). (b) A darker tone or darker color at the top of the picture or scenic element will tend to imply a top-heavy feeling of depression (*left*). The lighter tone or brighter color at the top gives a feeling of more solidarity and normalcy (*right*).

more of an illusion of depth. Painted on the studio floor, *false perspective* lines can reinforce a great feeling of depth. Lines can also be worked into other scenic elements. This kind of false perspective is limiting, however, in that the illusion works from only one specific camera location. (See figure 7-6.)

Tone and Color

The predominant tones determine, to a great extent, the overall emotional image of a production. Light tones result in a delicate, cheerful, happy, trivial feeling, whereas dark tones result in a feeling that is heavy, somber, serious, forceful. Tone

also affects balance. A dark tone carries more mass, weighs more, and can be used to balance a larger mass that is light in color or tone.

The position of various tones or blocks of dark and light mass in a picture also affects its stability and emotional quality. A dark mass at the top of a picture tends to induce a heavy, unnatural feeling of entrapment and depression; heavier tones in the bottom of a picture give it more of a stable base. (See figure 7-7.)

As mentioned in section 5.2, color is usually discussed in terms of three characteristics: **Hue** is the actual color base itself (red, green, purple, orange, and so forth); **saturation** refers to the strength or intensity of a color, how far removed it is from a neutral or gray shade); and **brightness** (or *lightness*) indicates where the color would fall on a scale from light (white) to dark (black). The considerations mentioned for tone apply to color; for example, highly saturated colors (a vivid red) appear heavier—for purposes of balance—than unsaturated colors (a grayish red).

Various hues are also subjectively classified as *warm* (yellows and reds) or *cool* (blues and greens). Warm colors appear to be "heavier" than cool colors. Much of the secret of achieving good color balance is the art of mixing various hues that are compatible, balancing highly saturated colors with grayer shades, and selecting the right brightness of a particular hue (for example, baby blue rather than navy blue).

All these elements of design—balance, line, tone—must be kept in mind as you look specifically at the elements of graphic composition and set design.

7.3 COMPUTER GENERATED GRAPHICS

Many years ago most TV station graphics consisted of title cards made by applying rub-on or stick-on letters to sheets of cardboard that were then placed in front of the camera. Occasionally, stations had "high tech" equipment—metal type (circa 1889) which, when pressed onto a sheet of acetate with pigment on one side, melted an impression of the type onto a card, usually burning the operator's hand in the process. If a chart or graph was needed, an artist drew it by hand, sometimes aided by a compass and protractor. Those days are long gone. Now most graphics are constructed with the aid of a computer.

The Hardware

In order to create computer graphics, you need both equipment (**hardware**) and computer programs (**software**) that can be used to make the hardware operate.

The Development

The first electronic graphics device, which appeared in the 1970s, was called a **character generator (CG).** A person sitting at a keyboard could type program titles or credits and they would appear on a TV monitor ready to be sent out over the air. The first character generators were fairly unsophisticated. They usually only had one or two white **fonts** and words that were typed could not be stored; they were typed as they were needed during the course of a program.

What led to their sophistication was the rapid advancement of computer technology. As the storage and manipulation capabilities of computers grew, the simple character generator became much more flexible. Fonts, colors, sizes, backgrounds, and other features emerged with great rapidity. In addition to creating titles and credits, these devices could be used to create graphs, charts, and other abstract designs. They became known as **computer graphics generators,** although they are often still referred to as *CGs.*

The original character generators were *dedicated, proprietary* systems. In other words, all they could do was create graphics for TV screens; they could not be used for other computer chores such as developing spreadsheets or communicating with modems.

Many of today's computer graphics generators are still proprietary because they work best if they are designed for one specific function. Creating the elaborate graphics seen on TV today requires a fast processor, a great deal of **random access memory (RAM),** and huge amounts of hard disc storage space. A dedicated piece of equipment can best supply what is needed.

However, nowadays, many personal computers (Macintosh, Amiga, IBM) are being used to create video graphics. This same computer can be used to compose TV station memos, create budgets, and bill advertisers. Few computers with graphics programs on them are used for such a variety of chores, however. TV stations, networks, and production houses have become so enamored with graphics that they use at least one computer full time to create them.

The Equipment

Whether graphics are created with a dedicated system or a personal computer, several basic pieces of equipment are needed. First, there is the **CPU** or **central processing unit.** This is the microprocessing heart of the computer that does all the actual "computing."

Second, there is a computer **monitor,** which looks like but is not the same as a TV monitor. Most computer systems have high quality **RGB** (red-green-blue) monitors that do not break the picture information down into the chrominance and luminance channels used for broadcast signals. The RGB monitor picture is not an **NTSC (National Television System Committee)** broadcast signal. With an RGB signal, both the color rendition and resolution are sharper than in a broadcast monitor or TV set, a definite advantage for creating graphics. Often, a computer graphics workstation will also include a black-and-white monitor for information that relates to instructions for the particular graphics program that is being used.

Third, there is the **keyboard,** an integral part of any simple computer. This is used both for typing instructions to the CPU and for typing text directly onto the

screen. Often a computer graphics generator will have a **mouse** that can be used to give the computer instructions or to undertake simple drawing. Drawing is more likely to be accomplished through a **graphics tablet,** also called a *data tablet* or *bit pad.* This tablet is used with a special electronic pen to enter digitalized coordinates. In essence, it converts the pen's touch on the tablet to a precise position (defined by x and y coordinates) on the computer monitor. Therefore it allows direct artist input to the computer using the electronic pen. It takes but a few hours for a graphic artist to get used to creating artwork by looking at the TV screen while "drawing" on a tablet located below the screen. (See figure 7-8.) A different type of drawing device found with computer systems is a **light pen** that directly touches the screen but operates on a principle similar to that of the graphics tablet.

Another component would have to be **input memory devices.** Most computers used a combination of **floppy disc drives**—input drives utilizing removable discs (either the familiar 5¼ inch or 3½ inch size) and internal **hard drive discs, CD-ROMs (compact disc/read-only memory),** and newer **optical disc** formats. In more sophisticated computer systems, another component is a **digitizing camera**—one that picks up picture information, either graphics material or a live scene, and immediately converts it to a digitized format that can be stored in the computer. Then the image can be manipulated by computer instructions—rotating images, squeezing and elongating the picture, changing colors, and so forth.

Because computer graphics generators do not send out an NTSC signal, the output must be changed to NTSC before it can be incorporated within a video system. Usually a special video board is installed in the CPU to accomplish this conversion,

FIGURE 7-8

A graphics tablet
and digitalizing pen
are basic tools for
any electronic artist.

although Amiga computers and some of the proprietary systems come with a built-in NTSC output. Sometimes this card is sold as part of the software package.

Obviously not all computer graphics systems have the same components. Ones that are going to be used primarily for opening and closing credits may have only a CPU, monitor, and keyboard. The more components, the greater the flexibility—and the greater the cost. Figure 7-9 shows a system that would lend itself well to both titles and drawings.

Software

Anyone who has mastered a word processing program will feel at home creating titles and credits with any of the many computer graphics programs on the market

(for example, Broadcast Titler, PrimeTime, Media Composer, or Video Titler). Although no two programs are alike, they are all menu driven. Operations such as choosing fonts, increasing or decreasing letter size, centering, underlining, and justifying are selected by typing on the keyboard or clicking the mouse. Words, pages, partial pages, or entire displays can be stored, retrieved, deleted, moved, or copied, just as they can be when you type a term paper using a word processing program.

Lettering Features

Because the words are being composed to be read from a TV screen, there are additional elements that are not regular parts of word processing programs. For example, because words must often appear over video footage, letters may need *borders* or

FIGURE 7-9

This DF/X equipment is part of an editing suite that includes a graphics table, a mouse, and a keyboard.

Photo courtesy of Digital F/X

shadows around them so that they stand out. Figure 7-10 shows a variety of CG lettering styles, some with borders or shadows.

Color is also important for TV lettering. Most programs have a large palette, often called a *paintbox* to choose from, and each letter can be a different color and have a different color border if so desired. Usually it is easy to change the color of letters if they do not look appropriate over whatever is in the background. (See figure 7-11.)

Graphics Features

Background creation is also part of graphics generation. Although words sometimes appear over video footage, at other times they need a colored background. The color palette is available to create these backgrounds, along with ones that look like wallpaper, candy sprinkles, tile, and other forms.

Drawings and other graphics use additional features of graphics programs. Usually the paintbox includes several size "brushes" so that the artist, using a mouse, graphics tablet, or light pen, can draw lines of various thickness. Some programs supply common shapes such as circles and squares to help artists construct their images. Others have model line and bar graphs to make construction easy.

Sophisticated programs allow the artist to rotate whatever has been drawn in order to see it from various angles. Shadows and light reflections can be incorporated to give a three-dimensional effect. Once an artist has drawn a particular figure, the computer can duplicate that figure anywhere else on the screen or make it larger or smaller. Figure 7-12 illustrates a number of these features.

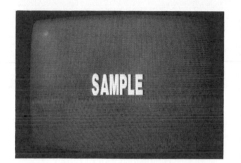

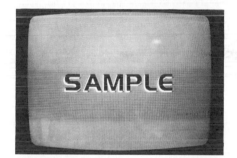

FIGURE 7-10

Some of the lettering
variations available
with many character
generators.

Top left: Helvetica
Bold type font.

Top right: Helvetica
Regular with border.

*Left, second from
top:* Helvetica Bold
condensed.

*Right, second from
top:* Helvetica Bold
expanded.

Left, middle: Handel
Gothic with drop
shadow.

Right, middle:
Handel Gothic with
border.

Left, next to bottom:
Futura Book with
drop shadow.

*Right, next to
bottom:* Futura Book
italics.

Bottom left: City
Bold.

Bottom right:
Bookman Bold, a
type font with
modified serifs.

FIGURE 7-11

Most character generators allow the operator to mix type fonts and styles and repeat type images in a variety of sizes and colors.

162

(a)

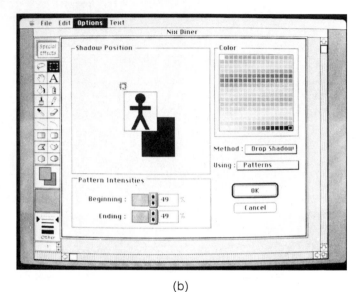

(b)

(c)

(d)

FIGURE 7-12

Moderately priced computer graphics programs can provide a wide variety of visual capabilities.

(a) All graphics programs are "menu-driven," which enables artist/operators to select many options (color, perspective, and shadowing effects in this example) from an on-screen menu. (b) In this example from *Pixel Paint* the artist positions the symbolic "sun" (located above and to the left of the stick figure) to determine exactly where the shadow effect (the large black rectangle) will appear on the finished art. (c) Original artwork can be created, usually using a mouse. In this *Adobe Illustrator* example, any individual detail—such as the bamboo leaves—can be repeated with a simple command. (d) Many variations of shading, texture, and color can be added to any original or "captured" artwork. (e) Starting with a conventional map, the artist can add any lettering, colors, special effects, and—in this case—distorted perspective desired. (f) The artist

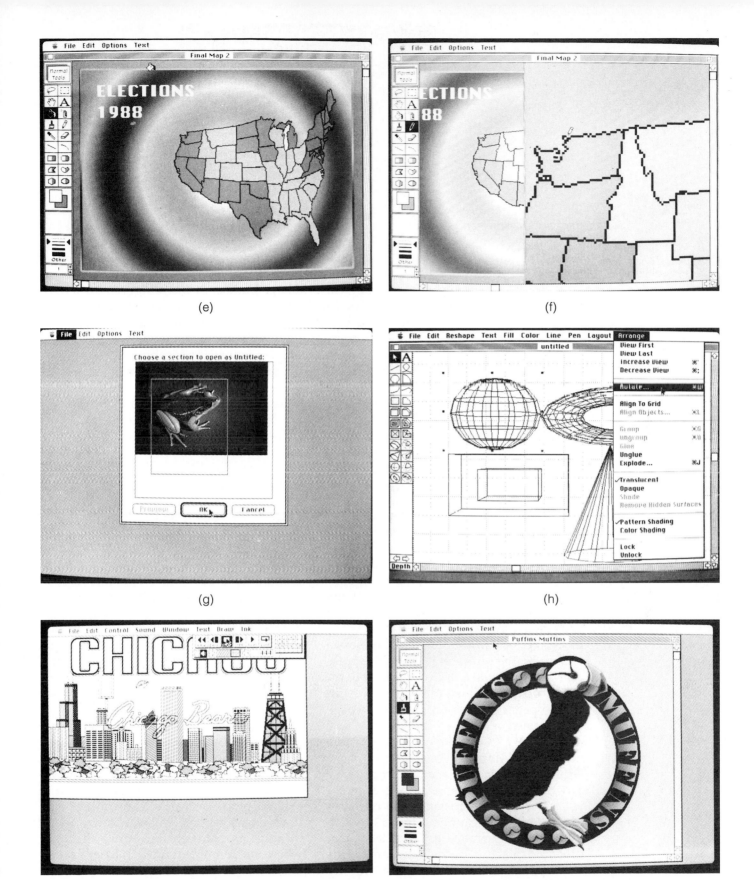

can work with magnified insets to change detail on any part of the artwork. (g) Using a series of grids and layout rectangles, the artist can size and position artwork in any desired configuration. (h) The *MAC 3-D* program allows the artist to create simulated three-dimensional models and rotate them to any desired perspective. (i) Simple animation effects can be created with modestly priced programs. In this *Videoworks II* sequence for example, the football (located below the "I" in "Chicago") is tumbling through the air. (j) In this finished piece of art, the original drawing of the puffin was created on *Adobe Illustrator* and the lettering was created, colored, shaded, and rotated into the circle by *Pixel Paint*.

Display Characteristics

Because the titles and graphics are going to be displayed on a screen, graphics programs include a large variety of display options. For example, you can tie together all the pages of closing credits so they *roll* from the bottom to the top of the screen as they are keyed over the closing shots of a program. Words can be made to *crawl* across the bottom of the screen as is done with stock and bond prices during a financial program. In the same manner, words or drawings can *wipe, cut, flip, spin, invert, warp, flash,* or look like a *page turn.*

Display characteristics can be programmed ahead of time so that when the credits or other graphics are called for, they will function flawlessly. For example, the speed of the roll (fast, medium, slow) can be predetermined as can the *dwell* time for the last page of graphics—the amount of time it stays on the screen before disappearing. However, provisions are also made so that the computer graphics generator operator can control when the graphics appear. For example, some programs have a **GPI (general purpose interface)** option that allows graphics to appear on the screen only when the operator hits the space bar of the keyboard. Many programs also allow you to skip certain pages of a series or rearrange page order easily.

Advanced Computer Graphics

Other sophisticated and/or proprietary programs allow for more advanced graphics. A system with **frozen-frame retrieval,** for example, can capture a frame of video information from any existing videotape or disc and place it in the computer. This frame can then be manipulated in any number of ways—the color can be changed, part of it can be magnified, it can be combined with letters, drawings, or even other video images. Similarly, a system with **camera capture** can use a digitizing camera, usually mounted on a camera stand in a graphics workstation, to take a picture of any visual—magazine artwork, a photograph. This material, too, can be placed in the computer and manipulated in a large number of ways. Figure 7-13 shows the process that went into creating a graphic for *Entertainment Tonight.*

Computer systems with a great deal of storage (usually gigabytes) can be used for complicated *animated* graphics such as those seen in commercials and moving logos. The reason that so much storage is needed is that the animation is built one frame at a time. Say, for example, that you wanted a star to move from the bottom left to upper right of a picture in one second. You could draw a star at the bottom left and another at the top right. The computer could then calculate the path from the bottom point to the top and make sure the star image moved the appropriate amount each frame so that its entire path was completed in one second. If you wanted the star to twist in the middle of the screen, you would need to give the computer more instructions. Each frame of movement is saved in the computer. One frame of video uses almost one megabyte of storage space. Therefore, at thirty frames per second, a five-second animation would use 150 megabytes.

Even more advanced is **morphing,** the transformation of one form into another. Morphing, too, is accomplished by changing each frame slightly. Figure 7-14 shows several frames of a commercial in which a car morphs into a tiger. Morphing was used extensively in *Terminator 2,* the most famous morphing shot being the one where the Terminator morphs from a piece of linoleum into a prison guard.

The Video Toaster

Somewhat in a class by itself is the *Video Toaster,* a computer system that has been

(a) A still photo of Madonna is retrieved from the video library. The first step is to use the graphics pad and pen to outline her head and block out all of the distracting background so that only the desired portrait remains.

(b) After a similar library shot of Roseanne Barr is retrieved and treated to remove the background, the two portraits are positioned for one of the planned on-air shots.

(c) In order to convey the atmosphere of Italy (the locale for the Madonna/Roseanne story), a small picture of the Leaning Tower of Pisa is pulled from the "flat art" file and placed on the copy stand.

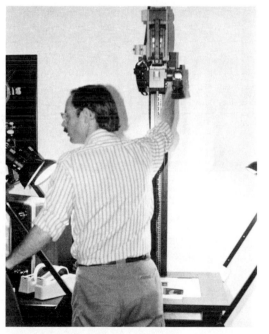

(d) This picture of the tower is shot with the video "capture camera," and the image can then be integrated into the other electronic graphics.

FIGURE 7-13

Many steps are involved in creating a series of graphics for a highly visual production such as *Entertainment Tonight*.

Photos courtesy of Paramount Studios, Los Angeles

(e) The tower is positioned and layered into an existing *Entertainment Tonight* mosaic.

(f) For one segment of the story, Roseanne's image is layered (matted) over the tower. The degree of blending and transparency of the images is controlled with the light pen and "paint" program options.

(g) For another segment of the story, a "Madonna" logo is retrieved from still art and shot with the "capture camera."

(h) The black-and-white "Madonna" logo is reversed, a drop shadow is added, and it is positioned over the tower.

**FIGURE 7-13
continued**

(i) and (j) Two of the on-the-air results with the electronic graphics keyed in behind the host.

FIGURE 7-14

This gasolene commercial uses morphing technology to turn a car into a tiger.

Photos, compliments of Exxon Company, U.S.A. © Exxon Corporation 1991

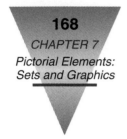
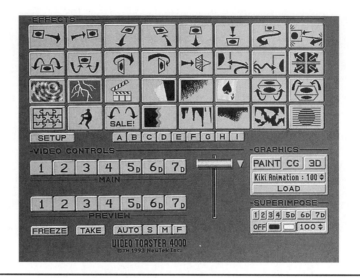

FIGURE 7-15

A graphics
workscreen
generated by the
Video Toaster.

Photo courtesy of
NewTek, Inc.

purchased by many schools, corporations, and even professional studios. (See figure 7-15.) Part of its success can be attributed to excellent marketing by NewTek Incorporated, the Kansas-based company that manufactures it. The company calls its Toaster a "studio in a box," and although it is not exactly that, at a price of $1,600, it can accomplish much of what used to need $60,000 worth of equipment.

Graphics Features

Most people use the Toaster primarily to create graphics. It includes 40 fonts, over 16 million colors, and a wide variety of digital effects transitions, some of them organic such as fire, smoke, clouds, and breaking glass. It boasts 125 built-in wipe patterns. It can *flip, spin, tumble, warp, scroll, crawl, key, peel,* etc. It enables the artist to draw irregular shapes and shade, tint, and colorize images. It includes still store, a frame grabber, three-dimensional effects, and limited animation.

Other Features

However, the Toaster is more than just a graphics program. It is the first computer video board to achieve meaningful performance in real-time of digital effects

and transitions between two moving video sources. In doing this, it does not really edit, but its seven-channel switching allows video images to be joined together. It can also use a camera as an input and can alter the image coming from the camera in a number of ways. For example, it can change a colored image to black and white or sepia-tones or make it look like a negative. It can also do **posterization** (reducing brightness levels to only a few so that the picture looks like a poster) and **solarization** (solidifying shades of color so that an image has high contrast). (See figure 7-16.)

Operation Parameters

The original Toaster could operate only by installing a Toaster board and software in an Amiga computer. NewTek has made a version for the Macintosh, but it is essentially an Amiga computer tied to a Mac. In other words, you still need to buy an Amiga computer even though you are intending to use the Toaster with a Mac. One of the strong points of the Toaster is that it provides high quality encoding so that its image can be compatible with NTSC video.

One of the "buyer beware" aspects of the Toaster is that in order to avail yourself

FIGURE 7-16

Solarization is a
process that can
be used for
stylized effects.

Photo courtesy of
Paramount Studios,
Los Angeles

to some of its features, you need to buy
other peripheral equipment. For example,
in order to use videotaped images, you
must purchase a TBC. NewTek has been
very good, however, about letting other
companies profit from the peripherals. For
example, a company called Digital Cre-
ations manufactures a TBC for the Toaster,
which it calls The Kitchen Sync. Similarly,
Cardinal Video Products makes the Bread-
board, which enables the Toaster to work
with a variety of switchers.

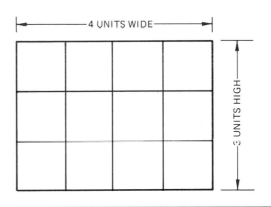

FIGURE 7-17

Regardless of the
size of the television
graphic—whether it
is four centimeters
wide or eight feet
wide—it must always
be in the three-to-
four aspect ratio if it
is designed to be
used full frame.

7.4 OTHER GRAPHICS

Sometimes it is necessary to use graphics
other than those created by a computer—
an award-winning photograph; a map of
the world that you want to show in its entirety and then zoom in on Egypt; a page
from an old manuscript. When this is the
case, you must prepare the graphic so that
it will look good on TV.

Aspect Ratio

To the extent possible, you should prepare
the material with a *three-to-four* **aspect
ratio**—the television screen is three units
high and four units wide. Nothing can be
done to change that ratio: regardless of the
size of the graphic, it still has to fit into that
three-to-four ratio. (See figure 7-17.) Computer graphics automatically give you that
aspect ratio, but graphics that come from
other places can be any size. If you are

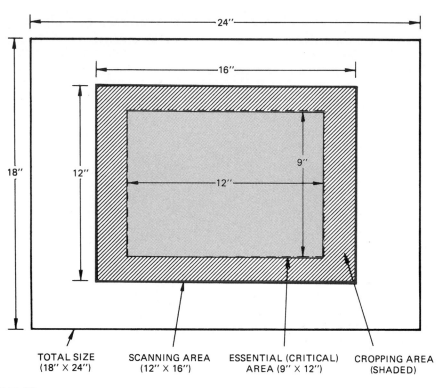

TOTAL SIZE
(18″ × 24″)

SCANNING AREA
(12″ × 16″)

ESSENTIAL (CRITICAL)
AREA (9″ × 12″)

CROPPING AREA
(SHADED)

FIGURE 7-18

Relationship of scanning area to essential area.

In this particular example, suppose you are working with a card that is actually 18″ x 24″. The scanning area is two-thirds of the total card size, or 12″ x 16″ (which includes the shaded area). The essential area is three-fourths of the scanning area (or half of the total card size); that is, 9″ x 12″ (indicated by the area in color). The cropping area (shaded) is the portion of the scanning area that may be seen by the television camera, but that may or may not be seen on the home television receiver.

starting from scratch, you can make sure you create the proper aspect ratio, but if you are using something like an old manuscript page, it is not going to be the proper aspect ratio.

However, you don't have to rule it out; you do have options. You can show only part of it; you can have the camera tilt from the top to bottom of it; or you can mount it on a larger board that is the proper aspect ratio and show borders around it.

Mounting Areas

In general, you should mount all graphics that are going to be used in a studio. This makes the graphics more stable and keeps the camera operator from shooting off the sides of them. The mounting board (usually a stiff cardboard) should be significantly larger than the actual graphic in order to allow for proper framing. Non-computer generated graphics are usually thought of in terms of total size, scanning area, and essential area. (See figure 7-18.)

All material that is prepared on a physical graphic card will not necessarily be seen on the home receiver. There has to be some room around the border of the card for numbering and identification of the graphic, handling, smudge prints, and so forth. Let us call this the *border* area and assume that it will not be used for any information at all. The camera will never intend to shoot this area. To give ourselves plenty of room, let us assume that this margin should be about one-sixth of the total card: that is, if the card is twenty-four inches wide, we will take off one-sixth, or four inches, from each edge. This leaves us with a total usable width of sixteen inches.

The remaining area that we have left is called the scanning area. This is the area actually to be scanned by the television camera. If we started out with a card that measured 18" by 24" and reduced that border one-sixth the dimension of the card on all sides, we should now have a scanning area of 12" by 16"—still in the three-to-four ratio.

Still, not everything in the scanning area will be transmitted through the entire system to reach the home TV set. The scanning system of the camera monitor may be slightly misaligned, so the camera operator will inadvertently cut off part of the graphic. The home TV set may clip off, or **crop,** some of the picture. To be safe, you should decrease the total width of the usable scanning area by taking off about one-eighth on all sides. Starting with our original card twenty-four inches wide, we would now have a remaining width of about twelve inches.

The remaining area is known as the **essential area.** All the crucial information that we want to transmit through the system must be placed in this zone. This amounts to about one-half of the original card size. It is still a three-to-four ratio. The information that is outside of the essential area but still within the scanning area (the shaded area in figure 7-18) may or may not be seen on the home receiver. Depending upon the various components in the total transmission system, some of this information may reach the home set; some of it will be cropped. This information, therefore, must be part of the total graphic design, but it cannot be essential.

7.5 GRAPHIC AESTHETICS

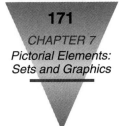
Regardless whether graphics are computer generated or physical, they should be pleasing to the eye and easy to read. Several factors are important for attaining this objective. They include the symbol size, simplicity and style, and color contrast.

Symbol Size

As a general rule of thumb, lettering on television should be *no smaller than one-fifteenth of the screen height.* If the critical area of a physical graphic card is fifteen inches high, that would mean that lettering could be no smaller than one inch. If no line is less than one-fifteenth of the height of the critical area (and assuming some space is left between each line of letters), this would mean that normally *no more than seven lines of information* should be included on a computer page or a TV graphic card. Of course, artistic considerations—balance and arrangement of mass—might dictate that much less material be used.

Given the ease of creating bountiful clean, crisp lettering with a computer graphics generator, the temptation is to flood the screen with information. But seven lines should generally be considered the maximum number of lines for a normal TV graphic. Think not of the high quality monitor directly in front of you in the control room; rather think of the myopic viewer at home sitting across the room from his or her slightly fuzzy old TV receiver.

Simplicity and Style

If there is one primary rule about the preparation of TV graphics, electronic or physical, it is simply this: *Keep it simple*— all lettering, all design elements, all artwork. The screen is too small and the scanning lines are too blurry to permit any fine detail work.

This is particularly true with lettering styles. Letters should be bold, thick, well-defined, with a sharp, firm contour. Elegant lettering with fancy serifs and swirls must be avoided (except possibly for large stylized two- or three-word titles). Letters should be of even thickness throughout—both horizontal and vertical lines should be the same. (Thin horizontal lines, for example, can be obliterated in the scanning lines.) Choose electronic fonts that are basic and uniform, such as *Gothic, Helvetica,* or *Futura.* (See figure 7-10.)

Any other artwork on a graphic card with lettering should also be kept simple. If it is too detailed, the audience will not get a chance to comprehend it; if it is too confusing and domineering, the audience will be distracted from the lettering.

All nonverbal graphics—pictures, cartoons, drawings, slides—must also be kept as simple as possible. Drawings or photographs showing a certain component or step in a process must show only what is absolutely necessary. One of the main problems in trying to use visuals prepared for other media (for example, charts from a book or photos from a magazine) is that they invariably contain too much detail. They are designed for a medium without the pressing temporal limitations of television. Usually they are visuals designed to convey as much information as possible in a single picture; they are designed for detailed study and comparison. Television, by contrast, may have to use three or four graphics sequentially to impart the same information. Do not try to crowd everything into one picture.

This admonition is particularly true with *maps.* It is safe to say that no prepared maps (designed for nontelevision application) can safely be used on television. Any television graphic that tries to squeeze in more than twenty-five words is really too cramped and the information is too small. Most maps have to be redone

FIGURE 7-19
Example of a simplified map appropriate for a television graphic.

for TV. (See figure 7-19.) Use only outlines of countries or natural geographical bodies and a few key labels or key locations. Keeping simplicity is often particularly difficult with computer graphics. There are so many temptations. But just because you have 16 million colors, 40 fonts, and 125 wipe patterns, don't feel you have to use them all. If you are just trying to capture the viewer's attention, you can flaunt a few special effects, but if you are trying to convey information, remember that often less is better.

Color Contrast

A third factor that can help determine the readability of either a physical or computer generated graphic is color contrast. Working with color graphics, it is important to use hues that contrast and complement each other without actually clashing. (See color plate B.) Artistic judgment and experience will help determine which hues go well together. It is often very effective to combine different saturation levels of the same or closely related hues.

Contrast in brightness levels also is effective in making certain segments of a graphic stand out.

With most basic computer graphics generators, thousands or even millions of colors are possible. Take time to experiment with your system and see what combinations of hues, saturation, and brightness work best for your purpose.

Video engineers like to have just a little white and a little black in a picture for reference points. Thus, a good graphic would be one that has two or three shades of brightness plus a little white and black for sparkle and interest. Avoid graphics that are all black and white or that consist entirely of high-contrast colors.

One problem to be avoided is the use of colors of the same brightness or saturation in preparing graphics. Two different hues (say, red and blue) will contrast best if you also consider differing levels of saturation and brightness. A dark brownish red will contrast better against a brilliant royal blue than against a dark navy blue.

In fact, contrasting saturations of the same hue (for example, a vivid chartreuse and a grayish olive green) provide considerable contrast. And even contrasting brightness or lightness of the same hue and saturation (for example, a light pink and a dark rose) provides essential contrast and legibility.

Working with graphics can be very rewarding. Computers have made the process fairly simple and fast, but the main responsibility, the creation of something that is aesthetically pleasing, rests in the hands and minds of human beings.

7.6 SET DESIGN

Set design, like graphics, has been invaded by the computer. **Production designers** and **art directors** frequently plan the overall look of a production and the specific set pieces by using computer programs. Graphics software helps them create a visualization of what will later become massive set pieces and furniture. Some programs allow them to "enter" a set and look at it from a number of different angles. Programs also help them keep track of what supplies will be needed to construct the sets, what the cost will be, and what is finished and yet to be completed.

For purposes of ordering different items, constructing needed units, and considering storage and construction, people involved with set design and execution will find it convenient to think in terms of three broad categories of scenery and staging elements: settings, set dressings and furniture, and hand props.

Settings

The term *setting* is usually used to refer to all the major scenic pieces that make up the background and surrounding environment of the scene. This category would, in turn, include about three different kinds of scenic elements: *standard set units,* such as flats, two-folds, and other standing background pieces; *hanging units,* including various cloth drops, hanging drapes, and the cyclorama (or cyc), that might cover two or three walls with a flat, neutral surface; and *set pieces,* which include pillars, steps and stairways, arches, platforms, wagons (platforms on casters), fences, lampposts, and so forth.

Set Dressings and Furniture

The terms *set dressings* and *furniture,* along with the label *stage props,* are used by different practitioners to mean slightly different things. Basically this category includes all those major items that are involved in *dressing* the set, filling out the naked setting represented by the flats and major set pieces. This includes all the major items of furniture (desk, lectern, chairs, tables, appliances, and so forth) and large exterior stage props (bicycles, cannons, trees, and other natural or man-made objects). The term *set dressing* is often used to refer even more specifically to those smaller items that are used to make the set look lived in—lamps, pictures, books and magazines, household plants, vases, and other furnishings. *Set dressings* and *stage props* come from different sources, depending upon one's ingenuity and budget: a studio's prop storage, secondhand stores, or one's own living room.

Hand Props

A specialized but extremely important category is that of *hand properties*—those items that are actually handled and manipulated as part of the television production. They include all those props needed for a dramatic production (telephones, bottles, kitchen tools, food, books, glasses, weapons), or for a commercial (the box of cereal or can of dog food), or for an instructional program (globes, models, chemistry apparatus). Obviously some of these items overlap with other set dressings, the distinction being that hand props are actually *used* in the program, rather than being planted as *decoration.*

7.7 STAGING REQUIREMENTS AND CONSIDERATIONS

Settings, set dressings, and hand props do not exist in a vacuum. They must be integrated with the equipment and actors that are part of any production.

Camera Movement

No matter what the set looks like, there must be provision for adequate camera movement. Several cameras will have to be free to have access from different angles in the setting. This usually poses no problems with settings that have few set units and very little furniture. A talk show with a desk and several chairs set against a cyc is easy for cameras to move around in. What creates problems are elaborate realistic settings with windows and doors and a great deal of furniture. For this reason, sets are usually constructed as just two-walled or three-walled sets. The open wall (the missing side of the set) is used for camera access. In three-walled sets, the walls do not have to be set at exactly ninety degrees; they can be left open at oblique angles so that the camera can have even more access. In some sets (occasionally a four-walled set may have to be used), it is possible to position cameras behind the flats or other scenic elements and shoot through a window, doorway, hole in the bookcase or fireplace, and other camouflaged openings.

Microphone Placement

The setting also has to have provision for adequate microphone placement and, if on a boom, movement. Although the wireless microphone (section 3.3) is increasingly used in studio dramas—soap operas and situation comedies—the beginning audio operator must learn how to cope with staging concerns involved with wired microphones. For most dramatic productions (since lavalieres usually are not worn, hanging mics result in bad audio, and hidden microphones are not encouraged), some sort of boom or giraffe or fishpole is used. This can lead to two kinds of problems.

First, if the set is small and the boom is large, there will be movement and coordination troubles; cameras will also have to maneuver around the boom and microphone cables; adequate room has to be left open. Second, the mic boom can cause bad boom shadows. If the lighting has not been carefully worked out with the precise boom placement in mind, there will be a strong possibility of unwanted shadows from the horizontal boom or fishpole. This could be more of a problem in a setting with a plain background than in a busy set that may make a shadow less noticeable. In most cases, however, either the mic boom or the lighting instrument will have to be repositioned somewhat or the light will have to be barndoored off the boom.

Lighting Instruments

Other lighting problems can be caused by certain kinds of setting arrangements. Occasionally, pillars or other foreground set pieces may be blocking crucial front lighting from a certain angle. Sometimes a strong key light may throw a very distracting shadow on a close-up shot of some small object; or if the talent is lighted too close to the set (flat or cyc), the key light may throw too much illumination on the set. One of the most common problems, however, is the blocking of the back light by a flat. If the flat is too high for the studio (a 10-foot flat might be high if the studio has a low ceiling), or if the flat is out too far into the studio from the back light, or if the talent is standing too close to the flat, it is going to be difficult to hit the talent with the back light. (See figure 7-20.) In this case, something—the back light or the flat or the talent—will have to be moved.

To minimize the problems between sets and lighting and make for ease of operation for both the staging and lighting crews, large set pieces such as flats are put up before lighting begins. However, furniture and set decorations are not put into place. This allows the lighting people to light according to the general placement of the sets without having to maneuver their ladders around pieces of furniture. Once the lighting ladders are put away, the set is

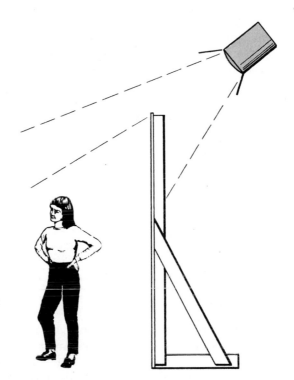

FIGURE 7-20
Back-lighting problems with scenic flat.

In this kind of situation, either the back light will have to be mounted higher, the light will have to be repositioned closer to the flat, the flat will have to be moved back (closer to the back light), or the talent will have to move forward, farther away from the flat.

dressed. Some minor lighting changes may then be made but these can usually be adjusted from the floor or with the aid of one small step ladder.

Talent Movement

Finally, the setting has to take into consideration all anticipated movement by the talent. How much action is required? Will several people be moving in the same direction simultaneously? How much space is needed for certain movement (a dance step or tumbling demonstration)? Is there plenty of room for all entrances and exits? Will the talent be forced to maneuver so close to the set walls that part of their lighting will be cut off? Or, if the performers work too close to the set, will they cast unwanted shadows on the flat or cyc? Once the director is satisfied that there is enough room for talent movement, lighting instruments, microphone placement, and camera movement, he or she is ready to look at the functional aspect of using scenery.

7.8 USING SETS AND SCENIC ELEMENTS

The physical manipulation and handling of all scenery units—construction, assemblage, and storage—is a major study by itself. Television scenery is closely related to stage and film scenery; anyone who has ever worked in technical theater or visited the back lot of a major motion picture studio has a feel for the scope of the scenery and props department. All we can do in this text is touch upon some of the basic elements involved in making scenery units, assembling them for studio use, and storing them for repeated use.[1]

Construction

The basic scenic unit for television, like that for the stage, is the **flat**—a cross-braced wooden frame faced with either canvas (which is lightweight, but too flimsy for repeated heavy use) or thin pressed board or plywood (which will take more abuse, although it is heavier to work with).

1. For a full discussion of scenery construction and use, consult any good theater stagecraft text or manual, such as Willard F. Bellman, *Scene Design, Stage Lighting, Sound, Costume and Makeup* (New York: Harper & Row, 1983) or Jay Michael Gillette, *Theatrical Design and Production* (Mountain View, CA: Mayfield Publishing Co., 1987).

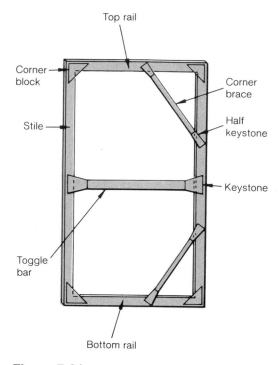

Figure 7-21
Construction of an ordinary flat.

Standard construction of a simple wooden flat consists of a frame made of 1″ x 3″ pine with ¼″ plywood for the corner blocks and keystones. The front of the frame is typically covered with canvas or with plywood (or pressed hardboard). If a solid wooden front covering is used, then the corner braces will not be needed.

The layout for a standard flat is shown in figure 7-21. Flats can be made in any size, but common heights are ten feet for larger studios and eight feet for studios with lower ceilings. Widths also will vary, although they are seldom broader than five feet (the width that one person can comfortably handle with arms outstretched).

Whenever wider widths are needed, flats can be hinged together semipermanently. Two flats hinged together are known as a *two-fold.* Three flats similarly

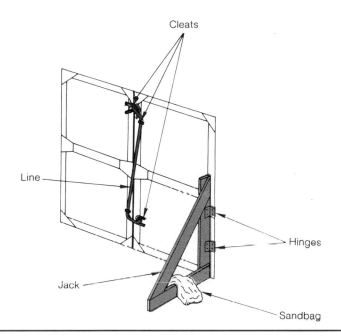

Cleats

Line

Jack

Hinges

Sandbag

FIGURE 7-22

Connecting and bracing flats.

Cleats on both flats allow the units to be lashed together by a line, which is permanently tied onto one of the flats. The jack is a hinged stage brace that, when weighted, forms a good self-supporting unit.

connected (seldom will you see more than three) are known as a *three-fold*. When a wider span needs to be covered, the flat units are temporarily lashed or connected together. (See figure 7-22.)

In addition to standard wooden construction, studios use other rigid but light-weight materials, such as foam board and corrugated feather board, for making flats and other scenic elements.

Construction of other set pieces (stairways, platforms, and so forth) is more complicated, requiring heavy bracing and sturdy framing for the amount of abuse and wear they will be subjected to. (See figure 7-23.)

Cycs can be either a permanent solid cyc (faced with plywood or some other hard surface, which may tend to give audio problems) or a cyc cloth (canvas, duck, or gauze, depending upon the desired texture and reflectance quality desired). Cycs as a rule are designed to be used while stretched taut, giving a smooth limbo background, although they may be hung loosely in pleats to give the appearance of opened drapes. Canvas cycs can also be painted and used as the backdrop for a set, as illustrated in figure 7-24.

Drapes, which are usually of a heavier material and often darker, can be either pulled taut or pleated, depending upon the desired effect. Darker, low-reflectance drapes are effective backing for cameo lighting. Drapes are usually used in smaller widths than a cyc and can ordinarily be easily rigged or hung for specific applications. A cyc, on the other hand, often is permanently mounted, covering two or even three walls of a studio.

If any amount of action or camera work is going to focus on the ground, the floor covering must be considered. Most studio floors are generic tile that blends in well with most productions. But a story line that calls for a realistic plot with dirt

FIGURE 7-23

A section of an
airplane fuselage
shows construction
that is typical
of specialized
set pieces.

Photo courtesy of
Universal Studios,
Universal City, CA

FIGURE 7-24

Canvas backdrop
painted to serve as a
street-front scene.

Photo courtesy of
Universal Studios,
Universal City, CA

FIGURE 7-25

Fiberglass "dirt skins" are made from burlap impregnated with fiberglass mixed with dirt or any other desired soil texture.

Photo courtesy of Universal Studios, Universal City, CA

or a sandy beach can cause problems. Figure 7-25 shows one answer—the use of a **dirt skin** to simulate a patch of natural earth. Similarly, natural vertical surfaces—cliff faces, rocks, mine walls—must be carefully constructed to simulate the real thing. These upright pieces, however, must be constructed from fairly rigid material such as fiberglass (see figure 7-26). A more common solution is to take the production out of the studio into the real world and use an actual beach, cliff, or mine for the shooting.

Assembling

Most flats are built with special hardware that facilitates easy temporary joining of two or more units. The stiles of the flats can be fitted with **cleats,** so that a line can be used to lash two flats together quickly. (See figure 7-22.)

Other methods of joining flats include the use of various metal fasteners (such as *L-plates*, which have drop-in fasteners and loose pin-hinges) and the use of large *quick-fix* clamps, which can be used to clamp the stiles of two adjoining flats together. Most flats also have some sort of bracing or supporting unit so they can be completely freestanding as a self-supporting unit. Several different types of stage braces are used. One of the most common is the **jack** or hinged wooded brace. (See figure 7-22.) When the flat is in place, the jack is swung out behind the flat at right angles to the front of the flat and held in place with stage weights or **sandbags.**

FIGURE 7-26

Rigid fiberglass pieces can be used to simulate the texture of mine walls or other rough surfaces.

Photo courtesy of Universal Studios, Universal City, CA

FIGURE 7-27

A metal brace used for semipermanent support of a flat.

Photo courtesy of Universal Studios, Universal City, CA

When flats are assembled for a set that is likely to remain in place for a prolonged period, they often are permanently secured with a stage screw. Figure 7-27 illustrates the use of a metal brace screwed into the floor for a set that is part of a long-running situation comedy.

Most set pieces are solid and freestanding units that need no special bracing when assembled for use in the studio. However, many of them—such as stairway units—do need to be fastened to other units or flats to make them as secure and immobile as possible. Door flats also need to be securely fastened to other set units to guarantee that the doorway will function properly without sticking or falling down when used. Some set pieces, such as *parallels* (collapsible platforms), can be partially disassembled and folded for storage. They must be carefully put together and securely set up before being used.

Storage

In many small stations and educational institutions, scenery storage can be a serious problem. There is never enough room to house everything that is needed, and scenery storage always seems to be one area that suffers the most. This can be a particularly critical problem because so many of the flats and special set pieces can be reused over and over in a variety of ways—with different set dressings—in a number of configurations. Yet, they have to be stored somewhere and catalogued for easy retrieval.

Flats and other narrow units are usually stored in racks, which are simple frames designed to hold a number of flats in an upright position. Each rack can be designed and labeled to hold similarly matched scenic units (for example, living room flats, office flats, green-speckled flats, log cabin flats, and so forth).

Props and other small items can be stored on deep shelves in the storage area. Again, it is important that each shelf and/or cubicle be clearly labeled: "telephones," "dishes," "bottles," and so on. Even furniture and other large stage props can be stored in multi-tiered shelves. Large overstuffed chairs, sofas, and heavy tables can be stored on the floor level; medium-sized chairs and tables can be stored on another level (four to five feet off the floor); and lightweight chairs and stools and small appliances can be stored on a third level (perhaps seven to eight feet above the floor).

Studio Techniques

In moving into actual studio usage, the director and staging director need to be aware of several other factors, including the floor plan, lighting effects, and special staging effects.

Floor Plan

First, as we have stressed throughout this text, the success of any television production is dependent to a great extent upon the discipline exercised in preproduction planning. As with the considerations of the lighting director, much valuable studio time and frustration can be saved by careful planning and plotting of the basic set.

A good floor plan allows the director to make the most economical use of all studio and staging space. Sets can be planned efficiently; equipment can be placed with precision. The director can plan how best to take advantage, for example, of the *cornerset*—a two-walled setting positioned in a corner of the studio—that provides good set backing for many types of productions (better than a flat backdrop), while allowing great depth and freedom of camera movement (more so than with a three-walled set).

A typical studio staging floor plan will include the placement of all flats and other set pieces and the exact location of all stage props and furniture. It is important that all flats and furniture be drawn to exact scale; otherwise the director's shooting angles, the talent's movement, and the lighting design will all be off. Computer programs designed to help develop floor plans are very helpful because they keep the scale consistent and can be used to "move" items around as often as necessary. Figure 7-28 shows a typical plot plan, drawn to the scale of one-eighth inch to one foot. Once the accurate floor plan is drawn, it will be used by the director, floor manager, audio person, talent, and even the lighting director (to confirm and complement the lighting plot). It is therefore essential that the plan be prepared with as much detail and precision as possible.

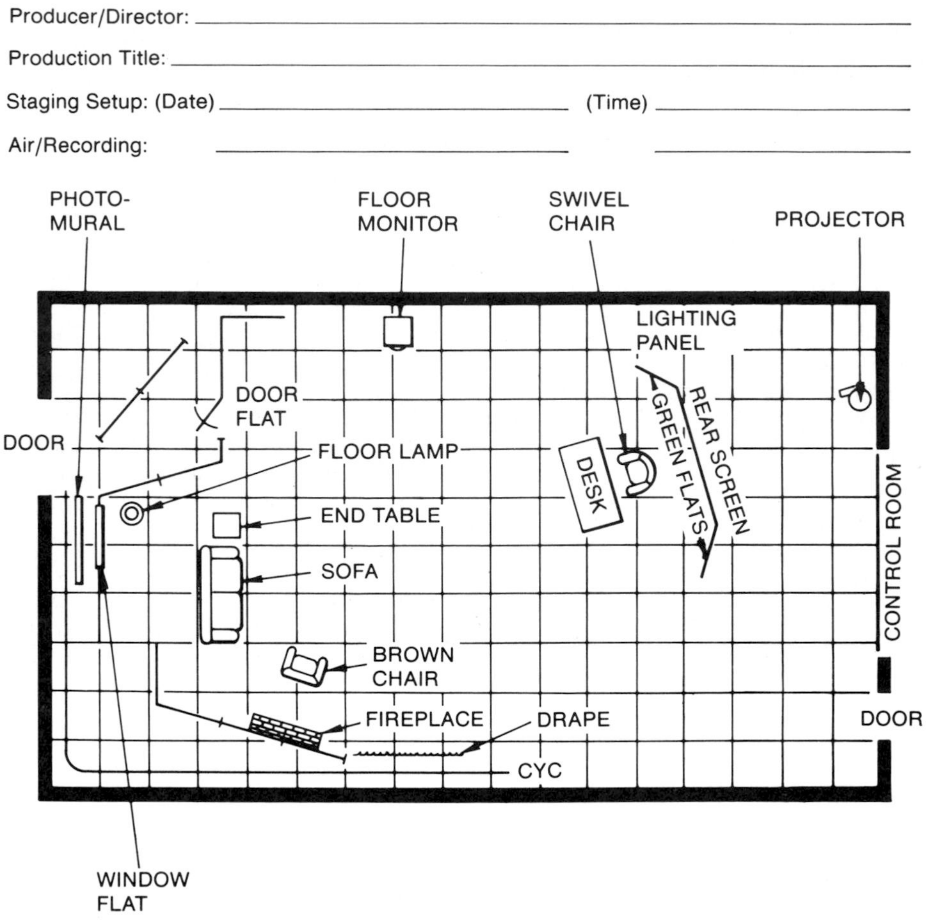

Producer/Director: _____

Production Title: _____

Staging Setup: (Date) _____ (Time) _____

Air/Recording: _____

PHOTO-MURAL   FLOOR MONITOR   SWIVEL CHAIR   PROJECTOR

FIGURE 7-28

Sample staging
floor plan.

In this particular
floor plan, the
squares on the floor
correspond to three-
foot tiles actually
laid on the studio
floor. In other floor
plans, a lighting grid
or pipe battens
might be
superimposed over
the studio layout.

LIGHTING PANEL

DOOR   DOOR FLAT   FLOOR LAMP   REAR SCREEN / GREEN FLATS   DESK

END TABLE

SOFA   CONTROL ROOM

BROWN CHAIR

FIREPLACE   DRAPE   DOOR

CYC

WINDOW FLAT

Lighting Effects

In addition to the regular lighting required for illumination of the production area, other special lighting effects should be considered as part of the overall staging design. We have already mentioned the use of the **cucalorus,** or **cookie,** pattern (section 4.4) to cast various shadow patterns (venetian blinds, prison bars, Moorish latticework, and so forth) on the set wall. (See figure 7-29.)

Colored gels can be used to throw colored lights on a plain cyc or other surface. Subtle lighting changes (with the dimmer) can be employed to change color or shadowing as dramatic action unfolds. Other creative lighting effects (determining shape and texture, modifying reality, and establishing mood) were discussed in section 4.3. Staging and lighting must be considered as one integral production element; they cannot be looked at as isolated, independent components.

Special Staging Effects

Several different types of mechanical and optical *staging effects* can be used. Although some of the effects depend upon expensive equipment and elaborate arrangements, others can be adapted to most studio situations.

FIGURE 7-29
Use of a cucalorus
pattern to project a
shadow on the back
wall of a set.

Large electric fans can create *wind* effects. Dry ice plunged into a tub of hot water creates *fog*. (Both of these effects cause studio noise that can be compensated for in a number of ways, including sound effects CDs.) *Lightning* and *explosions* are best suggested by lighting effects (off set) coupled with sound effects.

To produce a *fire* effect, shake silk strips on a stick in front of a spotlight to create flickering shadows or superimpose film footage of a flame over the set (since flame is translucent, the super effect works well). Again, use sound effects to present a total contextual effect. *Smoke* can be added by carefully pouring mineral oil in a container on a hot plate.

Rain can be simulated by preparing a **rain drum** graphic—a continuous loop of black paper with white streaks splashed on it rotated on a round surface (you can use an old base drum); super a slightly defocused shot of the drum over the scene (with the actors in wet clothing). Again, add sound for a total effect. *Mirrors* can be used in a variety of ways. For example, a large mirror suspended from a lighting grid can be used to get a shot looking straight down onto a demonstration table or into a cooking pot. Mirrors can also be used in musical productions. High and low shots—for example, dancers' feet on a bandstand program—can be obtained by using a double-mirrored periscope.

Gobos are another handy staging device that enable a camera to frame a shot through some special foreground design. The gobo is a cutout (for instance, a simulated gunsight or keyhole) that is positioned several feet in front of a camera; it is an obvious stylistic effect that can be used judiciously to good advantage. Other optical devices using special filters and prisms also can be utilized in more sophisticated situations.

Production Problems

Finally, mention should be made of several common troubles that periodically plague even the best staging plan. One is the difficulty of obtaining a consistent background from all angles. Whether a person is using a lighted cyc or a realistic set of flats, care must be taken to make certain that the set is evenly lit so that each camera, shooting from its particular angle, will be getting the same background shot. Also, care must be taken to ensure that the sets are wide enough—that there is enough cover at each end of the set—so that a camera shooting from outside angles will not be shooting off the set.

Troubles frequently occur with functional furniture. Chairs, stools, and sofas must be appropriately matched with talent. Some common furniture problems include: the *swinging swivel chair,* in which guests vent their nervous energy by rotating back and forth; the *precarious perch,* which involves sitting uncomfortably on top of a high, hard stool; and the *talent swallower,* overstuffed chairs and sofas that are so plush and soft that the person sinks down so far the director is left with nothing but a shot of knees. Make sure you use solid furniture that is comfortable but firm.

One last production problem that has ruined many a final take is the *forgotten prop.* In any kind of production that relies on hand props (dramas, demonstration shows, training programs), there is always the danger of failing to return a given prop to its starting point after a rehearsal. The gun must be returned to the bedside table; the magician's paraphernalia must be repacked and checked; a new set of vegetables must be prepared for the cooking demonstration; the toys must be put back in the clown's sack; and so forth. Both the talent and the stage manager should double-check after the dress rehearsal to determine that everything is in place for the final production.

SUMMARY

Good pictorial design—for graphics and sets—starts with consideration of both *informational* functions and *emotional* functions of the picture. Basic elements of design that should be considered in every production include *balance and mass, dominant lines,* and *tone and color.* Color components include *hue, saturation,* and *brightness.*

Computer graphics have progressed very rapidly, both in *proprietary* systems and in systems tied to Macintosh, Amiga, and IBM platforms. The hardware needed for a basic *computer graphics generator* consists of a *CPU,* a *monitor, disc drives,* and a *keyboard.* Also of value are a *mouse,* a *graphics tablet,* a *light pen, videodisc,* and *optical disc* players, *CD-ROMs,* a *digitizing camera,* and a *video board.*

Software programs are similar to those used for word processing in that they are *menu* driven, involve placement and selection of various *fonts,* and can store, retrieve, delete, move, and copy parts of a text. In addition, lettering programs can be used to create *borders* and select *color* and *backgrounds.* Drawing programs have *brushes* for various line thickness, and can create common *shapes* and *shadows* and *light reflections.* They also have possibilities for duplicating and enlarging elements of the drawings. Software programs also contain many *display* options such as *roll* and *crawl,* and these functions can be preprogrammed or operator controlled.

Advanced computer graphics include *freeze-frame retrieval, camera-capture, animation,* and *morphing.* The *Video Toaster,* with its multitude of colors, fonts, and effects has become very popular for graphics creation.

Sometimes physical graphics, such as photos or maps, must be used. They should be in the three-to-four *aspect ratio* and should be mounted to take into account *scanning* and *essential* areas. Easy to read graphics should contain no more than seven lines of text, should emphasize simplicity, and should use hues that complement and contrast with each other.

Set design has also been affected by the computer, which can help designers visualize design parameters. Scenery elements include *settings* (standard set units, hanging units, and set pieces), *set dressings and furniture,* and *hand props.* In designing a studio setting, consider also *camera movement, microphone placement, lighting instruments, and talent movement.* In handling pieces in the studio, you should know the basic *construction* of a flat, how flats can be *assembled,* and the best way of *storing* flats, set pieces, and properties. Some other studio techniques involve the preparation of a staging *floor plan,* use of *lighting* effects, other special *staging* effects, and dealing with basic problems of backgrounds, furniture, and props.

This chapter has covered the pictorial elements of graphics and sets. The next chapter will discuss how graphics and other inputs are joined together through the switcher.

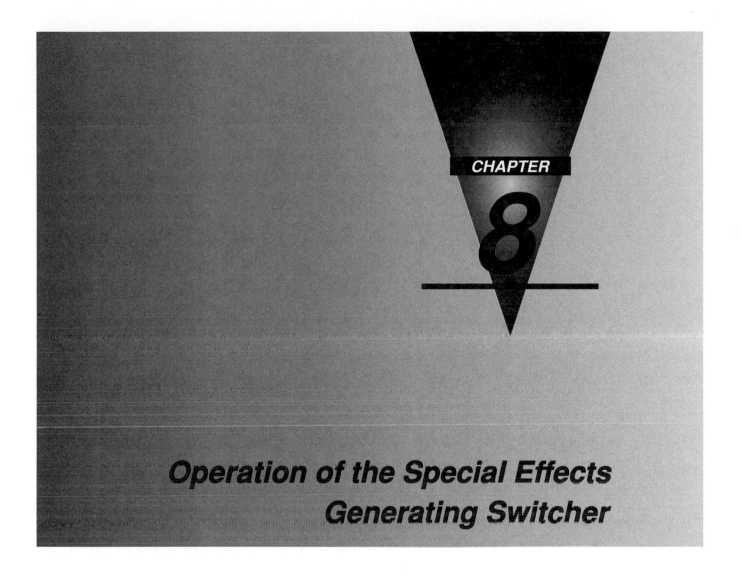

CHAPTER

8

Operation of the Special Effects Generating Switcher

A number of complex and impressive components are found in the modern video production center. One piece of equipment, the **switcher,** goes back to the very beginning of television. While retaining all its original functions, it has constantly been redesigned to greatly enhance its operational capabilities.

The video switcher, much like the audio console, has three primary functions. First and foremost, it is an *editing device,* developed to facilitate the time-ordered *sequencing of inputs* within a live, or live-to-tape, video production. To do this, the switcher serves a *channeling,* or routing, function—selecting a video source from all the available inputs such as cameras, videotape machines, remote feeds, character generators, and computer generated graphics.

Second, the switcher functions as a *mixing component* that can combine two or more picture sources by means of **superimpositions, key** effects, **wipe** transitions, and other **special effects.** Third, to accomplish some of these special

FIGURE 8-1

*Entertainment
Tonight* technical
director Wayne
Parsons working on
the Grass Valley 300
SEG/Switcher.

Photo courtesy of
Entertainment Tonight

effects, the switcher also functions as a *shaping device* that can alter not only the color and luminance quality of a picture but also its physical design and shape—for example, in executing various specialized transition effects such as page turns.

During the process of channeling, mixing, and shaping, the switcher must at all times be able to maintain the waveform and synchronization information of the various signals, so that its final *program output,* whether broadcast or recorded, can ultimately produce a picture on the **cathode-ray tube** of the receiving TV set. More and more during the past decade, traditional switcher operations and effects have been greatly augmented through the use of **digital video effects (DVE),** equipment that converts the basic **analog** video signal into a series of **digital**

signal pulses. (See section 8.4.) It is this digital processing that enables us to achieve the eye-dazzling computer effects that have become common in the past few years—the enhanced graphic designs and continuous-motion animation that generally surpass similar film-based visuals.

When these digital capabilities are added to the more traditional switcher functions, the unit is usually referred to as a **special effects generator (SEG).** (See figure 8-1.) Used in conjunction with a number of specific function modules, the unit can create and execute a wide range of video displays and transitions. Many of the *folding, zooming,* and *exploding* effects that serve as elaborate transitions from one picture to the next are built into the sort of SEG that is typically used in the production of sports events and game shows.

FIGURE 8-2

The Grass Valley
Model digital
switcher, shown
here at Hollywood
Digital, a west coast
postproduction
house, is the central
unit among a
number of
components used in
the final assembly of
major television and
cable productions.

Photo courtesy of
Hollywood Digital

Even more impressive effects are accomplished with switcher/SEG units that are designed to work within the disciplines of the **postproduction editing** process. Here, great amounts of time, talent, and money are lavished upon special animated effects that emphasize the creative use of color. The graphics one sees on television today are seldom the work of an artist with pen and brush; they are increasingly the electronic product of an artist/technician working with computer generated graphics (see section 7.3) or a SEG through the switcher.

In major postproduction houses the special effects generating switcher is the primary creative control factor among a number of other edit related components found within very sophisticated editing suites.

(See figure 8-2.) These "smart switchers" allow the operator to pre-program effects such as dissolves, wipes, tumbling cubes, flipping pages, and shrinking inserts. Effects that include timed transitions—such as an exact two and one-half second (seventy-five frame) wipe—can be similarly programmed into the switcher's microprocessor for later execution.

Many educational institutions find that budgetary restrictions make it difficult to keep up with such state of the art equipment. Schools and small-scale video operations are more likely to have modest switchers. It is therefore important to keep in mind that with the switcher, as with many other components, there are a few basic principles of design, function, and operation common to all units—no matter how simple or complex the construction. Once these essential principles are understood, you can more confidently approach the task of operating the impressive switcher units found in professional studios. Once you know what you are looking for, the process of understanding machine function is greatly simplified.

For example, the concept of video signal flow, as presented in section 5.1, is integral to understanding how the switcher serves as a channeling device. It is suggested that, before proceeding, you review both section 5.1 and section 5.2, which provide a background for understanding the nature of the color signal that our switchers will be controlling.

8.1 THE PRINCIPLE OF THE SWITCHER

The switcher in a network television studio is indeed an impressive instrument. With its multiple rows of buttons, switches, levers, and lights, it is quite a formidable piece of machinery. Despite all of its complexity, however, it operates on exactly the same fundamental principles found in the simplest units. Basically, the switcher can be thought of as a sophisticated *connection panel*—an electronic "box" where all the camera signals and other inputs come into one side of the box and the edited program is sent out of the other side. All the various buttons, levers, and knobs are just a means of taking video signals from several sources (cameras, graphics units, video recorders, remote feeds) and selecting those to be sent out as the *program signal*, or "program line out."

The basic elements of any switching device are represented in figure 8-3. A group of buttons (which can be depressed or "punched up") is arranged in simpler

switchers in two rows or **banks.**[1] The top row is designated as the *A* bank or **bus,** and the lower row is the *B* bank or bus. Each button is, in effect, the temporary termination point of a video cable leading back to a picture source (camera, video recorder, and so forth). The two rows are, in that way, identical. In figure 8-3, there is a position for each of three cameras and also a button for the **black** picture signal; the black picture is a fully synchronized signal with the luminance (brightness) information set at the lowest possible point. This is used whenever you want to send out a blank (black) picture.

When pushed down, a button makes contact with a separate video line running beneath the row of buttons correspondingly labeled *A* bus (usually upper) and *B* bus. The signal from the camera (or other source) connected to that button—for example, camera 3 on the *B* bus in figure 8-3—is then connected to the bus line. Only one signal source can be connected to a given bus at a time; the buttons are mutually canceling so that when a button is pushed, that action releases the previously depressed button. Therefore, each bus can have just one camera signal punched into it at any given moment.

The incoming picture source is thereby sent on "downstream" (try to envision the signal flow as flowing downstream from the original video source, merging with other tributaries and inputs along the way, to its terminus in a completed picture) to a **fader lever,** which is designed to control the strength of the signal output from each bank. Each bus has its own corresponding fader arm or lever. The fader functions just like a fader on the audio console, with each

---

1. Technically speaking, the mixing bar that connects the buttons under the switcher panel is the *bus*, and the row of buttons above the bus is the *bank*. However, in common usage, the two terms are used interchangeably.

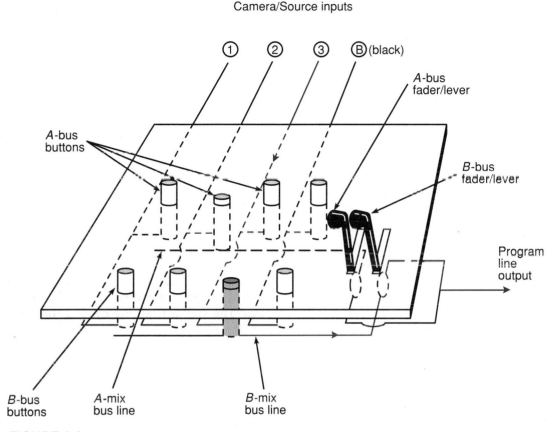

Camera/Source inputs

① ② ③ Ⓑ (black)

A-bus buttons

A-bus fader/lever

B-bus fader/lever

Program line output

B-bus buttons

A-mix bus line

B-mix bus line

FIGURE 8-3

Cutaway schematic drawing of a two-bus switcher.

On the *A* bus, camera 2 is punched into the mix-bus line. On the *B* bus, camera 3 is punched into the mix-bus line. Thus, with the fader arms in the down position (activating the *B* bus), camera 3 is providing the program line output. If the fader arms were to be moved into the up position (activating the *A* bus), camera 2 would then provide the program line output.

lever controlling the strength of the video signal flowing through its respective bus. Therefore, when the *A*-bank fader is activated, the signal from the *A* bus is sent out on the program line. When the *B*-fader arm is activated, the signal punched up on the *B* bank becomes the program output.

Although the early switchers had two separate fader bars as seen in figure 8-3, all units today are more like those seen in figure 8-4. They are usually locked together. In this manner when one fader is activated, the other will automatically be deactivated. Thus, when both fader arms are pushed up toward the *A*-bank position, the *A* bus will be activated and the *B* bus will be dead. By keeping the two fader arms locked together—moving them up and down simultaneously—we will always have one bus activated (sending out the program signal) while the other bus is dead. (Although, as we shall see, there are occasions when they are separated).

Therefore, as in figure 8-3, if both fader arms are placed in the *B*-bank position, the *B* bus will be sending out its signal as the program feed and the *A* bus will be inactive. Thus, the full video signal is being sent out from whatever picture is punched up on the *B* bank—in this case, camera 3. If you press a button on the *A* bank (for example, camera 2), there is no effect upon the line output because the *A*-bus fader is in its deactivated position. With camera 3 pressed on the *B* bank, you will see the picture from that camera on your line monitor. If you want to replace that picture with the picture from another camera (for example, if you want to go from camera 3 to camera 1), you would perform a camera **cut** (a **take**) by pressing the camera 1 button on the same *B* bank. With no loss of synchronization, you will see an instantaneous change of picture on the program line monitor—cutting from camera 3 to camera 1.

8.2 FADES, DISSOLVES, AND SUPERIMPOSITIONS

From its earliest film beginnings, the moving picture art has always made use of the gradual transition between pictures known as the **dissolve.** Related techniques include **fades** to and from black, as well as *superimpositions.*

Fade-Ins

Most video programs are begun with a one- to two-second "fade-in" from black to the first picture. (An instantaneous *take* from black to picture would seem very abrupt.) Figure 8-4 shows how the *technical*

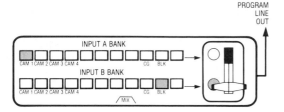

FIGURE 8-4

Simple television switcher.

This figure shows how the two mix banks on a simple switcher would be set up to execute a dissolve from black (or fade-up from black) to camera 1. The red tinted buttons indicate which input selector buttons would be pressed. "Black" is punched up on the *B* bank, and camera 1 is punched up on the *A* bank. The small red light just to the left of the fader lever in the *B*-bank position serves as a reminder of which bus is feeding the program line. As the fader arms are raised from the *B* bank to the *A* bank, the *A* bus will be activated and camera 1 will gradually be faded in and appear on the line monitor.

director prepares a simple two-bank switcher for an initial fade-in.[2] This follows the director's command, "Prepare to fade from black to camera 1." (See section 8.5 for a discussion of preparation and execution commands.) With both faders locked together in the lower *B*-bank position, the "black" button is pressed on the *B* bank and camera 1 is pressed on the *A* bank. Your program line monitor would at this point show a "blank" screen. At the command, "Fade from black to camera 1," or

2. Throughout this chapter, the term *technical director* (TD) will be used to denote the person who operates the switching unit. The term is derived from professional situations where the person given that title has a much larger engineering responsibility for supervising the entire technical staff and operates the switcher/SEG only at the latter part of the production effort. There are circumstances when a person may function only as the SEG operator and is usually then known simply as the *switcher*.

"Fade in camera 1," the technical director gradually moves the interlocked fader arms from the lower to the upper position (gradually reducing the strength of the *B*-bus signal and simultaneously increasing the *A*-bus signal with camera 1 punched up on it). On the monitor you will see the camera 1 picture gradually fade in and come up to full strength.

At this point, if the director asks for an instantaneous cut (take) to camera 2 or camera 3, it is accomplished by pressing the designated button on the *A* bank.

Dissolves

If, for any one of a number of dramatic or aesthetic reasons, the director wants to get to the next shot by momentarily blending the images of two cameras in a transition, you can utilize a *dissolve*. Assuming you have the switcher set up as shown in figure 8-5 (with camera 1 punched up on the *A* bank), camera 1 is on the line because both levers (locked together) are in the *up* position, so all the video signal is coming through the *A* bus (camera 1). When the director gives the preparatory command, "Prepare a dissolve to camera 2," you, as the technical director, will prepare the switcher by punching up camera 2 on the *B* bank; there is, of course, no change in the picture on the line monitor because all the signal is coming through the *A* bus (where camera 1 is punched up).

When the director gives the command, "Dissolve to camera 2," you move the interlocked fader levers downward, which activates the *B* bus while deactivating the *A* bus—thus decreasing the video signal from camera 1 on the *A* bank at the same rate that you are adding power to the picture (camera 2) on the *B* bank. When both faders are at the bottom position—fully activating the *B* bus and cutting out the *A* bus—you see only camera 2.

PROGRAM
LINE
OUT

193

CHAPTER 8
Operation of the
Special Effects
Generating Switcher

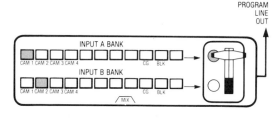

FIGURE 8-5

A dissolve on a two-bank switcher.

As a continuation of the switching sequence started in figure 8-4, the switcher is shown here as it would be set up for the next transition—a dissolve to camera 2. The camera 1 selector button is still punched up on the *A* bank (from the fade-in executed in figure 8-4) and is feeding camera 1 as the line output—since the fader arms have activated the *A* bank at this point. Punch up camera 2 on the deactivated *B* bank ("black" was previously punched up for the initial fade-in) and you are ready for your dissolve from camera 1 to camera 2. Simply pull the fader arms down from the *A*-bank position to the *B*-bank position and you have dissolved from camera 1 to camera 2.

But for a brief period, you had the two camera pictures overlapping during the *dissolve* transition.

It should be noted that for years motion picture directors, working in the dramatic idiom only, used what was termed the *lap dissolve* to denote the passage of time or a change in physical location from one scene to the next. With the advent of television with program forms such as music, news, and sports, the dissolve is more often used as a way of aesthetically *connecting* two visual ideas.

Superimpositions

If the director wishes to blend two images together and hold them in combination for a specific period of time, the result is termed a superimposition or, more often, a **super.** A superimposition is really nothing more than a dissolve that has been halted at midpoint. With both the *A*- and *B*-bank levers locked together at the halfway point—and different cameras punched up on the two banks—the switcher is simultaneously feeding 50 percent of the picture from the *A* bank and 50 percent from the *B* bank. The result is a "blended" picture with two half-strength, ghostlike images seen at the same time.

A good example of when to use such a super may be in a musical production—for example, a vocalist accompanying herself on the guitar. At a point dictated by the nature and tempo of the music, the director will have a wide shot on camera 1; then, telling the camera 1 operator to slowly pan left (moving the performer to the right half of the frame), a close-up shot of the singer's face, from camera 3, is supered in the left half of the frame.

If one or both of the camera shots in a super seems to be relatively weak in terms of brightness, it is possible to press a release button on the handle of the faders and separate the *A* and *B* levers. Each fader can then be adjusted individually to enhance its brightness level. This process is called *splitting the faders*. Since both pictures are only at half-strength when two pictures are *in super*, an obvious question might be: Why not split the faders on all supers—activating both buses all the way—and have the full value of both pictures? The best answer is that the resulting two-picture video level will often exceed what the video control system can handle. The effect is usually a *blooming* (or white domination) of the brightness scale of the picture. To achieve the best balance of the two pictures, ideally, the TD should have a chance to note the needed levels during a rehearsal period. However, because this is not always possible in live programs, we begin to see the inadequacy of our simple two-bank switching system.

There is one other transitional effect that our basic two-bank switcher is able to accomplish *after* the superimposition has been set up as the output of the switcher. Called an **undercut,** it is a matter of *retaining* one of the picture sources making up the super and *changing* the second picture by means of a simple camera cut procedure. As an example, let's say that we have started a program with the lettering of the opening title originating from the character generator (position #5 on the *B* bank) *in super* with a still picture being shot by *camera 1* (on the *A* bank). After our initial fade-in from black to camera 1 (on the *A* bank), you would then super the character generator (on the *B* bank) over the camera 1 shot by pulling the fader arms down to the halfway point. Next the director wants to replace the still picture (on camera 1) with a wide shot of the studio (which is on camera 2) but still leave the title supered. To accomplish this undercut, you would simply push the camera 2 button on the *A* bank—without moving the fader arms—and the studio shot (on camera 2) replaces the camera 1 shot *in super* with the title. It should be noted that the undercut works equally well with a very different two source effect called a *key* that will be covered later in the chapter.

Fade Outs

At the end of the program—or at the end of a major segment—the usual transition is a fade to black. The normal method of fading out is to use the black position on the inactivated bus as another camera source and dissolve to it. For instance, in figure 8-5, if the director called for a fade to black, you would first have to punch up "black" on the *B* bus. Then, on command, you would move both faders down to the *B*-bus position. In actuality, you would be fading out the *A* bus with camera 1 on it while you are simultaneously fading in the *B* bus with black (a synchronized signal with no picture) punched up on it.

If there are two picture sources *in-super* with both faders together at the midpoint position, a fade to black must be achieved by simultaneously moving each fader toward the bus that has had a black synch signal activated and away from the bank with the picture source. This is another application of the *split fader* technique described above. In effect, both buses have now been inactivated—no program signal is coming through on either bank—and we have black on the screen. If, however, you have gone the wrong direction with both faders, you will then have two very bright pictures on the screen. Another method of getting to black is to first fade out one of the two signals, and then fade that bank to black.

8.3 OPERATION OF THE SPECIAL EFFECTS GENERATOR

The visual transitions previously described are exactly those that were available to directors during television's formative years in the 1950s. The top network shows, from what is often called "The Golden Age of Television," did not have their creativity limited by what would today be considered a rather primitive switcher.

Evolution of the Modern SEG/Switcher

This is not to say that directors and technical directors did not wish for more flexibility. Supered titles always looked washed out. And even if you wanted to split the faders for added video strength, there was no way to *preview* a super in advance so as to set up the desired camera strength from each bus. Except for the super, there was no way to combine elements of two pictures

at full strength or show two sources on a split screen. There was no way to combine more than two pictures at once. So, the next generation of switchers was produced with an impressive array of special effects that not only solved these problems but also greatly enhanced the "visual vocabulary" of television.

The term *special effects generator (SEG)*, truly describes the functions and capabilities of the modern switching unit. Along with the basic cuts, dissolves, and supers, the simplest SEG can create, for example, *two- and three-source keys, chroma key effects,* and *pattern wipes* that are very impressive—although somewhat complicated from an operational standpoint for the beginning student. (See section 8.4.)

If, however, one approaches the SEG/switcher in a manner that seeks to understand the *functional logic* that goes into the creation of each individual effect, then the unit is not nearly so intimidating. Always try to picture the underlying video signal flow, and the basic operations should be much easier to follow. In other words, one should look for certain *patterns of operation* that apply to a number of different production functions. For example, whether you are doing a camera cut, dissolve, or wipe, you must first make certain that the correct camera or other picture source has been selected on the proper switcher bank. Only then can you proceed with the specific operations that will accomplish the desired effect.

The Grass Valley Group Model 100 Production switcher, as shown in figure 8-6, is in use in well over 5,000 production facilities throughout the world. With a price range and functional complexity designed for the medium-sized operation, it is perhaps the best known of all switchers used in industrial and educational institutions. With its impressive special effects capability and other electronic components relating to picture control, it has many of

FIGURE 8-6

The Grass Valley Model 100 switcher introduces considerable flexibility with its deceptively simple design.

Photo courtesy of Grass Valley Group

the features found in larger and more expensive units. Therefore, we shall use the GVG Model 100 as an example to show operational techniques that students will be using as they move into professional video activity of all types.

Specific Operational Techniques for Basic Transitions

Having previously outlined some of the general switcher operations in terms of fader bars, which always correspond to a specific *A* bank or *B* bank, we must now modify that generalization because on many of the newer switchers, such as the GVG Models 100 and 110, this is not the case. In the following example of the dissolve, the fader arms could be placed in either the upper or lower position prior to the beginning of the move. It would not matter at that point—as long as other buttons were preset properly.

Program and Preset

A careful look at figure 8-7 shows that there are two lower switching buses

(sometimes called *crosspoint buses*). These are labeled **program** and **preset.** (We shall for the moment ignore the additional *background* aspect of their function. We shall also for the moment ignore the *key bus* directly above.)

The main concept in this arrangement is that the upper *program* bank (the middle of the three buses) is *always* the bank that provides the source of the picture that is the *line output of the switcher.* And it follows, then, that the *preset* bank is where you press the button for the camera picture that will be the *next line output* following the completed transition.

Using the GVG 100 model, let us follow an example of a simple dissolve from camera 1 to camera 2. We would first go to the transition section shown at the right hand side of figure 8-7 and press the *mix* button just above *transition type* because with a dissolve we will be mixing two signals together. We also press the *background (bkgd)* button above the *next transition* section of the effects transition group of controls. (We will look at this in more detail later.) Next, with the fader lever in the *upper* position, the *camera 1* button is

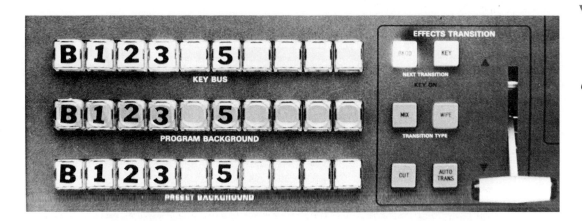

FIGURE 8-7

Operating buses of the GVG 100 switcher.

The "transition control section" is comprised of the individual buttons on each bank for input selection and the fader arms for dissolves and effects.

Photo courtesy of Grass Valley Group, Inc.

pressed on the upper *program* bank and the *camera 2* button is pressed on the lower *preset bank.* The camera 1 button on the program bank will glow brightly with what is called *high tally;* this reinforces what our program monitor tells us—that we are feeding a camera 1 signal on the program line. The camera 2 button on the preset bank glows with a softer intensity called a *low tally;* this indicates that camera 2 is selected to be the next camera on the air.

As we begin to move the fader downward, we will see a *green arrow* begin to glow at the place where the fader arm will be when we have completed the dissolve to camera 2. (This reinforcement of the direction of our lever move is important in more complex operations.) As we continue the fader movement downward, both the camera 1 and the camera 2 buttons will glow brightly as both cameras are seen briefly on the program monitor (a momentary superimposition) during the dissolve.

As the dissolve is completed and the fader lever makes contact at the lower position, we have put camera 2 on the air, and we see camera 2 on the program line monitor. But the surprising thing is what has happened to the two banks. The upper *program* bank now shows its *camera 2* button glowing brightly (high tally); and on the lower *preset bank,* the *camera 1* button (the camera from which we have just dissolved) is now glowing dimly (low tally). As we completed our dissolve, the two cameras switched positions on the buses, executing what is called a **flip-flop** because their positions as *line feed* and *off-line feed* cameras have just been reversed. Looking again at the switcher, we see that even though our fader is in the *lower position,* the line feed camera (camera 2) is shown on the *upper* bank, indicating it is on the *program* bus. It is the brightly glowing tally that reminds us which camera is our line feed and *not* of the position of the fader—as with older switchers.

Automatic Transitions

If we had wanted a dissolve lasting exactly two seconds, we could have used the **automatic transition** feature of the GVG 100 and not even used the fader levers at all (since the position of the fader arms no longer indicates which bus is on the air). We would start out by having the program and preset buses set up exactly as in the beginning of the previous example—with the fader arms in the upper position (although we could just as well have started with them in the lower position). We would then have used the **auto transition rate** controls at the upper right-hand corner of the unit. (See figure 8-8.) Keeping in mind the thirty-frames-per-second rate explained in chapter 5, we would use the *set* controls to put the transition rate at sixty frames.

In this same group of controls, we would use the *select* button to move the red indicator light to the *auto trans* position. The *mix* button for the "transition type" and the *bkgd* button for the "next transition" are still pressed (see figure 8-7). By pressing the *auto trans* button, we will achieve a perfect two-second dissolve from camera 1 to camera 2. The "flip-flop" will occur as before. The faders are not moved—although they can be used to *override* the automatic dissolve at any time.

For an instantaneous cut between cameras 1 and 2, we would only have had to press the *cut* button (right next to the *auto trans* button) instead of the *auto trans* button itself.

Wipe Transitions Between Cameras

In making a transition between two consecutive pictures, there are times when neither the take nor the dissolve is suitable. An example might be where you want to draw special attention to a picture or series of pictures. The *wipe transition* often accomplishes this perfectly—by letting the viewer see portions of both pictures as the separation line moves through the screen. Used excessively, the wipe calls attention to itself as a gimmick, but when used with discretion, it is an important part of a director's visual vocabulary.

Many production switcher/SEG units in use today have dozens of *patterned wipe* designs—ranging from the traditional vertical line moving horizontally across the screen (or the horizontal line moving

FIGURE 8-9
Corner insert.

This effect may
either be used as a
transition from one
camera to another or
to hold two pictures
on the screen for a
period of time.

vertically down the screen) to diagonals, diamonds, circles, and all manner of boxes, to the jagged shark tooth effect, which is the cliché of the late-night horror movie show.

Split Screens and Corner Inserts

Just as the superimposition may be thought of as a dissolve suspended in mid-transition, so might the **split screen** and **corner insert** (or any one of a number of special use inserts) be thought of as a wipe effect that has been halted in midpoint.

As a common application of a "suspended" wipe transition, the *split screen* is a means of combining two pictures with either a horizontal or vertical (and occasionally diagonal) line separating the screen into two distinct areas—with a different picture (from separate cameras or other video sources) in each part of the screen. By means of the special effects faders, relative sizes of the two pictures can be adjusted.

By manipulating the horizontal and vertical special effects faders separately, it is also possible to achieve a *corner insert*. (See figure 8-9.) This places the inserted camera picture in any quadrant of the screen. In a televised baseball game, for example, when you see the runner at first base within a small insert in the top right-hand corner of the primary "behind-the-plate" wide shot, you are actually seeing a corner wipe that has only been taken part of the way—in what could have been a full-screen wipe from one camera to another. Again, the exact size and proportion of the corner insert can easily be adjusted by the control levers.

A further technical advance is the *multiple-source split screen*. With this device, it is possible to split the screen into a number of individual sections, each with a separate picture. Again, these separate divisions can be positioned and shaped to meet a variety of artistic needs. When four picture sources are shown it is known as a **quad split.**

Another useful special effect is the **spotlight,** which enables the operator to dim the entire screen except for one circle of light that can be shaped, changed in

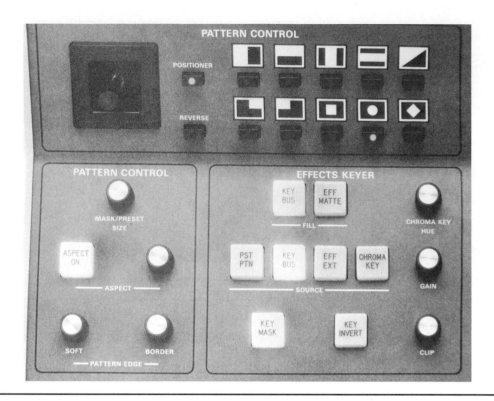

FIGURE 8-10

The "pattern control" section of the GVG 100.

The pattern control buttons allow the TD to select specific patterns for wipes and inserts. It also has controls that can further position and shape the patterns.

Photo courtesy of Grass Valley Group, Inc.

size, and positioned anywhere on the screen with a joystick. This effect can also be considered as a special application of the suspended wipe transition.

Execution of the Wipe Transition

The method of handling the patterned wipe transition is not too difficult once one understands the basics of the dissolve transition.

Returning to our specific example with the GVG 100, we first need to push the *wipe* button for "transition type" next to the fader arms (see figure 8-7), cancelling the *mix* transition button. On the "pattern control" section of the switcher (see figure 8-10), the *select button,* under the pattern with a confirming red light, determines the basic shape of the wipe. Keep in mind that the new video from the preset camera will appear in the *white* area of the pattern shown on the button. With the *center circle*

wipe, for example, the new picture will emerge on the screen as a circle in the middle of the picture; its image will be widened by the movement of the fader.

There is also a *reverse* option in which the *black* area of the pattern represents the new camera. Other controls allow for changes in *position* and *shape* of the circle or other selected design. You can also adjust how *hard* or *soft* you want the edge of the wipe to be and how wide you want to make the *border* between the two video source pictures. The *auto transition* feature discussed previously can be utilized for the execution of wipes as well as for dissolves.

Keyed Special Effects with Two and Three Sources

For the majority of multiple picture combinations the superimposition has been

FIGURE 8-11

Two monitors illustrating the difference between a super and a key.

The monitor on the left shows white lettering from a character generator supered over the woman's face. The right-hand monitor shows the same lettering keyed over the woman's face.

totally replaced by the *key* effect, which "cuts out" and combines solid images from two or more video sources.[3] The basic principle of the key is a process by which differences in brightness and/or color are used to insert one picture into another. Often the analogy of a "cookie cutter" is used to explain how one image electronically *dominates* all or part of a second background picture to produce a *key effect*, such as white letters over a studio camera shot. Unlike a superimposition where the two images bleed through onto each other, the key cuts a clean electronic hole into which it inserts its signal. Figure 8-11 illustrates the difference between a super and a key.

In many such effects, a *wipe pattern* is used to create the *outline shape*, and a *third source* is used as an input to fill the hole with another picture. Another version of this three-source effect, known as an **auto key** (formerly labeled the "external" key), uses one video source to establish the external shape of a letter or figure—in effect, stamping out an image much like a stencil might cut out a shape. The key effect then utilizes a third source to fill in the picture and color of the "stenciled out" part of the design.

However, for our example we will use the least complex of these special effects—white titles keyed over a camera shot. This is what is termed a **self key** (also known as a **luminance** or **internal key**) because the dominant brightness level of the lettering cuts its own electronic pattern in the background picture. However, even this simple special effect should always be previewed and adjusted before it is used.

3. Occasionally the word *matte* is associated with the *key* process. The term was derived from the traditional film technique that printed or "matted" inserts within the larger film frame.

Let us say that we are going to use our key at the beginning of a program. The director's command would be to "Prepare to fade up from black to a key of titles on the CG over camera 1." The technical director would press *black* on the *program (background)* bank, *camera 1* on the *preset (background)* bank and *button # 5* (for titles from the character generator) on the *key bus* (refer back to figure 8-7). In this case, camera 1 is our *preset background* and the character generator will be our *key* source. Our fader arms can be in either the upper or lower position to start the exercise. (Remember, their position does *not* relate to the bank that is feeding the program line.)

The two *next transition* buttons in the *effects transition* area allow us to select the source bus or busses used in the next transition or effect. In this case, we press *both* the *bkgd (background)* and *key* buttons because when we come up from black we are going to fade to a key consisting of *two* images, the preset background from camera 1, and keyed over it, the lettering originating from the character generator on the *key bus #5* position.

In the *effects keyer* section (see figure 8-10), we must press both *key bus* buttons because the *key bus* will be both the *source* and the *fill* of the effect. (If we were preparing a three-source key, we would punch up different sources for the source and for the fill.)

Once the selections have been punched up on the *preset background* bank (camera 1) and on the *key bus* bank (the character generator), the **preview monitor** will be displaying the key effect of those two sources (see the following discussion). Because the difference in brightness between the lettering and the background is always a matter of delicate balance, a look at this preview monitor will now tell us just what adjustments must be made. The **clip knob** sets the *brightness* threshold for the key source video, which allows the letters to "cut" the

electronic hole, and the **gain knob** sets the *sharpness* of the key effect itself. After viewing the result of these adjustments, the director gives the command, "Fade up on the key effect," and the technical director executes the fade-in to the effect by moving the fader arms from wherever they are to the opposite position. The key effect is brought up on the line, and we see the results on the **program (line) monitor.**

On the GVG model 110, there is a feature called **key memory** that is built into the unit. It will remember the *clip* and *gain* settings for a source image that has been used previously and noted. When that source is used a second time, the clip and gain settings will automatically be returned to their previously established levels. Other state of the art SEG/switchers have even more amazing electronic memory innovations (see section 8.4).

Picture Monitors

At this point it should be obvious that the video monitors in the video control room are essential to the proper use of the switcher in addition to camera operations.[4] For that reason it is important to discuss some of the specific monitors that were essential to the explanation of the above switcher operations.

Even in a moderate-sized studio, there may be up to a dozen different monitors, each performing an important individual function (see figure 8-11). Each video source will have its own monitor. Each studio camera, character generator, and video recorder will have a small individual monitor. In addition to these seven- to ten-inch units, there will be several larger monitors. The most

---

4. The video *monitor* is distinguished from the regular television *receiver* in that the monitor is usually a high quality unit with ability to reproduce fine detail. It receives a direct unmodulated video signal, as opposed to a modulated radio frequency signal. Thus, there is no audio and no channel-selection capability.

crucial of these is the *program (line) monitor,* which shows the actual picture that the switcher is sending to master control for live transmission or recording. This is the one that the director must watch constantly as a final check on the program picture content.

The other large monitor, often to the left of the program monitor, is the *preview monitor,* which is used heavily by the technical director to adjust keys and other special effects in advance of their use—and to show the director just how these effects or any upcoming shot will look. For some types of production, directors may ask for the upcoming camera shot to be displayed so that any need for minor adjustment can be more clearly seen.

In complicated network sports programs, this preview function may be done on separate **preset monitors** used just for effects. In some production systems, the preset monitors may be used to routinely preview the upcoming shot so that the director will always be able to see precisely what is going on the air next. There may also be a number of preview monitors for remote location feeds in addition to the basic preview monitor. In a live broadcasting situation, an **air monitor** always shows the actual broadcast picture.

8.4 ADDITIONAL SPECIAL EFFECTS AND DIGITAL APPLICATIONS

An additional component called the **downstream keyer** is increasingly being put to use as television production becomes more complex. It is used to add an additional effect to a video signal *after* it has passed through the primary selection and combination functions of a switcher. When viewed on a monitor, the output of the downstream keyer looks much the same as the output of the internal key component.

It is designed to insert captions or other key effects into the final output of the switcher and, as such, may also utilize sources such as a character generator or a graphics camera.

The *key memory* feature of the GVG Model 110 was previously described. Other state of the art SEGs have even more amazing electronic memory and execution innovations. For example, the Grass Valley Group Model 300 (see figure 8-12) offers a much more sophisticated memory feature called the *E-MEM,*[5] which can combine digitally produced animated graphics along with color, brightness, and other design information in its memory unit. With the pressing of a single button, the animated effect/transition can be recalled and executed with no other preparation or commands.

Other features of today's switchers include all sorts of ways to manipulate colors and shapes of backgrounds and borders. The actual *color* itself is adjusted by the **hue** control. The **chroma knob** varies the *intensity* **(saturation)** of a color (the "bluishness" of blue). And the **luminance** control can regulate the amount of brightness in the image. All these controls interact to a degree that can only be appreciated with hands-on experience.

Chroma Key

Now one of the most common of the electronic special effects, the **chroma key** is a matting process that has long been a staple of much video production. This is a technique in which a specific color—rather than a graphic design or pattern—is used as the electronic key to cut out part of the picture. (Any color can be designated to be used as the key; however, light blue or green is most often used because it is farthest from any skin tones.) Wherever the

5. *E-MEM* is a trademark of the Grass Valley Group.

FIGURE 8-12

A complete view of
the Grass Valley
Group 300
SEG/switcher.

Note signal control
displays and the
number of
switching busses.

foreground or key camera detects the designated hue (and chroma) in its picture, that video information is discarded and background picture signals are supplied from a second source such as a still-store device, graphics unit, camera, or VCR.

Probably the best known example of this process is seen nightly on the local weathercast during the news. The studio camera has a shot of the weathercaster standing in front of a light blue background (and not wearing any blue item of clothing). Through the switcher, this picture is combined with the computer generated local or national weather map that includes cloud movement and other animated effects. (See figure 8-13.) The result is impressive and depends upon the skill of the weathercaster in pointing out specific areas on the blank wall through the use of an unseen monitor.

Although the use of chroma key is widespread, it is not without numerous potential difficulties. The electronic equipment has to be delicately adjusted; lighting of the color background of the key camera has to be perfectly even; considerable attention must be given to selection of costumes and scenery. Slight problems in any of these areas lead to conspicuous troubles such as tearing of the foreground image, an obvious border around the foreground figure, discoloration, or indistinct contours.

Many of these drawbacks have been overcome by newer systems, such as *Ultimatte*,[6] which has supplanted or replaced chroma key in most major professional studios. In addition to conventional color matting features, Ultimatte can render not only highlights and reflections off of glass, but

6. *Ultimatte* is a trademark of the Ultimatte Corporation.

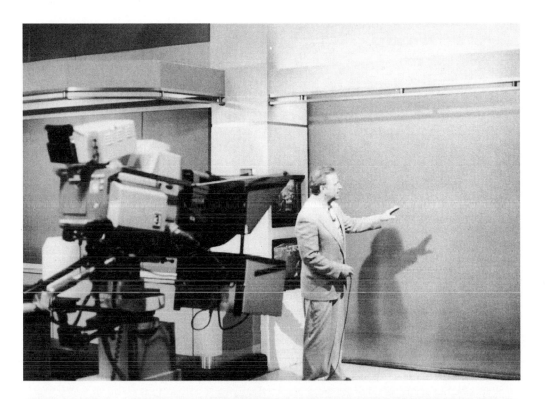

FIGURE 8-13
Chroma key.

Like all weathercasters, KABC-TV's Johnny Mountain actually works against a blank blue or green screen. The computer generated map and other animated effects are chroma keyed through the switcher as seen on the televised picture on the bottom.

Photo courtesy of KABC-TV

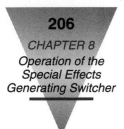

a. Representation of an analog signal waveform.

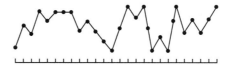

b. Analog signal as measured for digital conversion.

01100101 01010111 10000101

c. Example of computer readout of measured digital signal.

FIGURE 8-14

Comparison of analog and digital encoding.

(a) Representation of an analog signal waveform. (b) Analog signal as measured for digital conversion. (c) Example of computer readout of measured digital signal.

---

the actual glass object itself will be visibly matted over the background image. The process is sensitive enough that it can capture every strand of a person's hair and even wisps of smoke.

Digital Effects

Whenever the switcher (DVE) unit is used to *shape* the picture, it is almost always the result of some aspect of a *digital manipulation* process. With digital technology it is possible to expand the creative and production capabilities of television far beyond what had been possible earlier.

Unless otherwise noted, the audio and video signals described in chapters 2 and 5 are *analog* systems; that is, variations in electrical current actually represent and define the sound and picture. The brighter the image hitting the lens, the greater the intensity of the electrical signal. With *digital* encoding, on the other hand, the video

information is transformed into a series of *binary* (base-two) numbers. (See figure 8-14.) Each of the 400 plus picture elements that are spread across a single scanning line, for example (see section 5.2), is reduced to a brightness level on a *luminance scale* from 1 to 256. The video signal can thus be translated into a series of binary numbers expressed as off/on blips. (A point registering at a brightness level of 155 on the luminance scale, for instance, would be encoded as 1-0-0-1-1-0-1-1 in the binary system.)[7]

Once the television signal is encoded into a binary-digital format, the system has many advantages: (1) memory or storage

---

7. Binary encoding, of course, is what forms the basis for all digital computers and microprocessing equipment. It is built on the base-two counting system, which reduces all numerical information to a two-symbol number (using *zero* and *one*). Thus, all numerical data can be handled as a series of *off* (zero) and *on* (one) electrical connections.

capacity can be significantly increased; (2) the quality of the video information does not deteriorate as it is processed, amplified, channeled, duplicated, edited, and transmitted; and (3) most importantly, the signal information can now be manipulated, compressed, enhanced, and augmented in ways that are impossible with analog information.

Some of the digital switcher effects most often seen are *continuous image compression,* which enables the switcher operator to compress the full-frame picture down to the size of a tiny circle (at any speed, to any size) and—with a joystick—to place the shrunken image anywhere on the screen. This is what makes the squeeze zoom possible as a transition. *Image expansion* allows the director to take any segment of the video frame and enlarge it up to four times its original size (beyond which point it becomes unintelligible). A combined phenomenon is *image stretching.* Any portion of the picture can be expanded or compressed in any direction; ratios can be altered; graphics can be shaped to fit the picture.

Other transitional devices—in addition to effects such as the fold-over and squeeze zoom—include the *video split,* which literally can take a picture and pull it apart in the middle to make room for a new frame, and the *push-off,* which simply shoves a whole frame off the tube sideways while replacing it with another image (as opposed to the wipe, which does not move the two stationary frames involved in the transition).

The strongest impact of many of these advances has been in the areas of graphics as they relate to postproduction editing. (See section 7.3.) Once the basic video images have been recorded, the director can sit down with an editor and decide how to time each transition, when to compress this image and bring in another, whether to electronically zoom in on a particular frame, how to shape graphics as they are added later, and so forth. The video editor now has at his or her command more sophisticated and less expensive creative opportunities than film editors have ever enjoyed.

Other components developed through the application of digital technology include the *time-base corrector* whose importance to the videotape machine will be discussed in chapter 9, and the *framestore synchronizer* that helps to synchronize the process of inserting live video feeds from distant locations.

8.5 VIDEO PRODUCTION COMMANDS

In discussing audio production techniques (see section 3.5), we stressed the difference between commands of *preparation* and commands of *execution.* Nowhere is this distinction more important than in giving commands to the technical director. The preparation and execution of the various transitions and effects involves very differing amounts of time in terms of switcher operation. A straight take is instantly ready but a dissolve to a chroma key effect requires a number of operations, done in a precise order. The commands of preparation must allow for sufficient lead time. Such commands, given over the intercom system, allow camera, VCR, and graphics operators time for their own preparations.

One helpful rule is that the command of preparation for any straight take is "ready." The preparation for any dissolve, super, fade, or special transition or effect that involves getting something set or prepared on another bus, uses the command "prepare." (A few directors prefer to use the command "set up.") Although some directors use the term "standby" as a preparation for both takes and dissolves, this can be confusing to the crew. The use of correct terminology immediately lets the technical director know whether he or she simply has to get ready to push a button on the same bus or whether it is necessary to prepare or set up another camera or effect on another bus. The command sequence for a direct take from camera 1 to camera 2 is stated by the director as follows:

> **(Preparation):** "Ready camera 2" (or simply) "Ready 2"
>
> **(Execution):** "Take 2"

The word *ready* lets the technical director know that he or she only has to place a finger on the camera 2 button on the activated bus.

No matter how rushed the director may be or how fast paced the program may be, the director should never skimp on the command of preparation. If occasionally the director does not have time to give full commands, some abbreviation could be used:

> **(Preparation):** "Ready 2"
>
> **(Execution):** "Take it"
>
> **(or simply):** "Take"

If time is so short that even this much preparation is impossible (for example, shooting a game show, fast-paced panel discussion, or football game), the command of preparation still must be given priority:

> **(Preparation):** "Two"
>
> **(Execution):** "Take"

When such abbreviated commands are used successfully, it is usually in a situation where the director and the crew have worked together for an extended period of time. Even so, most directors will return to the safer, more complete commands when time allows.

A dissolve requires a different sounding command of preparation to allow the technical director time to prepare for a more complex series of actions. Assuming you already have camera 1 on line, the correct commands for a dissolve would be:

> **(Preparation):** "Prepare a dissolve to 2" (or) "Prepare 2" (or) "Set up 2"
>
> **(Execution):** "Dissolve to 2"

For a super, the actions are the same so the commands are much the same:

> **(Preparation):** "Prepare to super 2 over 1" (or) "Set up 2" (implying that camera 1 stays on the air)
>
> **(Execution):** "Super camera 2 over 1" (or just) "Super 2"

We depart slightly from the basic pattern whenever two cameras are to be *taken* together in a super or key. While these effects involve a movement of the control levers to set them up, the movement is not one of program execution. As previously outlined, the command of execution is a "take"—calling only for the pressing of the *line mix* output button or *take bar*. For this reason, the voice procedure in this case should be as follows:

> **(Preparation):** "Ready to take 2 and 3 in super"
>
> **(Execution):** "Take super"

The repetition of camera numbers in the command is optional, but does reinforce the intent of the command.

Much of the discipline necessary for keeping a program under control comes from this pattern of preparation and execution. The technical director must know exactly what is coming. Of necessity, this pattern must occasionally be broken—when complicated effects are called for. Usually a key, for example, must be preset several shots before its use. In this situation, after the command of preparation, there may be several intervening commands before the execution of the key. The command of preparation must be given far enough in advance so that the technical director has a chance to do the preset at a time most convenient during the ongoing program. The director keeps an eye on the preview monitor to see when the key is ready. The commands might be as follows:

(Advance preparation): "We're about to wrap so preview your key of camera 2 and credits on the CG"

(Ongoing shots in the program continue): "Ready 1, take 1 . . . etc."

(Immediate preparation): "Now set up a dissolve to the key of credits over camera 2"

(Execution of the key): "Dissolve to the credits"

Similarly, any command to preview and adjust—say, a corner wipe or an insert—in the coverage of a live event may be given well in advance of its eventual use on the air. There may be several intervening ad-libbed shots. This can be thought of as a nontime-specific command. For example:

(Advance preparation): "Preview a top-left corner insert, camera 3, of runner off first base, within camera 2"

(Intervening shots ad-libbed): "Ready 4, take 4, . . . etc."

(Adjustment of preparation): "Tighten the framing on camera 3 insert"

(Intervening shots ad-libbed): "Ready 1, take 1, . . . etc."

(Immediate preparation): "O.K. Now, ready to take corner insert"

(Execution of the effect): "Take effect"

One final note: Fades to and from black are handled in a manner very similar to the dissolve (the fade to or from black is in essence a dissolve to or from black). Due to the fact that a sync black picture has such a definite connotation of separation and/or conclusion, many directors reserve the term "fade" for use as a command only to dissolve to or from black. This serves as a safeguard to protect against any inadvertent dissolve to full-screen black.

As special effects generating switchers have become more complex, the numerous visual options available to the director have placed many demands upon the technical director. The director is obligated to use the clearest of command language, which in turn must be based upon an operational understanding of what is involved in achieving execution of those commands. Beyond common courtesy, there is a very practical aspect to this. Ill timed and poorly stated commands simply cannot be executed within the time framework that the director may have in mind. Such a disparity can have serious side effects, especially with live programming. Used well, today's state of the art switcher is an impressive instrument. For those learning its operation, the advice is much the same as with all television components. One first gains a clear understanding of basic technique and then extrapolates those fundamentals to more complex equipment. It is especially true with the switcher.

SUMMARY

The switcher is the key *channeling* and *mixing* device in the video signal flow system. In conjunction with the *special effects generator (SEG)* and *digital video effects (DVE)*, it is also involved in *shaping* the video signal.

The switcher can be thought of as a simple connection panel, with additional *banks* and *fader arms* added to increase the flexibility of the unit. The basic camera transitions and effects used on the switcher include the *take, dissolve, fade,* and *super.*

There are several variations of more complex switchers that, in conjunction with the various video *monitors,* enable the technical director to *preview* and *preset* certain effects. On many switchers *auto transition* is available so that transitions can be programmed to be of a specific length. Special electronic effects include *wipes, split screens,* *corner insert,* and *spotlight.* Also available are numerous *key and insert* effects and the *chroma key* and *downstream keyer.*

Effects that are possible because of *digital* technology encompass *image compression and expansion* and *image stretching*—as well as transitions such as the fold-over, squeeze zoom, video split, push-off, and numerous others.

Because the video switcher is a complex piece of equipment, the director must give precise instructions to the technical director.

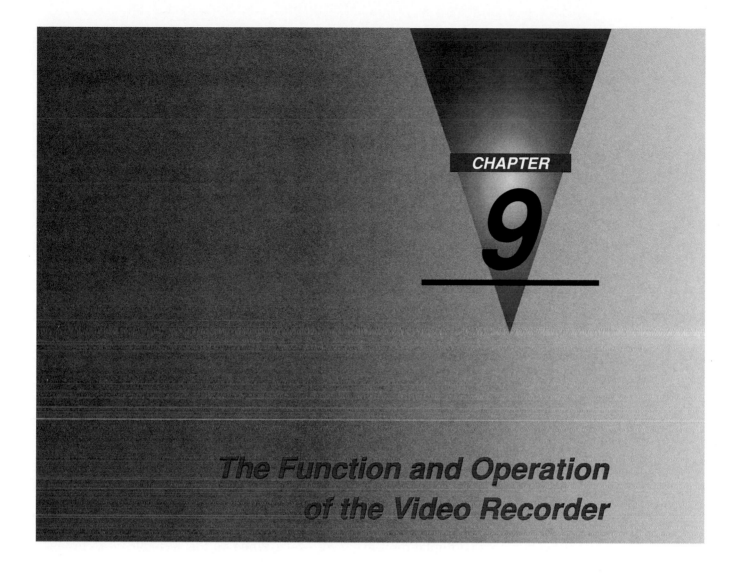

CHAPTER

9

The Function and Operation of the Video Recorder

I
n 1956 CBS first used videotape for the delayed rebroadcast of its newscast to the western states. The industry immediately saw the possibilities that tape provided for the *distribution* and *storage* of program material. The *editing* potential was obvious, but the technology had yet to be developed. In the intervening period, videotape has played an enormously important role in the development of the television industry because of the impressive advancements in recording as well as editing capabilities.

In televised news, a crucial aspect of production is to "get it on tape." The material can be later edited and in numerous other ways prepared for broadcast, but if there is not that first *acquisition* process, the story may not appear at all. Increasingly, raw footage is transferred by microwave or satellite directly from cameras in the field to recording machines waiting at a central studio location. After preproduction editing the program segments are again stored on individual videotape cassettes for flexible access during the live broadcast. Similarly, soap operas, situation comedies, and countless other types of production presently place large amounts of material on an *original master* recording for later work during the **post-production** process.

Until recently this production sequence has been entirely dependent upon the use of videotape at all stages. The constantly expanding use of videotape during the past decade was due to a number of improvements in the traditional NTSC signal. As these innovations are applied to videotape recording, they can greatly enhance the quality of the picture. (See section 5.2.) Instead of the video signal being combined into a **composite** form, it can now be improved by having the color and brightness elements separated into a **component** signal. (Some formats further divide the color signal into two parts.)

A change with an even bigger potential has been the move from the original **analog** waveform (reflecting the structure of lightwaves) to a **digital** form that is almost entirely immune from distortion or interference. Of even more importance, however, is the fact that this signal is one that can be controlled and stored through the use of digital computer technology. It is obvious that this advance has important implications for all stages of video production, from acquisition to editing and graphics production, even into segment delivery during production.

It should be noted, however, that while the promise of computer related digital production methods are very much on the minds of many in the TV industry, the excellent performance of tape-based equipment and the cost of replacing existing units are seen by many as an assurance that videotape will be a factor in at least some phases of production for most of this decade. The wall of high quality videotape machines shown in figure 9-1 extends another fifty feet beyond camera range. It is typical of the sort of investment found in major postproduction houses all over the country.

This latest equipment has been designed to cope with the variety of signal formats that are currently in use. Figure 9-2 shows the video portion of the rear connection panel of the one-half inch Sony Betacam DVW-A500. There is provision for analog video signals in either a composite or component form. (The *Betacam* component signal requires two lines for the color signal.) The component digital *serial* signal to the right requires only one cable and carries audio as well. The larger meaning of these labels is that this tape deck is able to convert any of the input formats to any of the output formats, and vice-versa. A look at the rear panel of a Panasonic MII AU-65H would reveal an ability to handle both composite and component signals as well as a compatibility with the S-video format which separates color and luminance in a slightly different manner.

While all this technology is currently in use by much of the industry, a total changeover to a component/digital signal is very dependent upon the timetable that is established for the introduction of the **high definition television (HDTV)** format to the American public. This much heralded, but somewhat delayed new video standard, is also referred to as the **advanced television (ATV)** format. It features an upgraded digital/component signal that utilizes roughly twice the number of scanning lines as the existing system. Current plans are for a screen ratio of 9 by 16 as opposed to the traditional 3 by 4 ratio of screen width to height.

The digital signal's compatibility with computer technology has been very important to the development of **nonlinear** video editing. With its ability to insert audio and video into existing segments (in much the same way that one adds an additional sentence to an already completed paragraph

FIGURE 9-1

These VCR machines are only a portion of those that fill a large room at a major postproduction company. Any one of them can be connected to a number of editing suites or interconnected for dubbing purposes.

Photo courtesy of Hollywood Digital, Hollywood, CA

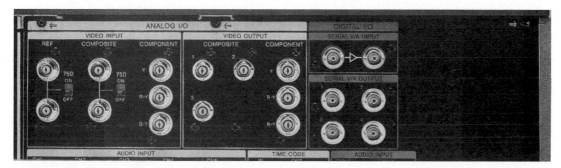

FIGURE 9-2

The Sony DVW-A500 Betacam not only hosts the latest digital/component technology, it is also designed to interact with other formats. Note the inputs and outputs for analog composite and component formats.

Photo courtesy of Sony Electronics, Inc.

with a word processor), it is bringing about some changes in the way much of today's video product is assembled. Some of the procedures relating to this new editing approach will be compared to traditional videotape editing in the next chapter.

9.1 PRINCIPLES OF VIDEO RECORDING

In this chapter we will first seek to provide a background to traditional videotape editing by presenting information on the operation and function of the equipment that is used in *recording* and *playing back* production video, whether it be for insert segments or entire programs. This equipment also serves as the basis for *storage* and *distribution* of the video product. In many cases, the equipment used for record and playback is the same as that used for editing and the construction of computer graphics.

The idea of video recording is based upon several aspects of the electromagnetic phenomenon. Chapter 5 presented a simplified model of how the three-chip camera creates an ongoing sequence of signals that are translated by the receiver tube into a color video picture. Although a brief recap of that material will be presented here, it is suggested that some may wish to go back to section 5.2 for an even more complete review.

A Brief Review of the Video Signal

The **CCD** chip, functioning as an **image sensor,** and the display picture tube **raster** (viewing area) are both organized into 525 horizontal scanning lines. (See figure 5-6.) Each of these lines is composed of more than 450 separate illumination points or picture elements. (This number can vary with the manufacturer.) Even though some of the top and bottom lines are used for synchronizing signals and information other than the video

picture, there are still roughly 250,000 separate picture elements or **pixels** that make up the mosaic-like electronic image.

As the lens focuses the incoming light from the subject onto the CCD image sensor, each one of the pixels is individually energized in direct relationship to the specific amount of light hitting the pixel. This process produces the signals that are the electronic version of the optical image focused on the face of the lens. In tube-type cameras, a stream of electrons (the **scanning beam**) is shot at the **target** at the front of the tube—essentially a similar plate of pixels—by means of electromagnets located just forward of the **electron gun,** which is the source of the electron beam. In the CCD camera, this "scanning" function is accomplished by vertical and horizontal **shift registers,** which in effect, collect the sequential output of the pixels.

This scanning process actually occurs in two phases. Starting at the top left of the picture, the odd-numbered lines are first scanned to produce a top-to-bottom picture **field**. Only one-half of the illumination points have been used to produce this picture. Once this half-picture has been scanned, the scanning beam starts at the top left of the picture again, and this time all the even-numbered lines are scanned to produce another picture field. There are sixty of these half-picture fields occurring every second. This odd-even field alternation, called **interlacing,** is designed to cut down on the unwanted "flicker" effect of the picture (sixty half pictures a second cause less flicker than thirty full pictures per second). This interlacing of fields adds up to a theoretical figure of thirty **frames** per second—although no complete frame ever really exists as a static entity.

Horizontal and Vertical Synchronization Pulses

Examining this process in greater detail, you will find that several additional factors are needed to ensure the stability of the picture. It is imperative that the scanning sequence in the camera, whether tube or chip type, be precisely synchronized at every stage of its journey—through the switcher, in all recording and editing equipment, during broadcast transmission, and at the home receiving set. A series of specialized pulses—generated independently of the color and luminance portion of the video signal—are utilized for this purpose. First, there is a **horizontal sync pulse,** which activates the video system at the beginning of each scanning line and turns it off for a brief retrace period **(blanking)** as the beam returns to the beginning of a new line on the left side of the picture tube.

At the completion of each field, there is a similar retrace period as the scanning beam returns to the top left of the picture. At this point, a **vertical sync pulse** is used to coordinate the start of each new field. While there are only two vertical sync pulses for every 525 horizontal sync pulses, they must nevertheless be considered as an extremely important part of the video sequence. Because it denotes the beginning of a new picture field, the vertical sync pulse has an important application in videotape editing.

9.2 THE ELECTROMAGNETIC BASIS OF VIDEO RECORDING

Previous sections of the text discussed how sound waves (section 3.2) and light waves (section 5.2)—through a series of transformations **(transducing)**—can be put into an electromagnetic form that is suitable for broadcast. By utilizing these and other qualities of magnetism and electrical energy, this complex broadcast signal can be permanently "memorized" for later use. As youngsters, many of us showed our friends how a magnet on the underside of a piece of paper can align iron filings into a magnetic pattern. The principle involved in that simple demonstration provides the basis for all audiotape and videotape recording.

The record-playback **head** on any tape machine is actually a magnet, and the tape is a polyester strip coated on one side with iron oxide particles. (On some of the newer high-resolution formats, metal particles are used.) If electrical energy—organized into a video signal—is fed into the head, the iron oxide or metal particles in the tape passing in contact with the head will be aligned into a continuing series of magnetic patterns. (See figure 9-3.) Thus, in the *record mode,* the resulting magnetic patterns are themselves a memory of the television signal. (The patterns are physically visible only if the oxide is treated with certain chemicals.)

In the *playback mode,* no electrical energy is sent to the magnetic head. Instead, as the tape moves across the head, the interaction of patterned iron oxide or metal particles in the tape and the magnetic head produces an electronic signal in the playback head that is a duplicate of the original input. This is how the "memorized" pattern on the tape produces the electrical signal that is transduced back into pictures and sound.

Occasionally, even with the best equipment, there can be some loss of quality. The tape itself may have imperfections that cause momentary breakup of the picture called **glitches.** The very process of having the tape pass through the system makes it vulnerable to small but destructive changes in speed. If any one of a number of setup adjustments is done incorrectly, quality can be seriously impaired. Eventually the iron oxide or metal particles are rubbed off and the tape physically deteriorates. But for the most part, state of the art video recording equipment is very impressive. It is reliable, with a high degree of fidelity to the original signal.

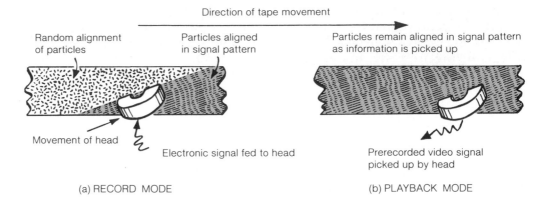

Direction of tape movement

Random alignment
of particles

Particles aligned
in signal pattern

Particles remain aligned in signal pattern
as information is picked up

Movement of head

Electronic signal fed to head

Prerecorded video signal
picked up by head

(a) RECORD MODE

(b) PLAYBACK MODE

FIGURE 9-3

Video recording and playback heads.

(a) **Record Mode.** The electronic video signals sent to the record head activate the magnetized head to align the iron oxide particles on the tape to retain a permanent (until erased) pattern of the recorded electronic video signal. (b) **Playback Mode.** The pre-recorded video signals on the videotape generate a small amount of electrical current in the playback head that is an exact duplicate of the original video signal.

Helical-Scan Videotape Recording Formats

The first professional videotape **quadruplex** machines used a two-inch wide tape. At one point of its movement, the tape curved around slightly less than one-half of a rotating disc containing four video heads, hence its name. Each head scanned only one-sixth of the picture making slow motion and freeze frame pictures impossible.

The answer to this and several other problems was to be found in the **helical-scan (slant-track)** videotape recorders developed in the late 1960s. Introduced originally as low-cost alternatives to the quadruplex machines, these recorders were at first only used for nonbroadcast applications such as college production courses and industrial training, as well as for an early form of off-line editing. In the intervening years the basic helical-scan concept has become the worldwide standard, giving rise to numerous formats differentiated according to tape size and signal type.

The U-Matic Format

In the early 1970s the Sony three-fourths-inch **U-Matic** format became the first broadcast quality helical-scan videotape unit. With its convenient cassette, it fit the needs of news and sports field production work and quickly became the standard. Its original analog/composite signal has been upgraded to an analog/component format known as U-Matic SP. The head assembly (figure 9-4) for the U-Matic is typical of all helical-scan machines.

Betamax and VHS

After several attempts to establish a consumer market with a home cartridge or cassette system, Sony finally succeeded with its **Betamax** format—followed closely

FIGURE 9-4
Helical-scan head
assembly of a
U-matic ¾-inch VCR
as seen from above.

Note the tilted,
round head
assembly.

by other manufacturers with the **VHS** system. In spite of a somewhat superior Betamax signal, the VHS system eventually eliminated Betamax because it was more widely marketed.

Super-VHS

In a very successful spin-off originally designed for the consumer market, the **S-VHS** format has become an important technology for a number of nonbroadcast applications due to its relatively low cost. While not a true component signal, its picture quality is achieved through the use of metal tape and a separation of brightness and color at certain phases of signal control.

The Panasonic AG-7750 shown in figure 9-5 has long been a workhorse in both educational and corporate production. Its latest model features an internal time base corrector that can eliminate most picture flaws caused by tape imperfections.

The 8mm Formats

The S-VHS system continues to be challenged by Sony's **Hi8** format. Both systems share the same signal and have connecting plugs that are identical. Sony's consumer level 8mm format, **Video 8,** also uses a metal tape. Its picture quality and small cassette make it an attractive acquisition mode camera for corporate and educational video applications.

Betacam

The original one half-inch professional Sony **Betacam** composite format has undergone many generational improvements on its way to recent models such as the DVW-A500. Its rear connection panel was earlier used at the beginning of this chapter (figure 9-2) as an example of maximum flexibility of design. It can input or output digital or analog signals in both the composite and component modes.

FIGURE 9-5

The Panasonic AG-7750 recorder is known as one of the workhorses in both educational and industrial production. Its S-VHS video signal achieves 400 lines of resolution and includes time code for editing. There are two hi-fi and two normal audio channels.

Photo courtesy of Panasonic Broadcast & Television Systems Co.

The M-II Format

The **M-II** analog/component format was developed by Panasonic and several other Matsushita related companies just in time for use by NBC at the 1988 Olympics in Seoul, Korea. It was designed to unite computer editing technology with a final videotape product. Its name is derived from its use of an updated version of the original VHS transport system with its distinctive "M" shape. (See figure 9-6.)

The C-Format

The **C-format** is the last remaining reel-to-reel tape system, still in use in many stations because of its reliability and durability. Through the late 1980s and into the '90s, this analog one-inch composite format remained the video editing and delivery system of choice at the network level for prime time programming. This was the unit that had supplanted the older two-inch quad format for broadcast purposes.

The Digital Approach to Recording Video

A number of steps during the past fifteen or so years point toward consumer and industrial communication systems that utilize digital computer technologies for their production and distribution. An **interactive** factor is also envisioned that will have a definite impact on consumer marketing of household products and on the way information and entertainment are distributed.

Although many people think of the **laser disc** copies of movies that started coming out in the late 1980s as being a

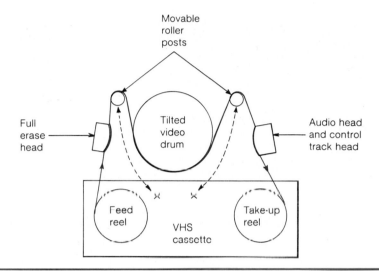

Movable roller posts

Full erase head

Tilted video drum

Audio head and control track head

Feed reel

Take-up reel

VHS cassette

FIGURE 9-6
The VHS "M" wrap system of transporting tape past the circular record-playback head after it has been retracted from the cassette.

digital system, they actually contain an analog signal. Video signals modulated into a laser beam are used to create pit-like variations on a photochemical layer on the record surface. When reflected later by the laser beam they can be amplified and modulated back into a video signal. Their uses in nonlinear editing will be covered in chapter 10.

Read Only Memory (ROM) Digital Discs

In addition to computer based games so popular with young people, a growing number of consumer oriented entertainment and informational **CD-ROM** discs that can operate with home computers are currently being sold at electronics stores. Many have interactive capabilities in that the observer/player has some control over the sequence of the programmed events. They are truly digitally based in every way and are actually a spin-off of the **nonlinear** recording and editing technologies that have been increasingly used for video production for several years.

Digital Recording and Playback

When potential program material is recorded in a digital medium, there are several phases involved. If its source is an analog signal, either live or from a previously recorded tape, it must be converted to a digital form. This process is referred to as **digitizing.**

Compared to the average personal computer, digital video storage equipment is somewhat of a mega-monster in terms of capacity. With existing technology, roughly twenty minutes of video accompanied by two channels of audio can be stored on one 3 gigabyte disc drive.[1] That storage rate is possible after the signals have gone through a process called

1. The book, *Digital Nonlinear Editing*, by Thomas A. Hanian, Focal Press, 1993, provides a good background on a range of technical matters relating to nonlinear editing. It discusses the number of *bytes* of information necessary for the storage of various levels of video information. Each byte is made up of eight *bits* of information in the 0 or 1 digital code. In one video frame a single byte could represent the gray scale value for one *pixel* of the total picture. The terms *kilobyte (KB), megabyte (MB),* and *gigabyte (GB)* denote the quantities of a thousand, a million, and a billion bytes of digital information. For its Media Recorder unit, Avid Technologies cites a capacity figure of 20 minutes of audio and video for a *3 GB drive*. Groups of these 3 GB drives can be connected for added capacity. Capacity can vary greatly according to the type of compression technology used in the storage process.

FIGURE 9-7

The Avid Media
Recorder is
specifically
designed as an all-
digital system to
replace videotape
in all recording and
production
distribution
functions. The VCR
unit is for the
process of
digitizing material
already on tape.

Photo courtesy of Avid
Technologies, Inc.

compression that greatly reduces the amount of digital information that is stored. Ultimately a **decompression** process is needed to restore the picture and sound back to its original form.

Several methods are used to accomplish this reduction and their use depends upon the needs of the final video product. Some methods sacrifice quality, while others determine those parts of the picture that are not changing from frame to frame, and do not store this *redundant* information. The ratio of the original digital information to its reduced stored content is an important factor. When compression is included in the process of editing for broadcast, a two-to-one (50 percent) ratio is considered appropriate because there is little discernable loss of quality. *Interactive video* productions designed for educational purposes may tolerate a fifteen-to-one ratio and still not detract from the product. Higher ratios with less loss are being developed.

Production Use of Nonlinear Digital Recorder Techniques

The Media Recorder (figure 9-7) manufactured by the Avid Corporation is an example of a whole new generation of facilities designed to receive live or taped inputs from studio or remote locations and digitize that input. Separate segments are automatically identified as **clips**, which can be then arranged in a **storyboard** sequence prior to the actual editing process.

The unit can accept composite analog video and two variations of component analog video along with two simultaneous analog audio signals. It uses the JPEG (Joint Photographic Experts Group) technique of compression for up to ten hours of storage on multiple disc drives. Its output can also be in any of the various formats of video.

The Helical-Scan Method of Videotape Recording and Playback

As with so many other technical innovations, the virtues of the videotape technologies may only be completely recognized after a period of transition to new equipment has begun. Editing, and as a result, all video production techniques were positively affected by the introduction of the improvements made possible by the helical-scan format. The number of machines currently in use and the numbers of personnel trained in all related technologies will insure the use of videotape for some time to come and therefore make it an area worthy of careful study.

Head Assembly
Many improvements in machine capacity were made possible by the innovative design of the helical-scan video head assembly. Each of the angled parallel lines shown in figure 9-8 represents one continuous scanning of the tape by one of the several video heads mounted on the circular drum (as shown in figure 9-9). Each single scan contains exactly the video information needed to record one complete 262.5-line picture *field*.

As the tape is pulled around the head drum, successive parallel angled (helical) tracks are scanned. In the *record* mode the heads are leaving a magnetized memory of the picture signal from the camera. In the *playback* mode, a still picture is produced when the tape movement is stopped because the video heads maintain a constant scanning speed on the diagonal of the tape. The heads scan the same area of the tape to reproduce the same picture field over and over again.

If the tape is moved at a slower-than-normal speed, a slow motion effect is achieved. As long as the revolving head speed remains constant, the video sync of the picture is maintained—no matter how fast or slowly the tape is pulled around the head drum. It must be remembered, however, that this 262.5-line picture *field* used to produce the *freeze-frame* or *slow-motion* effect contains only one-half of the video information necessary to reproduce a full 525-line picture *frame*. On consumer level machines this results in a somewhat washed-out picture. On professional units information is "borrowed" from an earlier frame and is used to fill out the rest of the 525-line "slo-mo" picture.

Transport Mechanism
The various mechanisms that move the tape from the feed reel to the take-up reel are called the *transport system*. Many hours of tape may pass through this very complicated assembly each day and the slightest deviation of speed or path can have serious negative effects upon picture quality. It is not surprising therefore that the transport systems on professional equipment are designed, manufactured, and assembled like an expensive watch.

The heart of the tape drive is the **servo capstan** mechanism that pulls the tape through the tape machine. It takes signals from the **sync pulses** on the **control track** of the tape itself to be able

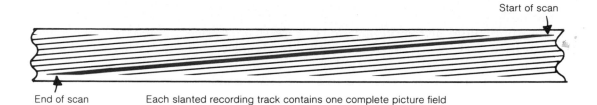

Start of scan

End of scan — Each slanted recording track contains one complete picture field

1
3
5
7
9

To line 525

The 262.5 odd-numbered scanning lines equal one picture field (½ frame).

FIGURE 9-8

Helical-scan slanted track.

The continuous video signal from one slanted video track contains enough information to record 262.5 odd-numbered scanning lines (one complete field) and to play back the field on the picture tube raster.

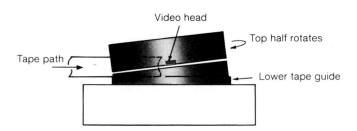

Video head

Top half rotates

Tape path

Lower tape guide

FIGURE 9-9

Helical-scan videocassette drum assembly.

The playback/record heads are attached to the rotating top half of the tilted head assembly.

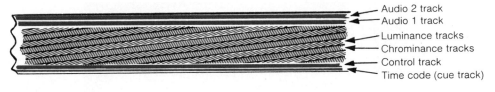

- Audio 2 track
- Audio 1 track
- Luminance tracks
- Chrominance tracks
- Control track
- Time code (cue track)

FIGURE 9-10

Configuration of ½-inch Betacam format (not to scale).

Note that alternate video tracks carry the luminance information while every other video track carries the chrominance signal.

to reproduce the exact speeds of the tape at the moment that it was originally recorded.

Figure 9-6 does not show the location of this transport unit, but it does show how, in the relatively simple VHS cassette format, the tape is pulled out of that cassette so that the tape can be partially wound around the tilted video drum.[2] The figure does show the *erase* head located "upstream" of the video head, and the location of the *audio heads* and *control track heads* that govern the speed of the tape as mentioned above.

9.3 VIDEOTAPE TRACK FUNCTIONS

Obviously a videotape has to contain more information than just picture signals. In

2. As with self-contained audio sources, the term *cassette* refers to a two-reeled unit in a semiclosed case; the videotape is not exposed to human handling. Once the cassette is inserted into its loading deck, the player mechanism automatically engages the tape around the recording head assembly. A *cartridge*, now used only for audio, refers to a single-reel container, which in effect, is a sealed supply reel; the take-up reel is enclosed in the player mechanism. When the cartridge is inserted into the player, it is automatically threaded; again, human hands do not become involved in the loading and threading operation.

the interests of simplicity, figure 9-10 shows the configuration of tracks used on an earlier Betacam format. Later VCR formats have additional audio tracks that are used for sound mixing during editing as well as for second language and descriptive applications.

The Video Track

The portion of the videotape that carries the series of slanted video scanning lines is known as the **video track;** this occupies roughly 80 percent of the tape area in helical-scan formats. It is here that the information dealing with the picture signal, color, and brightness is carried. Every second, sixty of the slanted tracks are scanned to produce sixty fields—resulting in the rate of thirty completely scanned picture frames per second.

As shown in figure 9-10, this older Betacam system used a two track system similar to those in use today. One video track carries the *luminance* (brightness) information, and the next track carries the *chrominance* (color) information. It should be noted that on professional machines there are also two "flying" erase heads—one for each track—revolving around the drum head to better accomplish the function of

224

FIGURE 9-11

Display of time-code information.

The SMPTE time code (hours, minutes, seconds, and frames) is displayed at the touch of a button.

the stationary erase heads shown in figure 9-6. Their ability to start and stop the erasing at a specific frame is essential to editing.

In addition to the video tracks, an increasing number of other tracks are simultaneously contributing to the picture and sound. In addition to the two or more *audio* tracks, there is a *control* track and a separate "address" or *cue* track at the bottom of the tape.

The Control Track

In sections 5.2 and 9.1, we described how the continuous display of the picture on a monitor is synchronized with the original camera picture by means of *vertical* and *horizontal synchronization* pulses. For every 262.5 horizontal pulses, there is one vertical pulse that initiates the scanning of either the odd- or even-lined picture field. When a broadcast picture is received, it is these sync pulses that "lock together" the camera or studio tape machine signal with the home TV set.

When the television picture information is recorded, these *sync pulses*—and some related information—are separated from the color and brightness signals and recorded on an individual band or *control track* of the tape. During the playback of recorded videotape programs, the sync

pulse serves an additional important purpose. The playback machine reads the signals and uses them to regulate the speed at which the *capstan* pulls the tape through the transport system—as well as the speed at which the video head wheel turns. This *servo control system,* in effect, tells the playback VCR exactly how fast the tape was moving when it was originally recorded.

The Cue Track

The title **cue track** is derived from a time when it was used for verbal editing cues. Now it is used to lay down the signal for an editing location system called the **SMPTE time code.**[3] This location system produces a digital clock-like numerical readout or *address* for each hour, minute, second, and frame recorded on the videotape. It can reflect the "real time" at which the tape was being recorded, or it can be added later, showing time elapsed from the beginning of a production or from some other reference point on the tape. The readout, as illustrated in figure 9-11, can

3. This editing location (address) system was so named because the technical standards were established by the Society of Motion Picture and Television Engineers.

be displayed on the picture monitor by a process similar to the way titles are matted over any picture source.

For some editing applications, the **window** display becomes a part of a **workprint** tape dub and is seen as a permanent part of the picture. Also, during the editing process, the time code can be viewed by means of LED (light-emitting diode) readouts located at the control panel and on the machines themselves. In most current editing systems a computer can "read" the unseen time code to locate predetermined edit points for the execution of cuts, dissolves, and special effects.

Time-code referencing is especially important for programs such as *Wide World of Sports*—or the Olympics—where tapes from a number of recorders in many different locations must later be edited together in precise chronological synchronization.

The Audio Track

The **audio track** hardly needs further explanation. The technology involved is exactly that of conventional sound recording. It must be noted, however, that the quality is somewhat less than that of professional audio equipment used in recording studios. The television industry is just beginning to take advantage of its capacity for stereo and high-fidelity sound—up to the 15,000-hertz level now heard on FM radio. As more home receivers are sold with this *MTS* (multichannel television sound) capacity, more stations and cable systems are making the necessary modifications for increased audio fidelity.

Most VCR machines designed for educational and industrial use formerly had a 5,000-hertz limitation, but newer equipment—including some of the Sony Hi-8 line—has capability for stereo and high quality **PCM (pulse code modulation)** audio. PCM sound, because it uses the 0-1 pulse codes, is recorded digitally.

9.4 VIDEO RECORDER OPERATIONS AND CONTROLS

The setup and operation of any VCR machine involves the use of components that generally fall under three headings: *connectors, control mechanisms,* and *visual indicators.* The arrangement, appearance, and even terminology may vary with the manufacturer—but once one knows what to look for, these basic components can be identified on any video recorder.

First, since videotape machines work in conjunction with other electronic units (cameras, switchers, microphones, other recorders, speakers, receivers, editing equipment, and so forth), as a primary step, you must be able to make hookups. Second, you must learn how to manipulate the collection of knobs, switches, levers, and push buttons that are used to start, stop, or change the basic audio and video functions of record, playback, and editing. Third, you must be able to monitor and understand those things that tell whether or not the machine is operating the way you want it to—feedback provided by items such as lights and meters.

Connections

In a studio situation where equipment and its related cables are permanently in place, the connection process takes place primarily at the patch bays where labeled receptacles indicate the sources and termination points of feeds. Often the camera, VCR, and other pieces of equipment are semipermanently connected, so you, as an operator, do not need to deal with the connections unless you do not obtain proper picture and sound.

However, much of the small format video for educational and industrial purposes—and much of the semi-EFP production for training purposes—involves a

FIGURE 9-12

The Sony EVV-9000.

What would appear to be a camcorder is actually a "dockable" Sony EVV-9000 video recorder mounted with a Sony DXC-325 camera. The camera can operate as a "stand-alone" unit or it can be connected by cable to a separate portable video recorder.

Photo courtesy of Sony

temporary "lash-up" of video recorders, cameras, mics, monitors, and associated gear in out-of-studio *field* locations. With most *camcorders* the connection between camera and recorder is permanent. In order to meet some dual needs, however, the industry has designed cameras and recorders having a "dockability" option. When docked together, you have a sophisticated camcorder. With the components disconnected, you have both an individual camera and a separate video recorder. If the camcorder shown in figure 9-12 seems to have an elaborate control panel for a camera, it is because the rear of the unit is actually a removable video recorder—the Sony Hi-8 EVV-9000. The front is a separate camera, the DXC-325. As a "stand-alone" camera, this sort of unit can feed into a recorder or even be used for field editing.

Even if the camera and recorder are together in a permanent or dockable configuration, other connections to mics, audio boards, monitors, and other pieces of equipment must be made. Whether in the studio or the field, the operational linking of components is most efficiently accomplished when three interacting factors are kept in mind:

1. The nature and purpose of all signal feeds
2. The direction and pathway of all signal flow
3. The structure of the connective hardware

If you know *what* your signal is supposed to do, it is easier to know *where* it should be going and *how* you are going to have to connect it to get it there.

Signal Flow

The first thing to keep in mind when making any connection is simply whether you are dealing with an *input* or an *output.* You should first look at a wiring diagram. If one is not available, the very act of making a sketch of the probable *sequence of signal flow* will bring some order to the process. Does the receptacle into which you are putting one end of a cable represent the signal output of a component? If so, with that connection made, the other end of the cable obviously becomes the new output of the signal—and as a result goes into an input receptacle to continue the movement of the signal. It must be emphasized that incorrect connections not only cause operational delay, they also can cause serious damage to equipment by overloading circuits.

Signal Levels

One of the main principles involved in the connection process is understanding the different types of signals that one deals with in making those hookups. In addition to knowing audio from video feeds, one must realize that some lines, such as **radio frequency (RF)** signals, carry both audio and video. (See figure 9-2.) Also different lines carry different amounts of amplification.

The basic concept of amplification differences was introduced when discussing audio patching in section 2.2. The same principle applies to the way in which the video recorder handles audio and video. The recorder has a provision for the input of an external microphone ("mic in"). This low-level signal is then amplified to *line level* within the machine before being recorded on tape. However, previously amplified signals (an audio recorder, for example) are only to be plugged into "line" audio inputs. If these are plugged into a "mic" input, you will get a distortion from the double amplification.

Connecting Hardware

Connective hardware for audio and video equipment involves a wide variety of receptacles and matching plugs. For example, *line video* may utilize a BNC, UHF, or RCA phono plug. *Audio* is usually handled by a phone plug, Sony mini-plug, or RCA plug. With low impedance mic lines,[4] a three-pin Cannon connector is quite common. See figure 9-13 for an idea of the most commonly used connecting hardware.

Adapters, Splitters, and Terminators

Because of all the differences in plugs and receptacles, the connecting process is greatly aided if one has a good supply of **adapter plugs** on hand (see figure 9-14). It should also be noted that a variety of cables are available with different connectors at the two ends. Such cables often make the most convenient types of adapter. With a variety of these on hand, one can quickly connect a number of components from different manufacturers with some degree of confidence. However, caution and common sense should always be exercised when making such connections. One simply cannot make a high impedance mic function with a low impedance cable by trying to use an adapter.

Attempting to connect two or more audio or video monitors to a single feed calls for the use of another type of specialized connector—a **splitter.** For instance, "Y" and "T" plugs allow you to tap into a line and send the signal to two different points—feeding one monitor while sending a signal onto another. The effect is much

---

4. Recall our discussion regarding impedance levels (section 3.1). In the studio, where the distance from the mic to the audio console may be up to fifty feet, a *low impedance* (low line resistance) cable and microphone are used. However, home VCRs and many industrial level recorders are designed to work with less expensive *high impedance* (greater resistance) lines and matching mics that are designed to carry not more than six to eight feet. A mismatch of lines and mics can cause hum or other distortion.

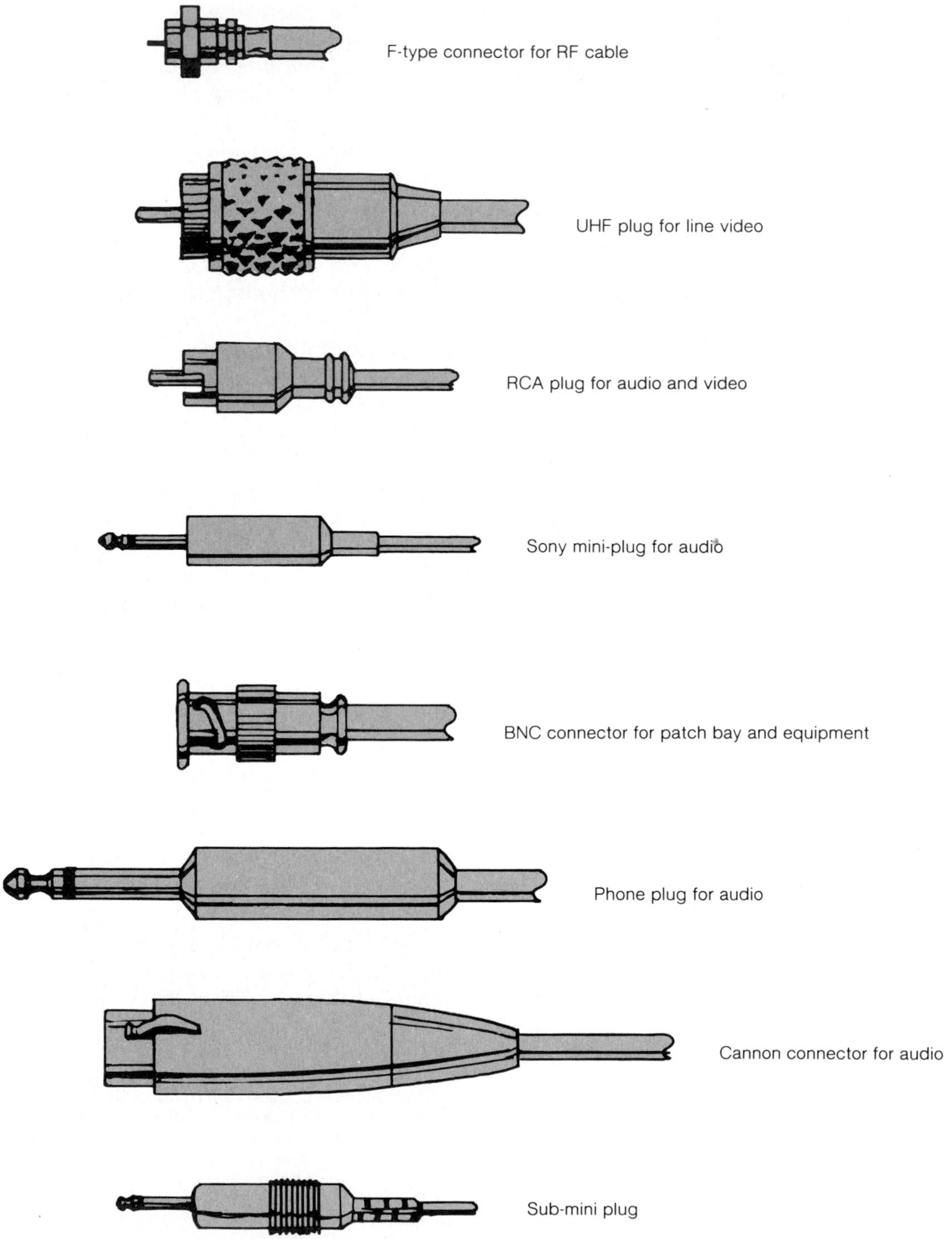

F-type connector for RF cable

UHF plug for line video

RCA plug for audio and video

Sony mini-plug for audio

BNC connector for patch bay and equipment

Phone plug for audio

Cannon connector for audio

FIGURE 9-13

Commonly used
audio and video
plugs and
connectors.

Sub-mini plug

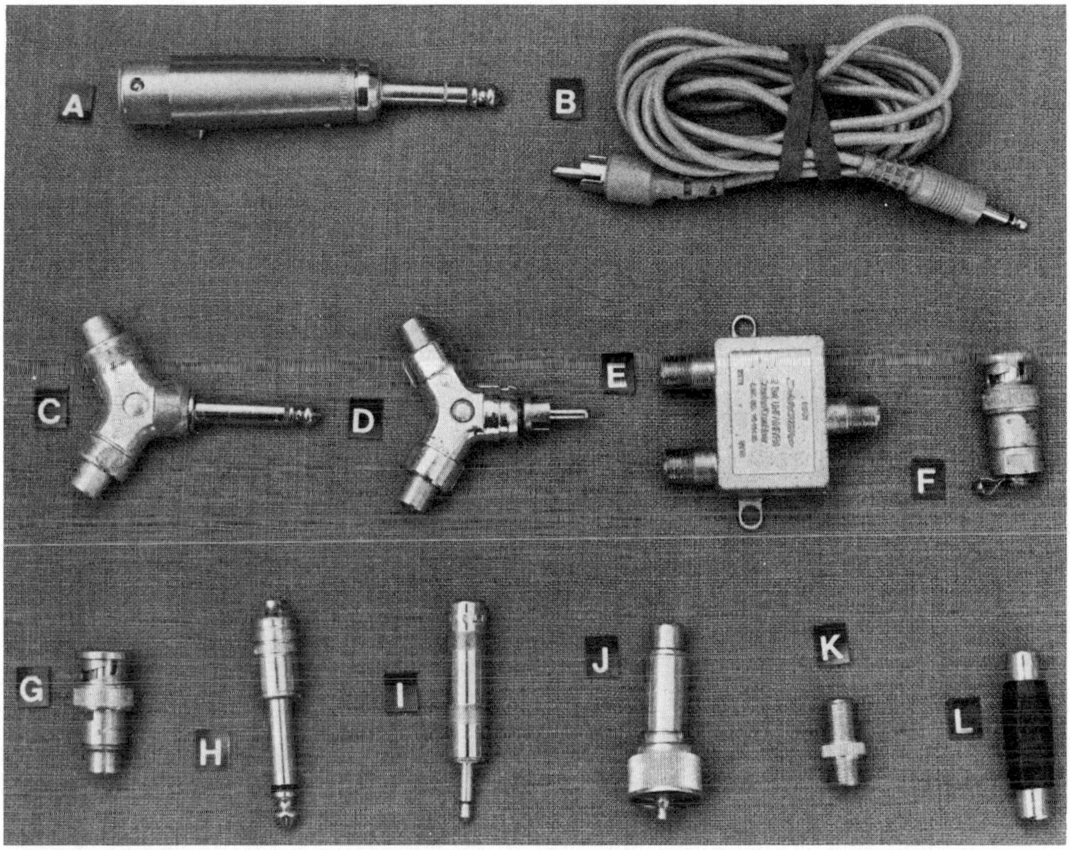

FIGURE 9-14

Some of the more common adapters, splitters, and terminators found in typical video and audio hookups: *(A)* convertor plug, female cannon to phone jack; *(B)* RCA to mini-plug convertor line; *(C)* phone jack to female RCA splitter; *(D)* RCA male to RCA female splitter; *(E)* RF (75-ohm) splitter; *(F)* BNC terminator; *(G)* RCA female to BNC convertor; *(H)* mini-plug to phone jack convertor; *(I)* phone jack to mini-plug convertor; *(J)* RCA to UHF convertor; *(K)* RF barrel plug; *(L)* RCA barrel plug.

the same as using an *RF splitter* on your home system to send an incoming cable TV signal to more than one receiver. However, splitting a signal does weaken its strength, and thus additional amplification may be needed. Most industrial video monitors can easily be set up in series so that the "video out" receptacle from one monitor can feed the same signal onto the next set. However, in this case, the final monitor in the chain must *terminate* the signal flow—either by a termination switch or a video termination plug. (See figure 9-14.)

Again, in thinking through the connections to be made with any system—regardless of how simple or how sophisticated the recorder and its components may be—it is important to think ahead and carefully plot out the types of connections to be made. Try to visualize all the related signal flows—as emphasized at the beginning of section 2.2—the *what, where,* and *how* of signal flow.

Controls

Regardless of the age or simplicity of design, the transport (tape movement) functions on all video recorders will have eight to ten basic controls. Normal speed playback is accomplished by activating the control labeled *play.* On many machines the recording mode is initiated by pressing *play* simultaneously with the *record* button; on other machines, just pressing *record* starts that function. On older and consumer level cassette machines, the *stop* control not only stops the tape movement, but it also causes the tape to unwind from the video drum and be retracted into the cassette. This allows the *eject* control to be used to remove the cassette from the machine. On these units "stop" should not be confused with the *pause* control that halts forward tape movement but produces a "freeze-frame" picture. The tape is still in contact with the heads that are in motion scanning the same slant track again and again. With these older machines the unit should not be left in this mode for more than a minute or so at one time as the heads are continually wearing away at the oxide on one specific track; tape damage and/or head clog can occur.

However, on all current professional models such as the Sony DVW-A500 (figure 9-15) designed for editing, the *stop* command will put the machine into a mode that leaves a still picture on the monitor. Even though the tape is in contact with the rotating heads, there has been a lessening of the tape tension to avoid causing excess wear. These late model

recorders also have another feature that automatically shuts off this stop/pause mode after it has been left alone for several minutes. The same feature is present in most camcorders also.

To get the tape quickly from one point to another, *fast-forward* and *rewind* controls are used. On some units, these two modes will produce a somewhat recognizable picture for "search" purposes. Many VCRs—especially those designed for editing—also will have *variable speed* controls that facilitate slow or sped-up motion, either forward or backward.

The *audio dub* (audio edit) control puts the audio record head into the record mode—without activating the video record heads. This enables you to make audio-only edits or to lay in a whole new audio track.

Tracking and Skew

One other control is important to accurate tape transport. The path of the tape around the video drum is crucial to the playback of a proper picture. Bands of picture distortion sometimes result when a tape recorded on one machine is played back on another VCR with a slightly different horizontal alignment. This problem can usually be corrected by an adjustment of the **tracking** control. The normal operating setting as determined by the factory is located at the top point (12:00 position) on the dial. The slight click one feels when passing this point is known as a "detent" position. After any tracking adjustment is made, the knob should be returned to this position for each new recording or playback.

On most professional units, there is an additional control for the tape transport called **skew.** When the top third of the picture appears to bend to the left or the right, it is usually caused by an incorrect amount of tension on the tape as it passes around the video drum. This is adjusted by means of the skew control knob. Keep in mind

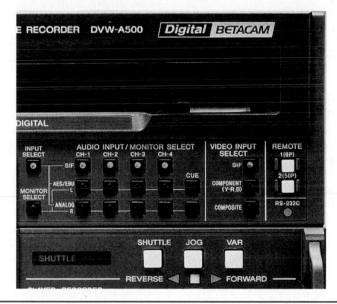

FIGURE 9-15

This is the full view of the Sony DVW-A500. The video connection panel was shown in figure 9-2 with a description of all the format capabilities. Note how all the controls are laid out in operational groups. (Bottom) See insert of audio and video input selection group from top right.

Photo courtesy of Sony

that this is a problem on the playback machine, not on the machine to which you are editing or dubbing. As with the tracking control, the knob should always be returned to the detent position before that same machine can be used for a subsequent recording or playback.

Selector Switches

As discussed previously, most video recorders are designed to function with a variety of different types of inputs such as a *camera*, the tuner in a *receiver/monitor*, or a studio *line* feed. There must, therefore, be an *input selector switch* that differentiates among the various levels and/or sync sources of these inputs. The advice of a studio technician may be needed to determine proper switch positions. Whereas a camera signal from the studio switcher would feed through the line input, a single camera might utilize some other selector position.

On some machines there is another switch that separately controls the use of internal or external *sync sources.* (On several VCR makes, the alternative to the external position is labeled "defeat.") This *internal sync* position allows the recorder to "strip off" any incoming sync signal and utilize the synchronization pulse from the machine itself during the recording process.

Visual Indicators and Meters

Our final area of concern is with visual monitoring and feedback indicators. Although these will vary from machine to machine, there are a number of controls that group together in operational units and directly relate to a visual readout—starting with the *pilot light* that indicates when the *power on/off* switch is activated. The most important of these are the VU meter (chapters 2 and 3), and the similar metered readouts that indicate video signal strength and the accuracy of video head tracking.

Automatic Gain Control

Most portable recorders have an **automatic gain control (AGC)** option for audio. When this is switched on, the AGC serves as a limiter that keeps incoming audio feeds within a range that does not exceed the capabilities of the recorder. However, the AGC often will automatically boost the "noise" of the line signal when there is momentarily no other incoming signal (a pause in the voice or music source), thereby recording an amplified hiss. The AGC selector switch allows you to defeat this feature.

Most machines will reflect their recording and editing functions with additional video control switches and indicators. There will be a *video control* knob that adjusts the level of incoming video—as well as a related *AGC off-on* switch that allows for automatic gain control of the video signal. These are usually grouped with the *video VU meter.*

Warning Indicators

An increasing number of portable recorders are including a number of warning lights and status indicators that provide several types of important feedback to the operator. Sometimes these are on the body of the camcorder, and sometimes indications appear in the camera viewfinder. On some machines, a *pause mode* light serves as a reminder that the heads are continuing to scan the tape. There are also lights that indicate the condition of the *battery,* the presence of moisture that is dangerous to the circuitry (*auto off*), a *tape supply* warning light that lets you know you are coming to the end of your videotape, and a *servo* lamp that warns of improper tape transport.

Counters and Location Indicators

Virtually all recorders have some sort of *counter* or other component that allows an operator to locate predetermined points on a recorded tape. On consumer models and lower end industrial units there is usually only a three- or four-digit readout that counts the revolutions of the take-up reel. Since the circumference of the tape on each reel will change as the reels unwind and wind, the operator must keep in mind that a given number of revolutions will indicate differing amounts of tape footage—depending upon how far into the program one is.

On most consumer-level VCRs there is a zero-point *reset* button that, on rewind, brings the tape back to the zero point and comes to an automatic stop. A somewhat more complex *memory control* permits the quick location of a series of selected points with the tape in the fast forward mode.

These controls are definitely useful, but as we shall see in the next chapter, it was the development of SMPTE Time Code that put the use of videotape on a very efficient basis. With its display of the precise hour, minute, second, and frame (figure 9-11) of any particular point on a tape, program segments could be quickly set up for broadcast. Of even more importance, however, were the obvious applications to videotape editing. What had previously been a slow, inexact, and expensive procedure quickly became one of television's most important tools.

There is a second location method that has a display that also looks very much like time code, but it operates very differently. Its numbering system is based on a count of the continuing sync pulses coming from the control track.

Both of these electronic digital readouts help the operator to "feel" the speed and direction of tape movement while operating the *variable speed* control dials. At the straight-up detent position, the tape is in "pause." The more you twist the dial to the right (clockwise), the faster the tape moves forward. As you turn the dial to the left (counterclockwise), the tape moves in reverse (rewind)—again with the speed determined by the extent you turn the dial. On most machines, speeds range from a very slow motion one-frame-at-a-time to five or more times normal speed.

9.5 SUCCESSFUL PERFORMANCE AND MAINTENANCE

The key to successful operation of the videotape recorder—whether for a student instructional project or the operation of the latest digital/component unit—is *familiarity* and *practice.* Instructions and specific controls will, of course, vary significantly from machine to machine. Become familiar with the ones you have access to. Make certain you have taken full advantage of the instructions and directions for the particular models you will be working with. Especially, follow the recommended care and maintenance instructions; this is particularly important for routine cleaning of the video heads. And then practice. Become familiar with the recorder. Under the guidance of a trained technician or instructor, work with the machine; experiment with it. Find out what it will and will not do. And then you should have the confidence and discipline to handle any video recording and playback assignment given to you.

A major part of your professional discipline will be care and respect for all production equipment—and the video recorder is one of the most expensive and delicate machines you will handle. Everyone will benefit if you follow a few common rules of preventative maintenance.

1. Videotape recorders require a constantly renewed supply of clean, cool, dry air. Heat, moisture, and cigarette smoke are damaging to all electronic equipment—especially VCR machines. Never place books, cassette cases, or papers on top of the recorder; it seriously inhibits the flow of air. Liquid containers and ashtrays—anywhere adjacent to video recorders—are simply disasters in the making.
2. Place a dust cover on the machine when it is not in use—but only after the unit has had time to cool off.
3. When a video recorder is moved, be extremely careful not to bump or jar the unit. Delicate components are easily damaged by slight shocks. Do not attempt to operate a recorder immediately after it has been moved from a cold to a warm environment.

4. Videotape should not be left in the recorder when the unit is not in use. Tapes should be rewound and properly stored in a cool, dry place.
5. Keep the recorder and tapes at a distance from other equipment that may be generating strong magnetic fields as these can erase the information on the tapes.
6. Do not tinker with various controls and functions without a clear purpose and idea of what you are doing. Do not fool around, for example, with the color lock control and other critical mechanisms. Maintenance personnel who are unaware of the misadjustments may spend hours trying to find and correct the resulting problems.
7. As the videotape operator, always allow yourself time to carefully think through all connecting and patching procedures—as well as the basic disciplines of machine operation. The time spent always pays off later in time saved.

SUMMARY

The video recording process involves an understanding of the entire electromagnetic concept. For our purposes, we have looked at two aspects of the electromagnetic phenomenon—*electronic principles* (such as the horizontal and vertical sync pulses) and *magnetic principles* (the electromagnetic properties of an electrical current rearranging iron oxide or metal particles) to record a video signal on videotape.

Just as the bulky and expensive *quad*-head machines have been supplanted by the *helical-scan video recorder*, the industry is now looking to *digital nonlinear* storage, editing, and production distribution. It is important that operators understand how the various *audio and video tracks* function as a part of the recording, editing, and playback process. Each tape has a carefully located space for picture information, *control track, cue signals*, and audio track(s).

Operational functions for VCR machines include three main considerations: *connections* (with cameras, switcher, line feeds, microphones, other recorders, speakers, monitors, editing facilities, and so forth); *controls* (for all operating modes such as play, record, fast forward, rewind, stop, pause, variable speed, dubbing and editing, input and sync selection, tracking and skewing adjustments); and *indicators* (lights, VU meters, counters, and so forth).

This information will be invaluable in chapter 10 as we continue looking at the video recording process as it applies specifically to electronic editing.

Video Editing: Equipment and Techniques

T hose pioneers who made the first silent films very soon discovered how powerful a *close-up shot* could be in the telling of a story. Since its beginning the theater had been limited to the aspect of the entire proscenium as its ongoing visual perspective. Considering audience-to-performer distance, most emotions had to be expressed by large arm and body movements. Film, however, could use what humankind has always used to communicate, the expressions of the eyes and facial muscles. The subjective and the objective aspects of the visual narrative could now be easily combined. By the 1930s the editing of motion pictures had become a truly creative art.

10.1 EDITING AS A FACTOR IN TELEVISION PRODUCTION

When television first began, much of what the audience saw was occurring at that very moment *live* in a studio somewhere. The director did the editing from the control booth, calling for the use of various camera shots as the program progressed. Then, as now, on the director's command the technical director used the switcher to connect the visual flow of the program by means of takes, dissolves, superimpositions, and fades to black. For network level musical and dramatic productions this approach necessitated a lot of prior planning. With limited amounts of rehearsal time, the problems that could arise during a live two hour drama would often negatively effect even the best-planned productions.

While the programs of the so-called golden age of television[1] were often very impressive, the networks eventually turned to the film industry for much of its dramatic and situation comedy programming. Many in the industry felt more comfortable with the idea that with the traditional single-camera film system of shooting, management could exercise more control over production, especially editing.

With the introduction of videotape, the nature of broadcasting (and eventually cablecasting) began to change again. New multiple-camera techniques that included live takes and later editing of material that had been recorded was used by situation comedies. While it is mainly the spontaneous nature of *real-time* production that has always given sports, news, and game shows an important sense of immediacy and realism, these program types also learned to take advantage of various aspects of video editing. Other types of video production are now entirely dependent on a final video editing process.

In a somewhat ironic move, those dramas, situation comedies, commercials, and rock videos that continue being shot on film have long since changed over to a process that puts the footage on videotape for all editing and effects work. Figure 10-1 shows a **telecine** suite where the film is not only transferred, but also where color corrections are made and other imperfections are eliminated. Operator skill and some rather expensive equipment are required, but the results are impressive.

New advances in computer-controlled digital editing technology are making further changes in the way that the product is assembled. **Nonlinear** editing is seen by many as a system that provides the operator with a number of advantages in solving the problems of increasingly complex productions. For some editors it is a system that allows them to work in a manner that is somewhat reminiscent of traditional film techniques in that video material can be inserted into an existing segment with no loss to that segment. Many people feel that the process of organizing images into a sequence is made easier through the use of video screen displays that can quickly show available pictorial options. This technology is currently being used to edit every kind of footage from movies to videotaped news. (See figure 10-2.) The first of the camcorders that record directly to internal magnetic discs are just now on the market.

---

1. The "golden age of television" is a term used about programming of the 1950s, and particularly refers to the anthology dramas such as "Marty" and "Requiem for a Heavyweight" that were produced and aired live.

FIGURE 10-1

This telecine suite is used to transfer increasing amounts of film into digitized video for postproduction editing, graphics, and other special effects work. The original quality of film is often improved by the operation of the *Ursa/Sintel Converter* in the background.

Photo courtesy of Hollywood Digital

FIGURE 10-2

Avid Technologies' *News Cutter* is a digital nonlinear editing system designed to allow news editors to produce news segments for direct broadcast. It has all the built-in tools for creating titles, dissolves, and wipes.

Photo courtesy of Avid Technologies, Inc.

In this chapter we will examine the procedures used when working in the traditional **linear** style as a basis for understanding the larger concept of how and why the purposes of all kinds of editing are accomplished. There will be a number of comparisons between linear and nonlinear techniques and equipment throughout. As stated in the previous chapter, many observers feel that videotape will be an important part of video production for a number of years, especially at educational institutions. The process of understanding both how and why editing should be used is such that there may even be certain advantages in having students first learn the disciplines of linear assembly.

Three Primary Categories of Editing for Video Production

Through the years, editing has been used in various ways for a variety of purposes and different types of programs. Sometimes the editing is completed after the main program is shot, sometimes it is accomplished prior to the taping of the major portion of the show, and sometimes the entire program is edited.

Postproduction Editing of Studio Based Production

The daytime "soaps" and some of the prime time situation comedies are shot using a multiple video camera technique. Two to three minute scenes are shot without interruption with the director calling the shots as in a live production. Later the segments are put into program sequence and slight errors such as a poorly lit close-up or a late entrance are corrected by editing in **pickup shots** that are re-shot at the end of the scene.

Daytime game and talk shows undergo a slightly less complicated process called **sweetening.** These programs are usually

taped start to finish, and it is not unusual to do five shows in one long production day. As stated above, *pickup shots* are recorded for insertion during a later editing session where a number of other small sound and picture corrections are made.

Some programs, such as rock concerts that are edited through the switcher and taped straight through from beginning to end, will have an additional camera separately **slaved** to an additional videotape recorder. This camera usually is assigned to hold wide-angle **cover shots** or get spontaneous **close-ups.** The director can later edit these shots into the program to smooth out or further enhance what is still basically a switcher edited production.

Preproduction Editing

In successful news programs the essential ingredient has always been fast-paced, well-edited film or tape footage. Similarly, magazine format shows such as *Entertainment Tonight* depend upon interesting, well-produced tape segments being fed into a *live-to-tape* program format. The *ET* show spends more than four hours each day prior to its studio assembly period preparing its animated graphics that appear behind the host and hostess. Like news, the video footage is edited right up until airtime. Both of the above program types, as well as a number of public affairs and corporate video formats, share the technique of maintaining a sense of spontaneity by balancing the edited segments with on-camera anchor/host *"wrap-arounds."*

Completely Edited Production

A single-camera technique is essential for some types of production whether the **acquisition mode** involves the use of film or video cameras. This approach, which grew along with the movie industry, is used for such diverse production work as serious drama, commercials, rock videos, and the currently popular reality based "police in

FIGURE 10-3

The AG A750 edit controller being used by these students is a very advanced piece of equipment as compared to editing methods that sustained television for many years.

action" shows. It also encompasses the documentary techniques that are applied to corporate and educational video. Camera work involves multiple takes of individual segments, shot out of sequence and often at different locations. It gives the director a much higher level of control over all aspects of the production but is expensive and time-consuming.

10.2 EDITING CONTROL SYSTEMS AND RELATED EQUIPMENT

All video editing currently being done can be divided into three basic categories. Each of these share a number of common characteristics but differ in some basic ways such as the medium that is used to store the video information, the system used to gain access to this footage, and the methods of controlling the edit/assembly process.

The Videotape Controller

The traditional *videotape based systems* transfer the materials selected from one or more cassettes of tape to a final edited version on an additional cassette. The selection and transfer process is manipulated by an **edit controller** that moves the tape containing the original material into position so that the edited recording tape can receive a succession of additional video segments in a planned sequence. As seen in figure 10-3, an operator controls tape in these two VCR machines from the controller unit. (Additional feed VCRs can also be used.) Every frame of both tapes contains

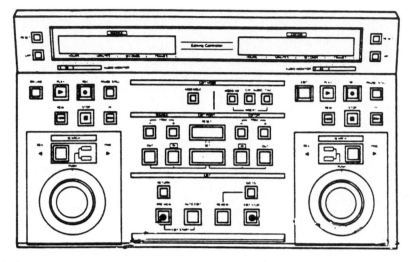

FIGURE 10-4

The face of the AG A750 edit controller is laid out in a convenient design that enables the operator to move source and record tapes quickly during the search process of assembly. Controls for preview, edit, and review of the edit are placed in the center of the unit.

Drawing courtesy of Panasonic Broadcast & Television Systems Co.

a **time code** numbered in frames, seconds, minutes, and hours. These numbers, in their digital form, are used by the controller in the process of locating segments and positioning the tape for edit.

The first step in any editing session must always be the process of **logging** the **inpoint** and **outpoint** numbers for each segment of tape that is being considered for use. The controller unit can use the time code **address** to locate the inpoint of an upcoming segment, moving the **source** (playback) tape to coincide with the outpoint of a previously recorded segment in preparation for the actual edit/transfer of video. This movement is termed the **search mode** and on professional models it is done with some precision by means of the time code numbers. But because videotape is a *linear* medium, considerable time is still spent in rolling the source tape into position to view a potential edit. Material

on that tape is usually in a very different order than the eventual sequence of its final assembly. Once the transfer is made to the edit tape it can be viewed in sequence with other edits, but that transferred segment can only be changed by replacing it with another segment of exactly the same length.

The Panasonic A750 Edit Controller shown in figure 10-4 is well known to editors working in the areas of corporate and educational video. The two round dials to the right and left of the unit are used to control the movement of tape at variable speeds during the search process. Controls for the *source* (playback) machine are on the left and controls for the *edit* (record) deck are on the right. The buttons just above the dials are for basic tape movement such as pause, forward, stop, rewind and fast forward. These buttons are identical on both sides.

FIGURE 10-5
Computer controlled units, such as this one manufactured by *Sundance Technologies*, are designed to let the operator create an edit decision list for later assembly by the same unit. After material on tape has been logged into the system it can be quickly and efficiently retrieved for this decision process.

In the center there are a number of control buttons that set the edit inpoints and outpoints once they have been located and the tapes are in position. At lower center are the controls that can initiate a **preview** of the edit before it is actually recorded, the **edit transfer** itself, and a **review** of that edit as laid down on the record tape. The two rectangular spaces at the top of the unit are where the time code readout is seen. Since source controls are always on the *left* of the controller, the video monitor that shows the source output will also be on the left while the record machine output will be seen on the monitor on the right. The process of aligning the two tapes relative to the recording and playback heads to

initiate the edit will be covered in some detail in section 10.4.

Computerized Control of Videotape

A new generation of controls was developed when it became evident that the digitalized time code on videotape could serve as the basis of an entirely new form of editing. The logging process becomes even more important with this approach. Every short segment of tape (often called a **clip**) is identified and logged into the database of the computer by reel number and clip name, as well as time code numbers for inpoints and outpoints.

In units like the one seen in figure 10-5 manufactured by *Sundance Technologies*, the

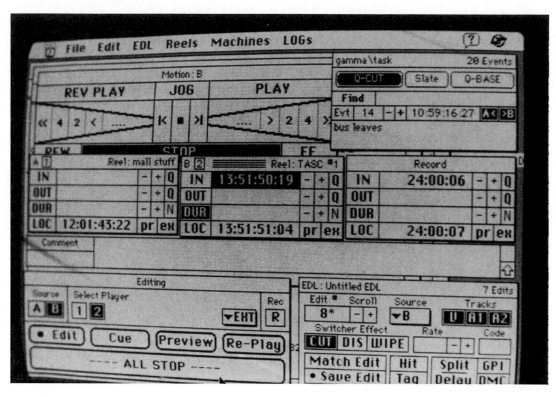

FIGURE 10-6

This video screen from the *Sundance Technologies* edit unit uses displays like the one shown here to provide quick access to the control options. During the logging process each clip is identified by time code numbers and other information. The operator uses either the keyboard or a mouse control to initiate the various operations shown on the video screen display.

operator uses a number of different workscreen displays and additional window overlays to select from the operational options. Using either a keyboard or a **mouse,** the operator places the movable cursor arrow over the visual **icon** that represents a particular operation and *clicks* the control to commence the operation—cut selection, forward movement, marking of the edit point, etc. For example in figure 10-6 the two triangular areas at top left are used to command the VCR machine to transport tape in forward or reverse at differing speeds. The mouse controlled indicator is placed at the number "4" within the *play* triangle and clicked to get a search speed

four times that of normal play. Just beneath this area is a time code status readout. At the bottom of the screen we see many of the controls used for the actual assembly. (It should be noted that on most units the control functions that are more easily executed through the use of the mouse can also be accomplished on the keyboard.)

The most important part of the editing procedure is not the actual transfer of each new segment. It is instead the *decision* by the operator to place most effectively each segment (clip) of video and audio into a meaningful sequence. As with tape controller systems, each edit is previewed and corrections are made before an individual

FIGURE 10-7

The Sony DME 3000 control board is designed to combine both the keyboard and the mouse in one improved unit. The round object in the photo is called a *trackball* and could be described as an upside-down mouse with increased capacity for movement.

Photo courtesy of Sony Electronics, Inc.

edit decision is entered. But with computer control, *all decisions* are entered into the computer before any recording is done. This allows the operator to go back and rework individual edits in light of later decisions. When source material is on a number of different tapes, multiple machines can be connected to save constant switching around of cassettes. It is also possible to program dissolves, wipes, and other transitional effects between segments if two source machines and a switcher are used.

Ultimately the data base of the computer will have been programmed with the final **edit decision list (EDL).** It tells the computer the time code numbers for the beginning and end points of each segment and also generates another set of numbers that determines any segment's position within the larger sequence of the program. When all is ready, the command is given and the computer controls the VCR machines as they assemble the entire production.

Some companies such as Sony have moved beyond the traditional keyboard and have come out with control boards specifically designed for this kind of computerized editing. The Sony DME 3000 controller shown in figure 10-7 has an improved version of the mouse cursor control built right into the unit. It is called a **trackball** and is sort of an "upside-down mouse." The palm of the hand is used to roll the ball creating a corresponding move of the cursor. Different surface areas around the ball are used to perform the click function. When a unit such as the Sony DME 3000 is used in conjunction with a Digital A500 Betacam recorder, the final production can be a computer edited, *linear* digital videotape.

Nonlinear Digital Video Editing

Although the signals were not digital, the first *nonlinear* editing units to be used commercially were available in the early 1970s. The *CMX 600*, developed by CBS and the Ampex Corporation, provided true **random access** to analog picture information stored on magnetic discs. Later, other companies utilized multiple videotape machines (all tapes containing identical material) and still others used laser discs to achieve the benefits of an instant retrieval of video. It is this attribute of random access to digitally stored video that has produced all the improvements found in nonlinear editing.

The differences between linear and nonlinear editing can be explained by using the oft-quoted analogy that describes a paragraph typed by an electric typewriter as being in linear form while a computer with a word processing program can operate in a nonlinear style. We can use the typewriter erase ribbon to delete a specific sentence, but another sentence of exactly the same length must be typed if we wish to make a correction. This is what an *insert edit* can accomplish on an edited videotape. However, with a word processor we can delete an entire sentence or any other group of words to make a shorter paragraph. We could also add several sentences and make a longer

paragraph. Previously existing material following our word insert is automatically moved forward to make room for the new material. This is possible because the digitized information is not permanently recorded on the disc and can be electronically located and moved around at millisecond speeds.

This is exactly what the computer platform can do with digitized video and audio. Once the video has been logged and identified by time code plus a few words of description, it can be quickly located, viewed, and placed in position for a potential edit. An editor can even program *several* alternative cutting sequences and view each of them in *real-time* before making the final edit decision. Nonlinear systems have created a whole new *computer workstation* approach for editing.

Generally two display screens are used when working in the nonlinear style. Figure 10-8 shows the setup for the *D/Vision Pro* unit. The screen on the right generally is used for a variety of pictorial displays such as a recorded outpoint and a new source inpoint. A number of other set displays are quickly available, such as the first frame from a group of twelve clips arranged in the sequence in which they were logged. The operator can then select one of these clips and view it in motion from fifty times play speed to slow motion.

The workscreen on the left is used to view a number of displays that control different phases of the edit process. The identifying time code numbers, titles, and usage notes that would be displayed on this screen let the operator move through the selection process with much more efficiency than with any linear system. Figure 10-9 shows the *main edit screen* for the D/Vision Pro. The very top line shows the edit menu. Below that, the left and right rectangles hold the controls for source and record (edit) video movement.

FIGURE 10-8

This D/Vision Pro is one of the new digital, nonlinear units designed for off-line editing. It takes advantage of the compression process to store multiple hours of footage into interconnected storage units. All video material is instantly accessible for the viewing of dissolves, wipes, fades, and freeze frames while the edit decisions are being made.

Photo courtesy of Touch/Vision Systems

The majority of the screen is taken up with the record **timeline** information. The horizontal bars are a visual display of a short segment of video and audio cuts shown together in a left-to-right time continuum. On this unit the video is indicated by its clip name as is the audio. The duration of the material displayed can be varied, but a ten second span is often used. For a preview of how a sequence of edits, overlayed titles, and up to six audio channels will play together, the segment is moved into the timeline part of the display. On cue, the operator sees and hears the preview while observing a vertical line that sweeps from left to right to indicate the relative position of what is being previewed at that moment.

This single main screen does not show all the operational displays that are used during editing. By using the mouse, the operator can activate a number of smaller "pop-up" **window** overlays that will appear within the larger screen. Such a window would be used, for example, in a final precise edit on the end of one audio track of music and the beginning of another.

For its advanced *Composer 8000* editing system (figure 10-10), *Avid Technologies* has designed its timeline displays

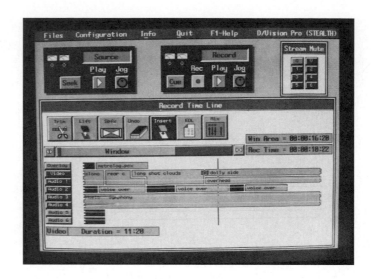

FIGURE 10-9

This main editing screen used by the D/Vision Pro unit provides the operator with many of the operating controls in the form of picture "icons" to facilitate quick access. At the top of the screen there are four other icons that each produce a "pull-down" window overlay of the listed functions. The horizontal rectangles in the lower half of the screen are a visual representation of audio and video tracks in what is termed a *timeline* display.

Photo courtesy of Touch/Vision Systems

FIGURE 10-10

This Composer 8000 from Avid Technologies is an extremely versatile nonlinear digital editing system with full off-line and on-line capabilities. It can edit 24 tracks of audio and 24 tracks of video. A number of transition video effects like wipes, peels, and centered zooms are available for use. These and many more features provide film and video professionals with the ability to go from rough cut to a top quality completed version of any production.

Photo courtesy of Avid Technologies, Inc.

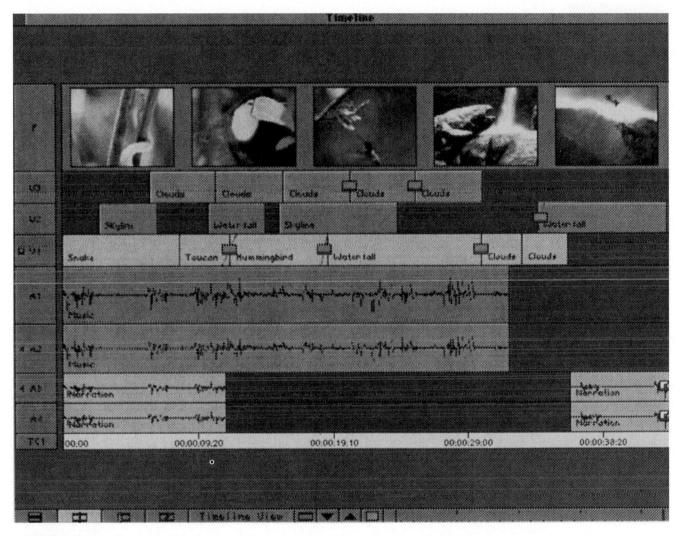

FIGURE 10-11

This timeline display used by the Media Composer 8000 provides a graphical view of the structure of a sequence being edited. The audio timeline shows the actual waveform of the sound. This illustration is only one of a number of full screen displays that the editor works with to produce the off-line EDL.

Photo courtesy of Avid Technologies, Inc.

to include still pictures that provide a graphical view of the structure of the sequence, in addition to the word description in the horizontal bar. Figure 10-11 is a display of the timeline edit mode for the Composer 8000. One can see that the audio timelines are in the shape of the actual waveform of the voice or music being heard. With this and other work displays, the editor can easily see and hear everything that is needed to program edits and special effects.

These two units described above, along with a number of others now in professional use, are differentiated by their ultimate purpose. The D/Vision Pro is designed to use its compressed/stored video primarily to create an *edit decision list*. This list is then used by a separate postproduction unit to assemble the final program on videotape or film for distribution purposes (broadcast, cable etc.). The compression process is such that any video output to electronic disc, while more than adequate for corporate video use, is simply not designed for broadcast. The unit is limited to that part of the total assembly process known as **off-line** editing, a trial and error procedure more fully described below.

On the other hand, while having all the features necessary for off-line work, the Avid Composer 8000 can also be used as an **on-line** edit unit to bring together, from its own edit decision list, all the special effects and other production elements into a final product on digital disc. In this form it can be broadcast or transferred, without any loss of quality, to disc, film, or videotape. There is one final technical note regarding the computer **platforms** that support the various systems and their individual software. All the Avid line products are designed to utilize *Macintosh* base as does the *Sundance Systems Group* and a number of others. *D/Vision* editing systems work from the DOS platform that is common to *IBM* and similar computers.

10.3 ON-LINE AND OFF-LINE EDITING

All single-camera productions, such as commercials, documentaries and rock videos, as well as many of the multiple-camera productions like situation comedies, undergo a two-phased production sequence. A weekly situation comedy may be shot over a period of a week or several weeks. Each night the **dailies**,[2] raw footage from the studio, are viewed by the producers who are usually also experienced writers. While a number of preliminary decisions are made at this point, the final shape of the program is achieved only at the end of camera production and only after several tentative **rough cuts** are viewed. The process of building these trial shows is the *off-line* editing phase previously mentioned. The process is directly derived from the **workprint** stage of film editing.

When all edit decisions have been agreed upon, they become the *edit decision list* previously mentioned. For simpler tape editing tasks, the EDL may only be some time code numbers on a piece of paper. When a computer is involved, it is usually a floppy disc containing time code numbers of the inpoints and outpoints for each cut and more numbers indicating the sequence in which those cuts will be placed. There is also further information regarding dissolve, cut, and wipe transitions as well as other special effects to be used in the final *on-line* assembly editing stage.

For most people the term on-line has come to denote *any* final assemble stage, even when there has been no off-line work done in preparation. Thus, a news producer or reporter hurriedly editing tape that has just arrived from a location shoot can also be said to be doing *on-line editing.*

10.4 LINEAR VIDEOTAPE EDITING PROCEDURES

It is probable that for the next several years a high percentage of students will receive their first editing instruction on videotape based linear editing equipment. This time

---

2. "Dailies" is a term brought to video from film production. The film shot each day would be processed at night and viewed the next day.

will not be wasted, not only because most of the basic concepts overlap, but also because there are many important fundamentals to be learned when one assembles an edited tape in the rather unforgiving linear manner.[3] The process still comes down to being able to electronically transfer a selected clip of video and sound and to do so starting at the precise endpoint of a previously recorded segment.

Some Preliminary Considerations

For the creative aspect of editing to be present, there must be a reliable and precise control over the point at which the new video clip is electronically transferred to the end of the previous clip. This also means that the exact beginning and end of any clip selected for editing (known as a *select*) must be similarly defined.

Use of Time Code

After some early hit-or-miss procedures that resulted all too often in failed or inaccurate edits, the Society of Television and Motion Picture Engineers (SMPTE) developed the previously mentioned time code system that located a precise point on tape in terms of hours, minutes, seconds, and frames (measured from a stated point at the beginning of the tape). (See figure 9-11.) These numbers can also be set to indicate the actual moment in local or international time that the recording was being made. An Olympic ski run of several minutes duration may be shot by as many as ten cameras as the skier moves down the slope. To recreate the run in its original time frame, the editor uses the second-by-second numbers to keep the shots in proper sequence.

3. Two good books that deal in detail with linear editing are: Arthur Schneider, *Electronic Post-Production and Videotape Editing* (Boston: Focal Press, 1989); and Steven E. Browne, *Videotape Editing* (Boston: Focal Press, 1989).

In older systems this information was recorded on one of the audio tracks. In newer systems it is recorded on its own track or in another section of the tape known as the **vertical interval.** This is the **retrace** area where the scanning process stops at the bottom of the frame and returns to the top of the frame. Because it uses the vertical interval, this type of time code is known as **VITC (vertical interval time code).**

A second type of time code functions in a slightly different manner. The sync pulse of the control track (see sections 5.1 and 8.1) serves as the basis of a digital readout in frames, seconds, and minutes. In many ways it can be used very much like SMPTE time code. This sort of control-track editing is very acceptable in training situations but has drawbacks because the frame location numbers are not permanently recorded on tape. They exist only in the edit controller and in relation to a movable "0" point, which can be changed by the operator at any time. The numbering system is erased each time the tape is removed from the machine but can be accurately restored if a definite "0" point is selected and reused at each editing session.

Assemble and Insert Edit Modes

The original industrial and educational level edit systems established two different modes for the transfer edit. To keep things simple, a primary **assemble** mode was to be used to lay each cut in a beginning-to-end sequence. To satisfy the basic needs of many productions there was also a second **insert** mode that could be used to replace a portion of any already recorded cut with a different cut placed within the existing inpoint and outpoint. It was to be used to add what the news people refer to as **B-roll** footage.

An example often seen on news programs would be a shot of a reporter interviewing the fire chief to get all necessary

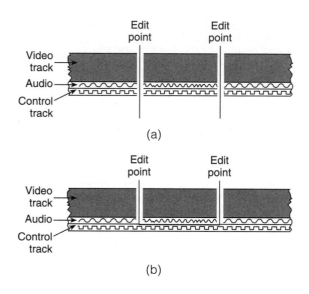

FIGURE 10-12

(a) **Assemble editing.** As each segment is assemble-edited, a new section of control track is laid down along with the video and audio signals. (b) **Insert editing.** After a continuous control track has been laid down, each insert edit attaches the video and audio signals to this existing control track.

information. This would be called **A-roll** footage. As this shot becomes visually redundant, *B-roll footage* of the fire is used to provide the audience with a sense of the nature of the fire itself. The interview sound from the A-roll continues to be heard. To accomplish this insert over existing video, the record machine must use the control track originally laid down for the conversation video so as to keep both the source and record machines in synchronization while the insert edit replaces that original video.

Operators very soon realized that insert edits were consistently more stable than assemble edits. The reason for this is that each assemble edit starts and ends a segment of control track with each edit. (See figure 10-12.) Editors began to use the insert mode for all editing—in effect, *assembling* in the insert mode. The required

continuous control track is accomplished prior to the edit session by recording a synchronous black picture. One can use either the output of a switcher or the internal synchronization (sync) signal that most VCR machines generate. With some equipment, an added benefit is that of being able to lay down time code while recording black.

Equipment Function

In its simplest form, editing can be done with just a few pieces of basic equipment. On the other hand it can also be done using a full complement of control room and studio equipment. The basic units needed are the *source* (playback) deck, the *record* (edit) deck, and the *edit control unit*. Usually, both the source and edit decks will have monitors so their outputs can be

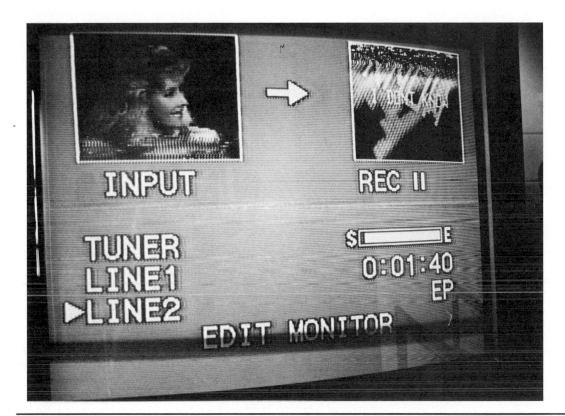

FIGURE 10-13

This monitor is used
to display both the
source and the edit
outputs for this earlier
consumer grade
editing system.

viewed. However, with some of the newer editing systems, both the source and edit outputs can be seen on one screen at the same time. Such a configuration is shown in figure 10-13.

Source Deck

Most source decks are basically like any other videocassette recorder, having the usual functions—fast forward, play, rewind, and so forth. One control that is particularly important to the editing function is the **tracking** knob. If tracking is not adjusted to match the setting on the original recording machine, a banding effect will occur—a severe picture breakup where a horizontal strip of the picture will lose its sync. With some equipment, there often is also a **skew** adjustment that

should be checked if the top portion of the picture tends to bend over in one direction or another.

Record Deck

The record deck is the one onto which the selected material is edited. Here one loads the tape with sync black and a resulting control track. This tape will become the **edited master tape.** This machine resembles a regular VCR but contains some extra electronics and function controls that allow it to accept signals that select and execute the editing procedure.

Edit Controller

The edit controller, as previously described in section 10.2, is the brains of the editing setup. From this unit the operator

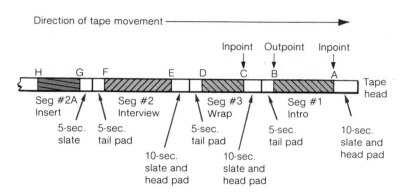

FIGURE 10-14

Recorded segments on the original master tape.

In this example, there are three segments of program material plus one insert segment to be edited in later. These are to be "assembled" in the order of the segment numbers.

executes the normal functions of both the source and edit decks (fast forward, stop, rewind, play, and so on). The type of edit—insert, assemble, audio-only—is also selected on the controller. On most units there are search dials for both source and record decks, although some controllers function with just one. These dials enable the operator to move the tape of either machine at varying fast and slow speeds as the footage is shown on the respective monitors. When an edit inpoint or outpoint is located by slow movement of the tape, the dial is used to bring the tape to a complete stop so that the new inpoint, for example, is seen in the pause mode (still frame) on the source machine monitor.

Basic Editing Procedures

In presenting the basic procedures and terminology of linear editing where assembly is done by means of a controller, we will use a simple editing situation such as one might find in field production or news work. Figure 10-14 indicates how four separate

camera segments might be recorded in the field on the *original master reel*. (In studying these illustrations, keep in mind that the direction of movement is from left to right as on all videotape machines. The **head,** or beginning of the tape, is seen here at the far right side of the page.)

Shot Order

Like single-camera film production, the individual shots are not necessarily recorded in the order in which they will be edited together. In figure 10-14, the segment (cut) numbers (1, 2, 2A, and 3) refer to the sequence into which they will eventually be edited. Segment #1 is the host introducing the program. Segment #3 is the host's conclusion or wrap-up. Shooting out of sequence would not be unusual. Program segment #2 (third in position from the head of the tape) is the host interviewing the guest. Consider segment #2A (the fourth segment to be shot) as being some footage that relates to the interview. It will be used as a *video-only insert* to replace ten seconds of the interview footage while the interview audio continues.

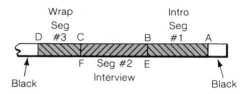

FIGURE 10-15

Program segments transferred to the edited master.

As the program segments (from figure 10-14) are assembled, the outpoint of segment #1 (B) is placed exactly at the inpoint of segment #2 (E) with other segments being similarly located as indicated.

At the head of each segment there must be eight to ten seconds of sync picture and sound identification of the upcoming segment. Known as the **slate** (see figure 9-14), this material consists of the camera pointed at a chalkboard or card with printed words such as "Segment 2, Take 1, Interview." The words should also be read aloud to confirm the audio level. With the tape still rolling, the slate is pulled away to reveal the host and subject for an additional brief period prior to the cue to begin. This short sequence and a similar continuation of picture at the conclusion of the interview are known as **head pad** and **tail pad.** The function of these pads is to provide an adequate margin of continuing sync picture signal, which as we shall see, is necessary to the editing process. Figure 10-15 indicates the order in which segments from the original master tape on the *source* machine will be transferred in program sequence to the *edited master reel* on the *record deck.*

Determining Edit Points

Prior to the actual assembly process, there is usually a viewing session involving the director, editor, and others responsible for the creative aspects of the program. This is called the **pre-edit session.** Its purpose is to check the tape carefully to determine not only what material will be selected for final editing, but also to designate the *inpoint* and *outpoint* of each segment that is to be edited into the finished program. In effect this is more or less a nontechnical *off-line* edit session.

We have established that segment #1 (figure 10-15) consists of the host/interviewer talking directly to the camera. Outpoint *B* is the end of a sentence introducing a second person who will appear with the interviewer at the beginning of segment #2. Our edit must allow for a normal time lapse between the end of this final sentence and the beginning audio of the next (interview) segment at inpoint *E*. A pause that is too long or too short would be unnatural and would distract the viewer. Our edit decision (sometimes called the **edit event**) in this case is relatively simple. Outpoint *B* will be established at a point that will allow for one-half second more of picture to follow the final word spoken. Inpoint *E* of the segment #2 interview will be set to allow an additional one-half second of establishing video ahead of the first audio.

Entering the Edit Points

The actual mechanics of using the controller to set up the edit are really not complicated. We must, however, make two assumptions in order to precede with our edit example. The first is that segment #1 has already been recorded with the slate removed and that several seconds of tail pad were included beyond the final spoken word at outpoint *B*. Now with record deck in a slow mode that permits words to be understood, the operator plays the end of the cut that has just been recorded, listening for the final word.

The technique is to use the dial to move the tape back and forth to find that word

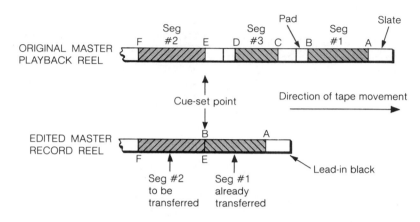

FIGURE 10-16

Playback and record tapes as they would be positioned relative to the cue-set point entered into the controller.

With segment #1 *(A-B)* already transferred from the original master (playback reel) to the edited master (record reel), the cue-set point is selected to determine the precise spot for the next edit of segment #2.

and then add fifteen frames (one-half second) of tape before putting the machine into the pause (freeze-frame) mode. Both the time code readouts and the video monitors provide important visual feedback for the operator during this process, especially if the pre-edit logging has been properly done.

Now the same procedure is used with the source tape controls to find an inpoint that is one-half second ahead of the first word of inpoint *E* of segment #2. This being done, the two VCR machines are set up as is shown in figure 10-16. Consider that the two arrows in the illustration indicate the two video recording heads in relation to the position of the segments on tape. The two video monitors will be showing something similar to figure 10-17.

To enter this edit point into the controller's memory, units like the Panasonic A750 will have a central *set button* (enter) located adjacent to an *in* and an *out* button on both the source and record sides of the

controllers. By simultaneously pressing the *set* and the *in* buttons on the source side of the controller and then the same two buttons on the record side, we have entered the edit point into the controller's memory. Tape on the source machine is then rolled to find the approximate end point of the new segment. Again the operator makes sure that there is an extra several seconds of picture beyond the last word. By then pressing the *set* and *out* buttons on the source side of the machine, a completion point for the segment has been set that allows some flexibility with the next edit.

Preview, Trim, and Execution of the Edit

The machines are now set up to perform an edit, but only in rare circumstances would an editor precede without first previewing the transition between the two cuts before going ahead. It is quite often the timing of the audio space between the

Playback   Record

FIGURE 10-17

Simultaneous display of picture information from both the playback (original source) and record (edited master) machines.

The operator watches the picture on the playback machine *(left)* while searching for the starting point of the next segment to be recorded. When located, the machine is put into the pause mode as seen here. During this search, the last frame of the previously recorded segment can be viewed on the monitor *(right)*. The operator can easily compare these two pictures while making the edit decision.

two segments that causes problems rather than the transition between pictures. The *preview* function can be accomplished without any actual transfer of the signal to the record tape. All editing units have controls that, when given the command, will roll both tapes to a *pre-roll point* shown in figure 10-18, pause there briefly, and then roll both tapes forward. As the tapes are getting up to playing speed, the record monitor shows the end of its segment and the source monitor shows material in front of the inpoint of the new segment. There must always be more than five seconds of continuous sync picture (or whatever is set up for the pre-roll time) at the head of the source tape or the preview function cannot take place.

If everything has been done correctly, the new segment will play to its outpoint as entered and come to a stop. If at the edit point something did not go as planned, it is possible to make an adjustment in the position of either of the two tapes to change the timing of the edit. Using our example, let's say that the one-half second of picture at the head of segment #2 (inpoint *E*) seems too short. One solution would be to use just a little more of the silent pad footage at the head of the segment. The **trim** control is designed to do just this by letting the editor program the edit to take place just a little earlier on the source tape. The trim control would be used to enter *minus* frames (lower numbers on the time code display) on the source side of the controller. (The end pad of the recorded segment could have been extended as another option.) If the editor is satisfied after a second preview and the

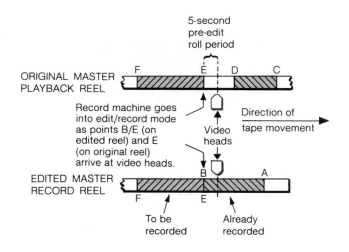

FIGURE 10-18

Tapes on the playback and record machines in position for the pre-edit roll period.

In this example, segment #1 *(A-B)* has already been transferred to the "edited master record reel" on the record machine. The next step is to transfer segment #2 *(E-F)* from the original master on the playback machine to the record machine at point *B*. For the edit to take place both the source and edit machines must first be rolled backwards for a precise number of frames and brought to a complete stop for a brief period. This move sets up the pre-edit roll period that gets both tapes up to proper playing speed. Generally five seconds or even less is sufficient for this purpose. On most machines this whole operation takes place automatically once the command is given to commence the edit.

edit itself seemed to go as planned, then the *review* control can be used to confirm the edit.

Insert Editing

With segment #2 transferred, the best option is to continue with segment #3 and then turn to the insert edit *2A* that is to be placed within segment #2. Such an insertion of video only is not difficult, but again there are some aesthetic aspects to be considered. The conversation in segment #2 may provide an obvious cue such as a reference to the item in the close-up shot to be inserted. Prior planning by the director would probably include having the interviewer say something like, "Now on this particular unit . . ." to serve as an inpoint. The outpoint could be a little more subtle. The important thing is to

have enough footage after the insert to re-establish the interview shot before the segment is concluded.

Figure 10-19 shows how, with these considerations in mind, the tapes would be set up in relationship to each other. Note the allowance for at least five seconds of picture head pad on the playback machine. This is necessary in order to assure proper picture sync at the time of the inpoint edit. As stated previously, the insert will begin eight seconds past the previously transferred edit point *B/E* and run for ten seconds. Insert editing is by no means limited to just video. The insert can obviously be video and audio combined.

A and B Roll Dissolve Transitions

Machine-to-machine edits as described up to this point can be used when the desired

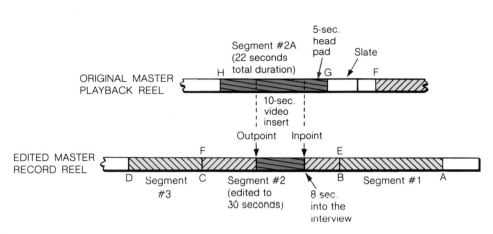

FIGURE 10-19

Playback and record machines set up for an insert edit.

The shot to be inserted (ten seconds from segment #2A) is to be edited into segment #2 *(E-F)* eight seconds after point *B/E* (the beginning of segment #2). The two VTR machines are rolled simultaneously from points at least five seconds ahead of the anticipated edit. The edit in and edit out commands can be executed either manually or by the edit controller.

effect is that of an instantaneous *take*. **Cuts-only editing** can be accomplished with nothing more than two VCRs and a controller. However, when dissolves or special effects are desired, the levers, buttons, and mix banks buttons of a **switcher** or **SEG** must be utilized. As in any dissolve or effect, this means there must be two simultaneous sources of video signal. Also, when mixing various video sources, the time-base corrector (section 5.1) must be used to guarantee that all video signals will lock up with no picture breakup.

To dissolve between two segments, it is necessary to have two separate tape feeds on *A* and *B* source machines. The technique is somewhat the same as in traditional *A* and *B* roll editing for film, where the final composite film is automatically printed from two specially edited film rolls. In television this system can either be set up for automatic computer control or be done manually at the switcher during the edit session. The basic principles involved in setting up the tapes are roughly the same in either situation.

When a dissolve (or wipe or other effect) between segments is planned, it is imperative to allow considerably more video pad (compared to editing a straight cut) following the outpoint of the first segment and preceding the inpoint of the second. For example, in the diagram shown in figure 10-20, the edit point *E/B* is the midpoint of a two-second dissolve between segment #1 and segment #2. However, both playback machines must feed a video signal to the record machine throughout the duration of the dissolve. Although only two seconds of pad from each segment are actually needed for the two-second dissolve overlap, it is always advisable to have extra-protection source video available. Most professional directors would not feel comfortable without a working margin of at least an additional three seconds added to each segment.

A sequence in which all the segments are to be connected by dissolves must be well planned to be recorded from beginning to end. Unless the dissolves are few

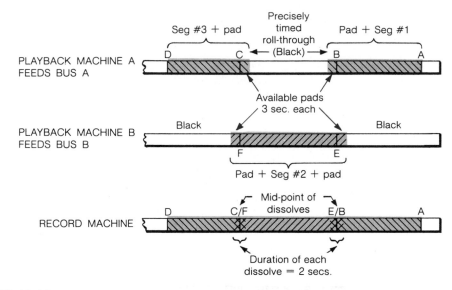

FIGURE 10-20

Three VCR machines set up for a dissolve edit.

In preparing the *A* and *B* playback videotapes, care must be taken to ensure that every segment and each "roll-through" (black space between segments) is precisely timed—including the exact pads that are wanted. As the two playback tapes are fed into the switcher, the actual dissolve edits (on noncomputer controlled editing units) are accomplished simply by using the fader arms.

and far apart, allowing for each one to be carefully cued-up well in advance, the only safe procedure is simply to designate points where the whole procedure stops for an ordinary edit while the B Roll is again cued. These types of problems are what led to the computer control of on-line editing and ultimately to nonlinear procedures where all of this is taken care of automatically.

10.5 A DEVELOPING CONCEPT OF HOW EDITING IS TO BE USED

The development of a wide range of digitally based technology is creating an entirely new approach to video production in terms of how and where it is used. The utilization of audio/visual training and communication systems in the business world was usually a matter of 35 mm slides, audio tapes, and some video. It is rapidly being replaced by what has become known as **desktop video.** With compact and reasonably priced equipment such as the *Avid Media Suite Pro* (shown with one of its work displays in figure 10-21), individuals are turning out very professional-looking informational productions for major corporations. Lettering in a variety of styles can be mixed with "pop-up" windows of full-motion digital video and other effects. Many in the video industry see increased career opportunities for those persons who have the technical and creative abilities to make the fullest use of this new generation of equipment.

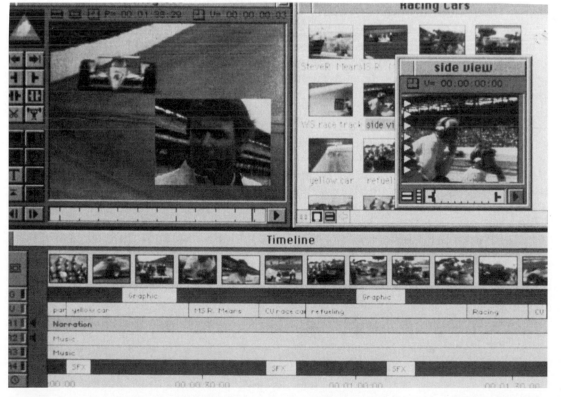

FIGURE 10-21

Desk top editing, the new look in corporate video production.

This Media Suite Pro unit from Avid Technologies demonstrates how nonlinear editing has made some definite changes in the way corporate America is communicating with its customers and within the company structure. More and more editors feel very comfortable working with this type of work display.

Photos courtesy of Avid Technologies, Inc.

SUMMARY

Most editing techniques and the equipment that has made them a functional part of television grew out of some obvious needs that became apparent as the industry developed. The original "edit as you go" style of earlier live television gave way to a number of impressive videotape based techniques that suited the needs of the growing audiences for sports, news, and situation comedies.

Videotape editing came to be seen as serving three distinct types of productions in somewhat different ways. The *postproduction* editing on situation comedies and soap operas takes individual short scenes and makes some minor corrections in both sound (applause) and picture (replacement for an out-of-focus close-up) and then is used to assemble all the parts into a whole. The *preproduction* work that puts taped news footage into short concise stories is the backbone of the news program. Newer program types such as the reality based "police in action" shows are shot with a *single-camera* technique that depends upon a *complete editing* job for final assembly.

For most its history, editing for television has been *linear* in structure. All footage existed on tape and, to view it, one had to roll through it in the sequence of its location on that tape. Editing of any complexity was divided into an *off-line* planning and trial assembly stage. This was followed by a final assembly stage termed *on-line editing*. The original *edit controllers* were eventually improved so that they could manipulate the tape with some facility. When *computer control* was added, an off-line editor still had to roll back and forth through tape but did so only for the purpose of creating a series of *edit decisions* that became the basis of the on-line assembly phase.

Nonlinear digital video editing makes possible the concept of *random access* to any frame of video that has been *digitalized* and placed on a *magnetic disc.* This means that an editor can instantly call up any segment (cut) of video and place it and other segments in a trial order for viewing in the off-line stage of editing. When this process has resulted in a final edit decision list on a digital disc, the on-line computer-controlled unit can perform the final assembly with both speed and technical perfection.

The equipment is truly impressive, but the lesson for students continues to be that technology is worthless without the creative knowledge that can make it live up to a worthwhile potential. Linear, tape-based equipment will very possibly serve as the introductory medium for students for a number of years to come. It has served the industry well for many years and its disciplines will continue to serve many students equally well during their transition to a working knowledge of more advanced facilities.

CHAPTER

11

Producing

The previous chapters have emphasized equipment—how it operates and how it can be used effectively to get across a message or create a particular mood. In this chapter and the next, we will be concerned with the overall process of putting together a program. This, of course, involves operating the equipment properly, both technically and aesthetically. But it also encompasses coming up with an idea, committing that idea to paper, making sure it can be accomplished given available resources, and then overseeing the whole project so it reaches fruition. Central to all this is the producer.

11.1 THE ROLE OF THE PRODUCER

Producers are in charge of the *overall organization* of a production, be it a network drama, a local station newscast, a cable TV sportscast, a syndicated game show, a public broadcasting music concert, or a corporate training tape. They are responsible for seeing that all the elements of a program—cast, crew, props, equipment, etc.—are in the right place at the right time. They often initiate a project and see that it is finished *on-time* and *on-budget*. Their most intensive work is accomplished during **preproduction.** This is the period when everything must be carefully planned so that **production** and **postproduction** can progress smoothly.

Hyphenates

In general, a producer handles logistics of a production while a director makes the creative and aesthetic decisions (see chapter 12). But sometimes a producer will be a **hyphenate**—a producer-director. In this case the producer will handle organization (primarily during preproduction) and then lead the cast and crew through the creative process of production and postproduction. Writers sometimes figure into the hyphenate role also with one person being writer-director, producer-writer, or producer-writer-director.

There are advantages and disadvantages to handling a number of different roles. Most people evolve into becoming hyphenates because they want *creative control.* A writer who has been displeased with how a director has interpreted his or her script will decide to become the director for the next script. Directors who feel they are unnecessarily curtailed by cost conscious producers may want to make their own decisions about how to prioritize spending. Producers who work hard to develop a project and raise the funding may want to ensure that their vision is carried out during the production phase.

Although being a hyphenate can lead to greater creative control, it is also more work. Given the time pressures of most TV productions, one person can become exhausted trying to polish a script, find Civil War–era guns, and plan camera angles all at one time. Also few people have all the aptitudes necessary to undertake multiple jobs. Someone who is highly skilled in getting the best performance possible from actors may not be equally skilled in handling financial statements. Multiple inputs, undertaken *harmoniously,* can also enrich a production. One person, given too much responsibility, can flounder—or become an ego maniac. Often the reasoned judgment that comes from bouncing ideas off others can lead to a richer end product.

Associate Producers

The nature and scope of the project also determine the number of roles that are needed. A talk show needs very little in the way of writing so a producer could easily handle what writing is needed. Sometimes producers have so much to do that they hire **associate** or **assistant producers.** For example, a game show may have one assistant producer whose job it is to acquire free prizes for contestants while another assistant producer is in charge of screening potential contestants. Whether someone is an assistant or associate producer is not related as much to what job they are in charge of as to their level of experience and skill; an associate producer is paid more than an assistant producer.

Line Producers

Some productions, primarily movies, have a **line producer.** This is a person representing the producer who is on the set each day, mainly making sure that all is progressing properly so the movie will be finished on-budget and in time for its scheduled airing.

Executive Producers

Executive producers oversee a number of different productions. For example, a production company (such as Carsey-Werner, owned by Marcy Carsey and Tom Werner) may have several network series (*The Cosby Show, Roseanne*) in production, in syndication, and in development. Each series has a hands-on producer, but the owners of the company, who made the deals with the networks and who are in the process of making other deals, make decisions regarding the overall scope and direction of the series—hence the term executive producer. Your instructor probably serves as executive producer for your class projects.

The number of producers needed for a production varies widely. A public access cable talk show may have one "guiding light" who produces, writes, and hosts the show and handles the expenses out of his or her own pocket. A network situation comedy series will have one or more executive producers, one or more producers, and a number of assistant and associate producers. But whoever handles the producing chores will find that somewhere along the way they are involved with scripts, budgets, personnel, production paper work, and schedules.

11.2 SCRIPTS

To be successful, even the simplest productions need something committed to paper to serve as a guideline. That something is referred to as a **script.**[1] The producer uses the script to organize the elements needed for the program and often to sell the idea of a series or program to someone who will pay the production costs. As with most other elements of TV production, scripts vary both in form and complexity.

Treatments

Most commercial network series start with a **treatment.** (See figure 11-1.) This is several pages, written in regular prose form, that tell the overall premise of the series, describe the main characters, outline the basic plots for several of the episodes, and highlight the strong points of the idea. A producer (or executive producer) from an outside production company (with a track record of success), can make an appointment to see the appropriate network executives for a **pitch** meeting—a session that lasts about half an hour during which the producer tries to convince the network executives that they should buy the series idea. The producer presents the information in the treatment orally and usually leaves the written treatment behind for the executives to study. If the network executives like the idea, they will commission (pay for) one or more complete program scripts. If they like the scripts, they will order a **pilot,** a produced program that is to be one of the series. If they like the pilot and decide to schedule the series on a regular basis, they will give the go ahead for more scripts and productions. Throughout this whole process the production company producer negotiates with the network regarding both creative and financial elements.

Many other types of programs also use treatments. Magazine, talk, and game shows that are planned for **syndication,** cable TV, or local broadcast often evolve from treatments presented to programming

263

CHAPTER 11

Producing

1. This book does not pretend to be a text in scriptwriting. What is given here is merely an overview of script forms. For more information on scriptwriting, see such books as Syd Field, *Screenplay: The Foundations of Screenwriting* (New York: Dell, 1982); Ronald D. Dyas, *Screenwriting for Television and Film* (Dubuque, IA: Brown and Benchmark, 1993); Jurgen Wolff and Kerry Cox, *Top Secrets: Screenwriting* (Los Angeles: Lone Eagle Publishing Company, 1992); Ken Dancyger, *Broadcast Writing* (Stoneham, MA: Focal Press, 1991); Peter Mayeux, *Writing for the Broadcast Media* (Newton, MA: Allyn and Bacon, 1985); and Ray DiZazzo, *Corporate Scriptwriting* (Stoneham, MA: Focal Press, 1992).

TREATMENT

"THE CAMPUS"

"The Campus" is a high energy series aimed at teens and young adults. It takes place on a college campus and features the adventures, problems, and experiences of four roommates.

Mark, a sophomore, is good looking and athletic. He is on the basketball team and seems destined to become one of its stars. He attracts coeds easily, but deep down he is uneasy with them. He comes from a wealthy family and seems to "have it all." However, he has trouble knuckling down and studying and is constantly on the verge of academic problems that will disqualify him from basketball. He's such a nice guy, however, that his friends try to come to his rescue and figure out ways for him to get through his classes.

Frank, on the other hand, has an easy time in classes, but always seems to have hard luck in social situations. He says the wrong things, wears the wrong clothes, spills his soft drink on a girl he is trying to win over, and generally falls prey to social indiscretions. He and Mark do not get along very well.

Juan tries to smooth the waters between Mark and Frank. He's not as bright as Frank or as athletic as Mark, but he's well rounded and a good mediator. He is on a scholarship and does not have much spending money. Mark sometimes tries to buy his allegiance by giving him material things, but Juan does not respond well to that. He works most evenings so does not have much time for social life.

George is the jokster of the group. In trying to make light of situations, he often utters what turns out to be prophetic philosophy. He likes to play practical jokes on people, especially Mark's girl friends, but he does not mean any harm. He is not particularly good looking, but he is a likable person.

In the first episode of the series, all four arrive back on campus for their sophomore year. Frank, Juan, and George had planned to room with each other and had thought their fourth roommate would be someone they had all befriended in their freshman year. However, that person has dropped out of school and Mark has been assigned to their room. He is unhappy about the situation. He thought he would be in special housing for athletes, but there had not been room for him.

Frank and Mark clash immediately and Frank goes to the housing authority to try to get Mark removed from the room. However, he is unsuccessful. Juan, realizing they will probably all have to live together, talks separately to both Mark and

1

FIGURE 11-1

The first page of a treatment that might be prepared by an independent production company to give to a network executive.

executives. In these cases the treatment will indicate the target audience, describe the overall idea for the series, and outline some of the planned segments. In addition, individual programs such as made-for-TV movies or documentaries often have a treatment as a starting point.

A newscast script proceeds very differently. If a network or station has decided to present the news, no one needs to spell out specific ideas with a treatment—the ideas come from the news of the day. The newscast script is written during the course of a day (or several hours) as the producer and news director decide what is the most important news. Reporters and writers put together individual stories and transitions between stories that are eventually read by newscasters. Usually the producer for a newscast is a *staff producer.* In other words, that person works full-time for the network or station overseeing one or more newscasts each day. This is unlike most network series, where the producer is a member of an *outside production company.*

Varying Script Forms

Because programs and circumstances differ, script forms also differ.[2] The type of script needed for a drama would be overkill for a talk show. A music video that is highly postproduced can use a script with less structure than a news script that must give accurate mistake-proof guidance for a live broadcast. Although many different script forms have evolved over the years, the main ones that you, as a television student, are likely to encounter are film-style scripts, two-column scripts, rundowns, outlines, and storyboards.

Film-Style Scripts

As might be evident from their name, **film-style scripts** (see figure 11-2) are the type that have been used for years to produce theatrical movies. The main characteristic of this script is that each scene is *separated* from the next so that each can be considered individually. Materials produced from film-style scripts are usually shot in a number of different locations with all the scenes from one location being shot on the same

2. A large number of computer programs are available to help television writers compose their scripts. Some of the most commonly used are *Scriptor* from Screenplay Systems, 150 East Olive Avenue, Suite 305, Burbank, CA 91502; *Superscript* from Inherit the Earth Technologies, 1800 S. Robertson Blvd., Suite 326, Los Angeles, CA 90035; and *Movie Master* from Comprehensive Video Supply, 148 Veterans Drive, Northvale, NJ 07647.

day or succeeding days. A script that highlights times of day, locations, and whether these locations are inside (interior-INT.) or outside (exterior-EXT.) can help a producer with preproduction planning. The producer uses the descriptive paragraphs to determine what will be needed in the way of props and set pieces.

Also, the director shoots each scene a number of times using only one camera. For example, the first time the camera might film a two-shot of a man and woman arguing. The second time the scene is shot, the camera would record a close-up of the woman delivering her lines and reacting to the man's lines. The third time through, the close-up would be of the man. Then, during editing, the various shots are cut together. The script form, by showing each distinct scene, helps the director figure out what to shoot. The dialogue is indented, keeping it separate from the writer's descriptive material about the scene. This gives the director room for notes and helps the actors pinpoint their lines.

Film-style scripts are very complete. They include all the words that will be spoken by the actors, describe all the primary action that will take place, and indicate basic moods and emotions. Of course sometimes the words are altered by the actors or director, and the interpretation and execution of actions and emotion is the province of the director (hence, the occasional conflict about *creative control*).

Just about anything that is shot single-camera can use a film-style script, but it is most often associated with dramatic productions.

Two-Column Scripts

The film-style script is not appropriate for multi-camera productions that are shot live or live-on-tape. The descriptions would get in the way and location does not change. More appropriate is the **two-column script** (see figure 11-3) that pairs the

INT. - ELEGANT RESTAURANT - NIGHT

Joan and Philip, both dressed in stylish clothes, sit at a table.
Philip has leaned forward and is talking softly to Joan. She is
leaning back and appears to be somewhat distant.

                    PHILIP
          I really want to come back, Joan. I miss the
          children and I'm tired of living out of a suit-
          case.

                    JOAN
               (sarcastically)
          That's tender.

                    PHILIP
               (exasperated)
          Now what did I do wrong?

                    JOAN
          You're just acting like your same old selfish
          self. Everything revolves around you. No
          consideration for me. Not even any sign of
          love.

                    PHILIP
          But, of course, I care about you. I don't need
          to tell you that.

                    JOAN
          That's a matter of opinion.

                    PHILIP
          Now you're being like your old sensitive self.
          I just don't get it.

                    JOAN
          That's right, Philip. You just don't get it.

Joan gets up from the table angrily and walks away. She realizes
she has forgotten her purse, returns for it, glares at Philip and
walks toward the door. Philip looks hurt and confused.

EXT. - CITY STREET - NIGHT

Christopher is seen driving his car, weaving in and out of
traffic. He pulls over to the curb and blinks his lights off and
on. A large dark figure carring a briefcase emerges from the
shadows, opens the car door, throws the briefcase in the car, and
receeds back into the shadows. Christopher drives off.

INT. - PHILIP'S OFFICE - DAY

Philip is going through a stack of papers, but he seems to be
having trouble concentrating. Mildred comes in the door with a
stack of phone messages.

FIGURE 11-2

An example of a
page of a film-style
script.

Note the separation
of the scenes and
the indentation of
the dialogue.

NIGHTLY NEWS

<u>VIDEO</u>	<u>AUDIO</u>
TAPE: OPENING CREDITS	SOUND ON TAPE. Runs :30. Ends with drum beat.
TWO-SHOT - STEVE AND SHARON	STEVE: I'm Steve Anderson. SHARON: And I'm Sharon Hendricks here with the latest news.
STEVE	STEVE: Fire fighters are still at the scene of a three-alarm fire on Market Street that destroyed two buildings earlier today. Fred White has this report.
TAPE: FIRE REPORT	SOT: Runs 2:56. Ends with "could have been a lot worse."
SHARON	SHARON: The Japanese are still trying to assess if any damage was caused by this morning's earthquake. The quake was
GRAPHICS: MAP OVER SHOULDER	centered two hundred miles from Tokyo and registered 7 point 1. Two strong after shocks have been felt.

FIGURE 11-3

A sample page from a two-column news script.

Note how the video and audio items line up with each other.

video elements on the left-hand side with audio elements on the right-hand side. The producer can find all the materials that will need to be gathered together, especially since elements such as music and insert tapes are capitalized.

The director, who must act quickly, can easily see what visual images should be on the screen as the talk progresses and can set up cameras for what will be coming next. Usually the left-hand margin of a two-column script is fairly wide so the director can make notes.

There are many variations on two-column scripts, depending on the type of program for which they are used. Some include every word of dialogue. Editorials and commercials, for example, need to be precise—no ad-libbing allowed. Dramas, such as soap operas, that are shot in-studio with multiple cameras can also use fully-scripted, two-column scripts. Other programs, such as magazine shows and newscasts, include all the words to be spoken by the anchors but just include basic information about edited field reports that are to be rolled in so that the director can bring them in and take them out without any flubs. Still others, such as talk shows and game shows, indicate the general topics to be discussed or questions to be asked because the answers, of course, can not be scripted ahead of time.

Rundowns

Rather than using a two-column script, some talk and game shows (and other programs for which little can be scripted ahead of time) use **rundowns.** (See figure 11-4.) These list the various segments that will be included in the program and are most often used for routine programs that

are produced on a daily or weekly basis, such as *Today* and *Meet the Press*.

Specific information is given for each segment. This information may vary from one form of program to another, but generally it includes the source for that segment (videotape roll-in, studio cameras, graphics, remote feed), what the segment contains, and how long the segment should run. If a program has a set length, such as one hour, the total running time may be indicated so that director can tell if the overall program is running short or long. Cues in and out of segments help the director prepare for transitions.

Producers use the rundowns to make sure all the guests are confirmed and ready to appear in the proper order. Usually these programs are directed by the same person day after day, so the director has a routine and is mainly concerned with knowing about anything unusual that is incorporated within a particular segment.

Sometimes rundowns include fully-scripted material that can be written ahead of time. When they do, they look somewhat akin to a two-column script in that they include a column for video and another for audio. The line can blur between a *detailed rundown* and a *nonspecific two-column list*, but how to categorize the script is not nearly as important as whether or not it is useful for the talent, producer, and director.

Outlines

The line also sometimes blurs between rundowns and outlines. **Outlines** list the various elements of a program but usually in less specific terms than rundowns. They are often used for pieces such as music videos (see figure 11-5) that are

RUNDOWN SHEET

"PROFILES" - NO. 37

SEGMENT	SOURCE	ITEM	SEGMENT TIME	TOTAL TIME
1	VCR	Opening Credits.	:25	:25
2	Cam 2 Host mic	Host welcomes Jane Collins from Personnel.	:20	:45
3	Cam 1,2,3 Studio mics Graphics for guest ID	Host and Jane discuss purpose of the department, how it interfaces with each employee, and its organzation. ENDS: We can see this on a chart.	3:00	3:45
4	Graphics of chart Studio mics	Jane discusses the chart of the department's organiza- tion.	1:00	4:45
5	Cam 1,2,3 Studio mics	Host and Jane discuss com- pany benefits. ENDS: Let's look at the tape your department produced about this.	1:30	6:15
6	VCR	Tape about benefits. ENDS: Music and copyright credit.	5:35	11:50
7	Cam 1,2,3 Studio mics	Host and Jane discuss how employees get additional information.	2:10	14:00
8	Cam 2 Studio mics	Host thanks Jane and closes program.	:30	14:30
9	VCR	Closing credits	:30	15:00

FIGURE 11-4

This is a rundown for one of a series of fifteen minute programs that might be produced as a corporate video to highlight the job functions of people within the company. Note that exact wording cues are written in some places so that the director can move smoothly from one element to another.

shot and then edited. Because of this, they can include some of the type of detail found in film-style scripts. The producer and director both have time to digest the information, and the shooting itself is usually undertaken with one camera from a variety of angles.

Documentaries often lend themselves to outlines. They can indicate general items, issues, or circumstances to be investigated, but the real conclusions and findings cannot be planned until the ma-terial has been shot.

Outlines do need to indicate to the producer the props, sets, locations, and other production elements that will be needed to ensure a successful shoot. They must give the director a general idea of what to shoot, but they allow plenty of room for improvisation.

```
                    MUSIC VIDEO FOR
                "I LOOK SO GOOD IN YELLOW'
                        BRIAN
```

The video will consist of four different set-ups:
     1. Brian, dressed in a variety of yellow clothes, lip
syncing in a nightclub setting.
     2. A chorus of children dressed in yellow singing the "Oo la
la la la la" refrain.
     3. Brian, dressed in a yellow shirt and lip syncing, walking
a dog dressed in a yellow dog jacket.
     4. The three back-up singers in a department store trying on
ugly colored shirts and finally finding yellow ones they like.

We will build two sets in the studio, one for the nightclub scene
and the other for the children's chorus. The nightclub scene
will have a 1940s look to it and will consist of a sequined
curtain and a floor stand microphone. The audience will not be
shown. An intense spotlight will highlight Brian's yellow
clothing.

The children's chorus (about twenty 8 to 10 year olds) will be on
risers against background flats that are painted with geometric
shapes in primary colors.

The dog walking scene will be shot on a street that has many
trees and colorful flowers that will show in the background.

The scene with the back-up singers will be shot in the men's
clothing store late at night when the store is closed.

As the track begins, we see Brian in the nightclub scene dressed
in yellow pants and a black shirt. As the first verse
progresses, he adds (in jump cut fashion) additional yellow
clothing--a shirt, shoes, a jacket, and finally a large floppy
hat.

At the first "Oo la la" chorus, we cut to a long shot of the
children singing.

Next, Brian is seen walking the dog. At first the dog is not
seen, but it is obvious from the leash and the way Brian is being
pulled that a dog is present. When the next "Oo la la" section
comes, the dog and its yellow jacket will be revealed. Both the
children and Brian will be heard for this "Oo la la," but the
children will not be seen.

The video returns to the nightclub lip syncing until the words "I
hardly know anyone who wears yellow shirts" at which point the
back-up singers are seen rummaging through shirts on a "sale"
counter in the men's clothing store.
```

**FIGURE 11-5**

An outline for a
music video.

Both general and
specific ideas are
given and the
various set and
remote locations
are enumerated.

                              **page 1**

## Storyboards

**Storyboards** (see figure 11-6) show pictures of each visual element and describe the actions and/or indicate the dialogue below each picture. They are usually used for short productions such as commercials or music videos. A drama could certainly be storyboarded, but it would involve a great deal of tedious artwork and pages and pages of paper. Sometimes directors will storyboard complicated scenes of a drama to better
```

FIGURE 11-6
A storyboard for a commercial.

This enables the director to visualize all the action and how it juxtaposes with the words. The accuracy of this visualization is much more important than any artistic considerations.

visualize them, but the storyboard, as a script form, is usually associated with short productions.

In general, directors like to work from storyboards because they are so *visual*. Although a director may superimpose his or her own ideas over the storyboard script, it gives a good starting point. Producers have to examine storyboards very closely to make sure all the props and other elements needed for production will be ready.

The type of script you choose to use—film-style, two-column, rundown, outline, storyboard—will depend on the type of program you are undertaking and the type of material you feel most comfortable with. Scripts are primarily a blueprint for production. People who try to shoot without a script are asking for trouble in the same way that builders would be asking for disaster if they tried to construct a house without following a basic blueprint.

11.3 BUDGETS

Students often do not give much thought to budgets because their monetary needs are small. The college provides the equipment; cast and crew members come from the class and do not need to be paid; props can be borrowed from dorm rooms or willing relatives. But in the "real world" of TV production, budgets are *very important*. A producer who goes over budget is not likely to stay employed. Moreover, budgets are usually part of the presentation package when a producer is trying to convince a network or syndicator that it should support a particular program idea.

Graduating students who understand the procedures of budgeting are likely to be looked upon as more *valuable* than graduates who have mastered only creative or technical talents. For that reason it behooves you to practice budgeting by figuring out what it would cost you to produce your class projects if you were doing them in the outside world.

Costs of Productions

TV production expenses are usually divided into **above-the-line** and **below-the-line.** The above-the-line costs are creative in nature and include the pay given to talent, producers, directors, and writers. Below-the-line costs are more technical in form and include the salaries of the crew, the cost of the staging area and equipment, and the money needed for supplies such as scenery and make-up.

Costs vary greatly depending on many factors—whether the crew is union or nonunion; the recognition value and reputation of the talent; the length of the production; the number of complicated effects needed; the part of the country or world in which the production is taking place; whether the equipment and facilities used belong to the production company or are rented from other companies.

Cast and Crew

Most major production companies, networks, and some local stations are unionized and agree to pay at least the minimum cast and crew wages stipulated by the various **unions** that represent the technical people—International Brotherhood of Electrical Workers (IBEW), International Alliance of Theatrical Stage Employees and Moving Picture Machine Operators (IATSE), etc.—and the **guilds** that represent the creative people—Screen Actors Guild (SAG), Directors Guild of America (DGA), American Federation of Radio and Television Actors (AFRTA), Writers Guild of America (WGA), etc. Every several years the unions and the producing organizations negotiate these rates. Over time the contracts have become quite complicated, but figure 11-7 shows

SELECTED TELEVISION INDUSTRY PAY RATES

Directors

If the program length is	the director is paid a minimum of approximately
5 minutes of less	$515 per day
over 5 minutes to 10 minutes	535 per day
over 10 minutes to 15 minutes	740 per day
over 15 minutes to 30 minutes	1785 per day
over 30 minutes to 45 minutes	1930 per day
over 45 minutes to 60 minutes	2400 per day

Producers

Producers are usually paid about the same as directors

Writers

If the program length is	the writer's minimum is a total of approximately
15 minutes of less	$4270
over 15 minutes to 30 minutes	7825
over 30 minutes to 60 minutes	14,225

Performers

If the program length is	principle performers are paid a minimum of approximately
15 minutes or less	$270 per day
over 15 minutes to 30 minutes	435 per day
over 30 minutes to 45 minutes	500 per day
over 45 minutes to 60 minutes	585 per day

If the program length is	bit performers with five lines or less are paid a minimum of approximately
15 minutes or less	$165 per day
over 15 minutes to 30 minutes	210 per day
over 30 minutes to 45 minutes	230 per day
over 45 minutes to 60 minutes	260 per day

If the program length is	off-camera announcers are paid a minimum of approximately
15 minutes or less	$150 per day
over 15 minutes to 30 minutes	240 per day
over 30 minutes to 45 minutes	295 per day
over 45 minutes to 60 minutes	335 per day

If the program length is	extras are paid a minimum of approximately
15 minutes or less	$70 per day
over 15 minutes to 30 minutes	105 per day
over 30 minutes to 45 minutes	120 per day
over 45 minutes to 60 minutes	135 per day

FIGURE 11-7

Selected TV industry pay rates (continued on page 274).

These are approximate rounded-off figures of pay for various union positions. Note that some of these people are hired by the day, project, or hour. In reality, union provisions are much more complicated, taking into account such factors as how long a person has been in the union, how many hours or days they work total, overtime pay, meal breaks, and working conditions. These figures are intended simply to help students approximate their production costs if they had to hire union people.

```
Musicians
     Major musicians are paid approximately the same as principle
performers,  Sideline musicians are paid $17.00 per hour.

Technical and Crafts People
     Technical director  .    .    .    .  .$30 per hour
     Lighting director  .    .    .    .  . 27 per hour
     Camera operator  .    .    .    .  . 27 per hour
     Audio operator .    .    .    .    .  . 30 per hour
     Audio assistant/Boom operator .    .  . 20 per hour
     Tape editor.    .    .    .    .    .  . 28 per hour
     Other technical personnel (graphics,  . 25 per hour
        VCR, teleprompter operators, etc.)
     Assistant director/Script supervisor  . 18 per hour
     Floor director .    .    .    .    .  . 18 per hour
     Stage hands  .    .    .    .    .  . 20 per hour
     Electricians  .    .    .    .    .  . 22 per hour
     Art director  .    .    .    .    .  . 37 per hour
     Set decorator  .    .    .    .    .  . 20 per hour
     Set painter  .    .    .    .    .  . 17 per hour
     Propmaster  .    .    .    .    .  . 20 per hour
     Costume designer  .    .    .    .  . 27 per hour
     Costumer  .    .    .    .    .    .  . 15 per hour
     Make-up artist .    .    .    .    .  . 18 per hour
     Hair stylist  .    .    .    .    .  . 16 per hour
```

FIGURE 11-7
continued

some of the major pay provisions for actors, directors, producers, writers, and technical and crafts people that should help students practice budgeting their own productions.[3]

Shoots that are non-union can pay whatever people are willing to work for, but the unions and guilds fine their own members if they work for anyone for less than union rates. Most of the truly skilled people are in the unions, so a non-union crew is likely to be less capable than a union crew. Of course, people who are highly prized within the industry can demand much higher pay than that stipulated by the union and guild minimums.

3. For more information on wages and salaries, see *Brooks' Standard Rate Book*, published each year by The Stanley J. Brooks Company, 1416 Westwood Boulevard, Suite 205, Los Angeles, CA 90024.

The trend within the television industry is to hire **freelance** cast and crew by the hour, day, or project as indicated in figure 11-7. However, sometimes people are hired on a more permanent basis, usually referred to as **staff** positions. A news producer, for example, would be hired by a local station to work with the local news day after day, year after year. That same station might have a staff director who directs a public service show one day and a children's program the next. Similarly five or six staff camera people might handle most local production—news, public affairs, children's programs—supplemented occasionally by freelance camera operators. Staff people usually receive less per hour than freelance people, but they are assured of steady employment while their freelance counterparts must be constantly seeking new jobs.

```
                    FACILITIES RATE CARD
```

```
Studio and Control Room Rental                    $250 per hour

(Includes a 35' by 35' studio with cyc, lighting grid and lights,
up to 5 microphones, and 3 industrial grade CCD cameras and a 12'
by 20' control room with an 8-in 4-out audio mixer, switcher with
2 effects buses, character generator, and 3/4" VCR.)

Additional Equipment

        Extra microphones    .    .    .    .    $10 each per hour
        Extra cameras   .    .    .    .    .     50 each per hour
        Teleprompter    .    .    .    .    .     35 per hour
        Digital video effects   .    .    .      50 per hour
        3-D Graphics generator  .    .    .      50 per hour
        Telecine   .    .    .    .    .    .     30 per hour
        1/2" S-VHS VCR .    .    .    .    .      15 per hour
        8mm Hi-8 VCR   .    .    .    .    .      15 per hour
        3/4" U-matic VCR    .    .    .    .      30 per hour
        1/2" Betacam VCR    .    .    .    .      75 per hour
        1" VTR     .    .    .    .    .    .     100 per hour
        D-2 VTR    .    .    .    .    .    .     150 per hour
        Cuts-only 3/4" editing  .    .    .      75 per hour

Set Pieces

        Easels   .    .    .    .    .    .      10 each per hour
        Plain flats   .    .    .    .    .      15 each per hour
        Chairs   .    .    .    .    .    .       5 each per hour
        Tables   .    .    .    .    .    .       5 each per hour
        Risers   .    .    .    .    .    .      10 each per hour
        Piano    .    .    .    .    .    .      20 per hour
```

FIGURE 11-8

A facilities and equipment rate card.

Studio rental fees vary greatly depending on the size of the studio, the quantity and sophistication of the equipment, and the part of the country where the facility is located. These figures are based on a facility that is similar to many TV studios located on college campuses.

Facilities and Equipment

Facilities and equipment are also major costs associated with production. If something is produced **in-house**—that is, within a production facility that has its own studio and equipment—the cost could be considered to be next to nothing because everything that is needed is already in place. However, the facility must be maintained and the equipment must eventually be replaced, so even a local public affairs show produced at a local station is usually "billed" (on paper only) for use of the facilities.

When a producer rents an outside facility, costs are real and can be easily budgeted. Most organizations that rent studios and/or equipment have a **rate card** listing the cost for a fully equipped studio or for the various pieces of equipment that the client might wish to use. The rate card shown in figure 11-8 lists the costs for a studio with three cameras and other commonly used production equipment as well as the rates for additional equipment. Once again, students can use these numbers to practice budget construction.

Supplies are figured at what they actually cost. If the production calls for a wig, the producer (or production assistant) must actually locate an appropriate wig and find out how much it will cost. One supply that is necessary for all taped programs is videotape stock. The actual cost of the stock will depend on which tape format is being used—¾-inch U-matic tape is more expensive than ½-inch VHS tape.

Constructing and Adhering to the Budget

Once all the information regarding costs has been gathered, the producer must actually construct the budget. It is laid out with the above-the-line costs separated from the below-the line costs. Figure 11-9 shows a worksheet that can be used for a typical TV production budget. Computer spreadsheets are particularly helpful for budgeting.[4] Using them, producers can determine what costs would be under various circumstances—with three cameras versus four cameras; hiring two different audio operators versus paying one audio operator overtime; with and without the scene that requires renting a helicopter.

The Role of the Unit Manager

The people working with or for the producer who deal the most with budgets are the **unit manager** and/or **production**

manager. Sometimes these titles are used interchangeably, but most commonly a person is called a unit manager if she/he works for a *production facility* and a production manager if working for an *independent production company*. For example, a unit manager might work for a network that produces some of its own shows and rents out its facilities and crew members to others (corporations, advertisers, production companies). The unit manager would be in charge of drawing up and adhering to the rate card and scheduling the facilities for use by both in-house producers and outside clients. This person has the responsibility for seeing that the production costs do not exceed the contracted amount paid (on paper or for real).

Production managers are usually associated with a *particular project* rather than a particular facility. They determine what costs will be incurred by the project in terms of people, facilities, supplies, and other requirements. Working closely with producers, they draw up the budgets. Then, during production and postproduction, they keep track of all expenses to make sure the budget is not being exceeded.

Budget Overruns

If a budget is being overrun, the producer is the one who must solve the problem. At times the producer can raise additional money to cover the shortfall; sometimes the producer can convince the director to work faster; other times some element of a program must be cut so that costs can be saved.

Budgeting is a difficult process. Costs must not be exaggerated or people will not be willing to undertake the production. But sufficient money must be provided so that the program is successful. As money becomes tighter, *more care* must be given to drawing up and adhering to the budget.

4. Computer budgeting programs made for the television and film industries include *Movie Magic, MacToolkit Film Budget, Turbo AD,* and *Cost Tracking.* All these can be purchased from Quantum Films Software Division, 8230 Beverly Boulevard, Suite 17, Los Angeles, CA 90048.

BUDGET WORKSHEET

Production Name_____

Producer_____

Director_____

Date(s) of Production_____

DESCRIPTION	ESTIMATE	ACTUAL	NOTES

ABOVE-THE-LINE
Producer

Director

Writer

Principle Performers

Bit Performers

Off-Camera Announcers

Extras

Musicians

Other

TOTAL ABOVE-THE-LINE

BELOW-THE-LINE
Crew
Technical Director

Lighting Director

Camera Operators

Audio Operator

Audio Assistant

Tape Editor

Graphics Operator

VCR Operator

Teleprompter Operator

Assistant Director

Floor Director

Stage Hands

Electricians

FIGURE 11-9

A budget worksheet (continued on page 278).

This worksheet should help you determine what the costs will be for your production. Use the space under each person or item to indicate how you arrived at your estimate; for example, 3 camera operators for 4 hours at $27 each = $324.

Art Director _____

Set Decorator _____

Set Painter _____

Propmaster _____

Costume Designer _____

Costumer _____

Make-up Artist _____

Hair Stylist _____

Other _____

_____

<u>Facilities</u>
Studio Rental _____

Extra Equipment _____

_____

_____

Set Pieces _____

_____

_____

_____

Props _____

_____

_____

Costumes and Make-up _____

_____

Tape Stock _____

FIGURE 11-9
continued

TOTAL BELOW-THE-LINE _____   _____

GRAND TOTAL _____   _____

11.4 PERSONNEL

In addition to seeing that the script and budget are generated, another major duty of the producer is hiring the various people who will be needed for the production. The most important person whom the producer hires is the director. Sometimes once the producer hires the director, he or she steps out of the hiring process and the director hires the rest of the cast and crew. Of course, if the producer, director, and crew members are all on staff at a production facility, no actual hiring takes place, but the producer may lobby to have the most appropriate (and skilled) of the directors and crew members assigned to the project.

Casting

If the project is a drama or sit com, **casting** is very crucial and producers often want to be involved. The usual procedure is that the producer and/or director draw up a list of the characters needed, along with their physical and psychological traits. (Often this is taken from the treatment or script). This list is given to various **agents** who then select actresses and actors they represent and send them to an audition where they read lines of the script. Then the director, producer, and others who have a vital interest in the production select the cast members. Sometimes specialized **casting agencies** are hired for productions with large casts, such as made-for-TV movies. The director may be involved with hiring the principle actors, but the casting agency alone fills the minor parts.

Although dramas present the greatest challenges for finding talent, other forms of shows also involve hiring or selecting talent. For example, great care goes into selecting contestants for game shows. The number of people wishing to try their luck on these shows far exceeds the number needed, so producers (or associate producers) look for people who are lively or unusual and who will perform well when the TV cameras are on. Talk show producers try to line up people who are well-known (or eccentric) and who will interact well with the host or hostess. Public affairs producers look for people with something to say who can present their points in a dynamic (or at least not boring) manner.

Actors who appear on dramas or sitcoms sign *contracts* that stipulate how much they will be paid and what their general obligations and working conditions are. Nonprofessionals should also be asked to sign **performance releases** (see figure 11-10) so that they can not come back at a later time and ask for money or other privileges. One student producer learned this lesson the hard way. He had a sword swallower appear on his student production and neglected to get the proper release form signed. Later he showed the production on a cable TV public access channel, and someone called the sword swallower to say she had seen him. The sword swallower, thinking the student was making huge amounts of money distributing the tape, sued for $100,000 in retroactive pay and residuals. Although the student managed to avoid paying the sword swallower, he had to hire and pay a lawyer to fight the suit. That student producer will never again forget to get each person to sign a release.

```
                    PERFORMANCE RELEASE


        In consideration of my appearing on the TV program

_____
                          (title)
and for no subsequent remuneration, I do hereby on behalf of
myself, my heirs, executors, and administrators authorize

_____
                        (producer)
to use live or recorded on tape, film, or otherwise my name,
voice, likeness, and performance for television distribution
throughout the world and for audiovisual and general education
purposes in perpetuity.

        I further agree on behalf of myself and others as above
stated that my name, likeness, and biography may be used for
promotion purposes and other uses.  Further, I agree to
indemnify, defend, and hold the producer harmless for any and all
claims, suits, or liabilities arising from my appearance and the
use of any of my materials, name, likeness, or biography.

Conditions:




Signature_____

Printed Name_____

Street Address_____

City and Zip Code_____

Phone Number_____

Date_____
```

FIGURE 11-10

A sample performance release.

All people who appear on a television program who have not signed official contracts should be asked to sign a form such as this.

Crew Selection

The producer for any show will definitely hire the production manager and assistant producers, if needed. She or he may also be involved with selecting camera operators, scenic designers, make-up people, and the like. One of the most important considerations is gathering together a group of people who work together harmoniously. Frequently producers and directors have people who they have worked with in the past that they want to work with again because they have a common understanding of the TV production process. This makes it hard for new people to break into the business, but it usually ensures a successful production.

If talent must be brought in from a great distance, if the production lasts for many hours, if any of the shooting is done at a remote location, then the producer must make arrangements for *transportation, lodging,* and *meals*. Creature comforts are definitely the domain of the producer.

```
        COMMUNICATIONS 350 - STUDIO PRODUCTION

                      GROUP 2

                       PROPS

   ITEM                WHO IS BRINGING IT            NOTES

   umbrella            Jorge M.

   world globe         Susan T.            will get from library

   purse               Kim S.

   waddling duck       Chris B.            bring it a week early
                                           to test it on camera

   lamp                Maria G.            get permission form
                                           signed by dorm coun-
                                           selor
```

FIGURE 11-11

A list of props as a student producer might prepare it for a class production.

11.5 PRODUCTION PAPERWORK

As previously mentioned, one of the duties of the producer is to make sure all elements of the program are in the right place at the right time. This usually involves making and double-checking *lists*. The type of lists needed vary from production to production. A drama will need lists that detail costumes, sets, props and who is responsible for each. (See figure 11-11.) An ongoing talk show will need a list of potential guests and dates when they are to appear. A game show will need a list of prizes that have been or may be acquired for free. Often the production manager draws up these lists because they relate closely to budget determinations.

Copyright Clearance

Producers must also keep track of **copyright.** Nothing that has been copyrighted (poem, short story, photograph, music, videotape footage) can be used on a show unless the owner has *granted permission.* Obtaining permission involves writing letters to copyright holders and then keeping careful track of what has and has not been cleared. (See figure 11-12.) Sometimes copyright holders specify particular stipulations, such as a special wording in a credit at the end of the program. Producers must make sure these requirements are executed.

The most commonly used copyrighted material in programs is music. Some TV stations pay **music licensing companies** (ASCAP, BMI, and SESAC) then have the right to use music represented by those companies, which is most of the popular music. However, most independent productions (including student productions) must clear copyright to use material that is not copyrighted.

Clearing copyright can be a difficult chore for the producer. Often just finding who owns the copyright can require extensive research. With music, the copyright holder could be the composer, the arranger, the publisher of the sheet music, the record company, or some combination of them. Usually when they are found, they want money, so copyright clearance can be *expensive.*

Date

Name
Licensing Department
Music Publishing Company
Street Address
City, State, and Zip Code

Dear Person's Name:

I am producing a student television production entitled ("Name of
Program") for which I would like to use part of your musical
composition ("Name of Music"), composed by (Name of Composer.) I
would like to acquire a non-exclusive synchronization license for
this musical composition.

I would like permission to use this material for broadcast,
cablecast, or other means of exhibition throughout the world as
often as deemed appropriate for this stuent production and for
any future revisions of this production. Your permission
granting me the right to use this material in no way restricts
your use for any other purposes.

For your convenience, a release form is provided below and a copy
of this letter is attached for your files.

Sincerely yours,

Your Name

I (We) grant permission for the use requested in this letter.

Signature_____

Printed Name_____

Title_____

Phone Number_____

Date_____

FIGURE 11-12

A sample of a letter
you might write to
obtain clearance
for music.

Music that is old enough to be in the **public domain** can be used without copyright clearance. Usually that means the composer has been dead at least fifty years, but sometimes a particular arrangement of a song can be copyrighted and the rights to that are held by someone who is still alive.

A way to get around copyright clearance is to have music composed specially for the production. This, too, can be expensive if the composer is to be paid. Student productions have an advantage in this regard because universities usually have music students eager for the experience of composing in return for a credit. There are also services that provide copyright cleared music very inexpensively.[5] The problem with much of this music is that it is not very distinctive—it all tends to sound alike.

The producer's problems are similar when it comes to videotape or film footage. If the opening credits require a shot of an airplane taking off, you can not simply tape a takeoff from some movie you have seen on TV and use it without permission. You could have someone take portable equipment to the nearest airport and shoot the shot or you could acquire it from a company that supplies stock footage.

Permission to use *written material* (poems, stories, charts) can usually be obtained from the publisher of the book in which it appears while permission to use a painting that is in an art book may require permission of the artist, the photographer who took the picture of the painting, the publisher of the book, the museum where the painting is hanging, or some combination thereof.

Record Keeping

The producer must keep careful records of legal documents (including actor contracts and performer releases), receipts for purchased supplies, damage done to sets or locations, and other paperwork that is generated during preproduction, production, and postproduction. This paperwork is necessary for a variety of reasons. First, if the producer leaves and a new producer is

5. Some libraries that supply copyright cleared music are Blue Ribbon SoundWorks Ltd. (404-377-1514); Canary Productions (800-368-0033); DeWolfe Music Library (800-221-6713); FirstCom/Music House/Chappell (800-858-8880); Killer Tracks (800-877-0078); Metro Music (212-799-7600); The Music Bank (408-867-4756); and Sound Ideas (800-387-3030). For more details see "Music Libraries," *AV Video*, September 1992, pp. 52-56.

hired, he or she will have the necessary information to continue production. It also supplies the cast and crew with specifics so they can do their jobs correctly. Some of the paperwork is used for tax purposes, while some is needed in case of (or hopefully, to prevent) lawsuits or investigations.

11.6 SCHEDULES

Scheduling is another part of the producer's duty. Sometimes this is relatively easy. An ongoing series produced in a studio is likely to tape at the same time each day or each week. The set will be the same each time, and for the most part, the cast and crew will remain unchanged. For such productions the producer usually posts a **call sheet** (see figure 11-13) on the studio door or somewhere that is easily accessed by cast and crew. This lists the time that everyone is to appear and gives a general idea of what will be shot. The time may generally be the same from week to week, but the call sheet takes into account aberrations. For example, if a complicated makeup job is called for in a particular episode of a series, the person being made up and the makeup person will need to report earlier than usual.

Scheduling is more complicated for a studio show that is produced only once. The producer must find a time or times when all the performers are available, often a difficult task because people appearing on a one-time only basis are likely to have other obligations. The producer must also work with the unit manager to assure that a studio will be available at a time when all the performers are free. If a producer wants a particular crew member, such as a certain audio operator, that further complicates the scheduling process.

CALL SHEET

Date_____

Program Title_____

Episode Number_____

Producer_____

Director_____

Studio Location_____

PERFORMERS

NAME   POSITION   REPORT TIME

CREW

NAME   POSITION   REPORT TIME

FIGURE 11-13

An example of a
call sheet.

Shoots that cover real events, such as news and sports, have their schedule set for them. The equipment and crews must be available and in place when the event takes place. The scheduling is easiest if the time of the event is known well ahead of time. However, news, by definition, does not occur that way. For this reason, most stations and networks have equipment that is dedicated to the coverage of news events.

Most complicated of all are programs that involve field production. Multiple locations are added to the problems associated with having cast and crew available. Also everyone is usually a long distance from the studio and cannot return for something that was forgotten. For these reasons, producers draw up thorough **shooting schedules** that list all the elements needed at each location. The process of producing and shooting away from the studio is discussed more thoroughly in chapter 14 dealing with field production.

SUMMARY

Producing is a crucial process that can make or break the overall organization and execution of a production. A producer is responsible for making sure that none of the details involved with a show are forgotten.

Sometimes producers are *hyphenates* and take on directing and/or writing chores as well as producing duties. Often they have a number of people working for them such as *associate producers, assistant producers, production managers,* and *line producers. Executive producers* oversee a number of projects.

Producers are in charge of making sure an appropriate *script* is generated. Often they must first sell the idea for a series or program to network executives by *pitching* the idea contained in a *treatment* and then making a *pilot.*

Different forms of scripts are appropriate for different types of programs. Dramas usually use a *film-style script* while news and information programs are more likely to use the *two-column script. Rundowns* are useful for programs, such as talk shows and game shows, that are similar from week to week and contain interviews and other unscripted material. *Outlines* are appropriate for music videos and other program forms that are rather nonspecific. *Storyboards* are most often used for commercials and other highly visual materials.

The producer is also charged with drawing up and adhering to the *budget.* A typical budget is divided into *above-the-line* and *below-the-line* costs and includes salaries, facilities, and supplies. People are hired on a *freelance* or *staff* basis and facilities usually have a *rate card.* Union and guild rates for various technical and creative positions come into play. *Unit managers* and *production managers* play an important role in budget creation and adherence.

The director is hired by the producer and both are often involved in hiring the rest of the cast and crew. *Casting* is a particularly important part of hiring that often involves agents and casting agencies. Nonprofessional talent should always be asked to sign *performance releases.*

Producers generate lists of things needed for the production to help people organize their jobs. They also clear *copyrights* and obtain music and stock footage.

Scheduling is another domain of the producer. This can be a fairly simple process for regularly scheduled, in-studio productions but becomes increasingly complicated for field production.

Directing Duties

T he **director** is in charge of everything that happens in the studio and control room. The producer may or may not be on the set, but even if the producer is present, it is the director who calls the shots, literally and figuratively.

Although the director is in charge, most productions utilize two other people who assist the director with directorial duties. They are the **associate director (AD)** and the **floor director.** If one were to think of the television director as the captain of the production team, then the two lieutenants would be the associate director and the floor director. The latter is in charge of virtually everything that takes place on the studio floor, while the former is the director's right hand and surrogate in all other matters.

The process of directing can be best understood by looking at what these three people are likely to do *chronologically* to put a production together.

12.1 OVERVIEW OF THE DIRECTOR'S DUTIES

A director is part artist, part manager, and part psychiatrist. Directors are the ones who make sure the production is aesthetically pleasing, who give the instructions to cast and crew, and who handle the reasonable (and unreasonable) demands or quirks of those involved with the production.[1]

During Preproduction

The discipline of thorough preproduction planning cannot be emphasized strongly enough. The success of every production is determined—to a very great extent—by the quality of the preproduction planning that the director has undertaken. For the purposes of organizing our thinking, it may be helpful to consider preproduction planning in five areas: script familiarization, facilities and equipment, cast and crew, production requirements, and script preparation.

Script Familiarization

In many academic and some professional settings, the director will also function as the producer/writer and thus, will have shaped the script from the beginning. In many other situations you, as director, will have the script handed to you and will take the production from there.

Your first concern should be to determine the *specific purpose* of the script. Ask yourself several questions: What is the objective of the program? How do you want the audience to be different when this program is over? Then you can begin to think in terms of the overall "feel" and image of the program. What kinds of settings, lighting, and graphics would be most effective in this particular *communication* process?

Next, there may be several immediate steps that need to be taken. Check the script for rough timing. Is the length alright or does it need to be cut or lengthened? The script should be put in its final television production format and duplicated for all personnel involved. Is any rewriting necessary? How many copies do you need?

Facilities and Equipment

Once you are completely comfortable with the script, you should be able to start specific *facilities planning*. In the case of a remote coverage of some event, you have to scout the location, of course. In other professional situations, you may have to make arrangements for the rental of actual studio facilities. How large a studio do you need? How long will you need the studio?

In most academic and training situations, the studio will be assigned to you for a definite period of time. In many institutions—even for training purposes—you will still have to fill out a **facilities request form** (often abbreviated **FACS**) reserving a specific studio and control room(s), cameras, microphones, video recorders, lights, sets, and other requirements (see figure 12-1). The items are requested for a particular production date and time. Failure to attend to such paperwork carefully at this stage can result in costly problems and misunderstandings later.

Cast and Crew

Again, in most academic situations, you may not have to be concerned with securing personnel. The technical crew may be assigned from your class or from some other participating class. There may be

---

1. Several books that contain good advice for directors are: Alan A. Armer, *Directing Television and Film*, 2nd ed. (Belmont, CA: Wadsworth, 1990); Steven D. Katz, *Film Directing Cinematic Motion* (Los Angeles: Lone Eagle Publishing Company, 1992); and Ron Richards, *Director's Method for Film and Television* (Stoneham, MA: Focal Press, 1992).

```
            FACILITIES REQUEST FORM
            YOURTOWN UNIVERSITY

Date Facilities Are Needed_____

Time Facilities Are Needed_____
  (Maximum is 4 hours unless special permission has been obtained)

Your Name_____

Address_____

Phone Number(s)_____

Student ID Number_____

FACILITIES REQUESTED
_____Studio
        _____number of cameras needed (maximum=3)
        _____number mics needed (maximum=5 lav, 3 stand, 1 boom)
          Indicate type(s)_____
          number of lights being used (maximum=20)
        _____news set
        _____talk show set
        _____other. Specify_____
_____Control Room
        _____audio board
        _____graphics generator
        _____switcher
        _____teleprompter
        _____record VCR
        _____roll-in VCR
        _____other. Specify_____
_____Editing Suite A
        _____U-matic to U-matic system
        _____character generator
        _____audio cassette player
        _____other
_____Editing Suite B
        _____Hi-8 to U-matic SP
        _____graphics generator
        _____CD player
        _____audio cassette player
        _____microphone
        _____other
```

FIGURE 12-1

A sample facilities request form that might be used by a university.

some occasions, however, when you will be involved in selecting specific individuals for particular crew assignments.

Casting for actors or other performers may also be done on an informal basis in the academic setting. You may work through the drama department, or you may prevail upon your personal friends. In securing such volunteer help, make certain that you have a firm commitment; many a student production has been ruined because some friend or casual acquaintance

FIGURE 12-2
Production conference with director, associate director, floor director, technical director, and lighting director.

backed out of a production at the last moment. In professional situations, of course, casting is quite an involved process (see section 11.4).

Production Requirements

Production requirements are what the bulk of this text has been concerned with. Now comes the job of pulling it all together. In any kind of major production, the director should plan on holding one or more *production conferences* involving the chief production heads—art director, lighting director, technical supervisor, associate director, floor director, and other key production persons. (See figure 12-2.)

You must now make sure that all the preproduction elements are properly requested and constructed. The *lighting and staging plans* are developed at this stage. If any special *costumes* or *props* have to be ordered or fabricated, they are initiated now. All *graphics* have to be ordered and

produced, either by hand or with the aid of a computer. Will you be shooting any *videotaped sequences* ahead of time? *Music* and *other special audio* selections must be chosen and/or ordered.

During all this preproduction process, you have to be working within a very tight interlocking schedule of *checkpoints* and *deadlines.* Many production elements cannot proceed until other items are taken care of first. Everything, therefore, must be scheduled days and weeks in advance. The exterior videotape cannot be shot until the costumes arrive. Set pieces cannot be constructed until the setting design is completed.

To protect yourself, you will put in *cushions*—a few extra days protection here and there throughout the schedule. In major productions, the intertwining complexities of the production schedule can become quite awesome. You cannot wait until the last minute to get things started.

Script Preparation

During all this activity, you also must be concerned with preparing your script for the day of production. How are you going to use your cameras? What kinds of transitions will best move the program forward without ambiguity? What will be the pacing you want to achieve? In short, what images and sounds do you want to create to achieve your purpose?

You should *mark* your copy of the script indicating which cameras you are going to use for which shots, what instructions the technical director and camera operators will need, where the audio cues will have to be, what cues the talent will need, and so forth. Most directors develop their own shorthand for marking their scripts, but some commonly used symbols are shown in figure 12-3. Depending on the program and the experience of the director, scripts are marked in varying degrees. A major studio comedy special might involve hundreds of abbreviated cues, instructions, and notes. With a fairly routine ongoing program, script preparation may take no more than a few pencilled reminders of unusual cues. (See figure 12-4.) As a beginning director, you will probably feel more comfortable with a heavily marked script. Just the process of noting all the commands you will need to make will help you when you are in the director's chair.

Once you have marked your script and thought through your camera shots, you can prepare **shot sheets** for your camera operators. These are abbreviated descriptions of every shot that a particular camera has to get. A shot sheet is compact enough to be attached to the rear of the camera where the operator can quickly refer to it. They are not particularly useful for interview shows where the director is calling shots on-the-fly depending on who happens to be talking. But they are very valuable for complex, fully-scripted programs where every shot

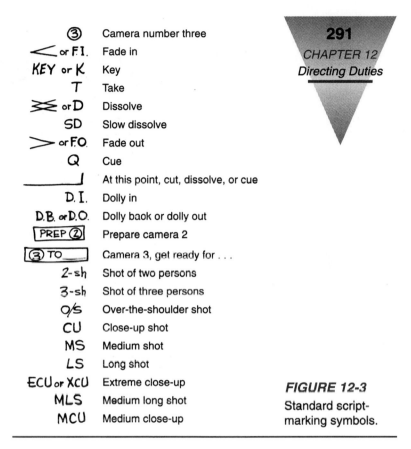

③	Camera number three
< or F.I.	Fade in
KEY or K	Key
T	Take
⋙ or D	Dissolve
SD	Slow dissolve
> or F.O.	Fade out
Q	Cue
⌐⎯⎯⎯⎯⌋	At this point, cut, dissolve, or cue
D. I.	Dolly in
D.B. or D.O.	Dolly back or dolly out
PREP ②	Prepare camera 2
③ TO⎯⎯	Camera 3, get ready for . . .
2-sh	Shot of two persons
3-sh	Shot of three persons
O/S	Over-the-shoulder shot
CU	Close-up shot
MS	Medium shot
LS	Long shot
ECU or XCU	Extreme close-up
MLS	Medium long shot
MCU	Medium close-up

FIGURE 12-3
Standard script-marking symbols.

has been carefully worked out by the director—and where the cameras will have to be moving quite a bit to get various shots as requested.

Figure 12-5 shows the three shot sheets for a three-camera drama. All the shots have been numbered in the order in which they will occur. In the illustration, all the shot sheets are shown on one page. In practice, these three sheets would be cut out separately, and each camera operator would have his or her own shot sheet taped or clipped by the viewfinder.

During Rehearsals

By now, you should have moved into rehearsals in one form or another. You should

NIGHTLY NEWS

Roll opening tape <u>VIDEO</u>

TAPE: OPENING CREDITS

Open mic

④ *2-sh*
② TWO-SHOT - STEVE AND SHARON

① *MS*
STEVE

PREP TAPE
Roll tape

TAPE: FIRE REPORT

30 sec.
③ *MLS*
SHARON

PREP GRAPHICS
K graphics
GRAPHICS: MAP OVER SHOULDER

<u>AUDIO</u>

SOUND ON TAPE. Runs :30.
Ends with drum beat.

STEVE: I'm Steve Anderson.

SHARON: And I'm Sharon
Hendricks here with the latest
news.

STEVE: Fire fighters are still
at the scene of a three-alarm
fire on Market Street that
destroyed two buildings
earlier today. Fred White has
this report.

SOT: Runs 2:56. Ends with
"could have been a lot worse."

SHARON: The Japanese are still
trying to assess if any damage
was caused by this morning's
earthquake. The quake was
centered two hundred miles
from Tokyo and registered
7 point 1. Two strong
after shocks have been felt.

FIGURE 12-4
This is an example
of how a novice
director might mark
a news script.

think in terms of several different kinds of rehearsals: **pre-studio rehearsals, floor rehearsals,** and **control room rehearsals.**

Pre-Studio Rehearsals
For many extensive productions, especially dramas and comedies, you will want to have some rehearsals prior to coming into the studio. Studio time is too precious to start from scratch with basic **blocking** (the positioning of actors). Using a rehearsal hall, an empty studio, or a living room, you can begin working with actors. Specific areas can be measured off and

CAMERA 1	CAMERA 2	CAMERA 3
3. LS, Mary in doorway	1. Wide Sh., Kitchen, hi-angle boom down.	2. CU coffee cup, pan to ash tray
5. LS, David in doorway	4. MS Mary. Follow her	6. MS Mary (she rises)
7. MS David (he walks into O/S)	12. 2–sh., Pan L as David crosses behind Mary	8. O/S Mary
9. O/S David	15. MS David. D.B. as he comes to her. Open to 2–sh.	10. CU Mary
11. CU David	17. CU Mary	13. MS David
14. MS Mary (she sits)	19. 2–sh. (tight)	16. MCU David (bust–shot)
20. Loose 2–sh. (Mary rises)	21. (Crane up) Hi angle 2–sh. D.I. & crane down to single of David	18. CU David
22. O/S Mary (in doorway). She walks toward David. David turns to camera.	25. Single David (wide). D.B., follow as he walks to Mary. Open to 2–sh.	23. 2–sh. as Mary turns
24. CU David	27. CU Mary's hands	26. (Hook wheels) 2–sh. D.I. to ECU Mary
28. 2–sh. Mary walks past camera. Hold on David	31. MS Alice	29. MS Mary
30. MS David. Pan to door as Alice enters	34. MS David (he sits)	32. Loose 2–sh. (Mary, David)
33. 3–sh., favoring Alice	37. ECU David	35. Loose CU, Mary
36. CU Alice	40. (Crane down) Loose MS Alice. Follow her to table. Follow action w/cup. Crane up & D.I.	38. ECU Mary
39. CU Alice		41. ECU Mary
42. Wide 3–sh., follow action		43. CU of knife

FIGURE 12-5
Representative shot sheets.

marked with masking tape or furniture to represent major staging areas, and much of your blocking of action can take place— as well as quite a bit of the dramatic interpretation and working on lines.

For nondramatic productions, there are also many good reasons for pre-studio rehearsals. Demonstration shows, educational programs, political broadcasts, and the like, can benefit from having an early **dry-run** session where the director and talent can work together on the basic staging of the program.

Studio Floor Rehearsals

When the director and the production crew start to work in the studio, the director usually will spend some amount of time on the studio floor before assuming the director's chair in the control room. Depending on the type of production, either the talent or the technical crew might benefit most from your presence in the studio. If the talent is particularly insecure or if the technical coordination of a production is really complicated, you might spend quite a bit of your time on the studio floor. On the other hand, if the talent is in control of the situation and the technical elements are no special problem, you probably would benefit from getting into the control room as early as you can.

The first rehearsal techniques you will be most likely to conduct from the studio floor will be a **walk-through rehearsal.** This might be either a *talent* walk-through (if they are not really sure of their positions and movements) or a *technical* walk-through (to explain major camera moves, audio placement, and scene changes). In many instances, the walk-through is a combination, taking both the talent and crew through an abbreviated version of the production.

Control Room Rehearsals

The full rehearsals are usually conducted with the director calling shots from the control room. The initial type of full-facilities rehearsal is called a **camera rehearsal.** For the first time, the camera operators are ready to operate the cameras and all other technical personnel are at their positions.

This first camera rehearsal may be a **start-and-stop rehearsal.** In this approach, you interrupt the rehearsal every time there is a major problem. You correct the trouble and then continue the rehearsal. It is quite a time-consuming process—although it can be effective if you have the luxury of enough studio time.

Another approach to the first camera rehearsal is the **uninterrupted run-through.** In this approach, the director attempts to get through the entire production with a minimum of interruptions. If time is short—and if problems are minor—you keep on plowing through the rehearsal regardless of what happens.

Finally, there is the **dress rehearsal.** Theoretically, this is the final rehearsal—a complete, uninterrupted, full-scale rehearsal after all the problems have been straightened out. In practice, this stage is rarely reached. Realities of the medium are such that there simply is never enough studio time to do as polished a job as you would want. In many instances, the director will wind up with a combination start-and-stop and dress rehearsal.

When time is short, you must economize and try to make the most efficient use of the time available. Do not stand around waiting for others to finish their jobs before starting your rehearsal; you can rehearse even while the lighting crew is still trimming the lights and while the audio engineer is establishing levels. In an abbreviated walk-through rehearsal, at least make certain you get through all the rough spots in the production; *rehearse the open and the close* and *the crucial transitions* that call for coordination of several kinds of movement. Pick your priorities; do not get hung up on small details (such as worrying about the possibility of a boom shadow) when you

have only a few minutes to work out major problems (the talent doesn't know where he or she should move next).

During Production

Finally, you are ready to start calling shots on your first production. First, try to control your physical anxieties. Regardless of what might be churning inside, try *not* to let it show. Force yourself to sit back and take a deep breath; let it out slowly; and coolly tell all the crew and the talent that everything will proceed confidently. Remember that the composure or anxiety you communicate to the crew will surely be returned to you.

Calling Commands

The first thing you need to do is start the VCR that is going to record the show. You do this by saying, "Roll record tape." When the tape has stabilized, the VCR operator will say "Speed," and you can then begin with the show. Give all your commands and directions as clearly as you can. Refer to talent (when talking to the floor director) by name—"Cue Dr. Morgan," not "Cue him"—to avoid misunderstandings. Refer to camera operators, on the other hand, by numbers; you are less likely to slip up and get confused. Make sure you use correct and precise commands of preparation to the technical director (see section 8.5) and to all other production positions; the commands of preparation are as important as the commands of execution.

Keeping the lag time of various equipment and personnel in mind, give your cues in a sequence designed to get things happening when you want them to. In opening your program, say "Hit music" and then "Fade in camera 2." It always takes a second or so before the music will be heard (if it is properly cued up), but the camera is there with the push of a

FIGURE 12-6
Director (center)
calling shots during
a production,
flanked by the TD
and AD.

lever. Similarly, always cue talent before putting his or her camera on the air. "Open-mic-cue-talent-dissolve-to-two" is often given as one command of execution. By the time the floor director reacts and throws the cue and the talent takes a breath and starts to talk, the camera will be on the air.

Watch and *listen* to your monitors. Always be aware of exactly what is going on over the air. If a picture is not what you want (what the viewer needs), then change it. The viewer watching his or her home receiver could care less about your sinus headache or your fight with the talent or the camera cable with the bad connection; all he or she knows is what comes out over the receiver, and if it is bad, it is bad.

Also, always check your camera and preview monitors before calling a shot to be put on the air. Make sure the camera you want to dissolve to or the special effects you want next are prepared and ready to be put on the air. You cannot afford to get buried in your marked script while ignoring the realities of the picture and sound you are sending out. (See figure 12-6.)

Planning Ahead
During the course of your program, always be looking ahead two or three minutes. What possible problems lie ahead? Did the mic boom get repositioned alright? Is everything set for the lighting change? Are the dancers prepared for their entrance?

If something should go drastically wrong, tell yourself you are going to remain

in control and salvage what you can. Camera 2 just went dead? Get a wide shot on camera 1 and keep going. The dancers just walked on the set ahead of their cue? The hostess will have to explain the best she can. The CG operator just hit the wrong button and lost your next two graphics? You will continue without them. Do not give up until the producer or instructor tells you to throw in the towel.

Finally, no matter what else happens, television—especially live TV and live-on-tape—is a *time-bound medium.* Everything has to fit into scheduled slots. If you are directing a program that is supposed to be exactly 7:30 long, that means exactly seven minutes and thirty seconds. When you are told you have five seconds to black, that means you fade it out and sneak out the music; you have no choice—unless of course, you know you are working with a flexible time slot.

After the Production

When the program is finished, let the VCR roll in black for about ten seconds and then say "Stop tape." Don't let either talent or crew leave their positions until the VCR operator has played back a bit of the tape to make sure it recorded. Then use the **studio address (talkback)** to thank the crew and talent. Assure them that everything went well. Keep your composure until you have a chance to collapse in private. Make certain you and your crew clear the studio and control room of all scripts, notes, props, and everything else connected with your production. Don't expect the next group using the studio to clean up your mess.

If there is any postproduction **editing** to be accomplished, your job is far from done (see section 10.1). If it is a simple matter of inserting a clean shot to cover the one bad blunder on the air, you may be able to get it done right away. If it is a major postproduction editing job of

assembling video pieces from several different sources, it will take quite a bit of scheduling editing sessions.

12.2 OVERVIEW OF THE ASSOCIATE DIRECTOR'S DUTIES

The director delegates various tasks to the associate director (sometimes referred to as the **assistant director**).[2] The position often carries quite a bit of responsibility for the production. In some situations, the AD will be responsible for setting up all the camera shots on the air or for calling out to the director what needs to be seen and heard next. If a program needs editing, the AD will keep notes regarding editing needs and may even be the person who oversees the actual editing process. In virtually every kind of studio operation, however, the AD's primary job will be that of timing the production. The AD will time individual segments during rehearsals, get an overall timing of the program, and then be in charge of the pacing of the program—speeding up or stretching as required—during the actual recording.

During Preproduction

In any major production undertaking, the AD will work with the director well in advance of the actual production period—attending production conferences, working with talent, and assembling props and other materials. During this preproduction period, the AD may also be able to start getting some rough timings of the

---

2. Depending on the actual production setup and the traditional organization of the studio/station, the AD may be labeled either "assistant director" or "associate director." The Directors' Guild of America officially refers to the position as "associate director" because the "assistant director" title is traditionally used in the film industry.

program and may begin to assemble notes on what postproduction editing will have to be done.

During Rehearsals

Once the production moves into the studio, the director often delegates numerous tasks to the AD. For example, the AD may be in charge of the rest of the crew—checking to make certain that everyone is present and reporting this to the director. In non-union or corporate productions, the AD may well be in charge of arranging substitute assignments, thus ensuring that every position is covered.

Keeping Critique Notes

During the rehearsals, the director will mention various production items that need attention before the actual take. The AD will jot down the "critique notes," as the director spots problems. Additionally, the AD should be making notes of similar items that might have escaped the attention of the director. If the AD notices a major item, it should be called to the director's attention before the rehearsal proceeds. Minor items are simply written down to be cleaned up later. The AD will be especially concerned with noting all the script changes that are made. The AD may also use the rehearsal period to time as much of the program as possible, including individual segments, tape inserts, and opening and closing elements.

Decision Making

Depending upon the production techniques of the individual director, the AD may or may not get involved with actually making production decisions. In some situations, the AD will be helping to compose shots for the director. The AD may also be making other suggestions regarding talent moves, graphics, script revision, lighting problems, or whatever else needs attention.

In other situations, the AD traditionally stays out of these kinds of directorial/aesthetic decisions and sticks closely to the note-keeping and timing functions.

Timing

During rehearsal the AD may also do some of the crucial timing that will be needed during the actual production of the program. For example, the final segment of a program might be very crucial to the understanding of the entire program and need to be aired in a specific way. The AD can time that segment and then **backtime** so that he or she knows exactly when the preceding segment must end so that the final segment can be completed properly. Then during production, the AD can give time signals to the talent regarding when they should wind up the next to last segment and begin the final segment.

Last-Minute Details

After the rehearsal and before the actual take, the AD will want to do several things. First, he or she must make certain that the director *follows through* on all production notes that were jotted down during rehearsal. Often, at this point, the director has a meeting with the entire crew to go over what needs to be changed before the program is actually taped or broadcast. This meeting is based largely on the AD's notes.

Next, the AD must make sure that everybody involved has all script changes marked down. As surely as one person did not get a crucial script change, that omission will lead to an on-the-air mistake. Additionally, the AD must remind the director of how much time is remaining before videotaping is scheduled to start or before the live program goes on the air.

During Production

Just prior to production, the AD will "read down" the clock, letting the director know how many seconds until air or until taping is to begin. Once on the air, the AD should remain alert to any and all potential problems—ready to call major troubles to the attention of the director; the AD must show *initiative* in this regard.

The AD should be following the director's marked script at all times, ready to give any assistance necessary. Again, depending upon the production complexity and studio philosophy, the AD may alert camera operators, audio personnel, character generator operators, and other crew positions to any special cues coming up in the script. In some network and station production situations, the AD will be giving the crew—including the camera operators—virtually all their instructions, based upon the director's script and rehearsals. The AD may even be giving "readies" and "prepares" to the technical director. This gives the director freedom to handle last-minute adjustments, make final artistic decisions, and call the actual takes on the air. In other instances, the director sets up all the shots and gives the "readies" and "takes" while the AD sits at the director's side reminding him or her of what is coming up next.

Timing Sheets

The primary job of the AD, of course, is handling *timing*. The AD must ensure that the entire production is the right length. Timing all of the segments to be electronically glued together in the editing session is an important consideration here. The AD needs some way of keeping track of the various timing notes and reminders. The digital clock readouts available in most control rooms are essential, but they are not of much use if the AD does not have some *organized* way of writing down the timing information.

One way is the use of a **segment timing sheet.** It may take several forms and be used in different ways. One sample format

is shown in figure 12-7. In this particular example, there are five columns for the AD to use. The first column is for a brief description of each segment in the program. The next four columns are for timing notations of one kind or another. "Unit" means the actual length of the *individual segment*. "Cume" is for the *cumulative time* of the program up to that point. The "Ideal" column is the estimated time that each segment *should* run; both the ideal unit-segment times and the ideal cumulative time should be figured out prior to setting foot in the studio. The "Rehearsal" column is for jotting down the unit times as various segments are worked through in a start-and-stop rehearsal. It is difficult to get an accurate picture of the actual cumulative times at this point, but the total of the unit times should give the AD a rough picture of how long or how short the program is likely to be. This column also allows the AD to figure backtiming so that certain segments start on time.

The "Dress" rehearsal column should give the AD a clear picture of how the actual cumulative times compare to the ideal times. The "Air" column is filled in as the program progresses. It lets the AD know how much to tell the talent to *stretch* or, in figure 12-7, how much to *cut* in order to come out on time. In this program, for example, we can see that several segments ran long, so the interview segment had to be cut short (from an ideal of five-and-a-half minutes to an actual five minutes).

There are many variations of timing sheets. Some will include *time in* and *time out* cumulative columns. Some will work with only one or two columns. This sample, however, should give the beginning AD an idea of what is needed to get the program timed accurately.

Talent Time Cues

The AD is also in charge of making sure the talent receives proper time cues. Either

SEGMENT (Description)	IDEAL (Unit) Cume.	REHEARSAL (Unit) Cume.	DRESS (Unit) Cume.	AIR (Unit) Cume.
1. TEASER	(:20) 0:20	:25	:25	:25
2. OPENING TITLES	(:30) 0:50	:40	1:05	1:10
3. INTRO	(1:05) 1:55	1:30	2:15	2:20
4. CHART	(2:00) 3:55	1:50	4:00	4:10
5. DEMO.	(4:00) 7:55	4:45	(4:15) 8:15	(4:20) 8:30
6. INTERVIEW	(5:30) 13:25	6:00	13:45	(5:00) 13:30
7. WRAP-UP	(:30) 13:55	:20	14:05	13:55
8. CLOSE	(:35) 14:30	:45	14:50	14:30
		16:15		
		(+1:45 over)		

FIGURE 12-7

Sample segment timing sheet.

In this particular example, we have a demonstration/interview program with several segments, which include a teaser, the opening titles, an introduction by the host, a 2-minute chart talk, a demonstration, an interview, the host's summary, and the closing credits. The ideal times are entered in the first column. During the stop-and-go rehearsal, various unit or segment times are obtained. By totaling these times in the "Rehearsal" column, we can see that the program is likely to run 1:45 (1 minute and 45 seconds) long. Adjustments are made—the interview segment is cut short—and the actual cumulative times are entered during the "dress" rehearsal and the actual "air" recording.

directly or through the director, the AD will tell the floor director when to give each time signal to the talent. Time signals are given to the talent in terms of *time remaining*. Thus, as we approach the end of a program, the AD will have the floor director signal the performer that there are "five minutes remaining," "one minute to go," "thirty seconds left," and so forth (depending upon exactly what time cues the talent, floor director, and AD had previously agreed would be used).

In many programs, such as the one illustrated in figure 12-7, the talent would need time-remaining cues in specific segments. Thus, working from the *ideal* times, the host would get, for example, a "thirty seconds remaining" cue at 3:25 into the program (as a reminder that there are thirty seconds left in the chart talk) and at 7:25 (thirty seconds left in the demonstration). The talent might want time cues to get out of the interview segment on time (that is, a 30-second cue at 12:55) or simply time cues to get through with the wrap-up summary on time (that is, a 30-second cue at 13:25). Care must be taken that the talent clearly understands what

these intermediate segment cues are so that they will not be confused with time remaining in the body of the program.

Program Time and Body Time

This brings up one other point of potential confusion. The AD must be concerned both with *getting the talent wrapped up on time* and with *getting the program off the air on time.* In figure 12-7 the talent needs a 30-second cue at 13:25 because he or she has to be completely wrapped up and finished at 13:55 (leaving the director thirty-five seconds for the closing credits). Also, the director has to have a 30-second cue at 14:00 in order to get the program off the air and into black at precisely 14:30. Thus, the AD has to work with both **body time,** the actual *length of the program content* including the host's closing summary but not the show's closing credits, and with **program time,** the *total length of the show* from fade-in to fade-out.

Also during the production, the AD will be taking notes for postproduction editing—both those items that the director points out that need to be taken care of (a missed shot, timing that was off a little, an opportunity to insert a reaction shot) and the items that the AD himself or herself notices that need to be corrected.

Finally, the associate director will be ready to take over at any time. The AD is literally the standby director. Should the director be unable to complete the program, the AD will assume responsibility for calling shots, and the production will continue.

After the Production

Once the production is completed, the AD still has a few obligations—especially in a training situation. The student AD should help clean up the control room of extra scripts, notes, and other materials, and debrief the director on any errors that occurred during the program.

A crucial postproduction job of the AD in many situations is the final editing session. The associate director may need to set up a schedule with the director for any planned editing. The AD may simply continue as the director's right-hand assistant in these assignments or, depending upon the nature of the production arrangements, the AD may be substantially in charge of the postproduction editing session—following the director's instructions, of course.

12.3 OVERVIEW OF THE FLOOR DIRECTOR'S DUTIES

The other right hand of the director is the floor director (also called the **floor manager** or **stage manager**).[3] The floor director is the director's surrogate to handle everything that happens on the studio floor.

During Preproduction

Ideally, the floor director will have taken part in production conferences preceding the date of studio production. He or she should meet the principal talent ahead of time in order to anticipate the kind of problems that may exist. However, often this is not the case, and the floor director is assigned to the production only a day or two before it is to be taped. In these cases, the floor manager should ask for a special meeting with the director to be brought up to speed on the requirements of the production.

During Rehearsals

Once the production moves into the studio, the stage manager is the primary contact

3. The official Directors' Guild of America designation is *stage manager*, but all three terms are used in various stations and studio operations.

the talent has with the rest of the world—the studio door is shut; the director is in the control room; all lights are focused on the talent who is left isolated, facing the cameras alone—except for the support of the floor director.

Talent Needs

There are two different kinds of talent needs that the floor manager should be aware of and ready to minister to. First, there are *emotional-physical needs.* The floor director has to be especially sensitive in this area. Is the talent physically comfortable? Can you offer him or her a glass of water? Can you get the talent out of the lights for a few minutes? What production mysteries should be explained to the talent?

This last point is important. Because the talent is not tied into the **intercom,** he or she is not aware of what is going on most of the time. Explain to the talent why there is a delay (a result of a computer graphics malfunction—not because the talent looked in the wrong direction during the rehearsal); explain why all the crew is laughing (at the AD's story—not at the talent's clothing). Try to put yourself in the position of the talent—isolated, in the spotlight, being stared at by the crew, and receiving no feedback as to what is going on.

Of course, sometimes performers are tied into the intercom because they are wearing an earphone for an **IFB—interrupted feedback system** (see section 3.6). In these cases, it is not as necessary to keep the talent informed of various production nuances.

The other kind of talent needs are more tangible *technical-production* requirements. The floor director must work these out with the talent on a program-by-program basis. What props must be available and where? Where is the talent to stand for this demonstration? What kinds of special cues might be needed? The details of each production must be worked out during rehearsal so that the talent is always sure of exactly what to do and the stage manager is always sure of what specific tasks and cues he or she needs to execute to get the talent's job done.

One inevitable production requirement, common to every program, is the communication of information to the talent through various hand signals and/or flip cards. (See figure 12-8.) During the rehearsal period the floor manager should demonstrate the various hand signals (stand by to start, begin talking, talk to this camera, speed up, thirty seconds to go, cut, and so forth) to the talent and decide exactly what time cues will be given. (See Appendix C for examples of the various hand signals.) During rehearsal, the floor manager should give the talent hand cues so they can become familiar with them. In doing this, the stage manager should always be in a position to be spotted easily by the performers. The talent should never have to turn his or her head to find the floor director.

Production Details

In addition to handling talent, the other main job of the stage manager is that of handling all production details on the studio floor. This area includes a variety of concerns: broadly supervising staging and lighting setups and handling all staging and lighting changes during the rehearsal; coordinating all audio, camera, and other facilities; directing all studio traffic; executing mechanical special effects; and every other production detail that might possibly occur.

The stage manager is ultimately in charge of virtually everything that happens on the studio floor, exercising dominion over all things technical—except the actual selection of shots for each camera. (In union situations, however, the stage manager may be restrained from crossing jurisdictional lines, such as giving orders to the

FIGURE 12-8

Floor director using hand cards to relay time signals to the talent.

Photo courtesy of KABC-TV, Los Angeles

lighting crew.) He or she must have a great deal of authority because virtually every other floor position is concerned with the production from only one specific viewpoint; for example, the camera operator, the audio technician, and the lighting director all have their particular perspectives to take care of. Perhaps each of these three will have selected the same spot on the floor to position a camera, a mic boom, and a light stand. It is up to the stage manager to coordinate these needs and decide what goes where.

The floor director is also the one who should obtain copies of the script and other specific instructions for various crew members and distribute them to everyone involved. The stage manager will obtain all physical (nonelectronic) graphics and props to be used in the production—making certain they are set up and arranged according to the script and the director's instructions.

The floor manager will plan and coordinate all movement. What props are to be placed where? What special effects will have to be cued? All physical graphics activity—moves, flips, pulls—will have to be planned and executed. If only a few things need to be moved, the floor director can handle them him/herself. However, if floor movement is complicated, grips and production assistants should be assigned to these various tasks and the floor manager will oversee what they do.

Last-Minute Details

After the rehearsals and before the final take, there are several things the floor manager needs to check. All sets, props,

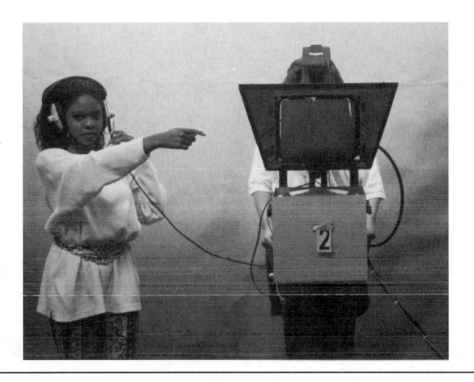

FIGURE 12-9

During production the floor manager gives cues to the talent, such as this cue to look at another camera.

physical graphics, and anything that is used during the body of the program should be in place, ready for the beginning of the production; all consumables need to be replenished—water in glasses, fruit, matches. The stage manager should generally console and reassure the talent that everything is fine and that they are doing great. He or she should also assemble the crew and make certain that everyone is ready and standing by for the beginning of the program.

During Production

The floor director's main job during production is to give hand cues to the talent and possibly move elements on the set such as props or charts (see figure 12-9). The stage manager must remain extra alert for any problems and double-check to ensure that all crew and talent are in their places, executing their cues. In general, she or he must guarantee that everything that was worked out during the rehearsal period is executed during production.

After the Production

The stage manager supervises the **strike,** helps collect the props, assists the staging and lighting crew in getting their elements properly stored, and generally polices the studio to see that everything is returned to where it belongs, ready for the next production.

In summary, the floor manager must think of himself or herself as *the* pivotal individual in charge of the studio—the person in complete control of all production elements. He or she must take the initiative in getting things done.

12.4 WORKING WITH TALENT

Now that we have given an overview of the jobs of the director, associate director, and floor director, we will turn our attention to specifics regarding three of the most important directorial jobs—working with talent, working with the crew, and (in the next chapter) considering creative aspects of the production. We will discuss these as duties of the director, although in reality some of them may be delegated to the associate director or floor manager.

The director's handling of talent is extremely important because the performers are what the viewing audience sees. If they view a lackluster acting job or a dull talk show conversation, the viewers will quickly change channels.

Directors must adapt their directing styles to fit their own personalities, the capabilities of the on-air talent, and the needs of the particular show they are directing. Some directors are, by nature, more authoritative than others, and give concrete, distinct direction. Others rely more on psychology and attempt to obtain superior performances by letting the talent feel they are the ones in charge of their own actions. Professional actors, such as those participating in a drama, require different handling than nonprofessionals who might be making a first-time appearance on a public affairs program. A children's program with many youngsters on it requires a more patient approach than a late-night talk show.

A distinction is often made between two groups of talent: (1) those in **presentational** or **reportorial** roles who serve essentially as communicators (see section 6.2), portraying no role except as a host or reporter; and (2) those in dramatic roles who are portraying some theatrical character. The first category is referred to as **performers** while the second group is referred to as **actors.** Although the two groups share many characteristics and concerns, it may be helpful to look at them separately in terms of what the director needs to understand and execute to maximize the performance of each person involved.

Directing the Television Performer

The category of performer includes announcers, hosts, narrators, reporters, interviewers, demonstrators, panel participants, and the like—talent who are communicating personally with the audience, usually addressing them directly.

Sometimes these people will be experienced pros who perform for the show week after week and sometimes they will be inexperienced guests at the television studio who may not feel at ease. As director you need to see that someone attends to the comfort and emotional security of all the performers. The floor manager will be very helpful in this regard, and a regular host can make guests feel at ease, but, as the director, you should make sure you meet and brief everyone thoroughly.

Explain the studio procedures, the nature of the program, and the intended audience. Go over the main purpose and points of the program so that everyone is in agreement as to how the program will proceed. Pass on information about commercial breaks, if any. Determine any special needs that the program or people in it might have. (See figure 12-10.)

You, as director, must emphasize to performers that their primary responsibility is to the audience. This performer-audience relationship is crucial to the success of any television program. Even though millions of people may be watching a particular TV program, the director must emphasize to performers that television is an intimate medium. It usually is received on a small screen, in the privacy of the home, as a rule by an audience of

FIGURE 12-10

Before the program is taped or aired, the director should discuss with novice performers the overall production process.

just a few people. The television performer is most successful when he or she conceives of the audience in that manner—three or four people sitting just a few feet away.

There are occasions, of course, when the TV camera is recording a performer who is playing to a large audience—the singer before a theater audience, the politician addressing his supporters, the minister preaching to a church congregation. In these situations, however, television is just an **objective** eavesdropper, covering an actual event. If the singer, politician, or minister is using television as a *reportorial* medium, addressing the audience directly and personally, then the director must help the performer adapt his or her style to a different audience relationship—more intimate, with direct eye contact, using a conversational tone of voice.

The director must also help the talent learn how to concentrate while on camera—how to focus on the material; how to ignore the technicians and assistants running around in circles; how not to be distracted by the lights, cameras, and mic boom.

Speaking Voice

The natural conversational speaking voice is one of the most elusive qualities the director needs to help the performer attain. The performer who can project the feeling of spontaneity and intimacy in his or her speaking style is on the way to capturing one of the most sought-after qualities of any television performer—*sincerity*. (As one comedian wisecracked, "If you can fake sincerity, you got it made.")

This is not to argue that the director should not allow the performer to exhibit enthusiasm or animation (if that is the person's natural style). It is only to point out that the speaker's *desire* to communicate with three or four people on the other side of the camera is, perhaps, the single most important ingredient in successful performing. If the director can affect the host/announcer/reporter/teacher psychologically so that he or she *sincerely* and earnestly *wants* to communicate (without an obvious artificial eagerness), then the performer should be able to succeed in that communication process.

Eye Contact

Just as important as vocal directness is the intimacy of specific visual directness—eye contact with the TV camera. In reportorial program formats when the performer (newscaster, TV lecturer, host, commentator) is speaking directly to the audience, the director should make sure the talent attempts to maintain a direct and personal eye contact with the camera lens at all times, looking straight into the heart of the lens.

This direct eye contact is the secret of maintaining the illusion of an exclusive relationship with each individual member of the audience. By looking directly into the lens, the performer is directly and personally addressing everyone who is in contact with the television receiver.

In maintaining the illusion of direct eye contact, the performer must become skilled, of course, in some of the artifice and techniques of the medium. In many productions the director will cut from one camera shot of the performer to another. The performer will have to re-establish eye contact with the new camera immediately. The director should always tell the stage manager when the cut is about to occur so that the stage manager can wave the talent to look at the new camera a split second before the camera cut is made. In some situations, the performer can make the transition look as natural as possible by momentarily glancing downward (or

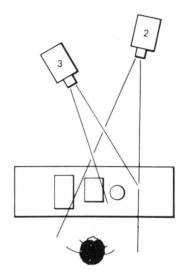

FIGURE 12-11

Camera pattern for shooting a close-up.

If the talent knows that camera 3 will be used only for close-ups of the objects on the table—and that camera 2 will always be getting the basic shot of the talent—then he or she will not have to worry about establishing eye contact with camera 3 every time the tally lights change. The talent can keep solid eye contact with camera 2.

upward)—as if glancing at some notes or trying to collect his or her thoughts—and then immediately establishing eye contact with the new camera.

The director can also inform the performer if one camera might be used exclusively for close-ups of some object he or she is demonstrating or discussing. If it is clearly explained to the talent that camera 3 will always be getting just a close-up of, for instance, the globe, then the talent need not worry about looking at camera 3 every time the tally lights change on the cameras. (See figure 12-11.)

Distracting Mannerisms

Because television is such an intimate, close-up medium, the director should make the talent aware that any visually or vocally distracting mannerism will certainly be captured with full impact. Some nervous mannerisms, such as a facial twitch or the unconscious habit of licking lips, may be hard to control. On the other hand, some fidgety distractions—such as playing with a pencil or pulling an earlobe—can be corrected if the director or stage manager discreetly calls it to the performer's attention. Many an audio operator has had a few hairs turn gray because a performer thumped his or her fingers on the table next to the desk mic or idly tapped his or her lavaliere while pondering a weighty question.

Vocal habits and mannerisms can also be distracting. The use of vocalized pauses (saying "um" or "ah") every time there is a second of dead air is a problem many of us share. The ubiquitous "I see" somehow always becomes part of the interviewer's basic vocabulary. (Why is it that in day-by-day conversation we seldom feel the need to say "I see" every time somebody makes a point to us, but as soon as we get on the air, it becomes part of the interviewer's response pattern?)

Scripted Material

Depending upon the specific program, the director and performers may be working from a full script (most likely a **two-column script**) or speaking extemporaneously from a semi-script, two-column script, or **rundown.** (See section 11.2.) Some performers, such as guests on a talk show may speak spontaneously or *ad lib* with no preparation at all. Many performers think they have to work from a full script—when they probably would be better off working from a rundown or some semi-scripted format. This enables the talent to have enough of a solid outline to speak with confidence; yet, by composing the exact words on the spot, they can add vitality and sincerity that is difficult to achieve with a prepared text.

The director can arrange to handle fully-scripted material in one of several ways. *Memorization* usually is required only for dramatic works and is best left to actors. Seldom can typical television performers deliver memorized copy without sounding artificial and stiff. The director is better off having them read from a physical script in their hands, from cue cards held next to the camera, or from a prompting device.

Reading directly from a *script* is satisfactory if the performers are quite familiar with the material and do not have to keep their eyes glued to the script. Some people can handle a script very well, glancing down only occasionally. Others, because of insecurity or nervousness, get completely buried in the script and never establish eye contact. If the talent does use a script, the director should make sure the pages are unstapled so the talent can slide the pages to the side unobtrusively without creating noise on the microphone. Someone should double-check to make sure the pages are in the right order before starting the final take.

The difficulties of working with a script can be avoided by using **cue cards,** but they have their own problems. Either the performer or some crew member will have to transfer the entire script onto large cue sheets (heavy oak tag paper or similar stiff stock). The cue-card holder also has to be trained to do a good job—holding the cards right next to the lens, reading along with the talent and raising each card to keep the exact line being read next to the lens, dropping each card silently, and positioning the next one. With a hefty stack of cue cards, holding them can become a very wearisome and demanding assignment. (See figure 12-12.) Cue cards allow for better eye contact than many performers can muster if they use hand-held scripts, but because they are beside the camera, the performers often appear to be looking slightly off camera.

FIGURE 12-12

Cue cards being properly held near the lens of the camera.

Cue cards have been largely replaced by the **teleprompter.**[4] This is a mechanical prompting device that attaches to the front of a camera. (See figure 12-13.) The prepared copy is projected onto a glass plate directly in front of the camera lens. Thus, the performer can read the copy while staring directly at the lens. The lettering is too close to the lens to come into focus from the camera's perspective. Sometimes the copy is printed out on long sheets of paper and run under a small camera that sends the signal to the glass plate. For more modern prompting systems, the copy is typed on a computer and then sent to the glass plate. Sometimes the same computer program that is used to generate the script can be used to create teleprompter material, eliminating the necessity of retyping the copy.

The exact spot on the script can always be positioned directly in front of the lens (by means of mirrors) so that the reader's eyes cannot wander away from the lens. (The astute viewer will probably catch the eyes scanning back and forth, however.) The main disadvantage of teleprompters is that they cost considerably more than hand-held scripts or cue cards.

Some experienced performers like to work from small note cards that they carry with them. It is a convenient and relatively unobtrusive way to handle material with

4. *TelePrompter* (TM) is a registered trademark of the Teleprompter Corporation, the first company to market prompting equipment successfully. Many companies now produce prompting equipment, but the title teleprompter has stuck and devices manufactured by other companies are often referred to as teleprompters.

FIGURE 12-13

Like many other prompting systems, this on-camera display unit reflects copy from a 15-inch monitor (bottom of picture) onto a mirror positioned in front of the camera lens. The camera simultaneously shoots through the mirror to pick up the talent's image.

confidence and ease because the talent can glance down at his or her notes when necessary but speak primarily directly to the camera lens.

Helpful Hints for Performers

A director can help performers come across effectively by giving whatever helpful hints are necessary. Not all of these will be necessary for all shows or all performers, but they are points that most directors will encounter at some point in their career.

Television is a close-up medium. In order to achieve good camera angles, people have to work in close together. One old television adage is, "If you ain't touching, you ain't close enough." Some performers feel uncomfortable with the close physical proximity they must maintain to other talent. As a result, they will start out in a chair close to the other talent but gradually, during the course of rehearsal and taping, move further and further away. The result is that a gap develops that looks inappropriate in the TV frame. (See figure 12-14.) The best way for the director to handle this is to explain to the performers the needs of the TV camera ahead of time. Then right before the program is to be taped, the director should double-check to make sure the distance is correct.

The director should also point out to the talent where the microphones and lights are and emphasize that the performers should not walk out of the light or out of the range of the sound pickup.

Performers should be advised not to acknowledge the floor manager's hand signals in any way (such as nodding their head) because this will show on camera.

FIGURE 12-14

Although these two people are sitting at what is normal distance for ordinary conversation, when the television camera frames both of them, there is an undesirable gap between them. They should be made to sit closer together.

The talent should be aware of where the stage manager is, but it is the stage manager's job to stand where talent can easily see him or her. Ask the talent if they want the stage manager to act as an audience member nodding encouragement and reacting to the performer. Some people find this helpful; others find it distracting.

Ask the talent to help you prepare for important shots by telegraphing them ahead of time. Talent that says, "Now let's look at the first demonstration . . ." warns you that a move is going to be made to the demonstration area. However, the performer should avoid giving direct instructions such as "Now, if I could just get a shot of this wristwatch!"

Ask performers not to make any big or sweeping gestures because the chances are that the camera will be on a fairly tight shot. Similarly, they should be careful with facial grimaces; there is a likelihood that the camera has a close-up of them.

If they are going to make a big move, they should lean into it gradually giving you and the camera operator ample warning. For example, if they are sitting in a chair and are ready to stand and walk over to the demonstration area, they should place both feet firmly on the floor, lean forward, put their hands on the sides of the chair, and *slowly* lift out of the chair. (See figure 12-15.) The camera is then able to follow them smoothly. In general, they should develop a habit of moving slowly as they go from one area of the set to another. This gives the camera operator a good chance of moving along gracefully. (And it always looks fast enough to the viewer.)

If talent is to hold up some object in front of the camera for a close-up, tell them to hold their arm tightly against their body to steady the hand. Even better, rest the object on a table or stand so there is no possibility of it moving.

FIGURE 12-15
Talent signaling his
intention to rise
by "leaning into"
the move.

Make sure talent knows not to handle microphones except hand or stand mics and to avoid playing with the mic cords. Also brief them on how to give an audio level. They should speak as they will speak during the program. Some performers will mumble a relatively weak audio check and then boom out on the air with their best basso profundo. A few will do just the opposite.

Again, not all performers will need all this advice. But it is all part of the *discipline* of performing.

Directing the Television Actor

Although we cannot begin to present a separate treatise on television acting, there are a few points that should be made. Assuming that you, as a director, will be working with skilled or trained actors, we do not need to get into the basics of acting methodology in this book.[5]

Many of the observations made regarding directing television performers apply equally to directing the television actor. Actors, too, must be concerned with their relationship with the audience (television is an intimate medium compared to the stage, or even to film); they must talk conversationally as their character would

5. Several books that can be consulted for overall information on acting are: John Harrop, *Acting* (New York: Routeledge, 1992); Hayes Gooden, *A Compleat Compendium of Acting and Performing in Two Parts* (Sydney: Ensemble Press, 1992); Paul Newman, "The Players," in Roy Paul Madsen, *Working Cinema* (Belmont, CA: Wadsworth, 1990), pp. 156-181.; and Brian Adams, *Screen Acting* (Los Angeles: Lone Eagle Publishing Company, 1987).

FIGURE 12-16

Differences in the scope of gesturing.

Left: A large sweeping gesture appropriate for the theater.

Right: A more subdued, intimate version of the same gesture appropriate for television.

talk; they need to learn to work with scripts; and they must be aware of the demands of the mics and lights and the hand signals of the stage manager.

However, acting involves special considerations, especially if the actors have been trained for stage acting and must be taught to adapt to TV acting.

The Missing Proscenium

First, and most obvious, there is no **proscenium arch**; there is no firm boundary separating the audience from the actors as there is on the stage. The audience perspective is switched every time the camera is changed. The director can move the audience ninety degrees with the push of a button.

In television, the viewer can be transported sideways, in or out, or (with the use of the **subjective** camera—see section 6.2) into the mind of the actor. (Even when a live audience is in the TV studio watching the taping of a situation comedy, the action is staged for the cameras and the television audience; the live audience is just watching the production of a program.) Actors must learn to adjust to this concept of moving audience perspective.

Limited Projection

Second, directors must help actors adjust to a small scope of projection. Instead of the exaggerated movements and sweeping gestures that must be seen in the back row of the theater, the TV actor has to restrict all actions and movement to the camera only ten feet away. (See figure 12-16.) Instead of projecting his or her voice so that every line is heard clearly sixty or seventy feet from the stage, the actor must restrict voice volume level—without losing emotion or intensity—for a pickup point only three or four feet away. Television is a close-up medium, and actors must adjust to this intimacy.

Blocking Precision

Third, directors must give a great deal of thought to *blocking*—the placing of actors and cameras in particular spots. Compared to stage, television placement and movements must be very *precise.* On the stage, each movement may be accurate to within a few feet. In television, the action must be measured by inches. If the actor's head is tilted at the wrong angle, the framing for a given shot may be off.

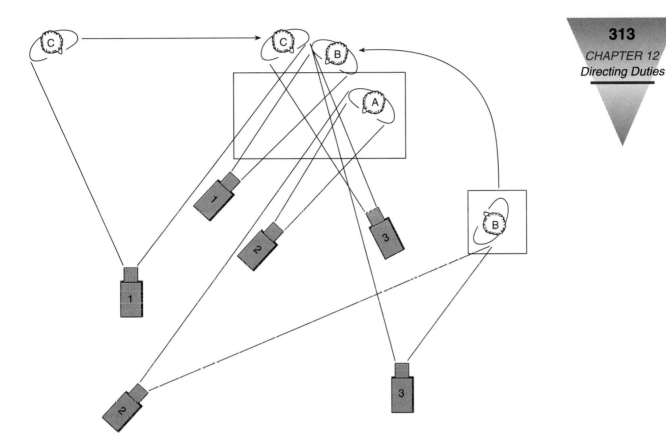

FIGURE 12-17

A blocking diagram as a director might draw it.

In this scene characters A and B are talking when character C comes in the door angrily and goes behind the sofa. Character B rises from the chair and goes behind the sofa where characters C and B argue. Character A reacts to the argument. Camera 1 pans with C as he moves from the door to behind the sofa and later has a close-up of B. Camera 2 shows A and B talking and then gets a reaction shot of A. Camera 3 follows B from the chair to behind the sofa and later gets a close-up of C.

Directors can help actors by thinking through blocking ahead of time. They should consider not only the relationship of the actors to the camera but also the relationship of the actors to each other. An actress who has to turn her head unnaturally in order to see the leading man is going to be too uncomfortable to deliver her lines well.

Sometimes directors have actors **cheat to camera.** An actor, in a two-shot for instance, will be directed to turn his or her face slightly toward the camera—rather than looking directly at the other actor straight on. Such *cheating* is not perceived by the viewer, but it does result in more of a head-on shot into the camera.

Directors often draw **blocking diagrams** to help them visualize the shots ahead of time. (See figure 12-17.) Using these diagrams, they can plan moves and think through how the people and the equipment will interact with each other. One useful blocking technique for directors is to *start* *blocking in the center of the program.* Pick the most crucial or difficult part of the production and figure out your camera pattern for that segment first. Once you know how that segment has to be blocked, you can figure backward to see how you will want to work your way up to that position. Continuing to work backward, you will be able to determine how you want to set up your cameras for the beginning of the program.

In planning multi-camera blocking, you must keep in mind that the action is continuous and you will not be able to stop to readjust the prop in someone's hand. You must also keep in mind the position of all the cameras so that they are not visible in any of the shots. And you must consider the position of actors and cameras so that shots can flow appropriately from one camera to another. With single-camera shooting, you can stop, but actors must perform in exactly the same fashion over and over again so that all takes are consistent (see section 14.9)

Pacing Precision

Fourth, television exists generally in a demanding and nonflexible time frame. Most dramatic programs have to be squeezed (or stretched) into given time slots—multiples of a half hour, minus requisite time for commercials. This means that a director may need to ask an actor to adjust pacing, speeding up or slowing down delivery of lines or action. This is especially a major concern with soap operas and situation comedies where there can be little flexibility in timing. It is less of a concern for filmed dramas, however, where the exact timing can be worked out in the editing process by cutting or augmenting silent footage, panoramic long shots, and chase sequences.

Out-of-Sequence Shooting

Filmed or single-camera videotaped dramas are almost always shot out of sequence.

There is no continuity of drama from the actor's standpoint. All the scenes in a given location are shot during the same setup. The director must help the actor assume the correct emotion for a scene that is unrelated to other scenes that have just been filmed. Sometimes multi-camera scenes are shot out of sequence, too, but the effect on the actors is not quite as jarring because the location does not change dramatically.

A Quick Study

Finally, compared to the stage and to theatrical motion pictures, television drama is a quick study medium. Whether working with single-camera or multiple-camera techniques, regular actors in a continuing series must learn up to an hour-long script every week—the equivalent of two feature-length motion pictures every month. For the actor in the hour-long daytime soap opera, the pace is even more demanding—up to a half hour of dialogue every day! Directors must realize the demands this places on actors and give them every opportunity possible to rehearse lines.

Thus, from a variety of viewpoints, the task of the television actor is quite demanding and complicated. Your job, as a television director, is to make the task as easy as possible for the inexperienced TV actor. The stage actor and motion picture actor will need guidance to help them adapt to the television medium, but even seasoned TV actors need care and consideration to do their best work.

12.5 WORKING WITH THE CREW

A director's style carries over to the crew as well as the actors. Some directors are authoritative and give precise instructions, such as specifying exactly how much **headroom** a camera operator should allow. Others let crew members make more decisions—the camera operator frames the shot and the director only intervenes if it is incorrect. Either method can work: the former assures quality control but can antagonize creative people who like to exercise their own judgment; the latter can lead to extra creative input that enhances what the director wants to do, but it can also lead to chaos if various crew members run counter to each other.

In working with crew, directors must be sensitive to lines of authority. Although directors have overall say regarding lighting, if they have a problem about the lights, they should talk with the lighting director, not the lighting assistant who is taking orders from the lighting director.

Crew Commands

During production, a director gives commands to many members of the crew. Each production is different, but a director might give different crew members the following kinds of commands:

Technical director—Various transitions, such as cuts and dissolves. The technical director will also set up special effects, but those are usually planned ahead of time because the director does not have time during production to give elaborate instructions as to what type of effect he or she desires. When the effect is needed the director will call for "effect 1" or "effect 5."

Associate director—Quick comments regarding things, such as pickup shots, that need editing. Actually, the associate director is more likely to be giving instructions to the director (such as time remaining in the program) than the other way around.

Audio operator—Fade music or other audio elements in and out; open and close mics.

Graphics operator—Change graphics and bring them in and out (unless they are brought in through the switcher by the technical director).

VCR operator—Start and stop the record tape and any roll-in tapes.

Lighting director—Bring up or fade out lights if lighting changes are part of the show.

Teleprompter operator—Usually this person rolls the script without instruction from the director, keeping pace with the talent. Commands would come only if there are problems.

Video control operator—This person, too, usually adjusts the luminance and chrominance of video inputs without direction, but if the director does not like the look of a camera, he or she might give instructions to the shader.

Floor director—Cues and timing information to relay to the talent.

Camera operators—Shot designations such as close-ups or wide shots and zooms or pans.

Boom operator—This person usually works independently following the talent, but the director might need to instruct the boom operator to raise the boom, if it or its shadow, looks as though it is going to appear in the picture.

Production assistants—These people may take their instructions through hand cues from the floor director or the director may need to tell them to flip charts or remove some prop.

Crew Interactions

Crew members who work with each other over and over for a continuing series often become like *family*. (See figure 12-18.) This has the same advantages and disadvantages as other family situations. They come to know each other well and can anticipate

FIGURE 12-18

The director (center)
should work to build
a spirit of
camaraderie among
the crew.

each other's moves. However, like brothers and sisters, they get on each others' nerves and develop rivalries and incompatibilities. The director, like a good mother or father, should realize that this will happen occasionally and try to make sure it has positive rather than negative outcomes. A disagreement on microphone placement between the audio person and the lighting director can be healthy because it can lead to better lighting and better sound. However, if the antipathy between the two grows to the point where the audio person purposefully places a boom microphone where he or she knows it will give the lighting director problems, the feud has gone too far.

The director must be sensitive to minor problems developing between crew members and nip them before they become major. Usually the best way is to sit the crew members involved down and have a frank, open discussion between them. Doing nothing and hoping the problem will go away rarely works.

When crew members have not worked with each other before, the director's job can be even more complicated. He or she must mould these people into a workable whole, taking advantage of the skills and personality traits each brings to the production. Initial rehearsals usually take longer when crew members are strangers because all of them are trying to find their specific roles. How much direction should the lighting director take from the floor director? Which of the camera operators should be given the complicated zooming shot? Should the audio operator use his or her own initiation in deciding how slowly to fade in the music or wait for specific instructions from the director?

The best way for the director to handle a *new crew* situation is to start the rehearsal session by holding a meeting and talking through the entire program, specifying each person's role at various points. As the rehearsal proceeds, changes and discrepancies will alter these roles, but at least everyone will have had the same starting point, and all people will have not only ideas about their specific roles but also general understandings about the roles of all other crew members.

A director should be able to assume that the people working on a production have both the *discipline and technique* to do the job. If any crew members are not exhibiting one or both of these characteristics, the director should have a talk with them, outlining expectations. If this does not work, the director should try to remove the person from the crew. However, in union situations (and student situations) this may not be possible. The director must then use psychological persuasion to motivate the person as much as possible.

Most production situations work very well, however. Cast, crew, and director develop a sense of unity and exhilaration wherein the sum of the whole is greater than any of its parts.

SUMMARY

The *director* is the person in charge during production, but he/she is often assisted with the directing chores by an *associate director* and *floor director*.

Adequate planning on the part of the director is necessary during preproduction. It is the time that the director must consider the specific *purpose* of the *script*, the *facilities* and *equipment* needed to execute it, the hiring of the *cast* and *crew*, *production requirements* such as lighting and graphics, and the *marking* of the script. The director then conducts various rehearsals—*pre-studio, studio floor,* and *control room* (in the form of *camera rehearsals, start-and-stop rehearsals, uninterrupted runthroughs,* and/or *dress rehearsals*). During production the director *calls commands* and *plans ahead* for shots and contingencies. After the production, the director may be involved in *editing.*

The associate director undertakes the preproduction tasks assigned by the

director, which may include working with talent or assembling props. During rehearsals the AD keeps *critique notes,* undertakes some *timing,* and makes sure *last minute details* are taken care of. Timing, with the aid of a *segment timing sheet,* is the AD's main job during production. He or she makes sure performers get proper *time cues,* and keeps track of *body time* and *program time.* After the production, the AD may be the one to handle editing.

The floor director may or may not be involved with preproduction. During rehearsals the floor director must attend to *talent needs,* both the *emotional-physical* ones (such as telling the talent what is going on) and the *technical-production* ones (such as explaining hand signals). The stage manager also oversees production details in the studio. During production, the floor manager gives *hand cues* to the talent. After production, he or she supervises the *strike.*

In working with television *performers,* those involved with the directing functions should give the talent tips about *speaking voice, eye contact, distracting mannerisms,* how to handle scripted material including the *teleprompter,* how to interact with lights and mics, and how to handle movement and studio procedures.

While directing *actors,* directors should help the actors be aware of the *missing proscenium, limited projection, blocking precision, pacing precision, out-of-sequence shooting,* and the need to be a *quick study.*

A director should facilitate harmonious relationships among the crew and make sure all crew members know their specific duties and the types of commands they will be given.

The director is also responsible for the artistic look of a program. Elements related to aesthetics will be discussed in the next chapter.

Directing Techniques

I n the last chapter we discussed the various organizational and people-related directorial tasks—in essence, those aspects that are the "part manager, part psychiatrist" facets of directing. In this chapter we will explore the "part artist" aspects of directing—ways in which a director can make a program aesthetically appealing and appropriate. Some of this appeal comes from the design of a production and some comes from camera angles and cutting techniques.

13.1 DESIGN ELEMENTS

Many productions have an **art director** or **production designer**[1] who works with the director to achieve an overall cohesion to the look of a show. Much of the concern with design involves sets and graphics, which have already been discussed in chapter 7 and lighting, which has already been discussed in chapter 4. However, attention must also be given to *costumes and clothing* and to *makeup and hair style.*

Costumes and Clothing

Costumes for program forms such as drama, comedy, music, and children's programs are an integral part of design, and if they are made from scratch, can be totally controlled.[2] The director and art director have less control over street clothing, especially that worn by guests who appear on a talk show. However, a director should talk to performers about dress because they will feel and act more comfortable if they know they are properly dressed for the occasion.

Clothing and costumes have to be considered in conjunction with the color scheme of the entire setting. The hostess for a local talk show should be told by the director not to wear a yellow dress if she is going to be sitting in a yellow chair because she will "disappear" into the chair. An actress's eighteenth century gown should not be sewn out of red cloth if the set is predominantly green (unless a Christmas aura is to be conveyed).

1. For most TV shows, the term used is "art director." "Production designer" is used for highly stylized productions that need a great deal of design coordination—mostly science fiction movies such as *Star Wars* and *Jurassic Park.*

2. It is not the province of this book to talk about how to make costumes, but for those interested in this subject, a good source is Rosemary Ingham, *The Costumer's Handbook: How to Make All Kinds of Costumes* (New York: Prentice-Hall, 1987).

Saturation

Unless a spectacular, deliberately colorful, dazzling effect is advised, the director should encourage performers to stick to clothing of a *dull saturation*—muted aqua rather than chartreuse, tan rather than brilliant yellow. Brightness and tonal balance also should be considered in terms of the overall emotional effect that is desired. Would dark, somber grays and browns be more or less appropriate than lighter shades and pastels?

Line

Line also is an important design consideration. Vertical lines tend to emphasize tall and slender proportions; horizontal stripes tend to exaggerate weight and mass. Performers who are concerned about appearing too heavy (and television has a tendency to make people appear a little heavier) should be advised to stick to vertical lines.

Contrast

Tell talent to avoid high contrast and extremes in color brightness. Remember that the television camera has a relatively limited contrast ratio (see section 4.2), which makes it difficult to handle white shirts against a dark suit. Try also to avoid high contrasts with skin tones. Dark clothes will make a pale person look even more pale; light-colored clothes next to a tanned complexion will make the skin appear darker. Blacks and other dark-skinned performers should be careful of light colored clothing that would tend to heighten the tonal contrast and wash out facial details in the dark areas.

Patterns

Generally, finely detailed patterns should be avoided. Whereas clothing with a rich thick texture will photograph well on television, clothing with a fine pattern usually will not because it is too busy and distracting and hard to make out once it has gone through the TV scanning process. (See figure 13-1.) Thin stripes, herringbones,

FIGURE 13-1

The fine design on a
blouse such as this
would be
substantially lost
once it is translated
into scanning lines.

and small checks can also create the **moiré effect**—a distracting visual vibration caused by the interference of the clothing pattern and the TV scanning lines.

Chroma Key

One other minor production consideration involves color. Inform talent if any **chroma key** effects are going to be used and tell them not to wear whatever color is being used for the chroma key—usually blue or green. (See section 8.4.) Anything, even a tie, that contains the key color will form part of the keying pattern, and the background picture will appear wherever the chroma key color clothing is otherwise visible to the camera. Imagine the effect when the newscaster has a scene from the battlefield keyed in behind him—and we see bricks and rubble appearing where his tie should be.

Detail

One costume element that needs to be considered for television and not for the stage is *detail*. Although you may be able to get

away with a few loose threads and a modern patch on the stage—where the nearest spectator is fifteen feet away—you cannot afford to try to fool the television camera, which brings the viewer only a few inches away. This is especially critical in costuming around the neck, shoulders, and chest areas, where the close-up picks up costume details with microscopic clarity.

Makeup and Hair Styling

The field of television makeup and hair styling is a specialized area that directors seldom get into, except to hire good makeup people.[3] Many productions (such as public affairs shows) do not require makeup. Guests can "come as they are" and look perfectly fine. However, many shows will look better if makeup is used

3. For more on makeup and hairstyling, see Vincent Kehoe, *The Techniques of the Professional Make-Up Artist* (London: Focal Press, 1985); and James Stevens Cox, *Hairdressing and Wig Making* (London: Batsford Academic, 1984).

for one of three functions: (1) to *enhance* appearance (improving the performer's basic physiognomy with color correction or a bit of powder on a bald head to cut down on its shine); (2) to *correct* appearance (creating the effect of pulling back protruding ears or straightening a broken nose); or (3) to *create* appearance (building a new character such as Frankenstein's monster or Mr. Hyde).

The object of television makeup for performers and for actors playing ordinary looking people is to have them look as natural as possible. A good, basic, unobtrusive makeup job should help enhance normal colors (evening up flesh tones); minimize any blemishes or distortions (covering up birthmarks, bags under the eyes); and emphasize good points. However, with the close-up lens any exaggerated makeup certainly would be perceived as unnatural.

For dramatic purposes, of course, much more makeup treatment is needed—getting into the third function of creating an appearance for certain characterizations. This includes collodion scars, nose putty, surface molding by plasticine and special waxes, and larger rebuilding jobs using latex prosthetics and face masks.

Makeup Application

Regardless of the extent of the makeup job to be performed, basic procedures should follow a fairly well-established pattern. Before applying any makeup, the face should be cleaned with either a moisturizer for dry skin, or an astringent (such as alcohol or witch hazel) for oily skin.

The primary makeup element is the *base.* This is the initial covering that is usually applied to the entire face or exposed area being treated (arms and hands and other parts of the body often need makeup treatment). This base is to provide the color foundation upon which all the rest of the makeup will be built.

Powder is usually applied next to set the base, dull any sheen or gloss, and help keep the base from smearing. Usually, powder that is a little lighter than the base color is applied.

Highlights and shadows are used to emphasize or minimize facial features. The forehead, nose, cheekbone, and jaw can all be highlighted with lighter shades or deemphasized with darker tones. Normally, *rouge* is next applied to the cheeks, nose, forehead, and chin as needed to give a healthy complexion and to counteract the flatness of both the base color and the evenness of the lighting.

Finally, special attention is given to those most expressive features of the face—the eyes and the lips. Specific drawing tools and accessory items are applied as necessary: *lipstick, eye shadow, eyeliner, eyebrow pencil, mascara,* and possibly *false eyelashes.* (See figure 13-2.) The extent of the use of these accent items depends upon the need for remodeling and the individual taste of the performer.

The director should ensure that makeup artists work closely with the lighting director for any production. The lighting director may be using colored gels, for instance, that could tremendously distort the effect desired by the makeup person. A green gel on a dark or black skin, for example, will completely wash out any color distinctions on the face. Generally—since most base color is in the reddish range—backgrounds should tend more toward blues and greens. But these subtleties must be coordinated with the lighting director.

Hair Styling Principles

In addition to the basic makeup job, hairstyling needs to be considered. Hairstyles with a definite shape or firm silhouette usually compliment the performer more than wispy, fluffy hairdos. Hair should be carefully combed because back light will tend to make loose strands stand out.

FIGURE 13-2
Makeup artist
applying final
touches with a
fine brush.

Photo courtesy of
KABC-TV, Los Angeles

Fancy hair treatments and fresh permanents should be avoided because they will make the person look unnatural.

If a person's hair needs to be changed entirely to fit a particular character role, the hair can by tinted or cut, or a wig can be applied.

Aside from extreme theatrical applications, the aim of good television makeup and hair styling, like that of good costuming, is simply one of accentuating the natural appearance of the performer for purposes of more accurate rendering by the electronic camera. For this reason, no makeup or hair styling job can be considered complete until it has been checked out on camera—under studio lighting conditions.

13.2 CAMERA AND CUTTING PRINCIPLES

While a director is directing a show, he or she should keep in mind a number of camera and cutting principles. Many of these involve **continuity**—a broad term that refers to keeping things the same throughout an entire program. These principles have developed over the years as part of a language of film and television. People viewing a movie or TV program expect certain conventions, and violating them confuses the audience. However, these principles are not laws of the land. In fact, they are made to be violated because sometimes you want to disorient (or frighten or shock) your audience. Music videos have certainly breached every camera and cutting continuity principle—and have done so effectively. But if a program is straightforward information or entertainment, a director should abide by the conventional language. In addition, understanding a principle better enables you to know how and when to violate it.

We will discuss a number of production conventions that directors should keep in mind. Although the focus of the discussion will be on multi-camera production, some of these conventions also hold true for single-camera shooting. Many of them are easier to obey in multi-camera shooting because all the shots are seen on monitors, and errors will be more obvious than they will be when shots are taken individually.

Shot Juxtaposition

Early filmmakers quickly came to the conclusion that when one picture is immediately replaced by another, an interaction occurs in the mind of the viewer that communicates something more than if each picture were viewed separately. This intriguing concept obviously can have direct bearing on the process of shot selection for any television program. Each shot must be thought of as being part of a flow of images, each with a relationship to the one that precedes it and the one that follows it.

For this reason, the succession of pictures should be motivated by the basic tenet, "Give the viewers what they need to see when they need to see it." To a great extent, this is determined by a juxtaposition of *collective* shots showing the whole picture—the relationship of all elements in the scene—and intimate *particularized* shots—giving the viewers the closer details they want. (See figure 13-3.)

The generalities of a scene or program situation are established by the **wide shot** (also referred to as a **long shot** or **cover shot**). Then the director cuts to a **medium shot** or a series of medium shots to give the audience particularized details. When something small or intimate needs to be seen, the director uses the **close-up.**

Of course, the terms *wide shot, medium shot,* and *close-up* are relative and vary from one type of program to another. The left-hand picture shown in figure 13-3 is probably a wide shot for a discussion program. However, if this were a children's program with toys to be demonstrated flanking the four people, this shot would be considered a medium shot. Likewise, the right-hand shot in figure 13-3 would be considered a close-up for a talk show, but for a drama in which the girl's earring played a major role, this might be the medium shot and the earring would be the close-up.

Nevertheless, the pattern of wide shot to medium shot to close-up should be observed so that the audience comprehends the total environment and can then relate to particular areas of that environment. Of course, as mentioned above, this "rule" is often violated for perfectly good reasons. Starting with a close-up of a dagger builds suspense and draws the audience into the

FIGURE 13-3

Comparison of wide shot and close-up.

Whether in a variety show, drama, or panel discussion, the same need exists to balance wide shots (*left*) with close-ups (*right*)

scene. Where is this dagger and why is it sitting there? Only after the audience's curiosity has been aroused does the director use a wide shot to reveal the location.

Camera Selection

Even with the opportunity to pre-plan or block out the camera work in multi-camera television programs such as dramas, the ongoing production technique forces the director to make some rather quick, on-the-air editing decisions because the exact moment of the take is crucial. With talk and game shows, of course, there is truly an ongoing series of changes in camera use every time someone new breaks in to talk. A basic challenge is to always have the proper camera ready for a shot at the exact moment the situation calls for it. On the part of the director, this requires an ability to be able to think *simultaneously* on at least two levels—what is on the air right now and what is going to be on the air next.

Thought Process

With a three-camera structure, the thinking process might work something like

this: Camera 1 is on the air. You, as director, have the choice of using camera 2 or 3 for the next shot. Camera 3, however, has just been used on the previous shot. Camera 2, therefore, has more time to make a framing adjustment or even change position. (See figure 13-4.)

By using the commands of preparation and execution properly (see section 8.5), the director can select the next camera to be used, allowing sufficient lead time to set the next shot. It is accepted studio procedure in a three-camera setup to place camera 1 on the left, camera 2 in the middle, and camera 3 on the right. This setup allows the director to keep track easily of the relative positions of cameras on the floor and the angle of shots available to them.

Obviously, cameras usually are not employed in a repeated 1-2-3-1-2-3 rotation. In order to observe the wide shot, medium shot, and close-up requirements of any program, at least one of the three cameras at any given time will usually be designated as a wide-angle cover shot camera. This is especially important in shooting unrehearsed programs such as

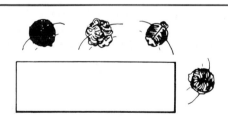

CAMERA 1
on the air

CAMERA 2
ready for next shot

CAMERA 3
has time to adjust
for its next shot

FIGURE 13-4

Sequence of camera shots.

In this illustration, the director has just used camera 3 (before taking camera 1); therefore, camera 2 will probably have more time to get the next shot lined up.

panel discussions where there are sudden changes of the individuals speaking. The technique on such a program is to cut to a wide shot on the change of voice if a close-up of the new person is not immediately available. The director then has a chance to ascertain who is talking and call for the close-up. The most glaring error on any kind of program is for an unprepared director to be caught with a speaker or performer still on camera when that person is no longer speaking or performing.

In a rehearsed program, when the camera blocking has been worked out in advance, the director can temporarily commit all cameras to close-up shots, having planned to return to a cover shot at a later specific time. Generally, however, the wide-angle and close-up shot balance requirements are such that at least one camera is always kept on a cover shot.

Crossing Camera Angles

Another principle involving camera selection deals with *crossing camera angles*. In many staging setups, the natural pattern will have two people facing each other. Shooting this situation with two cameras can get the best head-on shots by having the cameras shoot across each other's angles; that is, each camera should be shooting the person or object farthest away from the camera. The camera on the right should be getting the shot of the person on the camera left, and vice versa. (See figure 13-5.)

Shot Relationships

When changing from one shot to another, the two pictures should relate to each other in both an informational and aesthetic setting. The subject in two successive shots should maintain continuity in that it should be *readily recognizable*. You would not want to cut to such a different angle that the viewer would not immediately recognize the subject from the previous shot.

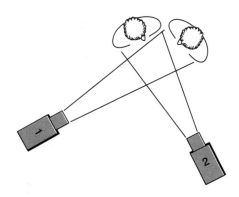

FIGURE 13-5

In order to get the best head-on shots, cameras should be set up so they shoot across each other.

Cutting Ratio

One of the most common errors of shot relationship involves wide shots and close-ups. If you were to cut from the left-hand shot in figure 13-3 to a close-up of the girl's earring, most of your viewers would be totally lost because they would not have noticed the earring in the wide shot. One good rule to follow is that you should always keep your camera cuts within a **three-to-one cutting ratio**; that is, do not take to a shot that is *three times larger* or *three times smaller* than the preceding shot.

Jump Cutting

For aesthetic reasons, you should avoid taking or dissolving between cameras that have almost exactly the same or matching shots. The result would be that the scene remains essentially the same, but the picture *jumps* slightly within the frame. On unrehearsed shows, the camera operators may inadvertently come up with almost identical shots; therefore, it is up to the director to watch carefully for this **jump cutting** on the control room monitors.

Position Jumps

Another problem to avoid is the **position jump**—having a primary subject jump

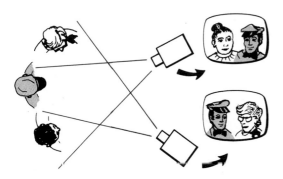

FIGURE 13-6
Subject jumping positions.

With both cameras shooting a standard two-shot, the central talent appears to jump from one side of the screen to the other as we take between shots.

from one spot on the screen to another position in the next shot—an apparent loss of continuity. This can occur, for example, if three people are lined up facing two cameras and each camera is getting a two-shot of two adjacent persons. The center person will be on the left of one picture and on the right side of the other camera's picture. (See figure 13-6.) This position jump can be avoided by having one camera go to a three-shot before cutting or, conversely, by cutting to a close-up single shot.

Axis of Action/Conversation

Another basic principle involves *screen direction*. In successive shots we want to make certain that all action is flowing in the same direction and that each screen character is facing in one consistent direction. If an imaginary line is drawn extending the path in which a character is moving, we can call this the **axis of action.** As long as all cameras are placed on the same side of this axis, the action will continue to flow in the same direction. If cameras are placed on different sides of this axis of action, however, the apparent screen direction will be reversed when cutting between

the cameras. (See figure 13-7.) Directors, therefore, always try to avoid having cameras **crossing the line.**

Closely related to the axis of action is the **axis of conversation.** If the imaginary axis is drawn through two persons facing each other, all cameras should be kept on the same side of this line. Otherwise the screen direction (the direction in which a person is looking) will be reversed when you cut to the other side of the line. This imaginary line—the axis of conversation—will shift, of course, as performers move. Figure 13-8 shows two common errors in crossing the axis of conversation.

Jump cuts, position jumps, and crossing the line problems are all examples of mistakes that are easier to spot in multi-camera production where the shots can be seen in relation to each other as they are being selected than they are in the field where shots cannot be compared. It is much easier for a director to accidentally cross the line when a long shot is recorded in the morning and its accompanying close-up is shot in the afternoon than it is for a studio director who is watching all the monitors.

Transitions

Many of the mechanics of continuity are carried out by the actual camera **transitions**—the manner in which the director changes from one picture to another. Over the years, these transitions have adopted meaning that audience members readily understand. The director must be aware of the psychological and grammatical impact of each—when to use one and when to use another. These transitions can be accomplished in postproduction editing as well as with the switcher during a multi-camera studio production.

Cuts

The instantaneous **cut** or straight take replaces one picture immediately with

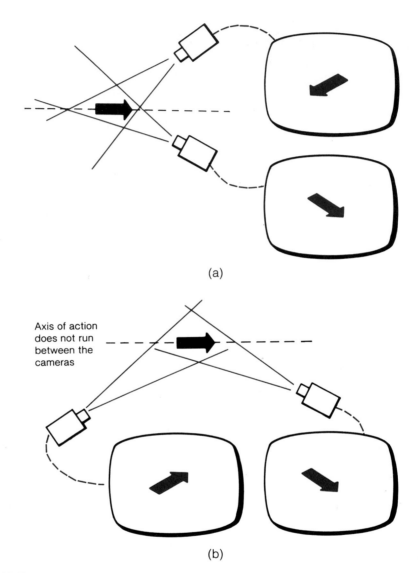

(a)

(b)

FIGURE 13-7

Axis of action.

(a) WRONG. If cameras are placed on both sides of the imaginary axis of action, the screen direction will be reversed when cutting between cameras. (b) CORRECT. When both cameras are on the same side of the axis of action, they will both perceive the action moving in the same direction.

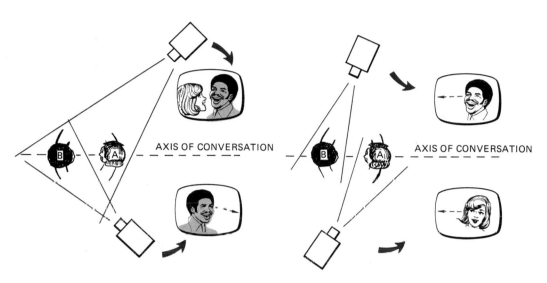

AXIS OF CONVERSATION

AXIS OF CONVERSATION

FIGURE 13-8

Axis of conversation.

In the *left* illustration, Actor B changes screen direction as we cut from one camera to the other. In the *right* illustration, both actors appear to be looking in the same direction, making it difficult for the viewer to establish the relationship between the two.

another. It implies that there is *no change in time or locale*. It happens right now. The audience is not moved anywhere, except to a different perspective of the same scene. It is the basic transition. It is the device that the audience has accepted since the beginning of the motion picture film for changing a point of view without making any major dramatic change. In terms of grammar, it is the end of a sentence—a period—and the beginning of a new sentence.

Dissolves

The **dissolve,** simultaneously fading out one picture and fading into another picture, creates a temporary overlapping of images. Dramatically, this implies a *change of place* or a *change in time* (usually a lapse of time). It shows a relationship with the previous shot, but there has been a change; the audience has been moved somewhere else or somewhere later in time. Grammatically, the dissolve corresponds to the end of a paragraph or possibly even to the end of a major section of a chapter.

In musical programs, the dissolve is often used purely for aesthetic reasons—a slow dissolve of a singer from a medium to a tight close-up profile, or a close-up of the dancer's feet dissolving to a long shot of the dancer. No change in time or locale is implied in this case—just a pleasant visual effect. In musical productions, the dissolve can be used as an artistic connecting or relating transition, whereas it has the opposite effect in dramas.

Dissolves are slow, and therefore, have an affect on the *pace* of a program. For example, an effective series of fast camera cuts can lose its intensity if a dissolve is suddenly used. If a director does not want to lose intensity, the dissolve should not be used. If the dissolve stops for awhile in the middle, creating a **superimposition,** this serves to intensify whatever is being expressed by the individual images.

Fades

A **fade** from a camera to black or a fade up from black implies a very *strong separation.* It is used in going from one segment of a program to another—from the talk show interview to the used-car commercial. Dramatically, the fade is the curtain falling—the end of a scene or an act. Grammatically, it would be the visual counterpart of the end of a chapter or story.

Defocus

One specialized transition that can be used with no fancy electronic effects is the **defocus**; the camera on the air defocuses and dissolves to a similarly defocused shot on another camera, which then comes back into focus. This usually implies either a *deranged state of mind* or a transition *backward in time.* As with other specialized transitions, it tends to call attention to itself and must be used very sparingly.

Wipes

The **wipe**—taking one picture off the face of the screen and replacing it with another—also calls attention to itself. Most of the time it has no special grammatical significance except to say, "Isn't this a *fancy transition!*" Some wipes, however, have developed grammatical significance. For example, in sports production, a wipe from the center to the sides indicates an instant replay.

Digital Effects

Digital technology has brought new dimensions to transitions. Graphics programs and digital manipulators used in conjunction with the switcher allow for an array of bursts, flips, tumbles, and spins. These are used mainly as attention-getters and are often employed during opening credits to *grab the audience.* They should be used sparingly during the body of the program because they draw attention to themselves and away from the content of the show.

Timing of the Transition

Understanding the different types of transitions helps to explain the *how* and *why* of changing cameras, but a word needs to be said about the *when.* Generally, camera changes must be adequately motivated; there has to be some reason for cutting at a particular point. The audience should want to see something else. ("Give the viewers what they need to see when they need to see it.") Without proper motivation, you should avoid the temptation to change the picture just for the sake of change. The following discussion on the timing of camera transitions applies equally to the timing of editing shots together in the postproduction process for single-camera production.

One of the strongest motivations for cutting is to capture action. When the action starts, you need a wider view. When the talent walks to a new area, you need an establishing shot. When cutting on action, you should always try to cut *just prior to the action*—not too long before it nor immediately after it. Ideally, as soon as the action starts, the audience needs to see the wider shot. Cutting to a movement that is in progress creates a jarring effect similar to a jump cut.

In a similar vein, you usually should not cut to a camera that is in the *middle of movement*—panning, tilting, zooming. Occasionally it is alright to cut (or preferably dissolve) from one moving camera to another that is moving in the same way. For example, if a camera is panning right, a cut can be made to another camera that is also panning right at the same pace. Cutting to a camera panning left or zooming in or to a stationary camera would be very jarring. But, of course, there are situations where this abrupt effect is desired.

During an interview or panel program, the strongest motivation for cutting is when a speaker *starts to talk.* The audience wants to see who is talking. The ideal timing of the take is precisely between the two speakers—not three seconds after the second speaker has started. As a practical matter, cutting during an ad-lib discussion program will usually involve a delay of a second or so. To counteract this, the director has to be sensitive to the body language and facial expressions of all participants (watching the off-the-air camera monitors). Who has his mouth open? Who just leaned forward? Who just took a deep breath? Anticipate who the next speaker is going to be.

Include appropriate, judiciously spaced **reaction shots** also. How are the listeners reacting? Which listener is especially animated? In timing reaction shots, *do not* cut at the end of an obvious statement or during a break in the speaking; it will look too much like a cut to the wrong participant. Reaction shots are most effective in the middle of a speech.

During musical numbers, time your cuts to fit the music. (In slower tempos, purely for an aesthetic "feel," dissolves may be a better transition.) The cuts should be crisp and clean, following a regular rhythmical pattern—cutting on the beat every four bars or eight bars—as the music dictates.

Now that we've discussed many of the elements that are needed for successful directing, let's take a look at how you, as a beginning director, might handle your first production—a fairly simple discussion show. An actual suggested discussion project is given in Appendix D, along with several other production project ideas.

13.3 PRODUCTION PROJECT: THE DISCUSSION PROGRAM

The discussion show, that sometimes maligned but nevertheless ubiquitous stalwart of television programming, provides an excellent format for understanding the fundamental principles involved in directing.

Staging

The majority of discussion shows utilize some variation of either one of two basic staging configurations: an *L-shaped grouping* that places the host on the end facing down a row of other participants (see figure 13-9); or a *semicircle,* in which the host is generally placed in the center (see figure 13-10). This conformity of staging is not as much a lack of originality on the part of the directors as it is their recognition that these seating plans provide an arrangement whereby the guests can best relate to each other and the host, and at the same time, provide the director with the best camera angles of the participants.

On these programs, four cameras are generally utilized. One of the cameras holds a wide shot of the entire group at all times and another camera holds a shot of the host for use at any time in the program. On a three-camera show, one camera will have to alternate between these two shots. The primary assignment of the other two

FIGURE 13-9

Typical setup for an *L*-shaped staging arrangement for a discussion program.

HOST

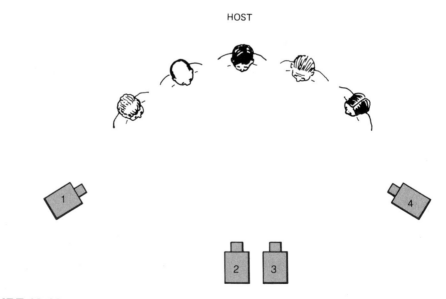

FIGURE 13-10

Camera pattern for semicircular staging.

In this typical "talk show" camera pattern, one center camera (either 2 or 3) remains on a cover shot of the entire group while the other center camera (3 or 2) holds a close-up of the host.

cameras is that of providing close-up shots of those persons facing their direction—by crossing their angles.

In a discussion program, the participants relate not to the audience but to each other, and as a result, face not to the front but in the direction of the persons to their right and left. Depending upon the role of the host/moderator, the other participants will tend to face in his or her direction during much of the program.

Lighting

Two suggested lighting plans for an L-shaped seating configuration have been presented as sample lighting plots in figures 4-22 and 4-23 (see section 4.5). A review of that section of material will be of value in the preparation of lighting plots for any of the several main seating configurations.

On a discussion program, care must be taken to ensure that the face, especially the eyes, is properly lit from all potential camera angles. The locations of the cameras provide a good guide to the location of the main lights in relation to the subjects. The amount of light reflected back from each subject to the camera must be individually balanced to produce an equal intensity. Differences in hair, clothing, and complexion can produce unsuitably dark or light close-up shots. When taken in succession, such shots are noticeably objectionable.

Shot Continuity

Earlier in this chapter, reference was made to *wide-angle, medium,* and *close-up* shots in terms of their respective abilities to communicate collective or particularized program information. Wide-angle *cover* shots are used within a program sequence to re-establish the relationship of program participants to each other and to the elements of the set. It is the *collectivizing* view of all those production values that contributes to the program as a whole.

By contrast, the medium and close-up shots are a *particularized* view of a person or object at a precisely appropriate point in the program sequence. As such, the information conveyed is selective and personal, even to the point of being intimate. The eyes and facial muscles add an important dimension to the total meaning of what a person is expressing in words. This is especially true of actors or other personalities who often speak in public or on television. For this reason, the most effective close-up shots are those in which the camera angle is not more than forty-five degrees from a head-on position. (See figure 13-11.)

Transitions

The most important production value on a discussion program is the precision with which the camera shots follow the spontaneous flow of the conversation. Each time a new person begins to speak, the camera on the air—whether a cover shot or a close-up—should include that person. To linger for more than a split second on someone who has just stopped talking or to cut to the wrong person is very distracting to the audience.

Ideally, each change of voice should be accompanied by a change of cameras to a close-up shot or one that predominately features the person talking. On a three-camera show that features four guests and a moderator, this is not always possible. By carefully watching the panel for clues as to who may be speaking next, the director may somewhat improve the chances of having the shot ready.

Most directors solve the problem by having a cover shot of the entire group available for use at all times. When a close-up shot of a new speaker is not

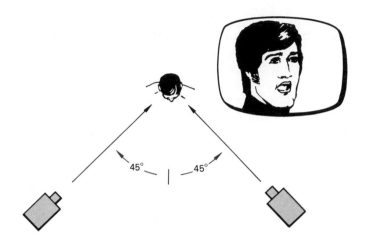

FIGURE 13-11

Optimum angles for close-ups.

Any camera getting a close-up shot should be as perpendicular to the talent as possible. The camera should not be more than 45 degrees from a head-on shot for a good close-up.

readily available, a take to the cover shot performs several important functions. Primarily, it gives the director a chance to be certain who is speaking before assigning a camera to the shot. In a fast-paced discussion, this alternative is the only way the director can stay with the quickly changing flow of conversation. Once the cover shot has been taken, the close-up need not be used immediately. The director can let the wide shot re-establish the collective aspect of the group while waiting for the end of a sentence as a convenient point to cut to the close-up.

During a discussion program, the situation often calls for shots other than a close-up of one participant in the total group. Shots including two or three persons not only add pictorial variety but are quite useful when several people begin a rapid interchange of short statements or questions and answers. Smaller group shots have an added dimension, showing the silent but often revealing expression on

the faces of persons other than the speaker. A brief close-up shot of someone moving his or her head in agreement or disagreement—a reaction shot—is especially useful when one person has been speaking for an extended period of time.

On the other hand, the director must be alert to group shots in which those persons who are not talking are looking away from the speaker. Whether or not intended, the visual effect is one of boredom and, as such, has a negative impact on the program as a whole.

Camera Blocking

The range of shots available to each camera in a program situation is dependent upon the two interrelated variables of camera and subject position. On a discussion program, where the staging options are somewhat limited, the director generally uses the seating arrangement as a starting point in the camera blocking process. Primary

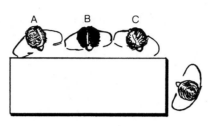

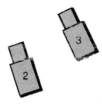

FIGURE 13-12

Camera patterns for *L*-shaped staging.

Plan A: *Camera 1* remains on a wide-angle cover shot. *Camera 2* gets close-ups of panelists as they face camera right and two-shots or three-shots of panelists. *Camera 3* gets singles of panelists as they face camera right and over-the-shoulder shots (with host in foreground).

Plan B: *Camera 1* gets close-ups of moderator/host, two-shots of host and panelist C, and singles and two-shots as panelists turn to camera left. *Camera 2* gets close-ups of panelists as they face camera right and two-shots or three-shots of panelists. *Camera 3* remains on a wide-angle cover shot.

---

camera positions can then be selected on the basis of the best angles for the close-up shots and the important requirement of wide-angle cover shots.

All the shot possibilities for each camera should be plotted so that each camera operator can work within the parameters of established shot assignments. Off-set visuals should be positioned for easy accessibility to camera positions—after the basic camera pattern has been established.

The use of a definite shooting plan aids in having critical shots available when they

are needed, and at the same time, helps in holding down the talk on the PL intercommunication system.

The direction of conversational flow may vary at different times during a program. For this reason, directors usually develop several shooting plans to cover all contingencies. Figure 13-12 shows two such plans that could be used in the coverage of an L-shaped arrangement. Plan A is designed to provide maximum close-up coverage of the three panel members, with the moderator being seen only on the wide shot on camera 1. Plan B is set up for situations in which the moderator takes a very active role in the program, and as a result, needs a close-up shot ready at all times.

Plan A has obvious limitations but has a basic utility in predictable situations such as a period in the program during which the host is bringing out individual responses from each participant. The beginning and ending of discussion programs usually assume this structure.

A director would probably quickly shift over to Plan B during the more active phases of the conversation. By holding camera 3 on a cover shot, camera 1 is able to get a close-up shot of the moderator. Camera 1 also has the option of getting close-up shots of those who turn camera left for a two-person conversation. In this situation, camera 2 then has the option of a close-up of the other person or a two-shot of both speakers. The reverse structure is also possible with camera 1 on the two-shot and camera 2 on the single of the person facing camera right.

Even taken together, these two shooting plans by no means exhaust the possibilities available within an L-shaped seating configuration. The use of camera 2 as a cover camera from either a left-side or right-side studio position opens up another series of coverage patterns. The suggestion of cameras 1 or 3 for cover shots stems from the fact that their angle to the set allows for a more interesting grouping of all participants in the frame. Each person's face occupies a larger proportion of the frame than in a wide shot from the center—which also results in empty space at the top and bottom of the frame.

In the press of a fast moving program, the director often is tempted to give up the cover shot and use that camera temporarily for smaller group shots and close-ups. It is an option that even the most experienced directors use with considerable care. Invariably, when all cameras are committed

to the three people who are dominating the conversation, the fourth (off-camera) voice suddenly starts speaking.

Calling Shots

In a discussion program, it is essential that preparatory commands always be used in conjunction with the commands of execution. An inexperienced director might be tempted to think that a needed shot could be put on the air instantaneously if only the command of execution were given. To do so, however, would be to increase appreciably the possibilities for error. The spontaneous nature of talk programs makes the command of preparation doubly important. The technical director needs this lead time to be certain that the right shot is readied. Of equal importance is the possibility that the camera operators need this time for final adjustment of the framing or as a warning to hold a shot they might otherwise be in the process of changing.

A good procedure for the director on a fast moving talk show is to give a "ready" for a probable next shot as soon as possible after the previous shot is on the line. This does not remove any option for a subsequent change in the upcoming shot; it simply aids the director in staying ahead of the action. An example of how the director can inform the crew of several probable courses of action would be as follows.

"Ready camera 3 . . . take 3" (cover shot). "Ready camera 2 on a close-up of guest C . . . camera 1, hold the moderator close-up, but be ready to move over to guest B."

In this situation, guest C has just interrupted the moderator. The director can afford to wait on the cover shot to see whether guest C will continue talking or whether the moderator will start talking again. At the same time, the director has noticed that guest B also is trying to break into the conversation.

Now that you understand the basics of directing a discussion show, you and your classmates should be able to undertake the program production project in Appendix D. This discussion format can be used for a repeated number of production exercises within the class. A minimum running time of five minutes for each exercise is suggested so that each director has an opportunity to become familiar with the pattern of the conversational flow and the related continuity of camera shots. A realistic element can be added by having the AD and the stage manager feed the moderator countdown cues for time remaining in the exercise. Directors should be prepared for the fact that the transition from the body of a program to the closing segment can be difficult unless cues and other instructions are given well in advance.

SUMMARY

Part of directing involves deciding on the aesthetic aspects of the program. Often an *art director* works with the director on the overall "look" of the show, integrating sets, graphics, lighting, costumes, and makeup.

Performers should be advised on their clothing so they do not clash with the set or disappear into it. The *saturation, line,* and *contrast* of what they wear should be considered. They also should not wear clothes that give a *moiré effect* or interfere with *chroma key.* Costumes should be neatly constructed because imperfections will show on the screen.

Makeup is used to *enhance, correct,* or *create* appearance. Often it is not needed for performers, but it is definitely needed when actors must look unusual. The primary elements of makeup are *base, powder, highlights, shadows, rouge, lipstick,* and *eye makeup.* Hair styles should fit the nature of the person and the overall program.

Directors must understand, and usually follow, *continuity* principles. In general shots should go from *collective (wide shot)* to *particularized (close-up).* Directors must always be thinking about which camera they are going to take next so that they do not get in a bind of not having the shot they need available. Camera angles should be *crossed* to create the best head-on shots. Directors should remember the *three-to-one cutting ratio* so that the audience keeps its orientation. Matching shots that appear to *jump* and subject *position jumps* should be avoided. Directors should also refrain from *crossing the line,* as it relates to the *axis of action* and *axis of conversation.*

In the area of *transitions,* directors should *cut* to indicate that there has been no change in time or locale, *dissolve* to signify change in place or time, *superimpose* to intensify an image, *fade* to create a strong separation, *defocus* to go back in time, and *wipe* to create a fancy transition. Transitions should occur to capture action, show a speaker starting to talk, establish a reaction, or follow the beat of music.

When planning a discussion program (or almost any type of program), a director should consider *staging, lighting, shot continuity, transitions,* and *camera blocking.*

CHAPTER 14

Field Production

M ost of what we have discussed in previous chapters has dealt with *live* or *live-on-tape multi-camera* productions shot in a studio environment. However, many productions are shot totally or partially in out-of-studio locations with one camera. This technique is often called **"film-style shooting"** because most motion pictures are shot with one camera that takes shots one by one from all the various angles employed in multiple-camera shoots. It is also referred to as **field production** because it takes place in the field rather than in a studio. Sometimes it is also called *remote* or *location* production.

There are numerous similarities between studio production and field production—mainly because much of the same equipment is used. A microphone is a microphone whether it is on a game show set or at the scene of a fire. Pictures should be focused and well-composed, and talent should maintain eye contact, whether in the studio or in the field. And yet there are many differences caused, to some degree, by the lack of control that exists outside of the studio. Many extraneous noises cannot be stopped; the sun and clouds cannot be controlled; crowds often cannot be maneuvered to remain outside of the camera's shot. In addition, postproduction editing takes on a much greater role because the single-camera technique obviously does not utilize the switcher during the production.

This chapter will concentrate on single-camera field production, looking at the similarities and differences between it and studio production. It is organized in the same manner as the rest of the book—beginning with a general introduction and then covering audio, lights, cameras, pictorial elements, video recording, editing, producing, and directing. In that way this chapter will serve as a review of the rest of the book, while at the same time, introducing concepts that are crucial to this increasingly popular form of production—for news and public affairs, dramatic programs, music videos, documentaries, corporate videos, instructional programs, and so forth. Suggestions for maintaining an efficiently operating crew and the related paperwork will also be covered.

14.1 INTRODUCTION

Field production, like its studio-based sister, requires both *discipline and technique*. It involves the development of a professional attitude and a knowledge of equipment and aesthetics. (See section 1.1.)

Discipline

In some ways field production requires more discipline because, once away from the studio, you cannot easily return for a forgotten item. Teamwork is a *must*; crews are usually smaller so it is hard to cover for anyone who is undependable.

One reason crews are smaller is that much less gear is involved. Only one camera is used to shoot, eliminating the need for all but one camera operator. No one is needed to operate a switcher; the camera

goes directly to the VCR because there is no need to cut between two or more cameras. Graphics are generally added during postproduction not during shooting.

Some crews are as small as two people—one to operate the **camcorder** (camera and VCR in one unit) and another to hold the mic and interview talent thus serving as producer-director-talent-audio operator. Other shoots have larger crews that include a producer, a director, an audio operator, a camera-VCR operator, someone to set up lights, someone to watch for continuity problems, and a production assistant or two to handle any other miscellaneous duties. (See figure 14-1.)

As with most task-oriented working groups, an efficient operation must have a clearly established plan for areas of responsibility and authority. Whatever the size of the crew, each individual member of the shoot should have a *clear idea* of his or her responsibilities—but with the understanding that flexible working arrangements may find each one helping out with other jobs.

One of the absolute essentials that all crew members on a field shoot must handle carefully is *cleanup*. If a crew member carelessly leaves a mic cable on the floor of the studio, someone else will probably find it later and put it away. But if a mic cable is left in the middle of a park, it will quickly disappear. Everything must be conscientiously disassembled, coiled, stowed away, and neatly packed—in part as a courtesy to the next people who use the equipment, and in part, because such care adds to the life of the equipment. Cleanup requires discipline. It is not glamorous work, but it must be done.

Techniques

Techniques are also very important for a field shoot. All crew members must know how to operate the equipment well. Miles

(a)

(b)

FIGURE 14-1

Crew configurations differ depending on the taping situation.

For the first taping (a) only two crew members were needed, because the footage was being shot silent to go with music during the opening credits. The director told the children what to do and the camera operator taped the material. For the second taping (b), which was much more complicated, five people attended—the producer who was coordinating with the people running the children's art workshop; the director; the audio operator; the camera operator; and a combination lighting person and production assistant.

away from "home base," they cannot turn to the instructor or technician when they have no picture in the viewfinder.

Field equipment, like studio equipment, changes rapidly. In fact, it did not exist at all during the first two decades of TV. Now, with each year, cameras, microphones, and lights become smaller, lighter, and "smarter" in that they are capable of allowing their users to increase creativity and flexibility.

Remote shoots are often more fun than studio programs simply because they are in unusual locations and offer interesting challenges. Anyone planning to be employed in television production should be carefully schooled in the disciplines and techniques of field production as well as studio production.

14.2 AUDIO

As with other technical components, many of the elements of field production audio are the same as those for studio audio; any differences are caused primarily by the uncontrollable elements of the outside world. As a starting point, ask the same questions concerning frequency, pickup pattern, impedance, and usage categories for both studio and remote productions (see sections 3.1 and 3.2).

Microphones

Sometimes the answers are different, however. Generally, microphones need to be more directional for remote locations because of all the extraneous noise. By the same token, mics that are less sensitive (and therefore need to be located closer to the talent) are desired because they will pick up less of the background noise.

Also, because of the transportation jolts and rough handling that field equipment is

subjected to, mics for remote shoots usually are of a more rugged design—**dynamic** rather than **condenser.** *Quality* and *frequency response* often have to be sacrificed for *dependability* and *ruggedness.*

Fishpoles and **hand mics** tend to be used most frequently in the field. The fishpoles (see figure 14-2) are common for dramas, where the mic should not be seen in the picture. Hand mics are common in interview situations, where the presence of the mic is accepted. Another type of mic, the **shotgun,** is used in situations where the subject being taped is far from the camera and cannot be miked easily (a lion in the jungle, or a man on a horse). Shotgun mics are highly directional and can pick up sound from long distances. However, because of the high directionality, they must be pointed at the subject accurately so that they pick up the desired sound. Wireless mics come in very handy when subjects need to move around a great deal.

At times you may want to attach the microphone to the camera to eliminate the need for someone holding it. This is usually *not* a good idea since the camera is located at some distance from the person talking and is likely to pick up noises close to the camera much more efficiently than it picks up the person talking. As a general rule, in the field, microphones should always be as close as possible to the people talking—closer than in studio production—because of all the background and extraneous noise.

Control Equipment

The sophisticated control room equipment that produces clean, well-balanced sound is not available at a remote site. There are no patch bays, equalizers, or separate audiotape recorders. Usually there is not even a board—just a "ballpark" meter and some cheap headphones. Audio on a remote is only *transduced* and

FIGURE 14-2

The audio operator is positioning the boom so that it will pick up sound as well as possible without getting in the shot.

Photo courtesy of Amy Phillips

recorded—and usually *monitored*. Channeling, mixing, amplifying, and shaping (section 2.2) are all accomplished in postproduction, and yet, great care must be taken to keep recording levels within a consistent range so that they can be matched when edited. Any differences in the levels of sounds will become very obvious when different shots are assembled together in the editing process.

One way to assure consistent levels is to utilize the **automatic gain control (AGC)** available on most tape recorders. This automatically raises the volume of sounds that are soft and lowers the volume of loud sounds. AGC is *not* always the solution to keeping audio levels within a consistent range, however. This is because AGC can be the cause of another serious sound problem encountered with outdoor audio. The AGC cannot

distinguish between desired and undesired sound; it boosts anything that is low. Therefore, when no one is speaking, the level of the background noise is automatically amplified—producing a hissing or roaring effect.

Because there is a built-in delay factor of one second or so, the effect is most noticeable at the beginning of segments or during long pauses. Attempts to erase this unwanted sound involve the risk of upcutting program audio.

Audio **balance** is particularly difficult if two people are talking and one has a very soft voice while the other has a booming projection. AGC cannot completely compensate. Sometimes the better solution is to record each person through his or her individual mic onto a separate track and then try to match the volumes in postproduction.

Audio Tracks

Most ¾ inch videotape recorders include two **linear** audio tracks, usually identified as *channel 1* and *channel 2*. Channel 2 is generally the better one to use for recording because on most common formats it is located as an inside track on the videotape. Channel 1 is at the edge of the tape, so it is more subject to any distortion if the tape wrinkles even slightly. Also, channel 1 is often used to record a separate time code, so many facilities routinely use only channel 2 for audio. However, if separate audio sources (such as loud and weak voices) need to be recorded in the field simultaneously, to be mixed later, the two channels should be used.

Many of the ½ inch and 8mm formats are capable of recording sound diagonally, in the same manner that the picture is recorded. One method of recording sound this way is referred to as **hi-fi** (or **AFM-audio frequency modulation**), and the other is called **PCM (pulse code modulation)**. Both of these methods allow for high quality stereo recording and playback. With hi-fi recording, the sound is recorded with the picture and *cannot* be separated from it during editing. With PCM, the sound is recorded on its own real estate and can be separated for editing purposes (see figure 14-3).

Sometimes you will be able to choose whether you want to record linear, hi-fi, PCM, or some combination of them. When you have options, you should note how the audio was recorded because this information will be needed when editing begins.

Portable Mixers

If you have a large number of different audio sources that need to be recorded at the same time, you will need to take a portable audio mixer on location with you. You can then feed several mics through the board, their levels can be set individually, and this mix-down can be recorded on the videotape on one of the linear channels or on the hi-fi or PCM track.

However, setting up such an audio board takes additional space and time, both of which are often unavailable on a remote shoot. Also, if the remote is taking place in a small area, you must be careful to listen for phase problems caused by placing the mics too close together.

Wildtrack

Audio operators on location should always make sure they record some separate **wildtrack** sound—background sound from the location recorded with no specific voices. Sometimes this is for a specific purpose. For example, a narrator may be standing next to a machine that is important to the story line but the machine has a distinctive sound. In the final edited program, shots that include the machine are to have a voice-over narration, which is to be recorded later in the studio. If the director wants to have the sound of the machine as a part of the background under the narration, then a wildtrack of that sound must be recorded for a later audio mix.

At other times the wildtrack sound is just general background noise that can be used to cover abrupt transitions during postproduction editing. Good sound operators will make a practice of recording numerous pieces of wildtrack sound as protection against unforeseen editing problems.

Extraneous Noise

The audio operator must also listen carefully to the sound that is occurring and being recorded while a take is being shot. The human brain *subconsciously* filters out unwanted sound. The noise of an airplane flying overhead often goes unnoticed by

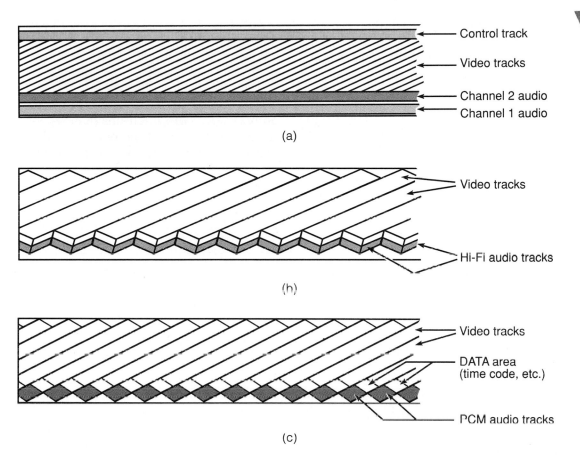

Control track
Video tracks
Channel 2 audio
Channel 1 audio

(a)

Video tracks

Hi-Fi audio tracks

(b)

Video tracks

DATA area
(time code, etc.)

PCM audio tracks

(c)

FIGURE 14-3

Three different ways that audio is recorded on field systems.

(a) Two linear tracks are available on some formats, including U-matic. (b) The hi-fi audio track rides with the video and cannot be separated from it during editing. (c) PCM audio is recorded on a slant-track following each video field.

two people engaged in conversation; they effectively hear only each other. But this **selective attention principle** does not work with videotaped presentation. An unnoticed airplane recorded on an audio track will come through loud and clear on playback. For that reason, the audio person must listen intently and stop production if an unwanted noise is too evident.

In many ways, a person operating audio on a remote shoot must have a disciplined "feel" for audio. He or she must have enough experience to know how something will sound in the final edited program.

14.3 LIGHTING

The basic **three-point lighting** approach (see section 4.5) is appropriate for remote shoots as well as in the studio. Likewise, **contrast ratio, color temperature,** and other principles of lighting (see section 4.2) apply, at least in theory, to location work. Once again, problems occur when dealing with uncontrolled situations. In this case, the problems associated with lighting indoors are quite different than those found outside.

Indoor Location Lighting

Since lighting grids are far from common in university classrooms, corporate offices, hospitals, and other locations, portable lighting apparatus must be brought to the remote shoot by the production crew. *Portable lights* (see figure 14-4) usually are mounted on stands that can then be placed in positions roughly approximating those of the basic **key, fill,** and **back** lights.

Often this is difficult or impossible to accomplish because of lack of space or because the light stands will show in the camera's picture. The back light is particularly tricky because it is essentially impossible to position it correctly without having the stand visible in a long shot. Occasionally, clip-on **internal reflectors** can be clamped onto a door or tall piece of furniture to serve as a back light. However, many remotes are shot with only key and fill lights.

In fact, many news shoots utilize only one light; it is mounted on the camera and is used only for basic illumination. The result is a very flat, nonaesthetic, washed-out effect—which is, nevertheless, better than shooting a silhouette.

The lighting instruments taken on a remote shoot are usually limited, too. **Scoops, ellipsoidal spots,** and even **Fresnels** (see section 4.4) are too bulky to lug along. And certainly the vast array of lights available in the studio cannot be taken. The main portable lights used are **broads** (see figure 4-12), but their beams are somewhat difficult to control.

FIGURE 14-4

This Lowel portable lighting kit contains the lights and supporting equipment needed for effective field production.

Photo courtesy of Lowel-Light

Lighting Control

Lack of a dimmer board adds to the control problems. In order to increase or decrease the intensity of a light, the stand must be moved in accordance with the principles of the **inverse square law** (see section 4.6). However, space limitations may hinder this. Space and time limitations also hinder the use of scrims, barn doors, flags, and other devices that could help diffuse or shape the light.

Power

Another big problem is securing adequate electrical power. A studio is specially wired in anticipation of the power that will be needed to meet extensive lighting demands. People's homes and offices are not. Lighting properly with key, fill, and back lights all plugged into one circuit is almost guaranteed to blow the circuit breaker.

For this reason, it is particularly important to learn ahead of time where the circuit breakers are, how many amps each circuit is rated for, and which outlets are on which circuit. You should also become familiar with the basic formula: *watts = volts × amps.* (This is often referred to as the "West Virginia" formula, *W = VA.*) The watts will be written somewhere on the lamp of your lighting instrument—usually 500, 1,000, or 2,000 watts. Amperes should be indicated on the circuit breaker—usually 10, 15, or 20 amps. Voltage is regulated by the power company and in most ordinary circumstances will be 110 volts. (In industrial settings, it may be 220 volts.) Therefore, if the circuit breaker is rated for 10 amps and the voltage is 110, you can plug in lights totaling 1,100 watts on that circuit. To be on the safe side, use a figure of 100 for the voltage (this also makes the arithmetic easier). So a 20-amp circuit could handle 2,000 watts.

However, you cannot assume your lights can use the whole circuit. The total wattage of all appliances and devices on the circuit must be taken into consideration. The office copier or the home refrigerator may be using the same circuit that you want to plug into. One group of students were taping a remote shoot at a factory; they had been recording without problems for an hour or so when suddenly the lights went out. Lunchtime had arrived and the employees began using the company microwave oven that was on the same circuit as the lights.

Usually you must plug in lights on at least two separate circuits, and generally, this means using plugs in two different areas. In many homes and offices, outlets in one room are all on the same circuit, and you may have to go several rooms down the hall to use a different circuit. This means you must take along extension cords.

Safety

The use of extension cords raises another question—the problem of safety. First of all, make sure that the extension cords you plan on using are rated for the electrical load you expect to plug into them. Using cords that are not heavy-duty will result in tripping the circuit breaker—or worse yet, overheating and starting a fire.

Also, electrical cable strung all over the floor is likely to cause people to trip—often unplugging the light and/or bringing down the light stand (as well as causing bodily injury). Where cords must be laid along the floor, covering them with a wide tape will help ensure that they will not be tripped over. Ideally, you should run the cords along the walls and up over door jambs. (See figure 14-5.) For these taping purposes, you must bring along heavy-duty tape—preferably something like *duct tape* that is a very strong adhesive. Where cords must be taped to painted surfaces, it is best to use *masking tape* that will not peel off paint when it is removed.

Lights also create a safety problem because of their heat. They should not be placed where someone is likely to bump into them accidentally. Also, they should not be placed where they are touching curtains or paper and could thereby start a smoldering fire. At the end of a shoot, they should be turned off *first* and packed away *last.* This gives them time to cool before crew members must handle them.

Available Light

One other problem associated with shooting indoors comes from available light. If at all possible, you should turn off all regular lights and just use the quartz lights from your remote lighting kit. However,

FIGURE 14-5
Crew member taping a power cord above a doorway to ensure that no one will trip over it during the recording.

sometimes available lights can be used for general illumination—if they are of a color temperature close to 3,200 degrees **Kelvin** (see section 4.2). Regular incandescent light bulbs can usually be used, but fluorescents should definitely be turned off. Not only will they result in a recording with a definite blue tint, they may also create a hum or buzz on the sound track.

Outdoor light coming through windows should also be avoided, if at all possible, because it is about 5,500 degrees K—far bluer than the 3,200-degree K quartz lights. The problem is not with the outdoor light itself, but with the fact that you are *mixing* types of light—daylight and quartz. If you set the camera's filter for quartz light and some of your light

source is from daylight, your footage will look blue. If you set the filter for daylight, the footage will be orange because you are using some quartz light. **Gels** are made to place on windows to change the color temperature of the outdoor light, but they are expensive and difficult to install. A simpler solution is to avoid mixing the types of light.

Outdoor Location Lighting

If you are shooting outside, your main source of light is the *sun*. This has both advantages and disadvantages. You do not need to worry about light stands or power requirements. However, you have no control over the sun. It changes position; it can be overly intense; it darts behind passing clouds. Its color temperature changes as the day progresses (ranging from 4,500 to 12,000 degrees K)—so that scenes shot at noon will not match scenes shot at 5:00 P.M. Not only will these scenes have a color switch, but they are likely to show different lengths of shadows, different molding of facial features, and different amounts of glare. This is a particular problem if long shots are taped at noon while close-ups, which are to be intercut, are not shot until 5:00 P.M.

Second Light Sources

Sometimes the sun is so bright that you need *extra* lights. This seeming contradiction is caused by the fact that a bright sun can wash out facial features. It acts, in essence, like a very bright key light. To counteract this, artificial lights can be added to create the effect of a fill. Of course, these lights have to be the same color temperature as daylight.

One way to do this is to cover the quartz lights used indoors with special filter gels that convert the 3,200-degree K light to 5,500-plus degrees K. However, the filters cut down on the efficiency of the

FIGURE 14-7

As an example of a technique used in portable lighting, these four 12,000-watt HMI instruments were focused through a scrim to produce a soft, flat illumination for an interior scene.

FIGURE 14-6

Fresnel *Mole Solarspot.*

This 2,500-watt HMI (hydrogen medium-arc-length iodine) light is used in field production where it is necessary to match the color temperature of sunlight. The control unit known as a *ballast* protects the lamp from sudden surges of power and provides for longer bulb life.

Photo courtesy of Mole Richardson

light, so more lights are needed than normal. Another way is to use **HMI** (hydrogen medium-arc-length iodine) lights that are made to produce 5,500-degree K light (see figure 14-6). These lights have a separate **ballast** that protects the lamp from power surges.

To minimize problems from the sun passing behind clouds and changing color temperature as the day wears on, large HMI floods can actually be used to create an artificial source of sunlight (see figure 14-7)—even for interior scenes.

If auxiliary lights are needed, getting power to them can be a problem. Powerful battery-operated lights do exist, but they are not commonly or inexpensively available.

A more feasible alternative for obtaining a second light from a different direction is to use a reflector. A commercially available *foil reflector* can be used to bounce sunlight onto a subject's face from almost any direction. (See figure 4-30.) And if the sun is behind the subject (functioning as a back light), the reflector placed in front of the subject can be used to provide a satisfactory key light. Even if a professional reflector is not available, any large piece of white material (a white poster board, for example) can be used in an emergency to provide some fill light from a complementary direction. Obviously, the more highly polished or reflective the surface of the reflector is, the more efficient it will be. (See figure 14-8.)

FIGURE 14-8

In this setup, reflectors are being used to bounce the sunlight onto the two actors sitting on the sand, providing both fill and back light.

Lighting Individual Shots

Overall, lighting can be one of the biggest headaches of field production. However, there is one very distinct advantage that location lighting has over live-on-tape lighting—location lighting allows each shot to be lit individually. When a studio program is shot with three cameras simultaneously, lighting must be general enough that it will provide acceptable illumination for any camera shot that is to be used. Often in multiple-camera shooting, compromises have to be made in setting the lights, and few shots are really properly lit. With location shooting, however, the camera is stopped after each shot, and the lights can be reset to light the next shot optimally.

14.4 CAMERAS

Most of the aesthetic principles of picture composition (see sections 6.2 and 6.3) apply in the field as well as in the studio. So do the general principles dealing with f-stops, depth of field, lens ratio, focusing, and filters. (See sections 5.3 and 5.4.)

Camera Controls

However, in a studio, once cameras are set, the characteristics under which they shoot remain fairly constant. White balance set at the beginning of a studio program, for instance, can be depended upon to give accurate color throughout a taping.

White Balancing

Such is not the case with field production. **White balance** must be reset frequently as lighting conditions change—because the white balance control adjusts the strength of the basic video level to suit the composition of the light that is available for an individual shot. It "reads" a designated item as *white* and then re-adjusts the electronics associated with the other colors so that they will render true color. (See section 5.5.)

As the sun peeks in and out of clouds, the light source changes and you need to readjust the white balance. The changes in the sun's color temperature over the course of a day also require changing white balance. Going from outdoors to indoors definitely requires repeating the white balance procedure.

Fortunately, white balancing is easy—just the push of a button on most cameras. In fact, some cameras automatically white balance as changes in color temperature occur. If the camera you are using does not automatically redo white balancing, however, your main white balancing problem may simply be remembering to do it. Also, you must remember to bring something white to the shoot to be used for **reference white**—a piece of paper, a white sweater.

Filters

A related item very easy to forget in the process of field shooting is the changing of the camera **filter** (see section 5.5). Most cameras have four filters—for instance, one for indoor quartz light (which also works for outdoor sunrise and sunset), one for sunny daylight, one for cloudy outdoor shooting, and one that acts as a cap.

When you move from outdoors to indoors, or vice versa, you must change the filter, or your footage will have a decided orange or blue cast. The outdoor filters are orange to compensate for the fact that quartz light is "orangish" and daylight is "bluish." The main difference between the *sunny daylight* and *cloudy outdoor* filters is the amount of **neutral density** in the filter. Neutral density lessens the intensity of the light by making the filter darker; therefore, the *sunny* filter has more neutral density than the *cloudy* filter.

Gain

Many remote cameras have **db (decibel)** gain switches to use in instances of low light. This boosts the electronics so that the camera "sees" better in the dark. However, using this switch makes the picture grainier and also shifts the color somewhat. It should be used only when it is absolutely impossible to add light—generally in the covering of a news story.

Power

Another problem in the field is the power source for the camera. Most cameras can be operated either on regular *AC* (household alternating current) or on *batteries*. Whenever possible, AC should be used because it is more reliable. However, cameras do add wattage to electrical circuits that may already be taxed from your portable lights.

Batteries have a disadvantage in that they do run out of charge—usually when you are in the middle of shooting your most important scene! If you do use batteries, make sure the battery is fully charged before you are scheduled to take the camera on location.

Secondly, while in the field, make sure you are not unintentionally discharging the battery when you are not shooting. By all means, disconnect the battery while you transport equipment from one location to another. Some cameras have a *standby* position that keeps the electronics operational but cuts down on battery use. This should be used while shots are being set up and rehearsed. Cameras differ as to how they conserve on battery power, so be sure to find out when the battery is and is not engaged on your particular camera.

Camera Mounts and Movement

Keeping a picture steady on a remote camera can be a problem. You usually do not have the luxury of the sturdy **pedestals** and **cranes** available in a studio (see section 6.1). What you are more likely to have is a three-legged **tripod** and/or a strong shoulder.

Whenever possible, the tripod should be used; it is steadier than the strongest of shoulders. Many student shots have been ruined because the camera operator or director did not want to take the time to put the camera on the tripod—thus fulfilling the axiom, "There's never time to do it right, but there's always time to do it over."

Pans, tilts, and zooms can all be executed very effectively on a tripod mount. However, assuming you do not have the benefit of a field crane (see figure 6-6), movements such as trucks and dollies do require the human body to simulate wheeled movement. Improvised dollies and trucks can sometimes be achieved with wheeled conveyances such as a child's wagon or a grocery cart.

Achieving smooth movement can be difficult, especially in a crowd. Shakiness in news footage is accepted by the audience because the camera is being used *subjectively*. It is the audience eye, showing people what they would see were they there—including the bumping and jostling. But, even so, camera operators should try to keep the picture as steady as possible at all times.

Camera operators and directors must also be willing to reposition the camera frequently for both aesthetic and informational purposes. This requires effort and muscle on the part of the person operating the camera, but it is needed for everything from reaction shots of the reporter re-asking questions to low-angle shots to convey a sense of power.

Camera Care and Maintenance

Care of the camera must also be a high-priority item for the camera operator. The high level of activity and unanticipated problems on any location production occasionally mean that some of the usual equipment precautions may be temporarily forgotten. Cameras are very vulnerable to the careless treatment they may be given on a field shoot.

The lens should be capped between scenes and whenever the camera is moved—because that is a time when light or stray objects such as pebbles can accidentally strike a camera. **Tube** cameras need particular protection from strong beams of light because these can permanently damage the tube. **CCD** cameras are not so affected, but they should still be protected from undesired elements.

Many types of professional location productions pose enormous engineering challenges for the optimum functioning and protection of cameras and other equipment. Special housings and mountings have to be used for many adverse situations: dust protection in arid country; heaters for arctic conditions; gyroscopic mountings for helicopter shots; and underwater housings for perhaps the most adverse environment of all. (See figure 14-9.)

In all probability, you will not be shooting in any of these extreme conditions for class projects, but whoever is operating the

camera should realize that he or she is in charge of an expensive piece of rather delicate equipment that must remain operational for many future projects.

14.5 PICTORIAL ELEMENTS

Pictorial elements receive less attention in remote shooting than in studio shooting. Graphics are usually added after the fact, and sets are determined by the nature of the location. Nevertheless, the basics of pictorial design exist in the field as well as in the studio.

Graphics

Graphics are essentially nonexistent in actual remote shooting. Some consumer cameras have built-in **character generators** so that graphics can be included during taping, but these are generally used only for slating/identification purposes. Occasionally, an on-set wall chart may be shot as a cutaway, but it is not likely to be designed for television, so the camera operator must frame it as well as possible under the circumstances.

If actual physical charts or illustrations are to be included in a program, they are better shot in a studio where lighting can be *controlled*. Most graphics, of course, are computer generated (see section 7.3). All of these will be incorporated into the program during the postproduction editing.

Sets

Sets, as such, do not usually exist either. The main reason you go on a location shoot is to obtain realistic scenery and settings that are not possible with constructed sets in a

FIGURE 14-10

Hallway to be considered for a location shoot.

How many problems can you spot if you plan on using this hallway for a remote production? How will the mixture of indoor and outdoor light affect color temperature and white balance settings? What can be done about the potential glare? How will the automatic iris function as the talent walks along the corridor—moving in and out of extremely bright spots? What will be the safest angles to use?

studio. However, when you are scouting to find proper locations, keep in mind the *pictorial design elements* discussed in sections 7.1 and 7.2. For example, yellow and reds are warm colors, and greens and blues are cool colors—whether they are in a studio or out in the country. Whether you are shooting indoors or out, the principles of balance and mass, lines and angles, always apply.

Unless you find some very cooperative people or you are willing to pay a great deal of money, you cannot usually change much in a location setting. You *can* clean up someone's desk so that the clutter will not be visually distracting; but you *cannot* readily change the color of the walls, the location of trees, or the placement of windows.

When shooting interior scenes, windows do present particular problems in that they cause glare and interfere with proper lighting. The best advice is to *avoid*

shooting into windows. However, it may not always be possible to avoid a passing shot of a window; perhaps it is absolutely necessary to pan with the talent while he or she walks across a room, passing in front of a window. In such a situation, you should consider disabling the automatic **iris** control; set the **f-stop** manually for the best interior (nonwindow) lighting and keep it consistent as the talent passes in front of the window. This will result in an overexposed background through the window, but the alternative (if the automatic iris is left on) is to allow the talent to turn to a silhouette when passing in front of the window.

In one sense, the setting is much easier (and less expensive) to deal with in a remote location than in a studio because very little, if anything, needs to be constructed. However, an improper setting can totally destroy the concept and atmosphere of your program. (See figure 14-10.) You can wind up with the wrong colors, architecture, period furnishings, traffic flow, backgrounds, and so forth. Therefore, you may have to spend many hours scouting and searching for just the right setting.

Real locations are invariably much "busier" than studio sets; they will have a lot of elements that are extraneous to what you will be taping—furniture, props, wall coverings, table objects, appliances, and so forth. As a result, you must pay particular attention to make sure you do not wind up with shots that have light switches or flower pots that look like they are growing out of someone's head.

FIGURE 14-11
Sony's Hi-8 format camcorder, the EVO-9100.

Photo courtesy of Sony Electronics, Inc.

14.6 VIDEOTAPE RECORDERS

Most modern-day field production is undertaken with camcorders, either Betacam, M-II, VHS, S-VHS, Video 8, or Hi-8. (See figure 14-11.) Therefore, the camera and recorder are the same piece of equipment, and the camera operator also becomes the videotape recorder operator. A button that is easily accessible when someone is holding the camcorder turns the recorder on and off. Sometimes ¾-inch U-matic equipment, such as that in figure 14-12 is used for field production and, when this is the case, the camera and recorder will be separate. The field recorder usually used for U-matic is smaller than the one used in the studio. It will only hold a cassette with twenty minutes of tape on it, not the thirty minute and sixty minute cassette sizes usually used in the studio.

Setup and Connections

In a studio setting, all the video equipment is more or less permanently connected. Such is not the case in the field. It is up to crew members to know how to attach all equipment. Although a camcorder may have a microphone attached to it, audio should be routed separately from an external mic whenever possible, because, as discussed previously, the microphone should be as close as possible to the talent. The VCR input for a microphone may be a *Cannon* connector, a *phone* plug, an *RCA*, or a *mini-plug*. (Review figure 9-13.) Make sure you check before you leave the studio/control room to confirm that the connector on the end of the microphone cable is the same as that required by the VCR. If it is not, change the microphone plug or get an **adapter** that will convert from one type of connector to the other. You will also want to connect headsets into the earphone output on the camcorder. Monitors are sometimes attached to VCR outputs so that the director can see what the camera operator is framing. The usual connectors for this are *BNC* or *UHF* (see figure 9-12), and again care should be taken to make sure the proper cables and connectors are brought to the remote site to connect the VCR and monitor. Monitors can be unwieldy because, when they are connected to the camcorder,

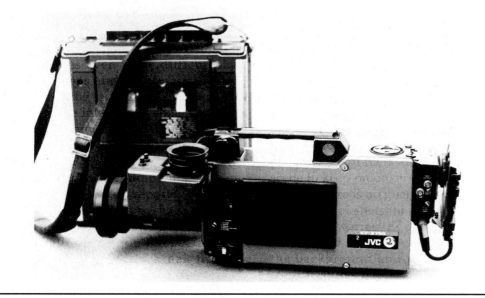

FIGURE 14-12

A typical early ¾-inch
U-matic video
recorder and camera
configuration.

they must be moved if the camera is moved. This can inhibit the camera operator's flexibility. The viewfinder of most camcorders can serve as a viewing device. After something is shot, the tape can be rewound and played back through the viewfinder so that the director can check it. This takes time, however, so many remote shoots take place without monitoring. This requires trust and complete communication between the director and the camera operator.

If the camera and recorder are separate, a **multi-pin connector** is often used to connect them. This contains, within one cable, wires for various functions—*video* (from the camera to the VCR); *audio* (in case a microphone attached to the camera is used); *power* (so that the VCR can operate from the camera's power source); *remote control* (so that the VCR can be operated by a switch on the camera); and *return* (so that the camera viewfinder can function as a monitor to view tapes after they are shot). Having a multi-pin connector gives a great deal more versatility to a production situation, but

multi-pin connectors are expensive and not all separate cameras and VCRs can accommodate them.

One good approach to the discipline of field production is to lay out all of the cables and connectors you will need for your particular assignment—and then plug everything together and operate it before you leave—just to make sure you have everything.

Taping Procedures

The camcorder/VCR operator should set the audio level and check all controls before taping begins. The operator should make sure the machine has been up to speed at least ten seconds before anything crucial is taped and, likewise, keep the machine running for about ten seconds after the shot is completed so that a strong control track will be available for editing.

The VCR should not be left in *pause* for long periods of time because this will wear the oxide off the tape and clog the video heads (see section 9.4).

FIGURE 14-13

This Sony EVO 9700 Hi-8 editing system is typical of what educational and corporate facilities use for linear editing.

Photo courtesy of Sony Electronics, Inc.

During taping, the person in charge of recording should be watching all the "vital signs," most of which appear on indicators in the viewfinder monitor—end-of-tape warning, battery condition, low light, and so forth. In most instances this person will also be framing shots and listening to the headphone to make sure the audio is recording properly. Because the person is doing so many tasks, he or she must be extra careful to make sure the recorder part of the camcorder is operating properly. The best of shots will be useless if they are not recorded properly and ready to be edited.

14.7 EDITING

Many of the options and operations of editing are the same for multi-camera and field production. The less expensive systems that use an **edit controller** and **source** and **edit decks** (see figure 14-13) are most likely to be found in educational institutions, while the professional world has largely moved to the newer, more expensive **nonlinear** digital editing systems (see figure 14-14). The editing procedures that involve **time code, assemble** and **insert** modes, determining edit points, previewing, trimming, reviewing, A/B rolling, and the like (see section 10.4) are the same regardless whether the source material was shot in the field or in the studio.

What is different, however, is the emphasis placed on the editing process, and the expanded role of audio editing.

The Editing Process

Because much of the editing done in conjunction with studio-based production is

FIGURE 14-14

This Avid system is typical of what is used for professionally produced programs.

Photo courtesy of Avid Technologies, Inc.

intended to correct mistakes made during production or put together short roll-ins to be played during production, the editing can usually be accomplished rather quickly.

Sometimes the one or two edits that are needed to improve a program can be accomplished right after production is finished while most of the crew is cleaning up. The program is then complete, and no one needs to give thought to further editing.

Such is not the case with material shot single-camera. The program is *literally* put together during postproduction—a process that is often long and drawn out. As all professional producers know, the process of "getting into" this final phase of postproduction is a crucial time. Much of the strength—and discipline—of a good producer is an ability to generate the sense of momentum and enthusiasm that is needed to complete a production. In live television, the relentless clock focuses everyone's attention; in single-camera postproduction, the constant pressure of a knowledgeable guiding hand is needed.

It may be difficult to understand the time frame that is necessary for the editing process; an inexperienced crew may initially waste a considerable amount of energy and effort. Usually, this phase passes as crew members become more efficient at their assigned responsibilities and the leadership and organization become more evident— just as they did during the shooting process.

Although many professional editing sessions involve only the producer or the director working in conjunction with the editor (or even the editor working alone with only a detailed set of notes), student postproduction sessions should, as much as possible, become a *learning process* for the entire team. Without proper organization, however, this process can drift into noisy chaos. The important thing is that there has to be someone who is acknowledged as being definitely "in charge." This may be the producer, the director, or the editor; but it should be the same person who has initiated and established the basic structure of the project.

FIGURE 14-15

For students, a two-person editing team can be a very efficient way to work. Many professionals, however, prefer to work alone whenever possible.

Editing sessions, which can last for hours, should be set up so that while the person operating the edit control unit is executing each transfer/edit, a second person or team is finalizing the next edit decision—locating the precise reel number, footage/revolution counter number, and exact word cue for the inpoint and outpoint. (See figure 14-15.) Other people can be working on constructing the graphics that will be used for the opening and closing. Still others can be composing and/or mixing music and other audio elements. As with the production phase, the producer and/or director should give each person a clear idea of what his or her role is in the postproduction process.

Audio Editing

For a studio production, audio is usually mixed while the program is being taped. Music is brought in at the beginning and end of the show, and sound effects are incorporated as the production is underway. Single-camera productions shot without benefit of a sophisticated audio board do not lend themselves to audio mixing during the production phase. Obtaining good dialogue, interview audio levels, or on-camera narration is all that can really be expected in the field.

As a result, for professional single-camera productions, audio editing is often undertaken separately from video editing. While one person is editing the picture and the principle dialogue shot in the field, other people are attending to music and sound effects. Dramatic productions are the most complicated from an audio point of view. Someone, often the director, must first determine where audio elements are needed. Where will the music be brought in and taken out? What sound effects are needed? Which sounds taped in the field need to be rerecorded because they are not good enough? Once all this has been decided, a musician is asked to compose the music, someone obtains effects from sound effects CDs or special libraries,[1] and sometimes some members of the cast are brought back into a studio where they record their lines over again—a process known as **automatic dialogue replacement (ADR).**

After all the sounds have been gathered, they are placed on a **multi-track** tape or in one of the digitized computer **workstations** that handle audio. Here the sounds are positioned so that they are heard where they are needed during the production. They are also **mixed** together so that they are in a proper volume relationship with each other. For example, the music should not be so loud that the voices cannot be heard, and the sound of a gunshot should be louder than the sound of rain in the background. The average TV drama, commercial, documentary, or top-flight industrial production has a final sound track that is the result of the skilled mixing of anywhere from sixteen to thirty-two separate sound tracks together onto the final mix track.[2]

Audio training facilities for most colleges and universities do not approach this level of sophistication—although inexpensive audio software that operates with off-the-shelf computers is enabling some universities to have at least semi-sophisticated audio mixing capability. Additionally, many TV production students have not had the opportunity for a substantial course in audio production.

---

1. Many commercial sources—such as APM's Broadcast One of Hollywood, Media General of Memphis, and Sound Ideas of Toronto—have extensive production music libraries available on CDs.

2. Some professional music recording sessions will use in excess of 100 different tracks. Quincy Jones, for example, has used over 200 in some sessions! This involves several *slave* tapes (up to twenty-four tracks each) that are pre-mixed before the final mixing session. Some audio consoles, however, can handle more than fifty inputs for a single mixing session.

Therefore, it is all the more important that the preparation for the sound track must start with the very first planning of the shape of the project. The director and producer should question each other continually as to the exact details of how each sound or combination of sounds (on-camera narrator, voice-over narrator, background noise, music, sound effects, and so forth) is to be achieved. Some of the sound work can be accomplished while production is still underway. For example, if you know you are going to need the sound effect of a dog barking, you can find it well ahead of the day you need to mix it with other sounds. One often hears the phrase, "We'll fix it in post . . ." This is an invitation to audio disaster. If you have not thoroughly thought out the procedure during preproduction planning, it is often too late to fix it in postproduction.

14.8 PRODUCING

As with studio shoots, producers are the people in charge of the *overall organization* of a remote shoot. Their busiest time is before the shoot actually begins, but they are responsible for making sure the production finishes *on time* and *on budget.*

Scripting

The same forms of scripts can be used for remote shooting as for studio shooting—**film-style scripts, two-column scripts, rundowns, outlines,** and **storyboards.** (See section 11.2.) For most forms of field production, the script is absolutely essential before planning or production can take place. Sometimes there is the tendency on the part of student crews to place a camera on someone's shoulder and assume that the location will provide the necessary material. More than one student production team has found that all of those great ideas they thought of back in the studio just seemed to disappear into thin air once they arrived at the shooting location. The very *act* of putting things down on paper is an important test of the feasibility of the operational plan.

There are times, however, in remote production when it is appropriate not to use any script at all. The most obvious example is when covering breaking news stories. But even then, some research can be undertaken ahead of time. Reporters usually keep track of the number of crimes that have been committed in a certain area, the backgrounds of the major political figures, the actions being taken by the local city council, and similar items. This material can be incorporated into what is reported from the scene.

Location Scouting

Producing a remote shoot is similar to producing a studio program in that all elements must be in the right place at the right time. However, this is usually much more complex for a remote shoot because everything is out of its usual habitat. Equipment logistics, travel arrangements, power supplies, coordination of props and talent all involve extraordinary consideration.

Finding a Location
One of the crucial initial steps a producer must undertake is to make sure someone selects and surveys the production location. For large dramatic productions requiring many locations, a person given the title of **location scout** will undertake the job of finding, visiting, and winnowing down the possible production sites. The location scout might find ten homes where a 1940s murder mystery could be shot. But some might be a great distance from where other scenes are being shot, some might be in noisy locations, and some may not have an appropriate looking porch. The location person will narrow down the choices and present them

to the producer and/or director. At this point most directors and some producers like to visit the potential sites to make the final selection. Having the camera operator along to give input on these location scouting trips can also prove invaluable.

Surveying a Location
For other types of programs you know approximately where you will be doing the shoot, and you go mainly to see the lay of the land. If, for example, you are interviewing a doctor about a new medical breakthrough, you will want to shoot at the hospital where the instruments used for the procedure will be available. You go there ahead of time to see how large the room you will be shooting in is, to find out where the electrical plugs are, to determine how you can best cut out background noise, etc.

Fast-breaking news stories are another matter. Obviously, it may not be possible to check out the location for these ahead of time. However, some places where news is likely to occur, such as the city council chambers or the police station, can be "cased" ahead of time and notes made so that crews that need to go there have some idea of what they will face.

If you shoot in a studio regularly, you are aware of the location of power outlets, the positions of the cameras, the types of curtains and set pieces available, the location of lighting instruments, and other similar information. With each remote shoot, these elements are different. That is why it is *essential* that the area be scouted ahead of time. If the only available plugs are out in the hallway and you have not brought extension cords for your lights, you will be faced with a major production problem.

When you go to a location, it is wise to have a list of things you want to check. A general *checklist* is shown in figure 14-16, but there will also be elements specific to each production that need to be discerned.

LOCATION SURVEY CHECKLIST

Type of material being shot_____

Time of shooting_____

Potential location of shooting_____

    Principal contact person_____

    Address_____

    Phone number_____

Camera:

    Where can the camera be placed?
    What, if anything, is needed in the way of camera mounting devices or platforms?
    What, if anything, is needed in the way of special lenses?
    Will any objects interfere with the camera shots? If so, how can this situation be corrected?

Lighting:

    What types of lights will be needed?
    Where can the lights be placed?
    What light stands or particular light holders will be needed?
    What, if any, special lighting accessories will be needed?
    How can any problems regarding mixing indoor and outdoor lighting be solved?
    In what ways will the sun's position at different times of day affect the shooting?
    What kinds of problems are shadows likely to cause?

Power:

    Is enough power available or will a generator be needed?
    Where is the circuit breaker box?
    Who can be contacted if a circuit blows?
    Which circuits can be used and how many watts can be run on them?
    How many, if any, extension cords will be needed?
    What power outlets can be used?

Sound:

    Are there background noises that may interfere with audio? If so, how can they be corrected?
    Where can the microphones and cable be placed?
    Are any particular microphone holders or stands needed?
    What types of microphones should be used?
    How much microphone cable will be needed?

General:

    Where is parking available?
    Where is the nearest telephone?
    If passes are needed to enter the premises, how can they be obtained?

FIGURE 14-16

A location checklist that is very useful when looking over an area that might be used for taping.

One of the first things you should do as part of a remote survey is obtain the name of a person who is in charge—someone who gives you the permission to shoot at any particular facility and someone you can contact when you arrive with equipment, someone to turn to quickly when any unexpected problems crop up. Who has the keys? Whom do you contact when you trip a circuit breaker?

You may wish to draw up a floor plan of the location and take Polaroid shots of the scene to share with other crew members and to remind you of important details as you plan specific shots. Or, better yet, take along a camcorder and tape the location.

If you are shooting outdoors, or if you are shooting indoors with any natural light, you will want to scout the location at the *same time of day* that you will be doing the shoot so that you can see exactly what you will have to deal with in terms of sunlight, shadows, and windows.

What about possible interruptions and conflicts? Do scheduled events at the location conflict with the shoot? Heavy equipment starting up? Airplanes taking off? If you are shooting on campus, for example, will the end of a class period send large numbers of people walking through the shot? What about those campus chimes? Make note of these items so you are not in the middle of a take when any of these noises occur. Listen for continuous extraneous noises such as an air conditioner or telephones ringing that will interfere with your audio. Try to obtain permission to turn them off while you are shooting. If you cannot, plan to work with more directional and less sensitive mics closer to the talent.

Stock Footage

Some productions require some shots that will be in difficult or expensive locations—an airplane that has crashed on a remote mountainside, a koala bear asleep in a tree. If the principal talent does not need to be in these shots, they can be obtained from pre-recorded material. Most professional producers turn to commercial companies that supply **stock footage.** The price is high (a minimum fee of $300 is not uncommon), but these companies have videotape and film to cover a wide variety of situations. News departments that used to discard their old news stories now carefully index them on computers and file everything they shoot for possible later use.

Students who cannot afford professional stock footage should first examine the resources of their own university. Sometimes some former student will have shot the local area from a helicopter and this footage will be made available for future student shoots. Large companies that turn out numerous public relations films will often allow use of portions of footage if credits are given. The copyright laws that govern the use of all stock footage are rather strict and should always be observed.

Budgeting

Budgeting for field production work is very similar to budgeting for studio productions, in that budgets include **above-the-line** and **below-the-line** categories. (See section 11.3.) The main difference is that different equipment will be used and a

greater emphasis will be placed on editing. Here are some equipment rental figures to help you budget for remote shooting:[3]

Low-end camcorders (VHS and Video-8)	$10 per hour
Higher grade camcorders (S-VHS and Hi-8)	30 per hour
U-matic recorders and cameras	45 per hour
Professional grade camcorders (Betacam)	120 per hour
Tripods	10 per hour
Portable lighting kit	40 per hour
Microphones	3 per hour
Character and graphics generator	50 per hour
Audio sweetening	70 per hour
Off-line editing	75 per hour
On-line editing	150 per hour

Conceptualization and Preproduction Planning

Before a program or segment of a program is taped on location, it should be conceived in its entirety. How each individual shot is planned and executed is dependent upon how it will be utilized in the final

3. These prices and the ones in chapter 11 were compiled from a number of rental catalogues including those of Cine Video, 948 North Cahuenga Boulevard, Hollywood, CA 90038; Birns and Sawyer, 1026 North Highland Avenue, Hollywood, CA 90038; Audio Services Corporation, 10639 Riverside Drive, North Hollywood, CA 91602; Artel Video, 1600 Broadway, Suite 1008, New York, NY 10019; Bexel Corporation, 801 South Main Street, Burbank, CA 91506; and Trans American Video, 1541 North Vine Street, Hollywood, CA 90028.

edited program. In other words, both planning and camera work must be carried out with the eventual editing process constantly in mind.

To aid in this process, video producers have developed a number of different forms. Some of the same paperwork used for studio production is used for field production. For example, performers should be asked to sign **performance releases** (see figure 11-10) and any music and other **copyrighted** material that is going to be used for the final edited production should be cleared (see figure 11-12).

However, because field productions usually involve a variety of locations and their inherent uncertainties, producers must examine the scripts very carefully to determine production needs and schedules.

Breakdown Sheets

If you are planning to shoot a complex production that involves a number of individual scenes shot in different locations, **breakdown sheets** are indispensable. They list—for each scene to be shot—a synopsis of the scene, the location, the people who will be needed, the props, and any special considerations. (See figure 14-17.)

Program material in extensive remotes is almost always shot out of order, so you use your breakdown sheets to juggle your production shooting and determine the order in which scenes will be shot. Usually the primary element for determining shooting order is *location*; all scenes occurring in the park will be shot at one time, even though they will be interspersed at various points throughout the program. However, sometimes the primary element for determining shooting order is the talent; if someone who is crucial to the production can only work one day, all the shots involving that person will have to be

BREAKDOWN SHEET

Program: __PARK MINI-DOC__

Location: __Park with a slide & swing__

Segment Number: __3__

Synopsis: __Mary Ellen talks of the need for greater__

__safety standards for playground equipment__

Cast	Props	Equipment
Mary Ellen Thomas	Jump rope	½" portable VCR & camera
Jason	Tricycle	Reflector
Tiffany		Mike & cable
Crew	**Special Needs**	**Comments**
Tom	Mike cable must be able to reach the slide	Should be shot at a time when children are there
Susan		
Tasha		

FIGURE 14-17

The breakdown sheet lists all the talent, crew, facilities, and other elements needed for every scene.

shot on that one day, even though this means traveling all over town. On rare occasions, shooting order may be determined by a prop; if you need to rent a vintage automobile, you might want to shoot all scenes with it on one day so that you can cut down on rental fees.

Sometimes lists of props, costumes, cast members, etc. are made from these breakdown sheets. These lists are similar to what might be made for a studio shoot (see figure 11-11), but usually there are more lists made because the elements needed for a remote shoot are more complex. For example, one list might include all the locales that the location scout needs to find; other lists might include all the animals or all the automobiles needed. Studio productions usually do not include these elements.

Shooting Schedule

Once the breakdown sheets have been made and assembled in order, a **shooting schedule** can be developed. This lists everything that is to be shot during each day, giving the description, the cast, and the location. It is used throughout the shooting and, of course, must be revised when production gets behind schedule. (See figure 14-18.)

Stripboards

Many producers (or their production managers) use **stripboards** to aid them with their shooting plans. Sometimes these are actual boards that can hold long strips of paper indicating the locations and characters needed each day. Computers are now heavily employed for all

SHOOTING SCHEDULE

Program: __PARK MINI-DOC__

Date	Time	Description	Cast	Location
4/20	1:00	Mary Ellen discusses playground equipment and safety needs (seg #3)	Mary Ellen Thomas Jason Sorkin Tiffany Barr	Alcove Park
4/20	2:30	Mary Ellen discusses need for flowers (seg #7)	Mary Ellen Thomas Mr. Hamilton	Patterson Park
4/22	11:00	Interview with park supervisor (seg #2)	Mary Ellen Thomas Dr. Belling	Dr. Belling's office, Park building
4/22	1:00	Interview with park planners (seg #9)	Mary Ellen Thomas Mr. Loomis Mrs. Robbins	Planning offices, Park Building

FIGURE 14-18

The shooting schedule is indispensable for coordinating location shoots on a major production.

forms of preproduction paperwork, including stripboards. Figure 14-19 shows a stripboard made with the aid of the computer program *Movie Magic*. When the production needs to be reorganized because some scene didn't get shot, the strips can be moved around by clicking on them with a mouse and dragging them elsewhere. Strips of the old-fashioned paper stripboard can also be easily moved, making stripboards a very flexible production planning device.

In addition, you can devise your own lists, forms, schedules, or pictures to help yourself conceptualize and organize your material. Like the major multiple-camera studio production, every hour spent in preproduction planning and scripting will save countless hours of valuable crew time on the shoot. Careful script preparation and preproduction planning are perhaps the most crucial *disciplines* involved in single-camera field production.

14.9 DIRECTING

Directing in the field is quite different from directing in the studio. There is no control room, so the director is on the location set in the midst of all the action, thus eliminating the need for a floor director. Also, because timing is usually not crucial for scenes that are later going to be edited, an associate director can be superfluous at a remote shoot.

However, there often is a person called a **script supervisor** or **script clerk**[4] who keeps notes and handles details so that what is shot can be effectively edited.

---

4. Generally, the term *script supervisor* is a film term, and *script clerk* is a video term. Historically, most of the people given these jobs were female, so the term *script girl* was used in earlier times. For many years, the script supervisor and script clerk were the only women on most film and video crews. Although the functions of script supervisor are very important, this is still a low-paying position.

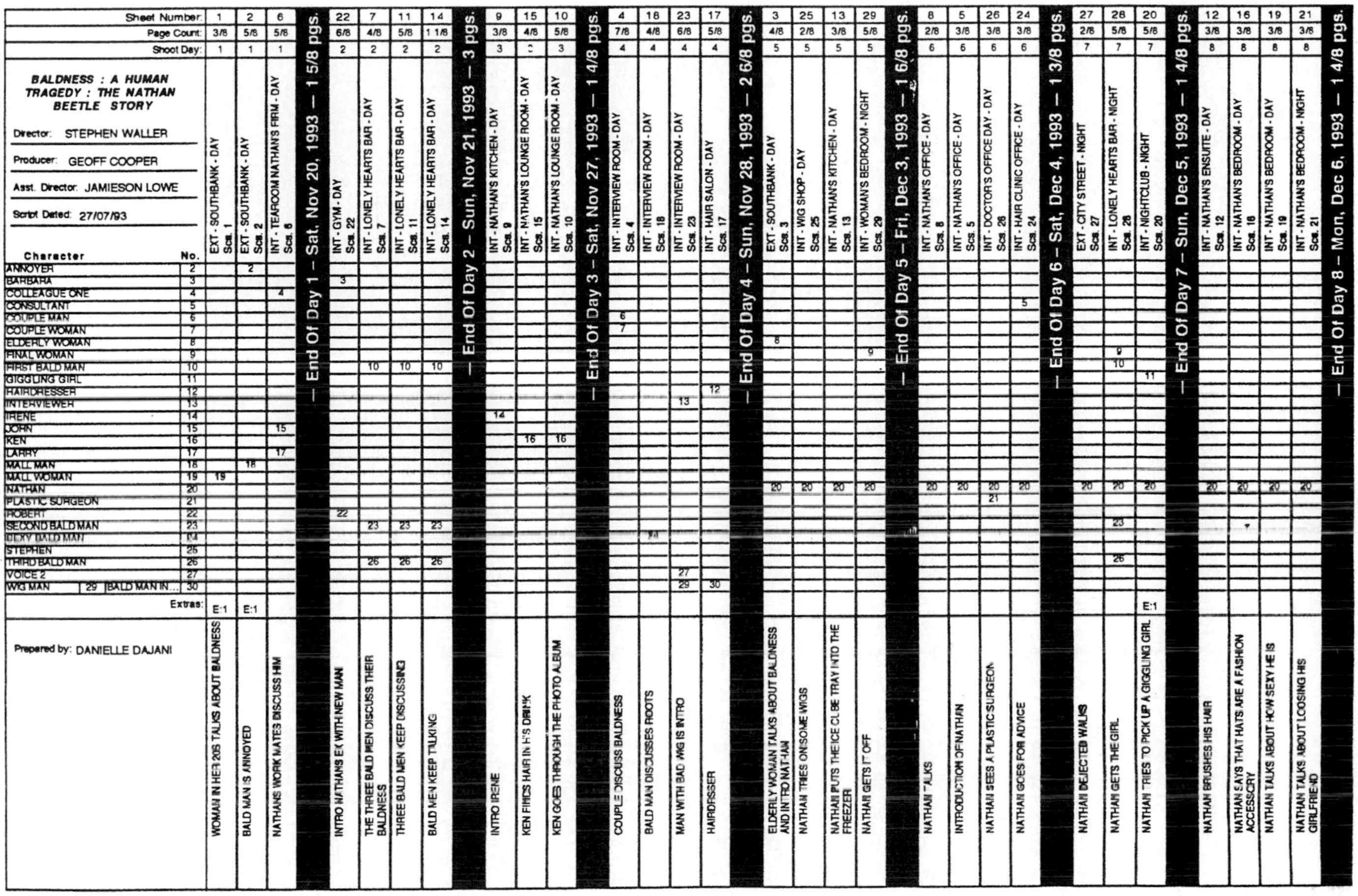

BALDNESS : A HUMAN TRAGEDY : THE NATHAN BEETLE STORY

Director: STEPHEN WALLER
Producer: GEOFF COOPER
Asst. Director: JAMIESON LOWE
Script Dated: 27/07/93

Prepared by: DANIELLE DAJANI

Characters (No.):
- ANNOYER — 2
- BARBARA — 3
- COLLEAGUE ONE — 4
- CONSULTANT — 5
- COUPLE MAN — 6
- COUPLE WOMAN — 7
- ELDERLY WOMAN — 8
- FINAL WOMAN — 9
- FIRST BALD MAN — 10
- GIGGLING GIRL — 11
- HAIRDRESSER — 12
- INTERVIEWER — 13
- IRENE — 14
- JOHN — 15
- KEN — 16
- LARRY — 17
- MALL MAN — 18
- MALL WOMAN — 19
- NATHAN — 20
- PLASTIC SURGEON — 21
- ROBERT — 22
- SECOND BALD MAN — 23
- SEXY BALD MAN — 24
- STEPHEN — 25
- THIRD BALD MAN — 26
- VOICE 2 — 27
- WIG MAN — 29 / BALD MAN IN... — 30

Shooting day breakdown:
- End Of Day 1 — Sat, Nov 20, 1993 — 1 5/8 pgs.
- End Of Day 2 — Sun, Nov 21, 1993 — 3 pgs.
- End Of Day 3 — Sat, Nov 27, 1993 — 1 4/8 pgs.
- End Of Day 4 — Sun, Nov 28, 1993 — 2 6/8 pgs.
- End Of Day 5 — Fri, Dec 3, 1993 — 1 6/8 pgs.
- End Of Day 6 — Sat, Dec 4, 1993 — 1 3/8 pgs.
- End Of Day 7 — Sun, Dec 5, 1993 — 1 4/8 pgs.
- End Of Day 8 — Mon, Dec 6, 1993 — 1 4/8 pgs.

Scene descriptions:
- WOMAN IN HER 20S TALKS ABOUT BALDNESS
- BALD MAN IS ANNOYED
- NATHAN'S WORK MATES DISCUSS HIM
- INTRO NATHAN'S EX WITH NEW MAN
- THE THREE BALD MEN DISCUSS THEIR BALDNESS
- THREE BALD MEN KEEP DISCUSSING
- BALD MEN KEEP TALKING
- INTRO IRENE
- KEN FINDS HAIR IN HIS DRINK
- KEN GOES THROUGH THE PHOTO ALBUM
- COUPLE DISCUSS BALDNESS
- BALD MAN DISCUSSES ROOTS
- MAN WITH BAD WIG IS INTRO
- HAIRDRESSER
- ELDERLY WOMAN TALKS ABOUT BALDNESS AND INTRO NATHAN
- NATHAN TRIES ON SOME WIGS
- NATHAN PUTS THE ICE CUBE TRAY INTO THE FREEZER
- NATHAN GETS IT OFF
- NATHAN TALKS
- INTRODUCTION OF NATHAN
- NATHAN SEES A PLASTIC SURGEON
- NATHAN GOES FOR ADVICE
- NATHAN DEJECTED WALKS
- NATHAN GETS THE GIRL
- NATHAN TRIES TO PICK UP A GIGGLING GIRL
- NATHAN BRUSHES HIS HAIR
- NATHAN SAYS THAT HATS ARE A FASHION ACCESSORY
- NATHAN TALKS ABOUT HOW SEXY HE IS
- NATHAN TALKS ABOUT LOSING HIS GIRLFRIEND

FIGURE 14-19

This computer generated stripboard was produced using the program *Movie Magic*.

Computer work courtesy of Stephen Waller

During Preproduction

Directors' duties during preproduction are similar to those for a studio shoot—familiarizing themselves with the script, planning for equipment, cast, and crew (section 12.1). The main additional chores revolve around those related to finding locations.

During Rehearsals

Rehearsing for a remote shoot should involve the same procedures as rehearsing for a studio program (section 12.1). However, because the amount of time you can utilize a remote facility is often limited, (you can't interrupt the work on a factory floor or monopolize the merry-go-round in a park) you often do not have the luxury of rehearsal in the field—which suggests that you substitute other creative alternatives. Can you at least have a **run-through** with the primary talent—to familiarize them with the actual location? How about rehearsing in a substitute location? Rehearsal hall? Your living room?

FIGURE 14-20

The slate should contain all the pertinent identifying information that will be needed for later editing.

During Production

On the day of production, many events occur that have nothing in common with studio production. First of all, the equipment must be packed and taken somewhere. The director must make sure that all crew members *double-check* that everything needed is packed and is in working order. If you get to a location site without any videotape, you are in big trouble.

Laying Bars

The taping procedure, itself, is quite different from that in a studio. If a camera has a **color bar generator,** at least thirty seconds of **color bars** should be recorded on the tape before anything else. This is to allow you or the editor time to adjust controls that will enable the tape to be played back with proper color balance during the editing sessions.

Slating

Each shot needs to be slated. As soon as the VCR is up to speed, one of the crew members (often the script supervisor or a production assistant) should hold a cardboard sign, small chalkboard, or professionally prepared **slate** in front of the camera. This should indicate the scene number, take number, director's name, and description of the shot.

The *scene number* should be the same as that on the script and the *take number* is the number of times that same material has been shot—take 1 for the first attempt, take 2 for the second, etc. While this written slate is being taped, the person holding it should read the information into an open mic so that both a video and audio slate are recorded. (See figure 14-20.)

Of course, this formalized slating procedure is not always possible—especially with fast breaking news. If a production crew has an opportunity to record a criminal being apprehended, you certainly would not want to take a chance on missing the crucial action while you prepare a proper slate.

Taping Procedure

Once the slate is recorded, with the camera still rolling, the director should say "Action," and after waiting several beats, the talent should begin.

	Slate	Count In	Count Out	Comments
University Security Office Seg 3 Shot 4 Take 3	Lt. Jones. 253 "My Job...	270... this problem."	Best one
Security Office Intro. Meyer Seg 3 Shot 1 Take 1	275 "Lt. Jones...	287... no parking."	
— Cassette #2 —				
Parking lot student #1 Seg 4 Shot 1 Take 1	025 "Well everyday...	037... no spaces."	Stumbled over words
Parking lot student #1 Seg 4 Shot 1 Take 2	045 "Everyday...	051... really mad."	
Parking lot student #2 Seg 4 Shot 2 Take 1	059 "I don't see	071... parking ticket."	

PRODUCTION __Campus Parking__   PAGE __2__

SHOOTING DATE __8 Nov__   PRODUCER __Evans__

FIGURE 14-21
Excerpt from sample production log

After the segment is taped, all talent on camera should hold their positions for at least five seconds while the camera continues to roll. These beginning and ending procedures are crucial for the editing function in that they provide both the necessary sync information and adequate **pads** for maintaining proper pace. (See section 10.4.)

If the director is satisfied with the take, he or she will proceed to whatever is being taped next. If the take is not acceptable, the shot will be taped over again.

Logging

Someone, usually the script supervisor, should keep a careful production log of every shot; this should include the scene number (which should be the same as the scene number on the script and the slate), take number, description, length of shot, and any special comments. (See figure 14-21.) The script supervisor should indicate if a take is bad, so that the editor does not have to bother looking at it. Often, particularly if the taping procedure is hectic, this **logging** is done after shooting is complete.

Continuity

In a complicated shoot, such as a drama, the script supervisor's main job has to do with keeping track of **continuity**. He or she makes notes concerning what the actors were wearing, where certain props were set, in which direction the action was flowing, how heads were tilted, and which hand actors used to make certain gestures. If the actor was wearing a tie when he knocked on the door in the scene shot on Monday, he should be wearing that same tie when he enters the living room in the scene shot on Thursday. If the interviewee's hand was clutching the book he was holding during the long shot, his hand should be around the book for the close-up that will be edited into the shot.

Shot Variety

Probably the most important production technique associated with field shooting is that of making sure enough varied shots are taken—mainly so that they can be used, if necessary, as **cutaways** during editing (to avoid **jump cuts**). If, for example, the taping involves an interview, the single camera will be on the guest throughout the interview. After the interview is over, the interviewer should be taped asking the questions over again. **Reaction shots** of both the interviewer and guest listening should also be taped. And close-ups of anything the guest talked about should be recorded. Take a long shot of the location with the two people appearing to be talking. Tape some over-the-shoulder shots and zoom-in reaction shots. In general, record as many different shots as you think you might conceivably be able to use in editing.

Dramatic scenes almost always include at least a cover shot of everyone involved, close-ups of each person delivering his or her lines, and reaction shots of each person.

During Postproduction

The directorial role during postproduction is obviously greater for remote shoots than for studio productions. In fact, if a program is truly live or live-on-tape, there is *no* postproduction. But material shot single-camera film style must be edited. In fact, the actual show is made in the editing room. Because of the generally uncontrolled conditions during shooting, postproduction can be quite a tedious prospect. It can also be quite rewarding, however, if preproduction and production have been carried out effectively—and the potential for a successful program is apparent.

Handling Talent

Most of what applies to talent in a studio production also is true for a remote shoot (see section 12.4). Sincerity and proper projection are important to any television performer. Constantly scratching an ear will be as distracting in front of the local courthouse as it will be in front of a studio talk show set.

However, in many ways performing at a remote site is more difficult than being on camera in a studio. For starters, there will be no teleprompter and probably no one to hold cue cards—which means talent must handle their own notes or script and they must know their lines and material well. There also are fewer crew members, which means fewer people to help out with talent requests.

Nonsequential Shooting

One of the hardest parts of remote shooting, though, is that scenes are shot out-of-order. This can create continuity problems and difficulties for performers.

Sometimes it is necessary for an actor to *switch emotions* on and off for the convenience of a shooting schedule. Often two scenes will be shot back to back because they are at the same location, but the emotional content of two shots may be diametrically opposed. An actor might be called upon to portray the emotion felt about the tragic death of a friend two days before the death of the friend has been acted out.

Even within one scene, lines are sometimes shot out-of-order. When actors' close-ups are shot, they deliver their lines often without benefit of cues and other lines in the rest of the scene. Frequently the characters they are supposedly talking to are not even on the set. Imagine professing mad passionate love—to a camera.

Because innumerable shots are taken of one scene, the actors must perform the same in each take so that the material can be edited together. This means they must follow blocking very precisely. An actor

FIGURE 14-22

Reporters and interviewers often have to tape reaction shots after the interviewed guest has departed. (*Left*) During the interview the single camera would have been behind the male interviewer, focusing on the female guest answering questions. (*Right*) After the guest has departed, the camera should be repositioned to shoot the interviewer repeating the same questions for later editing.

cannot walk beside the sofa in the long shot and behind it in the close-up because doing so would cause a continuity problem.

Of course, there are many professional actors (chiefly those who are experienced in film) who have learned to perform in this way. But crew members must let them have their "space" so that they can build up to the required emotions. This is part of the reason that **stand-ins** are used for camera rehearsals. The stand-in can concentrate on changing positions to meet technical and lighting requirements while the actor is off the set concentrating on getting into character and building emotion.

Taping out-of-order is a problem for talent in nondramatic shoots also. Because the camera is on the guest during an interview, the interviewer's face will not be seen. This means that after the interview has been completed, reverse-angle shots must be taped of the interviewer asking the questions over again. This is often very difficult for the interviewer. He or she must sit there and earnestly ask questions of a camera lens—because the person being interviewed has already departed. (See figure 14-22.)

This brings up a related *ethical* problem. How much can the wording of the questions change between what was asked during the actual interview and what is asked on the reverse-angle shots taped later? The answer should be, "Not much." If the question is changed significantly, the guest's answer may take on an entirely different meaning. Networks and stations have policies regarding the need to keep the questions the same. Because of this, a continuity person should listen to the original interview and jot down the exact wording of the questions that are asked. An audiotape recorder, of course,

can serve the same purpose. Then the interviewer can review the questions before the reverse-angle shots are taped.

Sometimes even more difficult than asking questions after the fact is the need to react after the fact. In almost all single-camera remote interviews, shots of the interviewer listening and reacting need to be recorded—usually after the guest has departed—so that they can be edited into the interview to prevent jump cuts. This requires the interviewer/reporter to just sit there looking at an empty chair and smiling or frowning every once in awhile; this is a difficult acting job—especially for novices. People tend to break up into laughter or to exaggerate movements such as nods of the head.

Equally awkward can be just standing doing nothing for the five seconds or so needed at the beginning and end of each take. Inexperienced talent will often loose composure during that time and ruin the take.

Uncooperative Talent

A common problem in many news or documentary shootings is people who do not want to be on television. Usually these are people who are in the news in a negative or controversial way and, as a result, try to avoid being interviewed. The degree to which these people should be pursued depends on the nature of the assignment, the context and reputation of the program, and the personalities of all involved.

Some people do not want to be on TV because they know they come across poorly. If these people are not crucial to obtaining the message, they should not be used—they may be self-fulfilling prophecies. And certainly, there is little justification for pursuing an interview with the grieving relative of a person who has just been killed.

Unwanted Talent

At the other end of the spectrum is the common problem of unwanted talent. Random people do not wander into a studio very often, but when a shoot is being conducted on a city street, the curious are bound to appear. If a drama is being taped, crew members (or off-duty law officers) are often hired for crowd control purposes—placed at the edges of the scene to keep onlookers out of the shot.

But there is no guaranteed way to keep people out of shots that involve fast breaking news stories. Egomaniacs and self-proclaimed clowns who strut around in the background and make faces (or obscene gestures) at the camera can be a real nuisance. If the director deals with these people in a firm but pleasant manner, such behavior can sometimes be modified.

Handling Crew

As with a studio shoot, the director must work to build *camaraderie* among the crew members. Poor interpersonal relationships can really damage a remote shoot because usually people cannot even get away from each other. In some instances they are stuck together for days or weeks.

Because the director is on the scene at a remote, he or she cannot give commands (zoom in, pan left) during taping—they would be picked up on the mic. Shot composition and other details must be worked out ahead of time by the director and crew.

Aesthetics

Most of the aesthetic principles regarding design and studio camera shots (see chapter 13) certainly apply in remote shoots. However, some of them take on an even increased importance. For example, the concepts of **axis of action** must be watched even more closely in a remote because so many shots are taped out-of-order. The director must be able to envision shots that will be edited together even though they may not be taped immediately after each other. For example, if a long shot of someone running is recorded before lunch and a close-up of the person running is shot after lunch, the camera must not **cross the line** of the long shot when it is used for the close-up. Otherwise, when the two shots are cut together, the person will appear to change direction.

Similarly, it is easy to shoot material that will violate the **three-to-one cutting ratio** when you do not shoot **wide shots, medium shots,** and **close-ups** one after the other.

But the compensating factor is that when you shoot single camera, you can take the time to carefully construct each shot so it enhances your message and appeals to the eye.

SUMMARY

Single-camera field production is both similar to and different from multiple-camera studio production. Both *disciplines* and *techniques* are needed to an even greater degree in the field because of small crews and distance from homebase.

Microphones most likely to be used are rugged *dynamic* ones used as *hand mics*, on *fishpoles*, or as *shotguns*. Audio boards are usually not taken on a remote. The *AGC* can be used to balance levels, although it will boost noise in addition to the wanted sound. Field sound is often recorded in a *linear* fashion, but some camcorders utilize *hi-fi* or *PCM* sound. Crews should remember to record *wildtrack* so it can be used for editing.

Often *three-point lighting* is difficult or impossible to accomplish because of tiny

shooting areas and lack of places to hang lights. The variety of lights available in a studio cannot be taken in the field; the primary type of light used on a remote is the *broad.* Care must be taken when plugging in lights to make sure they do not blow *circuit breakers,* and overall safety precautions must be taken. Color problems can occur if light is *mixed,* with some coming from incandescent lights and some coming from outside daylight. The best procedure is to use either indoor or outdoor light. If shooting occurs outdoors, the sun is the primary light source. However, often it is so bright that it must be supplemented with *HMI lights* or *foil reflectors.*

Cameras must be *white balanced* and the proper *filters* must be selected based on whether the shooting is occurring indoors or out. In the field, cameras are usually powered by *batteries* and the most common mounting device is a *tripod.*

Graphics are usually a postproduction function not dealt with in the field. Sometimes the location for the taping must be modified to meet the needs of the program, but elaborate sets are not needed.

VCRs are usually part of the one-piece *camcorder.* However, connections often need to be made to microphones and monitors.

Editing takes on a larger role with single-camera production than with multi-camera shooting because the show is put together in the editing room. The *mixing* of audio is of particular importance.

Producers have a great deal to do during the preproduction stage. Because of the complications of shooting in a number of different places, *breakdown sheets, shooting schedules,* and *stripboards* are useful. Someone must also scout the *location.*

Directors are always on the set because no control room is available. They must make sure scenes are *slated* and that head and tail *pads* are recorded. *Continuity* problems are likely to occur, and it is all too easy to shoot in a way that will create a *jump cut* or an unwanted *crossing of the line* in the editing room. Directors must be aware of the problems shooting out of sequence causes actors, and they must keep in mind the ethics of reshooting questions after the answers have been given.

A WRAP-UP

The traditional *wrap-up* is given to a performer about fifteen seconds before he or she has to get off the air. It means that there is very little time left to wrap things up, quickly summarize, and say good-bye. Perhaps it is appropriate that we wrap up quickly at this point.

This text has been concerned with the production *techniques* of production—both for studio productions and for field production. If it has been successful, it has also gotten into the *disciplines* of handling these various elements. Discipline has been defined in several ways throughout this text. As much as anything, it be considered a matter of attitude.

Attitude toward learning and improving is one major ingredient of discipline. If you truly want to learn as much as you can about the business of television, you will gain quite a bit from this course. You will observe intently. You will try conscientiously. One of the most important secrets of learning in a course such as this is the ability to admit areas of temporary ignorance and then ask questions or seek experiences to fill in those areas. If you are unsure about audio patching, ask to have it explained to you. If you are insecure with the switcher, get all the experience you can as technical director. Do not try to bluff your way through; no one gets very far in that manner.

Attitude toward communication is important. Unless you have a strong feeling for the pursuit of communication—unless you really have a deep desire to want to succeed in communicating a message—then you are in the wrong field. Television is not just a business of glamour or money or excitement. It is the business of communication. For example, every program starts with a specific purpose—a clear-cut idea of what is to be attained in the production. Until you begin program planning with this attitude, your productions may be slick and polished, but they most certainly will turn out to be meaningless and devoid of any substance.

Finally, *attitude toward a professional obligation* must be considered. The terms *professional attitude* and *professionalism* are bandied about with little thought as to their implications. We use the terms here to imply more than just a means of earning a livelihood. We challenge the student to think of professionalism in the original sense of the three learned professions (law, medicine, and theology), which carry a strong societal obligation. The true professional is one who is dedicated to high principles and a sense of community benefit. If you are committed to this kind of self-giving professionalism, you certainly will be more likely to leave your mark upon the field of broadcasting.

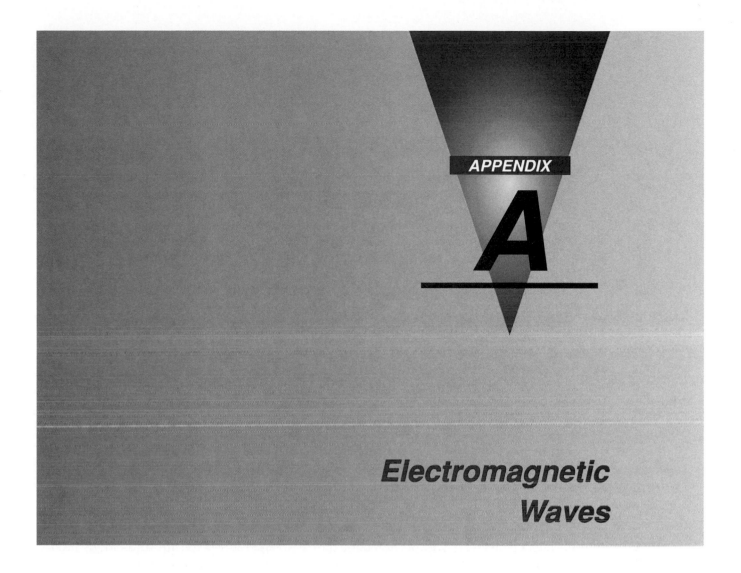

A

Electromagnetic Waves

The principles employed in the transmission of television picture and sound are extensions of several important discoveries made more than 100 years ago involving the related phenomena of electricity and magnetism. In 1856 James Clerk Maxwell expressed the theory that electrical energy existed within the universe in the form of oscillating waves. He further suggested that not only did these electrical waves travel at the same speed as light but also that they were physically related to light itself.

By 1887 Heinrich Hertz was able to prove the existence of waves of electrical force by developing the equipment with which to generate them. His experiments revealed that the waves had varying lengths and differing rates of oscillation. It was further seen that these two factors interact with each other in a mathematical relationship also involving the wave velocity.

Before proceeding, it should be pointed out that while the vibrations that constitute natural sound in some ways resemble the qualities of the waves of the *electromagnetic spectrum*, present-day scientific thinking considers each of these to be a separate phenomenon, existing side by side within the physical laws of the universe. Pressure sound waves can be transmitted only through the media of the atoms and molecules of solids, liquids, and gases; whereas electromagnetic waves can move also through the vacuum of space.

The analogy to water waves has developed as a convenient way of expressing the very complex properties of both of these forms of energy transmission. While sound pressure waves are relatively well understood, most scientists confess an inability to comprehend totally the nature of electromagnetic energy.

In any case, let us use the water wave analogy as a means of understanding the properties of both types of oscillations. Think of a series of ocean waves as seen from a cutaway side view. In the water there is a rubber ball that floats up and down with the crests and troughs of the passing waves but remains stationary in relation to a fixed point on the sand beneath. Riding just in front of a wave crest is a body surfer. If the person moves in a straight line, he or she will indicate the speed at which the wave is traveling relative to the shoreline. In our hypothetical ocean, all the waves come into the shore at the same speed. With this in mind, we can tell several important things by looking at the ball and the surfer. (See figure A-1.)

First, we can measure the distance from crest to crest to determine the *wavelength*. We then notice that this wavelength has a definite relationship to the number of times the ball goes up and down in a certain period of time. This crest-to-trough and back-to-crest rate of oscillation is the measure of *frequency*. If the wavelength were shorter (distance between crests), the ball would go up and down more often in the same period of time. (Do not forget that our waves move through the water at a constant velocity.) This is an important quality of waves of electrical energy—*the greater the frequency, the shorter the wavelength.*

Watching the up-and-down movements of the ball over a long period of time may give us one more important piece of information. The ball may continue its same up-and-down movement at a consistent number of oscillations per minute, but as the hours pass, we may notice that it is not going as far up and down. As in a real ocean, the height of the wave is often the result of energy expended by a storm out at sea. The height of the wave will decrease as the energy creating it decreases. In electrical energy wave theory, the *amplitude* or amount of oscillation is the result of the amount of energy applied to the wave.

The *velocity* of the wave is simply a measure of how long it takes the crest of a

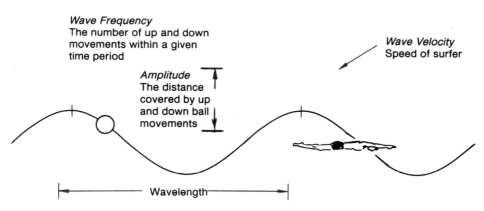

Wave Frequency
The number of up and down movements within a given time period

Amplitude
The distance covered by up and down ball movements

Wave Velocity
Speed of surfer

Wavelength

FIGURE A-1

Relationship of wavelength, frequency, amplitude, and velocity.

single wave to move from one given point to another. In the case of electromagnetic energy, this speed is constant—the same as the speed of light, roughly 186,000 miles per second. As with light, the direction follows that of a straight line. The complex exceptions to this general rule are such that they need not draw our attention.

The basic wave cycle that measures one complete oscillation from crest to trough and back to crest again is usually called a *hertz* in honor of Heinrich Hertz, who did much of the preliminary research in this scientific area. Because the number of cycles per second is so large in most scientific measurements, figures are usually expressed in *kilohertz,* or thousands of cycles, and *megahertz,* or millions of cycles.

Looking at the AM radio, we see that the carrier frequencies utilized for transmission are those of 540 kilohertz (540,000 cps) to 1,705 kilohertz. Each AM station occupies a band of frequencies

ten kilohertz wide. The station's call letters are identified with the midpoint of these frequencies. For example, KNX in Los Angeles, 1070 on the dial, actually utilizes 1,065 to 1,075 kilohertz for broadcast purposes.

In AM (amplitude modulation) radio, the broadcast signal is, in effect, added onto the carrier frequency and, in the process, variously alters the amplitude of the signal. It is this modulation of the amplitude that the receiver translates back into sound. (See figure A-2.)

FM (frequency modulation) radio uses much higher carrier frequencies, from 88 to 108 megahertz. Here, it is the frequency of the carrier signal that is changed by the modulation process and, in turn, translated or demodulated back into sound. (See figure A-2.)

As shown in figure A-3, radio and television occupy but a small part of the immense range of the known electromagnetic spectrum.

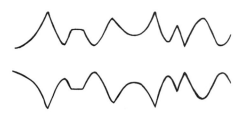

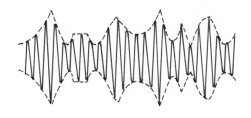

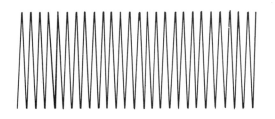

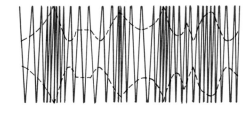

FIGURE A-2

AM and FM modulation of a carrier wave.

Top, the electronic signal coming from the microphone or recorder consists of electrical information that carries the original sound waves. *Bottom*, the unmodulated carrier wave is generated at a specific frequency in the electromagnetic spectrum.

Top, **AM Broadcasting.** The electronic signal can be superimposed onto the carrier wave by changing or *modulating the amplitude* of the carrier wave. (The dotted line indicates the original electronic signal.) *Bottom*, **FM Broadcasting.** The electronic information also can be combined with the electromagnetic wave by varying or *modulating the frequency* of the carrier wave. Where the original electronic signal is strongest (indicated by the pattern of the dotted lines), the frequencies are relatively compressed.

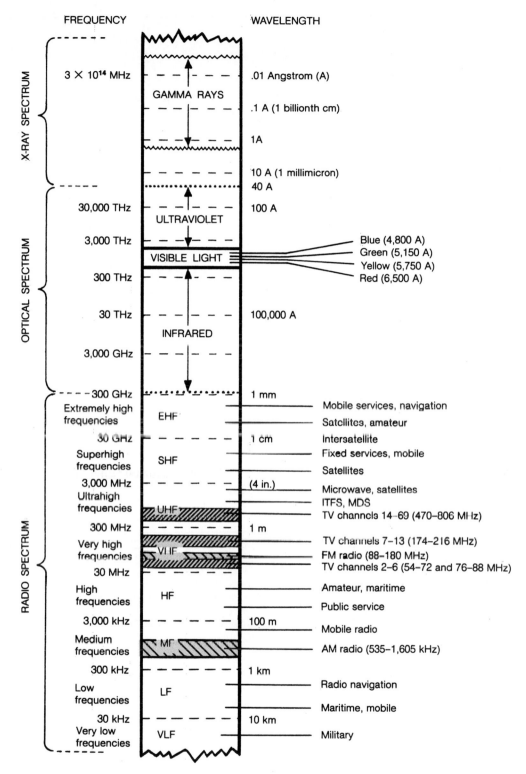

FIGURE A-3

The electromagnetic spectrum.

The entire electromagnetic spectrum includes waves that range from infinitesimally short X-rays measured in angstroms (1 angstrom equals 1 ten-millionth of a millimeter) to radio waves that vary in length from 1 millimeter to several miles. Radio and television broadcast services occupy only a very small portion of the radio spectrum. Most of the electromagnetic space is assigned to hundreds of various services—military, navigational, satellite, data transmission, cellular radio, amateur (ham) radio, cable TV distribution, fire and police services, CB radio, microwaves, short wave, mobile paging, and on and on.

The Overtone Series

I n the early chapters of this text, we explained in rather simple terms the process whereby the waveform of natural sound, known as pressure waves, is transformed for broadcasting purposes into the very different electromagnetic energy wave. The production use of microphones, speakers, and other audio equipment depends largely upon a good understanding of the qualities of sound itself. The water wave analogy used in Appendix A is of considerable help in examining these qualities.

The factor that distinguishes the tone of middle C on a piano from its higher neighbor, D, is its *frequency*. Whether it is the string on a violin, the reed on a clarinet, or the vocal cords of the human voice, each instrument has an element that is able to vibrate at varying rates of cycles per second. The relative size of the vibration is the measure of amplitude. If more force in terms of air pressure is applied to the reed, the vibration is bigger and the tone therefore is louder. The frequency, however, does not change. The pitch of the note stays the same—until the apparatus producing the tone (the clarinet's column of air or a violin string) is altered in shape or length to change the frequency of the vibration.

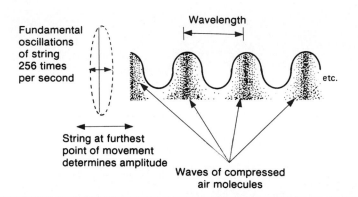

Wavelength

Fundamental
oscillations
of string
256 times
per second

etc.

String at furthest
point of movement
determines amplitude

Waves of compressed
air molecules

FIGURE B-1

Sound pressure
waves.

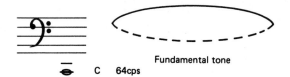

C   64cps

Fundamental tone

FIGURE B-2

Fundamental tone.

The *velocity,* or traveling speed, of a sound wave is relative to the density of the form of matter within which it moves. In the air, altitude and temperature can affect this speed. In fairly average conditions, the velocity of sound is 1,120 feet per second. With the increased density of water, the speed is 4,700 feet per second. In solid steel, for example, the velocity is sixteen times that which occurs in the air. Such velocities are a very minor consideration in broadcasting.

Our primary consideration is the effect of a vibrating instrument upon the molecules of the air. Let us take the example of a middle C tone struck on a piano. Actually, three middle C strings are set in motion when struck by the hammer, but let us follow just the action of one. The string is set in motion at the rate of 256 cycles per second. Each oscillation presses against the molecules of the air and creates a moving pressure wave. When 256 of these pressure waves strike the ear every second, we hear its frequency as being the same tone as a middle C on a piano. (See figure B-1.)

This simple example of the back-and-forth movement of the string is not a complete description of what is happening to the agitated string. Actually, a vibrating string further subdivides itself into smaller vibrating lengths that produce additional pitches or *overtones* or *harmonics* at higher frequencies. The main tone we hear is called the *fundamental tone.* As an example, we shall move two octaves down the piano keyboard to the low C that is written on the second line below the musical staff. Being a low fundamental tone, it vibrates at a frequency of only sixty-four times a second. (See figure B-2.)

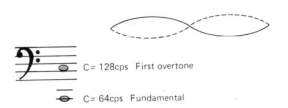

C = 128cps First overtone

C = 64cps Fundamental

FIGURE B-3
First overtone.

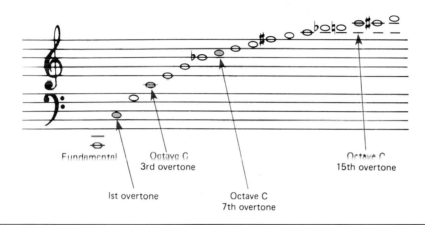

Fundamental

Octave G
3rd overtone

1st overtone

Octave C
7th overtone

Octave C
15th overtone

FIGURE B-4
Overtone series.

In addition to this main vibration of the string between its two endpoints, a series of smaller subdivisions occurs, each of which produces its own tone. The first subdivision divides the string in half and produces the first overtone. (See figure B-3.) Each subsequent subdivision separates the vibrating string into quarters, eighths, sixteenths, and so forth. (See figure B-4.)

The series of succeeding overtones are of far less intensity or loudness than the fundamental tone. Only the most discriminating ear even hears them as separate notes. Generally speaking, the lower overtones predominate, with the higher frequencies becoming almost inaudible. It is the resonating quality of each type of instrument that determines the presence or absence of overtones. The fundamental tone of A, at 440 cycles per second, on a violin will resonate and thereby reflect certain overtone frequencies better than others in the series as a result of the very design of the instrument. A metal flute playing the identical tone will resonate an entirely different series of overtones. It is this differing profile of selected overtones from among the entire series that determines the distinctive tonal quality of an instrument. The electronic synthesizer artificially creates tones closely resembling real instruments by manipulating the overtone series. In the same manner, it can create tonal effects previously unattainable on conventional instruments.

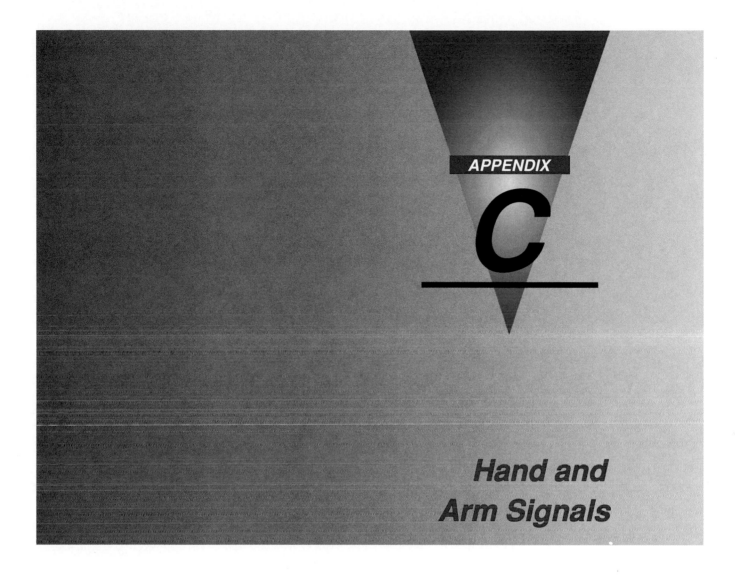

APPENDIX

C

Hand and
Arm Signals

In a production situation, the hand and arm signals of the stage manager are simply a visual extension of the director's commands. Most of these gestures were developed during the early days of radio. A few have been altered somewhat for use in television production. The following examples (see figure C-1) show the signals most generally in use today.

CUE	MEANING	DESCRIPTION
STAND BY	Ready to start show Ready to record Quiet on the set	Stage Manager raises hand in air, with fingers pointing upward
YOU'RE ON TAKE YOUR CUE	Start talking Talent is on the air	Points to performer or live camera
GET CLOSER TOGETHER	Talent, performers or reporters too far apart Get closer together Get closer to object of interest	Stage Manager plays an invisible accordian, bringing palms together repeatedly
GET FARTHER APART	Talent too close together	Stage Manager moves hands together, back to back, then spreads them sharply apart

FIGURE C-1
Television hand signals.

CUE	MEANING	DESCRIPTION

**TALK TO THIS CAMERA
CAMERA CHANGE**

Changing cameras

Stage Manager swings
hands through a wide
arc from camera that
is on the air to the
camera that will be
on the air

**STRETCH IT OUT
SLOW DOWN**

Talking too fast

Move hands as if
pulling taffy apart
or stretching rubber
bands

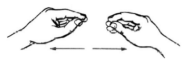

SPEED IT UP

Talking too slow
Running out of time

Move forefinger in
circles

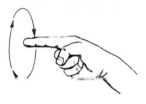

**O.K.
ALL IS WELL
YOUR POSITION IS
FINE**

Well done
Stay right there

Form an "O" with
thumb and forefinger
with other three
fingers raised

FIGURE C-1
continued

CUE	MEANING	DESCRIPTION
FIVE MINUTES TO GO TWO MINUTES TO GO ONE MINUTE TO GO	Time cues to end of show	Raise hand with corresponding number of fingers spread apart or raise flash cards

HALF A MINUTE TO GO	Time to end of segment or end of show	Cross forefingers or forearms at midpoint

WRAP IT UP	10 seconds left Come to a conclusion	Rocking or shaking of clenched fist

CUT FINISH OFF THE AIR	Segment or show is over	Stage Manager slashes own throat with fore-finger or edge of hand

FIGURE C-1
continued

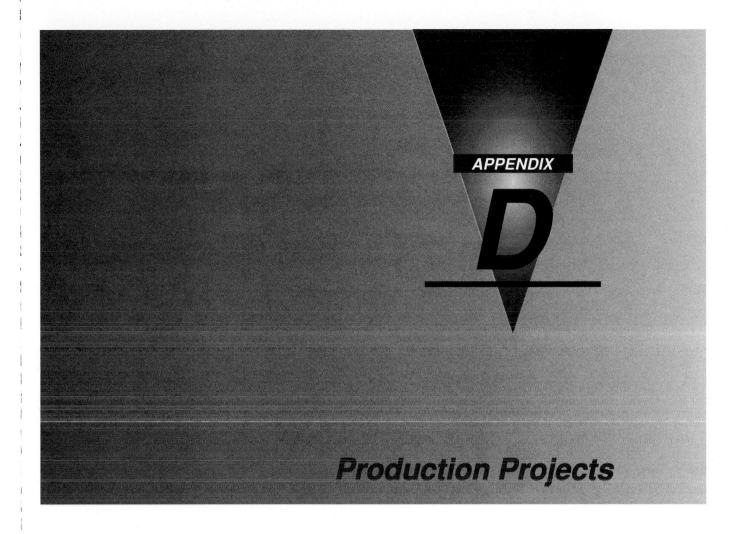

APPENDIX

D

Production Projects

D-1 CLASS AUDIO PRODUCTION PROJECT

COPY: "INTEGRATED SOUND CORPORATION" COMMERCIAL

MUSIC: UP FULL, 10 SECONDS AND UNDER.

ANNC. # 1:   THE <u>INTEGRATED SOUND CORPORATION</u> IS PLEASED TO PRESENT ITS <u>HOME</u>

       <u>STUDIO</u> SOUND SYSTEM, FEATURING A CD PLAYER, DIGITAL TUNER,

       TURNTABLE, AND CASSETTE DECK, ALL HEARD ON SPEAKERS WITH 120 WATTS

       OF POWER FOR EACH STEREO CHANNEL. THESE COMPONENTS FEATURE A REMOTE

       CONTROL OPTION FOR YOUR CONVENIENCE.

MUSIC: UP FULL, 5 SECONDS AND UNDER.

ANNC. # 2:   DO YOUR OWN HIGH QUALITY DUBBING TO CASSETTE FROM RADIO, CD, OR THE

       TWO SPEED TURNTABLE. THE FIVE-BAND GRAPHIC EQUALIZER LETS YOU SHAPE

       THE SOUND TO YOUR TASTE. SPEAKERS EACH HAVE A TWELVE INCH WOOFER, A

       FIVE INCH MIDRANGE AND A THREE INCH TWEETER.

MUSIC: UP FULL, 5 SECONDS AND UNDER.

ANNC. # 1:   THE <u>HOME STUDIO</u> SOUND SYSTEM REPRODUCES FREQUENCIES AS LOW AS 20

       CYCLES PER SECOND WITH A HIGH END OF 20,000 CYCLES PER SECOND. THIS

       IS SLIGHTLY GREATER THAN THE RANGE OF HUMAN HEARING. THE RESULT IS

       A LIFELIKE "OPEN" QUALITY THAT FILLS THE ROOM WITH A SOUND OF

       UNEQUALLED FIDELITY AND CLARITY.

MUSIC: UP FULL, 5 SECONDS AND UNDER.

VIDEO	AUDIO
ANNC. # 2:	OTHER FEATURES INCLUDE DIGITAL TUNING THAT LOCKS ANY SELECTED FREQUENCY TO A PRECISE QUARTZ-CRYSTAL REFERENCE, ELIMINATING DRIFT IN ANY OF THE TEN AM AND TWELVE FM PRESET STATIONS. THE <u>HOME STUDIO</u> MULTIPLE FACILITIES UNIT COMES IN EBONY, LIGHT OAK AND MAHOGANY FINISHES. SEE YOUR <u>INTEGRATED SOUND</u> DEALER TODAY TO EXPERIENCE THE <u>HOME STUDIO</u> FOR YOURSELF.
MUSIC:	UP FULL, 5 SECONDS AND OUT.

D-2 PRODUCTION PROJECT: DISCUSSION PROGRAM

OPENING AND CLOSING FORMAT

VIDEO	AUDIO
WIDE ESTAB. SHOT CAM 2	<u>MUSIC</u>: ESTABLISH FIVE SECONDS AND UNDER
C.G.: TITLE, KEYED OVER CAMERA 2	<u>ANNC</u>: "Frame of Reference," an information service program designed to explore the multifaceted issues that affect us, both as individuals and as members of an increasingly complex society. Here with our guests is the "Frame of Reference" moderator,_____. <u>MUSIC</u>: OUT
MCU, CAM 1	<u>MODERATOR</u>: Our area of examination today is_____. To help us in gaining a greater understanding of the problems that

(CONTINUED)

VIDEO	AUDIO
	are involved in this issue are three people who hold somewhat
	differing views on the solutions to those problems. Seated next
CU CAM 3	to me is_____from_____.
CU CAM 2	Our second guest is_____ who
	represents_____.
CAM 3	Our final guest, who is from_____,
	is_____.
WIDE SHOT	As a way of establishing the background to today's issue, I would
	like to address my first question to_____.
	(BODY OF PROGRAM TO CONCLUSION OF DISCUSSION)
CU MODERATOR	MODERATOR: With that last point we must, for now conclude our
CAM 1	discussion of_____. The issue is a large one and
	our program time is, unfortunately, limited. I would like to thank
	our guests_____,_____,and
	_____for joining us today and for measurably
	adding to our collective knowledge of this controversial issue.
	This is_____. Good-bye until next week.
EXTREME WIDE SHOT CAM 2	MUSIC: ESTABLISH FIVE SECONDS AND UNDER

VIDEO	AUDIO
KEY CREDITS	<u>ANNC</u>: As a program, "Frame of Reference" does not attempt to establish any final solutions to the problems under discussion. Our goal is that of presenting well-informed opinion leaders to our viewing public so that each individual can come to his or her own conclusions. Next week our "Frame of Reference" will encompass the matter of ____ _____. Be sure to join us then.
	<u>MUSIC</u>: UP FULL TO CONCLUSION
FADE TO BLACK	<u>MUSIC</u>: FADE OUT

D-3 SCRIPT FOR FULL-FACILITIES PRODUCTION EXERCISE

VIDEO	AUDIO
CG FRAME OF REFERENCE	<u>MUSIC:</u> ESTABLISH, THREE SECONDS AND UNDER
	<u>BOOTH ANNC:</u> Should the United States government ban sale and manufacture of pesticides for export that are banned in this country? Kenneth Anderson is joined by experts on both sides of this important question on "Frame of Reference," Saturday afternoon at four on KCSU-TV.
PUBLIC SERV. VCR :30	<u>SOUND ON TAPE</u>

(CONTINUED)

VIDEO	AUDIO
STUDIO NEWS ANNOUNCER	<u>ANNC:</u> Tonight on the six o'clock news we have the latest statement by the president on the new crisis in the Middle East. . . . A report from Washington on new plans for the homeless. . . . Another aftershock hits quake prone southern California . . . and Sportscaster Stan Dilbeck has a report on the Matadors and their chances for a winning season.
STUDIO PROMO ANNOUNCER **Computer graphic, Johnson** **Second graphic, time**	<u>ANNC:</u> Tonight at nine our program series, "The Magnificent Burden" presents an account of the triumphs and defeats of Lyndon B. Johnson. As a man forced to assume power in a time of crisis, he was often admired and criticized for the manner in which he took over the responsibilities of leadership. Many of his proposed social reforms were diminished by the demands of a war that seemingly could not be ended.
PROMO ANNOUNCER	<u>ANNC:</u> Coming up in just a moment we have something in a lighter vein on "Campus Rock and Country." Host Charlie "Red" Stewart presents the Grass Valley Boys singing "It's Pure Pleasure," Bonnie Street does her version of "The Sadness of My Life," and that new group, The Electric Car, performs their hit, "Turn on the Lights Again."
STATION ID	They get it all together on KCSU-TV here on campus channel forty two.
VCR	<u>SOUND ON TAPE</u>

D-4 DRAMATIC PRODUCTION: "IT'S A DATE"

In blocking out any studio production that involves considerable movement of people to various parts of the studio, a storyboard (see figure D-1) can be immensely important. This is especially true of any dramatic presentation. The storyboard presented shows the framing of the main shots of the dramatic sequence as the actors assume new positions in relation to each other. A number of other shots should also be planned to adequately follow the flow of conversation.

FIGURE D-1
Storyboard for "It's a Date."

VIDEO	AUDIO	(Approx. 4 Min.)

HARRY: (TALKING TO NANCY, WHO IS OFFSTAGE) I see where old Harold Osgood is fighting with the university again.

NANCY: (ENTERING FROM DOOR, CENTER) What, dear?

HARRY: Councilman Osgood objects to the fact that taxpayers' money is being spent on a college course called "The Crisis in Human Sexuality." He says that it's part of a plot to destroy the morals of American youth.

NANCY: (WALKS TO FIREPLACE) Oh, it's probably just one of those courses that teach people how to get along with one another.

HARRY: (SARCASTICALLY) Yeah, I'll bet it is. I can just imagine how they're telling them to get along.

NANCY: (WALKING TO SIDE OF COUCH) Oh, Harry, it's not that. Those kind of classes just help people to establish their personal identity . . . you know, who they really are.

HARRY: Well, when I was in college no professor had to tell me who I really was.

NANCY: I remember very well what kind of a guy you were. (KIDDING) You were a big hunk, that's what you were.

VIDEO	AUDIO

HARRY: (SMILING) Oh, come on, Nancy, so I was <u>cool</u>. That's all . . . no big deal.

NANCY: (SITTING NEXT TO HIM) Well, it just might have done <u>you</u> some good to have taken one of those courses. Things are different now with men and women, Harry. We're not living in the 1950s.

HARRY: Yeah, a lot of good it's done . . . a bunch of so-called liberated females running around. . . .

NANCY: (INTERRUPTING) Harry, they don't run around. They do a lot of constructive things. Why only last week. . . .

KIM: (INTERRUPTING FROM OFFSTAGE) Daddy, what time is it? (ENTERING SOMEWHAT BREATHLESSLY) Derek will be here any minute.

HARRY: (STERN BUT FATHERLY) It's seven twenty-five, and who is Derek?

KIM: He's only this really neat guy, that's all. Can't you just <u>chill out</u>, Daddy?

NANCY: Kim, you know that your father always thinks of your dates as being direct descendants of someone out of <u>The Night of The Living Dead.</u>

(CONTINUED)

VIDEO	AUDIO
	KIM: Well he's not. He's really nice. He writes on the school newspaper and he's also very into video.
	HARRY: Well, if he's somehow made you suddenly aware of the discipline of time, he can't be all bad.
	KIM: Well, he's very . . . you know, intellectual. He knows <u>all</u> about music and things.
	HARRY: Yeah, I can imagine. I remember that football player friend of yours. From the way he carried on a conversation you felt that his IQ number was about the same as his coat size.
VCR Insert	<u>MUSIC</u>: HEAVY METAL STYLE AS IF FROM OUTSIDE.
Off-road	<u>SFX</u>: SQUEALING TIRES COMING TO A STOP
Vehicle Parks	
	HARRY: (CONTINUING) Yeah, well at our school football players . . . say, what's that noise?
	KIM: Oh, that must be Derek. Will you go to the door? I'm not quite ready yet! (EXITS)
	NANCY: Well, we should be thankful that Derek at least comes to the door . . . not like the boy who sat in the driveway and honked. (WALKS TO DOOR)

VIDEO	AUDIO

(HARRY PUTS DOWN THE NEWSPAPER AND SLOWLY STANDS UP SHAKING HIS HEAD.)

NANCY: (OPENING DOOR) Hello, I'm Kim's mother. You must be Derek. Won't you come in? She will be right out. Harry, this is Kim's friend, Derek. I'm afraid that Kim hasn't told us your last name.

DEREK: Uh, Derek's O.K. . . . or, Rick.

(THERE IS AN AWKWARD 3-SECOND PAUSE WHILE ALL TRY TO THINK OF SOMETHING TO SAY.)

NANCY: Well, it's so nice to meet . . . . . .

HARRY: (OVER NANCY'S LINE) Is that coming from your car?

DEREK: That's my van, man, it sleeps two.

HARRY STARTS TO SAY SOMETHING, THINKS BETTER OF IT, AND QUICKLY TRIES TO COVER HIS STARTLED EXPRESSION. DEREK WALKS OVER TO CAMERA RIGHT COUCH AND JUMPS OVER THE BACK TO SIT DOWN.

DEREK: (CONTINUING) Like, I do a lot of camping. It's really great with my tape deck out in the woods.

(CONTINUED)

VIDEO	AUDIO

HARRY: (STRAIGHT, BUT WITH A TOUCH OF SARCASM AS HE AND NANCY SIT DOWN) Yes, I guess you could really get back to nature.

(NANCY GIVES HIS ARM A WARNING SQUEEZE.)

DEREK: That's Wretched Yellow playing "Let's Boogie Till 1999." It's their big hit. Great guitar. (HE BRIEFLY PANTOMIMES A GUITAR PLAYER.)

NANCY: Kim tells us that you write for the school newspaper.

DEREK: Yeah, like I write a column called "Makin' It On Disc." They wanted me to call it "Pickin' the Platters," but I thought it sounded kinda' corny.

HARRY: You're right, it just doesn't have the same ring to it.

NANCY GIVES HARRY ANOTHER WARNING SQUEEZE.

DEREK: What do you do, Mr. Olmstead?

HARRY: Well, I . . . uh . . . I'm a loan officer at First Federal.

DEREK: Oh yeah, Kim told me. Well, I guess everybody has to do something.

HARRY: (REACTING) It may seem sort of quaint, but in today's society. . . .

KIM: (INTERRUPTING AS SHE ENTERS FROM CAMERA LEFT) Hi, Derek. (SHE CROSSES TO HIM AS HE STANDS.) I just love your jacket. It's really neat. Hey, we better go.

NANCY: Wait a minute. Where are you two going?

KIM: To the movies. We can either see a musical, "The Monster on Lead Guitar" or "My Secret Swedish Summer." They say it's a beautiful, artistic movie about this couple in love. . . .

HARRY: I don't think I want to hear . . . I can already guess.

NANCY: Isn't there something else playing?

DEREK: Yeah, but they're just like what's on television. Kim, let's go to the monster movie. They say that Lulu Bash is fantastic in the death scenes. She does karate moves and, like you know, plays the love theme from the movie on her guitar.

KIM: Oh Wow!! Well, we better go. See you later. (EXITING) Everybody at school has seen it by now. We just have to go.

NANCY: Don't be too late, dear.

KIM: I won't. (OFFSTAGE) Bye-bye.

WHEN THEY ARE GONE, THERE IS A PAUSE AS NANCY AND HARRY LOOK AT EACH OTHER.

(CONTINUED)

HARRY: (LAUGHING RUEFULLY) Well, what do you think?

NANCY: Oh, he's alright, Harry. He's just at that age. (SHE SITS NEXT TO HIM.)

HARRY: I guess you're right. I hope so anyway. Say . . . how would you like to sneak off and see "The Monster On Lead Guitar"?

NANCY: (LAUGHING) How about something really wild, like, "My Secret Swedish Summer"? (SHE GIVES HIM A HUG.)

MUSIC: BRIEFLY FADE ROCK MUSIC UP FULL AND OUT.

(END)

D-5 FIELD PRODUCTION EXERCISE: "THE STOLEN ITEM"

This is a generic script—the specifics are to be filled in by the students undertaking the production. The item to be stolen can be anything—a book, a teddy bear, a ball, a girlfriend. Obviously, the dialogue can be changed, and extra dialogue can be added. The basic shot structure should remain the same because it presents a number of common production problems related to continuity, shooting angles, and pacing. The shots, however, will not be taped in the order listed. The order given is the sequence for the final edited product.

"The Stolen Item"

EXT. SOMEWHERE - DAY (SCENE 1)

1. LS establishing that the MAIN CHARACTER is doing something with an object.

2. MS of main character continuing to do something with the object.

3. CU of object the main character is working with.

4. MS as main character picks up his belongings, including the item, and exits screen left. The camera follows part of the way with a pan and then stops and allows the main character to exit the frame.

EXT. MAIN LOCATION - DAY (SCENE 2)

5. LS as the main character enters the frame, sits down, and places his belongings, including the item, near him.

6. CU of the item.

7. MCU of the main character as he becomes preoccupied with something.

8. CU of the THIEF looking at the item from behind some cover.

9. CU of the item from the thief's point of view.

10. CU of the thief as he moves toward the item and out of frame.

11. MS (reaction shot, cut-away) of the main character's FRIEND approaching and seeing what is happening and reacting in a startled manner.

12. MS of the thief stealing the item and sneaking off to the right.

13. MS of the friend running toward the main character, alarmed. The friend goes out of frame.

14. MS of the thief running away with the item.

15. Re-establishing shot of the friend joining the main character who stands up.

16. CU (over the shoulder) of the friend:

FRIEND

A thief just stole your item.

17. CU (reverse over the shoulder) of the main character appearing confused and then understanding:

MAIN CHARACTER

What? Oh, no. Someone stole my item.

18. Re-establishing shot as the main character and his friend run out of frame after the thief.

Glossary

A

A-roll In news production, the main tape reel that usually contains an interview or a report over which some illustrating B-roll material may be laid.

above-the-line Costs for creative and performing personnel (such as the producer, writer, director, musicians, and actors).

acquisition mode The means used to gather material before it is edited; examples of acquisition modes are film, Hi-8, and Betacam.

actors TV talent who perform as someone other than themselves.

adapter plugs Connectors that convert from one type of connector to another, e.g. from phone to RCA.

additive A color system that combines two colored lights to form a third.

address The time code information for a particular frame; i.e. its hour, minute, second, and frame location.

address system Those editing components with their numerical readout, based on either the SMPTE time code or upon the vertical sync pulse on the control track, that allow for the precise location of each recorded picture on a given reel of videotape.

ADR See *automatic dialogue replacement*.

ADT See *advanced television*.

advanced television A term for high definition television.

AFM See *audio frequency modulation*.

AGC See *automatic gain control*.

agents People who find work for actors, writers, and others engaged in creative aspects of the media business.

air monitor 1) In video, the TV set that shows what has been transmitted or what is the output of the videotape recorder. 2) In audio, the speaker that allows an operator to hear the transmitted broadcast signal.

amplify To magnify an audio or video electrical signal for mixing, distribution, and transducing purposes.

analog A process in which the electromagnetic output varies as a continuous function of the input creating degradation as the signal is reproduced.

announce booth A soundproof room where performers speak into a microphone.

aperture The opening in the camera lens that determines how much light will pass through.

arc A combination trucking, panning, and dollying movement in which the camera is moved in a semi-circle around a subject while the camera head is always pointed toward the subject.

arm move To move the boom arm of a crane left or right.

art director A person who deals with the look of sets and other artistic aspects of a television program.

aspect ratio The ratio of the height of a television screen to its width.

assemble An editing mode where various segments are added together sequentially in the final program order; the control track of the source tape is transferred along with audio and video information to the edit tape.

assistant director See *associate director*.

assistant producer See *associate producer*.

associate director The person who keeps track of timing for a program and assists the director in other ways.

associate producer A person who helps the producer with any of a number of production chores.

asymmetrical balance An informal arrangement in which an important object placed close to the center of the picture is balanced by a lightweight object some distance from the center.

audio board See *audio console*.

audio console The piece of equipment that is used to gather, mix, and amplify sounds and send them on to their next destination.

audio control booth The room where all audio signals are controlled and mixed.

audio frequency modulation   A diagonal method of recording audio on a videotape in which the sound cannot be separated from video for editing; also called hi-fi.

audio track   The portion of a videotape or audio tape that holds the sound information.

auto key   A special type of key effect in which one source is used to establish the external shape of the key.

auto transition rate   The control on a switcher that is used to determine how fast a switch from one picture to another takes place.

automatic dialogue replacement   Rerecording dialogue for a production after the principal shooting is over because, for some reason, it was not recorded properly when it was shot.

automatic gain control   An internal control device, for either audio or video signals, that automatically increases or decreases (as needed) the strength of the incoming sound or picture in order to maintain optimum signal strength.

automatic iris control   A setting on a lens that continuously alters the diaphragm to create the best exposure possible.

automatic transition   A feature on many switchers that allows dissolves, wipes, and other transitions to take place for predetermined durations without the use of the fader levers.

auxiliary send   A special audio feed that goes to an earphone worn by a performer in the studio so that he or she can hear the program signal.

axis of action   An imaginary line that extends the path in which a character or object is moving, with the result that if one camera is on one side of the line and another is on the other side, cutting from one camera to another will make the person or object appear to change direction.

axis of conversation   An imaginary line that connects two persons talking to each other, with the result that if one camera is on one side of the line and another is on the other side, cutting from one camera to another will make the person appear to change position.

B

B-roll   In news production, material that relates to what is being reported that is placed over a certain portion of the audio in order to illustrate it.

back light   A highly directional light coming from above and behind a subject, adding highlights, shape, and separation from the background.

background light   General lighting on the set behind the talent.

backplate   The part of a condenser mic that is electrically charged.

backtime   The process of timing a piece of audio and/or video so that it can be started at a precise time and end at the properly appointed time.

balance   In audio, the achievement of the correct ratio among several sound sources.

balanced   Audio cables that have three wires, one for positive, one for negative, and one for ground.

ballast   An attachment to an HMI light that protects it from surges in power.

bandwidth   The number of frequencies within given limits that are occupied by a particular transmission.

bank   A row of buttons representing various video inputs on the switcher.

barn doors   Movable metal shutters, attached to the front of a lighting instrument, that are used to limit the area of the projected light.

base light   The basic lighting needed for adequate illumination to achieve a technically acceptable television picture.

batten   A counterweighted lighting grid that can be raised and lowered so that lights can be worked on near the studio floor.

beam splitter   The optical device in a color camera, consisting of a prism and mirrors, that separates the incoming visual image into the primary colors of blue, red, and green.

below-the-line   Costs for technical and production personnel and for equipment, facilities, and services.

Betacam   A broadcast quality ½-inch component camcorder manufactured by Sony.

Betamax   A consumer level ½-inch tape format developed by Sony that no longer is being manufactured.

bit   One on or off digital pulse.

bit rate reduction   Limiting the amount of digital information that must be transmitted by transmitting only that which changes from one element, such as a video frame, to another.

black   Technically, a synchronized video signal that contains no picture information—a blank screen.

blanking pulse   A signal that momentarily turns off the scanning beam in a camera tube or TV set so the beam can retrace its path before starting to scan another line.

blocking   Careful planning and coordinating of all movement and positioning of talent and production equipment.

blocking diagrams   Drawings made by directors to help them visualize where actors and cameras should be placed.

body time   The length of a program not including closing credits and titles.

boom   1) Any device consisting of a movable base, an adjustable stand, and a long arm for suspending a microphone above and in front of a performer. 2) An arm of a crane that can be used to move a camera up and down or sideways. 3) To move a camera with a boom arm.

breakdown sheets   Sheets of paper that list what will be needed for each shot, such as actors, props, and special effects.

brightness   An indication of where a color would fall on a scale from light (white) to dark (black).

broad   A rectangular-shaped floodlight.

bus   The mixing bar that connects the buttons representing various video inputs on the switcher.

C

C-clamp   A metal clamp with a pivot adjustment for attaching lighting instruments to a lighting grid.

C-format   A 1-inch videotape format that uses reel-to-reel recording.

call sheet   A posted list that lets cast and crew know when and where they should report.

cam   A type of camera mounting head that consists of a flat plate that rests between the camera and the mount and enables the camera to move various directions.

camcorder   An integrated unit that contains both a camera and videotape recorder in one housing.

cameo lighting   A type of lighting where the performer is lit but the background is not.

camera   A piece of equipment that contains an imaging device that changes light into electromagnetic energy.

camera capture   A camera that can digitize a photo or other artwork so that it can be manipulated within a computer.

camera chain   The electronic camera plus associated equipment such as the sync generator and camera control unit.

camera control unit   Electronic control equipment that is used to regulate all the engineering functions, such as luminance and chrominance, of each camera.

camera mount   The support arrangement that holds the camera mounting head and the camera itself—usually a tripod, pedestal, or crane.

camera rehearsal   The first rehearsal where the camera operators and other technical personnel are operating their equipment.

Cannon connector   See *XLR connector*.

capacitor   The part of a condenser mic that stores electrical energy and permits the flow of alternating current.

cardioid   A microphone that picks up sound in a heart-shaped pattern.

carrier frequency   The specific portion of the electromagnetic spectrum assigned by the Federal Communications Commission to a radio or television station for transmission of its modulated broadcast signal.

carrier wave   The specific range of frequencies used to carry an electronic signal from a transmitter to a receiver.

cart machine   Audio or video equipment that records or plays back material on tape that is on a continuous loop in a self-contained unit.

cartridge   An audiotape or videotape recording and/or playback tape container that holds the tape in a continuous loop on a spool.

cassette   An audiotape or videotape container that holds both the supply reel and take-up reel in a self-contained case.

casting   Deciding who will act various roles in a television program.

casting agencies   Companies that can be hired to select people for various roles in a production.

cathode-ray tube   A TV reception device in which an electronic beam can be focused to a small cross section on a luminescent screen and can then be varied in position and density to produce what appears to be a moving picture.

catwalk   A walkway suspended below the studio ceiling that allows lighting personnel easy access to lighting instruments.

CCD   See *charge-coupled device*.

CCU   See *camera control unit*.

CD player   Equipment that plays back discs on which sound has been recorded digitally.

CD-ROM   Compact disc/read-only memory; a computer input device that can be read but not written to.

central processing unit   The part of a computer that calculates and stores information.

channel   1) The specific pathway used to get a signal from source to destination. 2) To move signals from one place to another.

channel fader   The part of the audio console that controls the volume for one particular input such as one microphone.

character generator   A special electronic effects device with a typewriter-like keyboard that can produce letters and numerals directly on the television screen.

charge-coupled device   A microchip, consisting of a photodiode and transistor, that is used to pick up picture information.

cheat to camera   Having an actor face slightly toward camera rather then directly toward another actor, in order to get a better camera angle.

chroma key   A special effect whereby a special color (usually green or blue) is used as a key to determine what picture information is to be cut out of the picture with the foreground image.

chroma knob   The control on the switcher that varies the intensity of a color.

chrominance   Information pertaining to the color characteristics of a video signal.

cleats   Pieces of metal on the back of a flat that are used to join two flats together with a rope.

clip   A short segment of videotape that is usually edited into other taped material.

clip knob   A special effects generator adjustment that can set a threshold level for a particular video variable such as luminance value for a key.

clip LED indicator   A light-emitting diode that, when flashing, confirms that the audio levels on an audio console have been properly set.

close-up   A view of a subject from a relatively short distance.

coaxial cable   Standard camera and video cable with a central insulated conducting wire and a concentrically arranged outer wire.

coil   The part of a dynamic microphone that vibrates within the magnet setting up an electrical charge.

color bar generator   The part of the camera or switcher or other piece of equipment that produces the basic colors—red, blue, green, yellow, cyan, and magenta.

color bars   An electronically generated pattern of vertical color strips, which when sent through the switcher, can be used to standardize and calibrate the color values of all cameras and monitors.

color temperature   The relative reddish or bluish quality of a light source, as measured in degrees Kelvin.

complementary colors   Yellow, cyan, and magenta.

component   A video system that records chrominance and luminance information separately.

composite   A video system that records chrominance and luminance information together.

compression   A technique for placing more video information in less space by including only elements that change from one frame to another or by reducing the quality of what is shown.

compressor   An electronic device used to lessen the distance between the highest and lowest audio volume levels.

computer generated graphics   Visuals that are created and manipulated with the aid of computer digital technology.

computer graphics generator   An electronic device that can be used to manipulate lines and forms to create visuals that can be changed in a number of ways such as stretching, shading, and repeating.

condenser mic   A high quality mic whose transducer consists of a diaphragm, backplate, and capacitor.

continuity   Maintaining a consistent and unobtrusive progression from shot to shot in terms of screen direction, lighting, props, and other production details.

contrast ratio   The relationship of the brightest area to the darkest area in a given camera shot, as determined by reflected light readings.

control booth   The room where all video signals are mixed; the director and technical director (and other crew members) control all program elements from this location.

control room rehearsals   A rehearsal with the director seated where he/she will be calling the shots, rather than in the studio.

control track   The portion of a videotape that contains the sync information that keeps all elements in a proper timing relationship.

controlled-beam spotlight   See *spotlight*.

controller   See *edit controller*.

cookie See *cucalorus.*

copyright The exclusive right to a production or publication.

corner insert A special effect with one input inserted into a specific quadrant of the picture.

cover shot See *wide shot.*

CPU See *central processing unit.*

crab A camera movement left or right that is similar to a truck but is accomplished when the driver of a crab dolly coordinates the wheels so they go in the right direction.

crab dolly A small studio crane that can move on tracks.

cradle A type of camera mounting head with a curved bottom that rests on the camera mount and enables the camera to move various directions.

crane 1) A large camera mount with an extended boom arm or tongue for a camera and a seat for a camera operator, all placed on a large, four-wheeled base. 2) To move the boom arm of a crane up and down.

crop To cut off the edges or border of a picture.

cross-key A lighting technique that uses multiple key lights aimed onto the set from different directions.

crossed-pairs mics See *X-Y mics.*

crossing the line Having one camera shot come from one side of the axis of action/conversation and another camera shot come from the other side.

CU See *close-up.*

cucalorus A metal or wooden cutout pattern that is placed in front of a spotlight to produce a shadow effect on a scenic background.

cue To prepare an audio or video source for a precise start at some predetermined point.

cue button A control on an audio board that allows an operator to hear a sound without transmitting or taping it.

cue cards Sheets of cardboard with the script written on them that are held next to the camera lens so that the talent can look at the camera and read the script.

cue channel A separate route on an audio board through which sound can be heard but not mixed or transmitted; it is used to prepare sound before it is to be aired or taped.

cue track The part of a video tape on which time code can be laid down.

cut An instantaneous change from one video source to another.

cutaway A shot of something that is not directly visible in the shot before it; used to avoid jump cuts.

cuts-only editing Editing where various shots are butted against each other without any dissolves, wipes, or other special effects.

cyc A large, continuous, smooth backing—usually made of cloth—that may cover two or three walls of a studio.

cycle per second A basic unit of frequency measurement for electromagnetic and acoustic waves; now usually referred to as *hertz.*

cyclorama See *cyc.*

D

DA See *distribution amplifier.*

D-1 A digital component video recording format developed by Sony.

D-2 A digital composite video recording format developed by Ampex.

D-3 A ½-inch digital composite recording format developed by Panasonic. Note: A recent competitive product from Sony, the ½-inch Betacam DVW-A500, has a digital component format with additional analog composite and component capability. It is not marketed with a D number.

dailies Unedited film or tape that the director and others look at after it is shot to see what material can and cannot be used in a final production.

daily hire Employment by the day rather than as a full-time staff member.

dB See *decibel.*

decibel 1. A unit of measurement of sound that compares the relative intensity of different sound sources. 2. A unit of measurement for video that relates to the output gain of the video imaging device.

decompression Restoring electronic information back to its original form after it has been compressed so that more can fit into storage.

defocus A camera transition in which the picture on the on-air camera becomes fuzzy.

demodulate To remove a broadcast signal from its carrier wave so that it can be reproduced.

depth of field The distance between the nearest point at which objects are in focus and the farthest point at which objects are in focus.

desktop video Editing and graphics equipment that takes up only a small amount of space and can be used in the home.

diaphragm 1) The vibrating element in a microphone that responds to the compressed air molecules of sound waves. 2) The adjustable mechanism that controls the size of the lens aperture.

digital A process that uses discreet on and off steps so that individual elements of picture or sound can be controlled and material can be reproduced without degradation of the signal.

digital video effects Special effects accomplished through digital technology whereby discrete elements of the video can be manipulated, resulting in pictures that change size, move across the screen, and so forth.

digitizing Converting analog information to digital information.

digitizing camera A camera that picks up graphics or live video information and converts it into a digitized format that can be used in a computer.

dimmer board A lighting control unit, operated on the same principle as a rheostat, that determines the intensity of a light by controlling the amount of electric current flowing to the instrument.

directionality In referring to microphones, the sides from which the mic picks up sound effectively.

director The person in charge of everything that takes place in the studio or on a remote and during the editing process.

dirt skin Material used to simulate a patch of natural earth.

dissolve A simultaneous fading out of one picture while fading in to another.

distribution amplifier A power amplifier that increases signal strength as an electronic signal is traveling from one place to another.

dolly To move the camera and its mount closer to (dolly in) or farther from (dolly out) the subject.

double headset system An audio intercom system that provides two earpieces to one person so that a boom operator can hear the director in one earpiece and program audio in the other.

downstream A term used to describe any process that occurs beyond a given point in terms of signal flow; for example, the audio console is downstream of the patch bay and a downstream keyer manipulates the signal after it has left the switcher.

downstream keyer Part of a switcher used to place an image (usually credits or other words) over a picture after it has gone through all other switcher manipulations, such as setting a corner insert.

dress rehearsal The final, full rehearsal before the actual production take—using all sets, props, and costumes—designed to be conducted straight through without interruption.

dry-run A session where the director and talent work together on the basic staging of a program without any technical facilities.

dub 1) To make a copy of a tape or disc. 2) A copy of a tape or disc.

DVE See *digital video effects.*

dynamic mic A rugged microphone whose transducer consists of a diaphragm connected to a movable coil.

E

earphone A small audio speaker that fits in the ear.

echo Sound that has bounced off a surface once.

ECU See *extreme close up.*

edit controller The electronic editing console that actually operates both the source deck and edit deck and is used to execute edits.

edit decision list A log of all recorded segments as they will be assembled during the postproduction editing process.

edit deck The VCR onto which material is transferred from the source deck(s) during the editing process.

edit in point The place on a tape where an edit is to begin.

edit event The decision of where a particular edit should start and stop.

edit out point The place on a tape where an edit is to end.

edit suite A small room where postproduction editing takes place.

edit transfer The actual edit when material from one tape is transported to another.

edited master tape The final version of a program—the tape that is edited on the record deck.

editing Putting together pieces of a program by means of electronic transfer.

EDL See *edit decision list.*

EFP See *electronic field production.*

electret   A type of condenser mic with a permanently charged backplate.

electromagnetic spectrum   The continuous frequency range of wavelengths that includes radio waves and light waves.

electron gun   The part of a television camera tube or receiver that shoots electrons to the target of the tube or the face of the TV set.

electronic field production   The use of a single video camera to record any kind of program on location for later editing in the postproduction process.

electronic news gathering   The use of portable equipment to record news events and other actualities; it is a single-camera technique resulting in a fast and mobile professional operation.

ellipsoidal   A spotlight with a reflecting mirror at the back of the housing that enables it to create a very directional, well-defined beam.

ELS   See *extreme long shot*.

ENG   See *electronic news gathering*.

equalize   To emphasize, lessen, or eliminate certain audio frequencies.

essential area   The center portion of a graphics card that contains all the critical information that must be seen on the receiving set.

establishing shot   A long shot used at the beginning of a program or segment that relates program elements to each other and orients the audience.

executive producer   A person who oversees several TV productions.

extender   A part of a lens that doubles the focal length.

external reflector   A spotlight in a small housing that has no lens.

extreme close-up   A shot, usually of a person, that shows less than the person's full face.

extreme long shot   A shot in which the characters are so far away that they are not distinguishable as specific individuals.

F

f-stop   A notation that indicates the size of the lens opening; the higher the f-stop number the smaller the opening and vice versa.

facilities request form   A sheet that someone fills out in order to reserve studio and/or equipment time.

FACS   See *facilities request form*.

fade   The gradual bringing in or taking out of an audio or video source.

fade time control   On cameras that can fade up to or from black, a control that governs the amount of time it takes the camera to get from black to full picture or vice versa.

fader   1) The audio console control that raises and lowers volume by controlling the amount of resistance going through the system. 2) On a switcher, the lever that controls the amount of video signal flowing to a specific bus.

fc   See *footcandle*.

feedback   1) In audio, a high-pitched squeal that results from accidentally feeding a program monitor into a live microphone, causing an instantaneous overamplification of the system. 2) A video effect caused by re-entry of a video signal into the switcher with subsequent overamplification that can make the video appear to go to infinity.

field production   Television production, usually consisting of single-camera recording and postproduction editing, that takes place outside of the studio.

field   One half of a television picture, consisting of alternate scanning lines, lasting one-sixtieth of a second.

field of view   The size or scope of a shot, indicating how much is encompassed.

fill light   An unfocused and diffused light used to complement the key light, coming from the side opposite the key to fill in dark areas and soften the shadows.

film-style scripts   Scripts that are organized by scene with description written the width of the paper and dialogue centered in the middle.

film-style shooting   Taping the way movie makers have traditionally filmed by using one camera and resetting the camera and lights for each shot.

filter   A glass or gelatin element mounted in front of a light or in front of a camera imaging device that compensates for changes in color temperature, or in other ways, changes the color of the light.

fishpole   A small light-weight arm to which a microphone is attached, to be hand held by an audio assistant outside of the picture frame.

fixed-focal-length lens A simple lens that is one specific focal length, such as 25 mm.

flag A rectangular, cloth-covered or metal frame placed in front of a lighting instrument to produce a precise shadow on one side of the light beam.

flat A standard staging unit, constructed of a wooden frame covered with cloth or hardboard, often used to represent walls of a room or the exterior of a building.

flip-flop A term to denote the action of certain switchers (with program and preset buses) that, at the conclusion of a dissolve, automatically switch the illuminated buttons on the buses to indicate that the input on the preset bus has now become the program feed.

floodlight A diffused light that covers a wide area.

floor director The director's key assistant in charge of all production concerns on the studio floor.

floor manager See *floor director*.

floor rehearsals Rehearsals where the director is in the studio rather than in the control room.

floppy disc drive Part of the computer that holds removable discs.

flying spot scanner A machine that produces a high quality transfer of film to videotape.

focal length The distance from the optical center point of a lens, when it is set at infinity, to a point where the image is in focus on an imaging device such as a CCD.

focal plane The place in a camera where the image is picked up—for example, the CCD chip, the target of a tube, or the frame of film.

focus To make an image look sharp and distinct.

follow shot A camera shot whereby the camera follows the subject, usually keeping the same distance from it.

follow spot A light of high intensity that is most commonly used to follow a performer as he or she moves around a stage area.

font A complete set of type of one style.

footcandle A unit of light measurement equivalent to the amount of light falling upon a surface one foot away from a standard candle.

frame One complete television picture, consisting of two fields, lasting one-thirtieth of a second.

frame-accurate editing A method of editing wherein the frame selected as the inpoint for the edit actually is the inpoint of the edit; this method uses SMPTE time code.

frame synchronizer The electronic component that takes outside video sources such as satellite feeds, analyzes their sync pulses as compared with studio sync, converts the signals to a digital format, adjusts the differences, and therefore can route all signals through the same switcher.

freelancers People who work by the hour or day on one project at a time and are not employees of any particular organization.

frequency The number of oscillations per second (hertz) of an electromagnetic wave that, in the audio range, determines the pitch of the tone and, in the light range, determines color.

frequency response The range of audio frequencies that a particular piece of equipment is capable of reproducing.

frequency response chart A graph that shows how well a microphone or other piece of audio electronic equipment picks up various different frequencies.

Fresnel A light with a well-defined lens; the beam width is varied as the bulb is moved toward and away from the lens.

frozen-frame retrieval A computer feature that can capture a frame of video information from a videotape, digitize it, and place it in the computer.

fundamental The main frequency of a particular sound.

G

gain Volume of an audio signal or amount of amplification of a video signal.

gain knob An adjustment on the special effects generator that is used to determine the sharpness of a key.

gel A thin translucent, colored material such as gelatin or plastic that can be mounted in front of lighting instruments to produce specific color effects.

giraffe A small boom that consists of a counter-weighted arm supported by a tripod on casters.

glitch A momentary breakup of a television picture.

gobo A scenic cutout unit that is positioned several feet in front of a camera to provide foreground design, depth, and framing interrest.

GPI General purpose interface; a graphics option that enables pictures to appear only when the operator cues them in some way, such as hitting the spacebar on the keyboard.

graphics tablet A pad used in conjunction with an electronic pen to enter coordinates into a computer to create drawings.

grid Pipes near the studio ceiling from which lamps are hung.

group assign switch A control on each input channel of an audio board that allows the operator to group some audio inputs together so they can be controlled separately from other audio inputs.

group master fader A volume control on an audio board that handles a subgroup of input channels before they are sent to the master fader.

guilds Organizations that set wages and working conditions that producers must adhere to for people (usually above-the-line people) that they hire.

H

hand mic A microphone that a person holds to speak or sing into.

hard disc drive An internal part of a computer that holds information that can then be put into the cental processing unit.

hard drive See *hard disc drive*.

hardware Refers to equipment as opposed to the material played on the equipment (software).

harmonics See *overtones*.

HDTV See *high definition television*.

head 1) The mechanism that connects the camera itself to the camera mount. 2) The magnetic element in a recorder that rearranges iron particles on a tape so that information can be stored. 3) The beginning of a tape.

head pad Material at the beginning of the shot that will not be used in the final edit but which will give the necessary synchronization information to make the edit stable.

headroom Space between the top of a subject's head and the upper edge of the camera frame.

headset The apparatus (worn over the head and consisting of an earphone and mouthpiece) that connects all production personnel on the intercom network.

helical scan A videotape recording format that lays down the video information in a slanted pattern on the tape.

hertz A basic unit of frequency measurement for electromagnetic and acoustical waves, named after Heinrich Hertz.

Hi8 A Sony 8mm tape format that is an improvement on the Video 8 format in that it uses metal particle tape and a wider luminance band.

hi-fi A diagonal method of recording audio on a videotape in which the sound cannot be separated from video for editing; also called AFM.

Hi-Z See *high impedance*.

high definition television A television system that uses over 1,000 scanning lines resulting in a sharper picture than the NTSC system; it also involves a wider screen ratio.

high impedance A characteristic of microphones that have a great deal of opposition to the flow of alternating current through them and therefore must have short cables; they are less likely to be used in professional situations than low impedance microphones.

high-key lighting Lighting that is generally bright and even, with a low key-to-fill ratio.

HMI light A hydrogen medium arc length iodide lamp that is balanced for daylight and is often used outdoors as a supplement to the light from the sun.

horizontal synchronization pulse The portion of the sync signal that controls the sweep of a scanning beam from left to right.

hot patch A connection made from a light to a non-dimmed circuit.

hue The actual color base, such as red, green, or orange.

hyphenate A person who undertakes two jobs, such as producer-director or writer-director.

Hz See *Hertz*.

I

icon A picture (usually seen on a computer screen as part of a computer program) that represents a particular procedure and can be turned on with a mouse so that the procedure can be executed.

IFB See *interrupted feedback system*.

image sensor The part of the camera on which the picture is gathered and focused after it has gone through the lens.

impedance Opposition to the flow of an audio signal in a microphone and its cable.

incident light Light coming directly from the source of illumination.

in-house Producing a program using equipment and facilities that belong to the company desiring the production.

inpoint The precise spot on both the source tape and master tape where an edit is to begin.

input channel On an audio board, the control into which a source such as a microphone or tape recorder is plugged.

input memory device Something that places information into a computer, such as a floppy disc or CD-ROM.

insert An editing mode where new material can be placed in previously recorded material because only the audio and/or video material, not the control track, is transferred.

Instructional Television Fixed Service Television channels, usually used by educational institutions, in the 2,500 megahertz range that need a special receiver to be viewed.

interactive Methodology whereby the person operating a media program has control, to some extent, over the content of the presentation.

intercom A closed-circuit audio network connecting all production personnel with headsets.

interlace The process of combining two television fields into one frame by first scanning all the odd lines and then scanning all the even lines of the frame; this process has less flicker than would scanning all the lines from top to bottom in one pass.

internal key See *self key*.

internal reflector spotlight A bulb with a reflector unit and focusing lens built into it.

interrupted feedback system An audio setup that allows the talent, wearing a small earpiece, to receive instruction from the director or hear program audio.

inverse square law A principle of physics that states that when the distance between a light (or an audio source) and its point of perception is cut in half, its intensity will be increased fourfold.

iris The part of the lens that allows light to pass through.

J

jack A hinged stage brace attached to the rear of a flat.

jump cutting Taking between two cameras or editing in such a way that the connecting shots have almost identical views of the same object and the result is that the object appears to jump slightly for no apparent reason.

K

K See *Kelvin*.

Kelvin The scale of measurement used to measure frequencies so that color temperature can be determined.

key A generic term for any number of special visual effects whereby video signals from two or more sources are electronically combined in such a way that one image looks like it has been cut out and placed on top of the other image.

key light The primary source of illumination falling upon a subject which is highly directional and produces a definite modeling or shaping effect with well-defined shadows.

key memory A feature on a switcher that remembers the clip and gain levels that have been set for a particular key so that the next time that key is used the values will be correct.

keyboard A typewriter-like device used to put words into a computer.

kicker Additional light, usually a spotlight, coming from the side and slightly to the rear of the subject.

kinescope An old-fashioned film recording of a TV program made by adapting a film camera to record from the face of the TV tube.

kook See *cucalorus*.

L

lapel mic A small mic that can be clipped inside clothing or to a tie or lapel.

laser disc A recording disc similar in structure and operation to the compact disc (CD) that records both video and audio to be read by a laser beam.

lavaliere A small mic that can be worn around the neck on a cord.

LCD See *liquid crystal display.*

lead room Additional framing space in a camera picture on the side toward which a subject is looking or moving.

leko See *ellipsoidal.*

light meter A photoelectric device that measures the amount of light falling upon a specific area.

light pen An electronic pen-shaped device that is used to touch the screen of a computer to draw various figures.

light plot A floor plan that indicates the lighting requirements—location, type, and function of each instrument—for every staging area in the studio.

lighting director The person who oversees the lighting of the set and makes lighting changes, if they are needed, during production.

lighting grid A permanent arrangement of pipes suspended below the studio ceiling on which lighting instruments can be hung.

limbo lighting A type of lighting where the performer is seen clearly but the background appears to be vague or nondescriptive.

limiter An electronic device used to cut off audio levels when the volume is too strong.

line level An audio amplification level for equipment, such as a videotape recorder or an audio tape recorder, that has already been amplified.

line monitor See *program monitor.*

line producer A person who is on the production set representing the producer by making sure the program finishes on time and on budget.

linear 1) A type of editing in which the material is put together from beginning to end; if changes are needed, everything after the change must be re-edited. 2) Audio tracks that run horizontally on an audio tape or videotape.

liquid crystal display Chemical elements that display black or a particular color when power is applied.

Lo-Z See *low impedance.*

location scout Someone who looks for appropriate places to shoot a remote TV production.

logging Writing down what is on a videotape including the content of each shot, the inpoints and outpoints, and comments about the quality of the shot.

long lens A long focal-length lens with a narrow viewing angle; it includes relatively little in the picture and tends to compress distance.

long shot See *wide shot.*

low impedance A characteristic of microphones that have little opposition to the flow of alternating current through them and therefore can have long cables and be of high professional quality; low impedance mics are generally in the 150- to 350- ohm range.

low-key lighting Lighting that is dark and shadowy with a high key-to-fill ratio.

LS See *long shot.*

luminance Information pertaining to the brightness characteristics of a video signal.

luminance key See *self key.*

lux A unit of light measurement equivalent to the amount of light falling upon a surface one meter away from a standard candle; approximately ten footcandles.

M

M-II A broadcast quality component camcorder manufactured by Panasonic and JVC that utilizes two chroma channels and one luminance channel.

M-S mics A coincidental stereo mic setup that involves three microphones arranged like an inverted T.

macro A special position on a lens that enables it to focus close-ups of small objects at short distances.

magnet The part of a microphone that creates a field that produces an electric current.

masking plate Part of the TV set that focuses the electrons as they strike the phosphor coating on the front of the tube.

master control room The primary engineering control center where all video and audio signals are ultimately channeled; program input, camera controls, video recording, and transmitter distribution often are handled from this location.

master fader The volume control on an audio board that is located after all the input channel controls and after the submaster controls.

matrix touchscreen displays A computer control methodology whereby changes can be made by touching the computer screen.

medium shot   A view of the subject from a comfortable distance between a long shot and a close-up.

mic level   An audio amplification level for equipment, such as microphones, that has not received prior amplification.

mid-side mics   See *M-S mics.*

minus decibels   Sound levels to the left of the 0 level on a VU meter.

mix   To combine and balance two or more audio signals through an audio console or two or more video sources through a switcher.

mix bus   Audio inputs that can be controlled in such a way that several sounds can be raised and lowered in volume in relation to each other.

mixing   The combining and balancing of two or more audio sources through the audio console or two or more video sources through the switcher.

modulate   To alternate a carrier frequency in order to superimpose a video and/or audio signal for broadcast purposes.

moiré effect   Distracting visual vibration caused by the interaction of a narrow striped pattern and the television scanning lines.

monitor   1) An audio speaker used to check the actual sounds being mixed. 2) A video display device that features a high quality television picture that has not been modulated to an RF signal. 3) To listen to or view sound or picture as it is being manipulated.

morphing   Gradually transforming one digital image into another by making a series of slight changes in the first image until it takes on the characteristics of the second image.

mount   See *camera mount.*

mouse   A rolling ball or moving instrument that is used to move elements around on a computer screen or to respond to computer questions or instructions.

movieola   A piece of equipment used to edit film.

MS   See *medium shot.*

multi-pin connector   A connector that allows video, audio, power, and remote control to flow through it between a camera and a VCR.

multi-track   Tape or a tape recorder capable of holding a large number of audio signals, such as eight, sixteen, or twenty-four, in parallel with each other.

multiple-camera production   Conventional television production, either in a studio or at a remote location, where several cameras are used simultaneously to pick up the action or performance; the pictures from the various cameras are edited instantaneously as the program progresses.

music licensing company   An organization that collects money from stations or production groups that use music and then distributes that money to composers and record companies.

N

National Television System Committee   A TV industry body that developed the basic technical standards used in American TV today, including the color standards that are usually referred to as NTSC standards.

negative/position selector   A switch on a video camera that changes a positive picture to its negative.

neutral density   Material in a filter that reduces the amount of light hitting the camera tube or CCD without affecting the quality of the color.

niche programming   Television programming, usually on cable TV, that is directed at a select audience rather than a general audience.

noise   Unwanted sound or static in an audio signal or unwanted electronic disturbance or snow in a video signal.

nonlinear   A type of editing in which the program does not need to be edited from beginning to end; material can be laid down in any order and can be added to, changed, or deleted without having to edit all over again from the point of the change.

normalled   Having a certain output on an audio patch bay permanently wired to a given position on the console so that a patch cord is not needed to make the temporary connection.

NTSC   See *National Television System Committee.*

O

O/S   See *over-the-shoulder shot.*

objective   A camera viewpoint where the camera acts as observer or eavesdropper in that no one directly addresses the camera.

off-line   A basic electronic editing process whereby original footage is transferred to a workprint that is used for making editing decisions.

off-mic Distorted sound that occurs when noise from outside a mic's pickup area is transduced and amplified.

omnidirectional A microphone that picks up sound from all directions.

on-line A concluding electronic editing stage in which all editing takes place on the finished master tape.

optical disc A computer or video disc that can hold motion picture as well as still photo information.

outlines A general listing of what will be included within a program, usually in sentence fragment or paragraph form.

outpoint The precise spot on the source tape and/or edit tape where an edit is to end.

over-the-shoulder shot A camera shot looking at one person framed by the back of the head and shoulder of another person in the foreground.

overtones Acoustical or electrical frequencies that are higher than the fundamental tone.

P

PL See *intercom.*

pad 1. An audio component that can reduce the strength of a preamplified feed so that it does not exceed the volume limits of a control channel. 2. In video, extra material at the beginning or end of the shot that is needed to maintain sync in editing.

pad switch A control on an audio board that selects the proper amplification for certain audio equipment such as a guitar.

pan 1) To turn a camera horizontally by rotating the camera mounting head. 2) A control on the audio board that is used to determine the balance of sound between the left and right channels. 3) A rectangular-shaped floodlight.

pan handle The handle extending toward the rear of the camera with which the camera operator controls movement of the camera.

pantograph A scissors-like spring, counterbalanced lighting mount that is attached to a grid and enables lights to be pushed up or pulled down to varying heights.

parabolic dish A large curved surface that collects sound and reflects it to a microphone.

patch bay See *patch panel.*

patch cord A cable with connectors on both ends that is used to go from one connector on a patch bay to another.

patch panel A board with numerous terminals (inputs and outputs) through which various audio, video, or lighting signals can be connected by patch cords to other channels or circuits.

PCM See *pulse code modulation.*

peak In audio, to reach the highpoint of volume level for a particular sound sequence; the ideal place to peak is at the 0 position on the VU meter.

pedestal 1) A heavy camera mount that facilitates easy raising or lowering of the camera head, usually with a counterweight system or with compressed air. 2) To move the camera head up or down with the pedestal mount. 3) The brightest part of the darkest part of a video signal as seen on a waveform monitor.

perambulator boom A large three-wheeled movable platform that holds a mic operator and a mic in such a way that the mic can follow action throughout a studio.

performance release A form signed by people appearing on TV giving the production company the right to distribute their performances.

performers TV talent who are on as themselves, not acting the part of someone else.

persistence of vision A human phenomenon whereby the brain retains images for a short period of time so that still images that are projected very quickly look like moving images.

perspective In audio, the matching of visual and sound distance.

phantom power Current sent to a condenser mic from the audio console.

phase control A control on a piece of audio or video equipment that changes the positive portion of the sine wave to negative and the negative portion to positive.

phasing The relationship of the positive and negative portions of the sine waves of two different electrical signals to determine to what extent their oscillations are synchronized.

pickup pattern The specific directions from which a microphone gathers sound.

pickup shots Material recorded after an entire program or sequence is recorded so that it can be edited in to correct some element of what was shot.

pickup tube A transducing device within a camera that changes light energy into photoelectrical energy through the use of a target and an electron beam that scans the target.

pilot A taped production of one representative program from a proposed series of programs.

pin To focus the rays of a spotlight to a narrow beam of intense light.

pitch A meeting during which people with a program idea try to convince other people to buy their idea.

pixel The computer-derived term for "picture element" that designates the smallest addressable triad of phosphor dots on a picture tube or CCD that can be manipulated and illuminated.

platform A particular computer system, such as the McIntosh platform or the Amiga platform.

playback To retrieve electronic signals from a tape or disc and turn them into sound and/or images.

plus decibels Sound levels to the right of the 0 level on a VU meter.

polar pickup pattern The directional sensitivity of a microphone as shown in a chart.

polarity reversal Interchange of the black and white aspects of a picture, thus attaining a negative image.

pop filter A metal or foam ball placed over the top of a mic to minimize plosive sounds.

position jump A cut between two cameras in which a person or object appears to change position from one side of the screen to the other.

posterization Reducing brightness levels on a video picture so that it looks like a poster.

postproduction A time after TV program material has been shot during which it is edited.

postproduction editing The electronic editing process that takes place after the individual program segments have been produced and recorded.

preamp An electronic device that can magnify the low signal output of microphones and other transducers before the signal is sent to a mixing board or to other amplifiers.

pre-edit session A meeting held before editing occurs at which the director, editor, and others involved in the creative aspects of the production meet to discuss what the final edited program will look like.

prepreproduction The period during which preparation and planning are undertaken for a television program.

pre-roll The period of time in the editing process when both the source deck and edit deck back up (usually about five seconds) and then move forward in sync to get up to speed.

presence The authenticity of a sound in terms of perceived fidelity and distance.

presentational See *reportorial*.

preset bus The switcher bank that controls the picture that will go on the air after the one that is currently on the air.

preset monitor The monitor that shows the output of the preset bus—the source that will be going on-air next.

pre studio rehearsals Rehearsals with talent in a rehearsal hall or other location before coming into the studio.

preview To look at an edit before it is actually transferred to make sure it is correct.

preview monitor A large monitor that can be used to look at any camera picture or video effect before putting it on the program line.

primary colors Red, blue, and green.

private line See *intercom*.

proc amp The electronic component that takes the composite video signal from the switcher, stabilizes the levels, and removes unwanted elements.

process amplifier See *proc amp*.

producer The creator and originator of a television program, usually in charge of elements such as writing, music clearance, financial considerations, and hiring the director.

production The stage during which all the shooting for a TV program is undertaken.

production designer A person in charge of the overall look of a film or video.

production house An organization that produces various types of television material—commercials, corporate videos, broadcast programs, educational programs.

production manager A person who works for an independent production company determining costs that will be incurred by a particular production.

program bus The switcher bank that controls the actual picture being sent out on the air.

program line out The final output of an audio board or of a switcher that shows what has been mixed through the console or switcher.

program monitor A large monitor that shows what is being sent out over the air or to the videotape recorder.

program speaker The main monitor in an audio booth that outputs what has gone through the audio console.

program time The total length of a show.

proscenium arch   In the theater, the arch that separates the stage from the auditorium.

public domain   The legal condition covering copyright that says that when material is old enough it can be used without copyright clearance being obtained.

pull focus   To change the focus of a camera lens from one extreme to the other in order to shift attention from one object to another (either in the foreground or the background).

pulse code modulation   An audio digital signal that is recorded diagonally on videotape separate from the picture information.

PZM mic   See *surface-mount mic.*

Q

quad split   A special effect in which the TV screen is split into four sections, each showing a different picture.

quadruplex   An older videotape recording format that used four rotating heads in a pattern transverse to the movement of the videotape.

quartz light   A highly efficient lamp with a high-intensity tungsten halogen filament in a quartz or silica housing.

R

radio frequency   The carrier wave on which radio and television signals are superimposed for transmission.

rain drum   A rounded surface on which black paper streaked with white is turned to simulate rain.

RAM   See *random access memory.*

random access   The ability to bring up video and/or audio information instantly, in any order, from a disc or similar storage device without having to wait for tapes to rewind.

random access memory   The part of a computer system that holds information that is needed or being worked with at a particular time.

raster   The viewing area of a camera picture tube.

rate card   A listing of costs for renting equipment or a facility.

reaction shot   A shot that shows someone responding to what someone else is saying or doing.

record   To use audio and/or video electronic signals to arrange iron-oxide particles on the magnetic recording tape or laser inputs on a disc so that they can be retrieved later.

reference white   A white object, such as a piece of paper or a t-shirt, that can be used on location to white balance a camera.

reflected light   Light bounced back from the surface of an object.

reflector   A rigid piece of material—often foil but even white cardboard will work—that can be set up to reflect sunlight onto the subject on a field shoot.

remote   A television production, usually directed from a portable control room, that takes place outside of a regular studio.

reportorial   A camera viewpoint wherein the talent talks directly to the audience through the camera.

retrace   The area in the scanning process where the electron beam is turned off so that it can move from the bottom of the screen to the top to begin scanning another field.

reverberation   Sound that has bounced off a surface or various surfaces more than once or sound that has been processed so it sounds like it has bounced off surfaces.

review   To look at an edit after it has been transferred to make sure it was executed correctly.

RF   See *radio frequency.*

RF mic   See *wireless mic.*

RGB   Refers to the primary colors red, green, and blue; used to label the noncomposite outputs of a color camera or computer.

riding gain   Adjusting volume through an audio console during a production or taping.

riser   A raised platform, usually made of wood, on which talent can sit or stand.

rough cut   A loose assemblage of video and audio that will eventually become the edited master of a program.

routing switcher   An audio device that allows for two or more inputs to be fed into the input channel of an audio board.

rule of thirds   A principle of composition that divides the TV screen into thirds, horizontally and vertically, and places objects of interest at the points where the lines intersect.

rundown   A list of various segments that will be included in a program.

run-through   A rehearsal of a production that may not involve all cast and crew.

S

SA See *studio address.*

S-VHS An improvement on Panasonic's VHS tape recording format.

safety chain A steel chain on a lamp housing that should always be attached to the lighting grid so the light will not fall if it comes loose.

sampling Selecting certain portions of something, such as a large number of small parts of an electromagnetic signal.

sandbag A heavy weight placed on the brace of a flat to hold the flat in place.

saturation The strength or intensity of a color—how far removed it is from a neutral or gray shade.

scanning area The portion of a graphic card that actually can be seen by the camera imaging device.

scanning beam The stream of electrons that goes across the camera tube or receiver tube in order to change light energy into electromagnetic energy or vice versa.

scanning lines The number of times an electron beam moves from left to right as it goes from the top to the bottom of the television screen.

scoop A floodlight that contains a single bulb in a bowl-shaped metal reflector.

scrim A translucent filter, often made of fiberglass or fine screening, used in front of either a spotlight or floodlight to soften and diffuse the light quality.

script The written guideline from which a TV program is produced.

script clerk See *script supervisor.*

script supervisor A person who keeps notes during production so that continuity is maintained and the material shot can be edited properly.

search mode The part of the editing system that enables the operator to move the source deck and edit deck forward or backward at varying speeds to locate the precise point for editing precision.

SEG See *special effects generator.*

segment timing sheet A form that helps the AD keep track of the running times of various portions of a program so that they add up to the proper overall time required.

selective attention principle The ability of the human ear to filter out unwanted noise so that a person can concentrate on the particular sound he or she wants to hear.

selective focus The technique of using a shallow depth of field to deliberately keep either foreground or background objects out of focus, in order to concentrate attention on a particular object that is in focus.

self key A key effect in which the dominant brightness level cuts its own pattern over the background.

servo capstan The part of a recorder that pulls the tape through the machine at the proper speed.

set light General lighting on the scenery or other background behind the talent.

shape To alter an audio signal by controlling volume, filtering out certain frequencies, emphasizing upper or lower pitches, creating an echo effect, and so forth.

shift registers The part of a CCD camera that collects the output of the pixels and transfers it to wire.

shooting schedule A sheet that lists what is to be accomplished each day of production and the major elements needed in order to accomplish it.

short lens A short focal-length lens with a wide viewing angle; it includes quite a bit in the picture and tends to exaggerate distance.

shot sheets Lists that the director makes that can be attached to the back of each camera so that the camera operators know what they will be shooting.

shotgun A highly directional microphone used for picking up sounds from a distance.

silhouette A type of lighting where the background is lit but the performers are not.

single-camera production Television production in which one electronic camera is used to record all of the action in a manner similar to traditional film production—one camera is repositioned for each shot, and the individual shots are then electronically edited together in the postproduction editing process.

skew A VCR control that adjusts the tension on a tape to correct for when the top part of a video picture appears to bend to the right or left.

slant-track See *helical scan.*

slate An identification procedure whereby date, scene, segment, and other information necessary to tape and film editing are recorded at the beginning of a designated camera sequence.

slave To send the output of a camera being used in a multi-camera production to its own separate videotape recorder.

SMPTE time code A frame location address system, developed by the Society of Motion Picture and

Television Engineers, that can label and find any section of a videotape by hour, minute, second, and frame.

snake   A connector box that contains a large number of microphone input receptacles.

software   Refers to program material (either computer or television) that is played on hardware (equipment).

solarization   Giving a video picture high contrast by solidifying shades of color.

source   In electronic editing, the VCR or tape that contains the original raw footage that is to be edited.

spaced mics   A stereo mic setup that uses two mics placed parallel to each other facing into the set.

special effects   Fancy electronic video transitions and methods of combining video sources such as wipes, keys, page turns, and so on.

special effects generator   The part of the video switcher that can be used to create special electronic effects.

specifications   Technical facts about electronic equipment such as power consumption, impedance, and frequency response.

specs   See *specifications.*

split-pair mics   See *spaced mics.*

split screen   A special effect with the screen split into two or more sections, with a picture from a different input filling each portion of the screen.

splitter   A connector that is used to send an output signal to two or more different inputs.

spotlight   1) A concentrated light that covers a narrow area; it usually provides some means for varying the angle of the illumination by moving the bulb within the housing. 2) A special effect in which one part of the picture is lighter than the rest of the picture.

spread   To focus the rays of a spotlight to a relatively wide area so that the light is less intense than when the light is in the pinned position.

staff   People who are employed by a particular production organization and receive regular weekly wages regardless of what project they are working on.

stage manager   See *floor director.*

stand-ins   People who take the place of actors during technical setups so that actors can prepare their lines.

start-and-stop rehearsal   A full facilities rehearsal with cameras operating, designed to be interrupted to work out problems as the production progresses.

stereo   See *stereophonic sound.*

stereophonic sound   Audio that is recorded, transmitted, and played back through two separate (left and right) channels to simulate binaural hearing.

still frame   Repeated scanning of a single video frame, while holding the videotape stationary.

stock footage   Scenes of various types that can be purchased to insert into a production.

storyboard   A series of simple drawings or computer generated frames that lay out visually the content of a commercial or program.

strike   Cleaning up a set after a production.

strip lights   A series of pan lights or low-wattage bulbs mounted in a row of three to twelve lights in one housing, used as a specialized floodlight for lighting a cyclorama or other large background area.

stripboards   Large boards or computer generated sheets that summarize the scenes, locations, and actors needed for each day of production.

studio   The primary room devoted to television production containing all the paraphernalia for sets, lighting, cameras, microphones, and so forth—the space where all acting or performing takes place.

studio address   A public-address loudspeaker system, allowing those in the control room to talk directly to the studio floor.

studio talkback   See *studio address.*

subjective   A camera viewpoint wherein the camera is an actual participant or actor in a dramatic sequence, viewing the scene from the standpoint of a person who is involved.

submaster   See *group master fader.*

submastering   Controlling groups of sound inputs, such as separate inputs from each percussion instrument in an orchestra, separately from other groups of sound inputs, such as all the strings.

super   See *superimposition.*

superimposition   A picture resulting from the simultaneous display of two pictures that are half way through a dissolve.

surface-mount mic   A flat microphone that consists of a thin pickup plate that, when mounted on a table or ceiling, uses the surface it is mounted on to collect sound waves.

sweetening   Improving sound and/or video during the editing process.

switcher   1) A video mixing panel, consisting of selection buttons and control levers (fader arms), that permits the selection and combining of incoming video signals to form the final program picture. 2) The person who operates the video switcher, usually the technical director.

symmetrical balance   Formal arrangement, usually with the most important element centered in the picture and other equal objects placed equidistant from the center.

sync generator   The part of the video system that produces a synchronizing signal (sync pulse) based on the basic 60-cycle alternating current (in the U.S.), which serves as a timing pulse to coordinate the video elements of all components in the video system.

sync pulse   A signal that operates in relation to the 60-cycle alternating current that is placed on videotape as a timing coordinator.

synchronizing generator   See *sync generator.*

syndication   A process by which programs are distributed to individual stations that air them when they wish as opposed to network programs that are generally aired by all network affiliated stations at the same time.

T

tail pad   Material after the end of a shot that will not be used in the final edit but will give sync information so that the edit remains stable.

take   An instantaneous change from one video source to another.

talkback   See *studio address.*

tally lights   Small red indicators on each camera to let the talent and camera operators know which camera is on the air.

tape switch   A control on an audio board that selects proper amplification for the input of a tape recorder.

target   The part of a television camera tube that is scanned by the electron beams.

TBC   See *time base corrector.*

technical director   The production person who operates the switcher.

telecine   The equipment used to transfer film to video.

telephoto lens   A lens with a very long focal length, used for close-ups of objects from a great distance.

teleprompter   A mechanical device that projects the moving script, via mirrors, directly in front of the camera lens.

three-band equalizer   Part of an audio console or a separate piece of audio equipment that can be used to emphasize, lessen, or eliminate various audio frequencies in three different sections—high frequencies, middle frequencies, and low frequencies.

three-to-one cutting ratio   A principle that states you should not take to a shot that is three times larger or three times smaller than the preceding shot.

three-to-one rule   A microphone placement principle that states that if two mics must be side by side there should be three times the distance between them that there is between the mics and the people using them.

three-point lighting   The traditional lighting setup that incorporates a key, a fill, and a back light.

tilt   To pivot the camera vertically by pointing the camera mounting head up or down.

time base corrector   The electronic apparatus that takes the video feed from the video recorder, encodes that signal into a digital form, and then reconstructs an enhanced control track and video signal for distribution and playback.

time code   See *SMPTE time code.*

timeline   The part of a computerized editing screen that shows the segment of audio (in waveform style) or video that is being worked on or that the operator wants to see for some other reason.

timing   Setting electronic parameters so that mic signals or camera signals from a studio go through their cables and reach their destinations at the same relative time.

top hat   A circular metal object placed in front of a light in order to pinpoint the light onto a particular area of the set.

trackball   A type of a mouse that consists of a ball that is moved by the hand in order to move the computer cursor.

tracking   The VCR control that adjusts the video head to put it in the optimum position when a tape is played back.

transduce   To receive energy in one form (sound waves or light energy) and convert it into another form of energy (electromagnetic signals).

transfer editing   The electronic rerecording (or dubbing) of video and audio information from an original videotape to a second tape for assembly in a program sequence.

transitions Methods, such as dissolves and wipes, for getting from one shot to another.

treatment Several written pages that describe the main premise and elements of a series or program.

trim 1) To add a few frames or subtract a few frames from an edit. 2) To make final adjustments on lights.

tripod A three-legged camera mount, sometimes with casters, that facilitates camera movement.

truck To move the camera and its mount laterally to the right or left.

tube See *pickup tube.*

two-column scripts Scripts with video in the left-hand column and audio in the right-hand column.

twofold Two flats hinged together.

U

U-matic The ¾-inch tape format.

unbalanced Audio cables that have two wires, one for positive, and one for both negative and ground.

undercut To change one video source of a two-camera super or other effect instantaneously while the effect is on the air.

uninterrupted run-through The rehearsal of an entire show without stopping for anything except major problems; minor problems are fixed later.

unions Organizations that set wages and working conditions that producers must adhere to for people (usually below-the-line people) that they hire.

unit manager A person who works for a production facility who draws up a rate card and schedules facilities.

V

vectorscope A specialized electronic monitor that graphically displays the saturation levels for each of the three primary and three complementary colors.

vertical interval The area in the scanning process where the electron beam turns off to retrace from the bottom of the screen to the top so that it can begin to scan another field.

vertical interval time code Information about hours, minutes, seconds, and frames that is placed in the area of a TV signal where the electron beam has turned off so that it can retrace from the bottom to the top of the screen.

vertical synchronization pulse The portion of the sync signal that controls the movement of a scanning beam from top to bottom.

VHS A consumer level ½-inch tape format developed by Panasonic; stands for video home system.

Video 8 A consumer level videotape format developed by Sony that uses tape that is 8mm wide.

video output control A control that increases the gain of a video signal so that a camera can obtain a picture in low lighting conditions.

video track The part of a videotape that holds the picture information.

videotape A plastic tape, coated with iron oxide, that can magnetically record audio, video, and control track information.

videotape recorder A magnetic-electronic recording machine that records audio, video, and control signals on videotape.

VITC See *vertical interval time code.*

voice levels The talking that studio talent does before taping so that the audio technician can set proper volume controls for the microphones that will be picking up the talent's audio.

volume unit meter A display meter that shows the relative volume of an audio signal.

VTR See *videotape recorder.*

VU meter See *volume unit meter.*

W

walk-through rehearsal An abbreviated rehearsal, conducted from the studio floor, to acquaint the talent and/or crew with the major outline of the production.

warning lights Lights on a camera or within the viewfinder that warn that something is wrong or about to go wrong, such as insufficient lighting or a low battery level.

waveform monitor A type of oscilloscope that displays the brightness of all picture elements and, like a VU meter, allows the operator to keep the elements with highest intensity from exceeding the capabilities of the equipment.

wavelength Measurement of the length of an electromagnetic wave from one theoretical crest to the next.

white balance An adjustment process through which light reflected from a white card in a given lighting situation is used as a reference point; in this setup mode, the camera automatically balances the red and blue intensities with the available light.

wide-angle lens See *short lens*.

wide shot A view of the subject from a relatively great distance.

wildtrack Background noise recorded at a site so that it can be mixed in with other sounds during postproduction.

window 1) A part of a computer screen that is used for a particular application and usually can be expanded and contracted so that the various aspects of that application can be undertaken. 2) A portion of a tape output that shows time code on top of the picture.

wipe A video transition whereby one image is gradually pushed off the screen as another picture replaces it.

wireless mic A microphone with a self-contained miniature FM transmitter built in that can send the audio signal several hundred feet, eliminating the need for mic cables.

workprint A copy of original tape footage that is used for interim editing so that the master does not need to go through the wear and tear of the editing process.

workstation Audio and/or video equipment that can be contained in a small space, such as a table top, to manipulate sound and/or picture with the aid of computer technology.

X

XCU See *extreme close up*.

XLR connector A professional quality balanced connector with three prongs.

XLS See *extreme long shot*.

X-Y mics A coincidental stereo mic setup that uses two cardioid mics placed like crossed swords.

Z

zoom lens A variable-focal-length lens that, through a complicated optical system, can be smoothly changed from one focal length to another.

zoom ratio The ratio between the widest angle a particular zoom lens is capable of and the narrowest angle it can capture.

Bibliography

Adams, Michael H. *Single-Camera Video.* Dubuque, IA: William C. Brown Publishers, 1992.

Anderson, Gary H. *Video Editing and Post-Production: A Professional Guide.* White Plains, NY: Knowledge Industry Publications, 1988.

Alten, Stanley R. *Audio in Media,* 3rd ed. Belmont, CA: Wadsworth, 1990.

Amyes, Tim. *The Technique of Audio Post-Production in Video and Film.* Stoneham, MA: Focal Press, 1990.

Armer, Alan A. *Directing Television and Film.* Belmont, CA: Wadsworth, 1990.

Armer, Alan A. *Writing the Screenplay: TV and Film.* Belmont, CA: Wadsworth, 1988.

Arnold, Richard L. *Scene Technology.* Englewood Cliffs, NJ: Prentice-Hall, 1985.

Benson, K. Blair. *Television Engineering Handbook.* New York: McGraw-Hill, 1986.

Blank, Ben, and Mario R. Garcia. *Professional Video Graphic Design: The Art and Technology.* White Plains, NY: Knowledge Industry Publications, 1986.

Blumenthal, Howard J. *Television Producing and Directing.* New York: Harper and Row, 1987.

Brown, Blain. *Motion Picture and Video Lighting.* Stoneham, MA: Focal Press, 1992.

Carlin, Dan, Sr. *Music in Film and Video Productions.* Stoneham, MA: Focal Press, 1991.

Compesi, Ronald J., and Ronald E. Sherriffs. *Small Format Television Production: The Technique of Single-Camera Television Field Production.* Boston: Allyn and Bacon, 1985.

Di Zazzo, Ray. *Corporate Scriptwriting.* Stoneham, MA: Focal Press, 1992.

Dominick, Joseph R., Barry L. Sherman, and Gary A. Copeland. *Broadcasting/Cable and Beyond.* New York: McGraw-Hill, 1993.

Dyas, Ronald D. *Screenwriting for Television and Film.* Dubuque, IA: Brown & Benchmark, 1993.

Electronic Industries Association. *Consumer Electronics in Review.* Washington, DC: Consumer Electronics Group, 1991.

Gross, Lynne Schafer. *Telecommunications: An Introduction to Electronic Media.* Dubuque, IA: Brown & Benchmark, 1995.

Gross, Lynne S., and David E. Reese. *Radio Production Worktext: Studio and Equipment.* Boston: Focal Press, 1993.

Gross, Lynne S., and Larry W. Ward. *Electronic Moviemaking.* Belmont, CA: Wadsworth, 1994.

Head, Sydney W., and Christopher H. Sterling. *Broadcasting in America.* Boston: Houghton Mifflin, 1990.

Huber, David Miles. *Audio Production Techniques for Video.* Indianapolis, IN: Howard W. Sams, 1987.

Hyde, Stuart W. *Television and Radio Announcing.* Boston: Houghton Mifflin, 1987.

Jurek, Ken. *Careers in Video: Getting Ahead in Professional Television.* White Plains, NY: Knowledge Industry Publications, 1988.

Kehoe, Vincent J. R. *The Technique of the Professional Make-Up Artist.* Stoneham, MA: Focal Press, 1985.

Kennedy, Tom. *Directing the Video Program.* White Plains, NY: Knowledge Industry Publications, 1988.

LeTourneau, Tom. *Lighting Techniques for Video Production: The Art of Casting Shadows.* White Plains, NY: Knowledge Industry Publications, 1987.

Mathias, Harry, and Richard Patterson. *Electronic Cinematography: Achieving Photographic Control over the Video Image.* Belmont, CA: Wadsworth, 1985.

Mayeux, Peter E. *Writing for the Broadcast Media.* Boston: Allyn and Bacon, 1985.

Merritt, Douglas. *Television Graphics—From Pencil to Pixel.* New York: Van Nostrand Reinhold, 1987.

Millerson, Gerald. *Technique of Lighting for Television and Film.* Stoneham, MA: Focal Press, 1991.

Millerson, Gerald. *TV Scenic Design Handbook.* Stoneham, MA: Focal Press, 1989.

Nisbett, Alex. *The Use of Microphones,* 3rd ed. Stoneham, MA: Focal Press, 1989.

O'Donnell, Lewis B., Philip Benoit, and Carl Hausman. *Modern Radio Production.* Belmont, CA: Wadsworth, 1990.

Rice, John F., ed. *HDTV: The Politics, Policies, and Economics of Tomorrow's Television.* New York: Union Square Press, 1990.

Richards, Ron. *Director's Method for Film and Television.* Stoneham, MA: Focal Press, 1992.

Schneider, Arthur. *Electronic Post-Production and Videotape Editing.* Boston: Focal Press, 1989.

Stuxal, John G. *The Age of Electronic Messages.* New York: McGraw-Hill, 1990.

Vane, Edwin T., and Lynne S. Gross. *Programming for TV, Radio, and Cable.* Boston: Focal Press, 1994.

Watkinson, John. *The Art of Digital Audio.* Stoneham, MA: Focal Press, 1992.

Wershing, Stephen, and Paul Singer. *Computer Graphics and Animation for Corporate Video.* White Plains, NY: Knowledge Industry Publications, 1988.

Whittaker, Ron. *Video Field Production.* Mountain View, CA: Mayfield, 1989.

Wood, Donald N. *Designing the Effective Message: Critical Thinking and Communication.* Dubuque, IA: Kendall/Hunt, 1989.

Wurtzel, Alan. *Television Production.* New York: McGraw-Hill, 1989.

Zettl, Herbert. *Sight-Sound-Motion: Applied Media Aesthetics.* Belmont, CA: Wadsworth, 1990.

Zettl, Herbert. *Television Production Handbook.* Belmont, CA: Wadsworth, 1992.

Index

control, 203
generation of, 111
key, 201
on a monitor, 158
and special effects, 188, 206
on video track, 223
Lux, 123

M

Macintosh, 123, 158, 168, 248
Macro lens, 123
Magnet, 24, 46–47, 215
Magnetism, 375
Makeup, 321–22
Makeup artist, 95, 281, 322
Maps, 172
Masking plate, 112
Masking tape, 347
Mass, 154–55, 171
Master control, 14, 37, 56–57, 102
Master fader, 28
Matrix touchscreen display, 38
Matsushita, 218
Maxwell, James Clerk, 375
MC, 14
Media Composer, 159
Medium shot, 122, 139, 324–25, 333–36, 373
Meet the Press, 268
Megahertz, 377
Microphone, 23–25, 36, 42–56
    and the audio board, 28–29
    elements, 45–46
    in the field, 339, 342–44
    impedance, 46
    level, 30
    output, 25
    pick-up patterns, 42–45
    placement, 51–54
    in relation to sets, 174
    in relation to the intercom, 57–58
    stereo, 55–56
    in the studio, 11–12, 14, 60–61
    as a transducer, 23–25, 102
    usage categories, 47–50
    use of, 50–51
    on a VCR, 227, 355
Mid-side mic setup, 56
Mini-plug, 227, 355
Minus decibels, 34
Mirrors, 183
Mix bus, 29
Mixing, 22, 29, 102, 187–88, 343–44, 360
Modulation, 24, 111, 379

Moiré effect, 321
Monitor, 202–3
    audio, 22, 33, 343
    with cameras, 104–6, 202–3
    computer, 38, 158
    in the control booth, 12
    in the field, 355–57
    video, 102
    with a videotape recorder, 14
Mood, 69
Morphing, 164
Mouse, 158, 159–60, 242–45
Movement, 140, 144–45
Movieola, 9
MS, 139. *See also* Medium shot
M-S mic setup, 56
MTS, 225
M-II, 110, 212, 218, 355
Multichannel television sound, 225
Multi-pin connector, 356
Multiple-camera lighting, 83–86
Multi-track tape, 360
Music, 281, 290, 359–60
Music licensing, 281

N

National Television Standards Committee, 18, 158. *See also* NTSC
NBC, 218
Negative/positive selector, 125
News director, 265
News producer, 274
NewTek, 168–69
Niche programming, 7
Nightline, 9
Noise, 24
Nonlinear editing, 236–38, 244–48, 258
    camcorder development for, 110
    CD-ROM as spinoff of, 219
    characteristics of, 18
    with computers, 212
    professional use, 357
Normalled, 28, 56–57
NTSC, 18, 104, 111, 158–59, 168, 212

O

Objective viewpoint, 137–39, 142, 305
Off-line, 17, 248, 253
Off-mic, 53
Olympics, 218, 225
Omnidirectional mic, 36, 44, 47, 50, 55
On-line, 17, 248, 258

Program output, 188
Program time, 300
Projection, 312
Props, 176, 181, 184, 281, 290, 302–3
Proscenium, 235, 312
Public domain, 282
Pull focus, 119
Pulse code modulation, 225, 344
Push-off, 207
PZM mic, 49

Q

Quadruplex, 16, 216
Quad split, 199
Quartz lights, 77, 97, 347–48
Quick-fix clamps, 179

R

Radio frequency, 112, 227
Radio frequency mic, 50
Rain drum, 183
RAM, 157
Random access, 18, 244
Random access memory, 157
Rank-Syntel, 17
Raster, 214
Rate card, 275–76
RCA plug, 227, 355
Reaction shot, 331, 334, 370
Read only memory, 219
Reality, 69
Record deck, 250–52
Recording, 22, 35–36, 102, 214, 219–23, 343
Reel-to-reel, 56
Reference white, 351
Reflected light, 64, 66–67
Reflected light meter, 86
Reflector, 93, 349
Rehearsals, 291–94, 296, 300–303, 316, 367
Religious production, 8
Rembrandt, 78
Remote production, 17, 339
Remote survey, 363
Reportorial viewpoint, 137–39, 141, 304–6
Resistance, 34
Reverberation, 33
Reverse-angle shots, 371
Review, 256
RF, 112, 227
RF mic, 50
RGB monitor, 158

Riding gain, 35
Riser, 143
Robotic camera control, 136
ROM, 219
Roseanne, 263
Rough cuts, 248
Routing switcher, 28
Rub-on letters, 157
Rule of thirds, 144
Rundown, 268, 307, 360
Run-through, 367

S

SA, 57–58. *See also* Studio address
Safety chain, 88, 96
SAG, 272
Sampling, 18
Sandbags, 179
Saturation, 106–7, 156–57, 172–73, 203, 320
Scanning, 110–12, 214–15
Scanning area, 170–71
Scanning lines, 18
Scenery, 176, 204
Scenic designer, 281
Schedules, 283–84
Scoop, 73, 80, 83, 85, 93, 346
Screen Actors Guild, 272
Screen direction, 327
Scrim, 73, 93, 346
Script clerk, 366
Scripts, 263–73, 307–9, 360–61
    AD use of, 298
    and casting, 279
    director familiarization with, 288
    director preparation of, 291
    floor director use of, 302
    with preproduction, 366
    and talent, 370
Script supervisor, 366, 368–69
SEG, 188–89, 195–203, 257. *See also* Special effects generator
Segment timing sheet, 298
Selective attention principle, 345
Selective focus, 119
Self key, 201
Semiconductor, 30
Semi-scripted format, 307
Servo, 221, 224, 232
SESAC, 281
Set design, 173–74
Set dressings, 173–74
Set light, 82
Sets, 151–57, 173–84, 353–55
    design of, 173–74
    floor manager responsibilities for, 302–3

T

X

Y

Z